CHICAGO'S BEST-KEPT

SECRETS

CHICAGO'S BEST-KEPT SECRETS

Mike Michaelson

SECOND EDITION

PASSPORT BOOKS
NTC/Contemporary Publishing Group

Library of Congress Cataloging-in-Publication Data

Michaelson, Mike, 1934–
    Chicago's best-kept secrets / Mike Michaelson. — 2nd ed.
        p.   cm.
    Includes index.
    ISBN 0-8442-9647-3
    1. Chicago (Ill.)—Guidebooks.   I. Title.
    F548.18.M49   1996
    917.73'110443—dc20   96-14742
                                                                   CIP

Editorial writer: Frank Sennett
First edition: David Michaelson
                Michael Sweeney
Editorial research and production: Glynis A. Steadman
                                    Miranda Nagy

Published by Passport Books
A division of NTC/Contemporary Publishing Group, Inc.
4255 West Touhy Avenue,
Lincolnwood (Chicago), Illinois 60646-1975 U.S.A.
Copyright © 1996 by Mike Michaelson
Printed in the United States of America
International Standard Book Number: 0-8442-9647-3

17   16   15   14   13   12   11   10   9   8   7   6   5   4

CONTENTS

INTRODUCTION

Since the previous edition of this guide, momentous changes have altered the face of Chicago. Navy Pier has emerged as a lively entertainment complex, combining the best of what it had—a beautiful domed ballroom and incomparable views of the city skyline—with a host of new diversions. These include a major concert stage, shops, pubs, restaurants, street entertainers, skating rinks, weekly fireworks displays, the relocated Chicago Children's Museum, and a landmark 15-story-tall ferris wheel that glitters year-round along the Chicago lakefront, in winter like some gigantic holiday ornament embedded along Lake Michigan's shore.

The John Hancock Center finally completed renewal of its lower facade, opening a sunken patio off Michigan Avenue, with tables set in front of a soothing fountain that is virtually a wall of water. Included in the make-over was the opening of a new pair of eateries, notably a second branch of L'Appetito, a wonderful spot to buy Italian groceries and sandwiches fashioned from imported meats and cheeses.

Fronting the Wrigley Building and Tribune Towers and reaching northward along Michigan Avenue are enormous new planters that are kept bright with showy seasonal blooms. Flags fluttering in the breeze on the Michigan Avenue bridge over the Chicago River are a legacy from the sprucing up the city did to welcome international soccer fans to the 1994 World Cup matches.

Chicago Stadium, where John F. Kennedy once rallied, Joe Louis fought, Elvis Presley swiveled, and Michael Jordan did what he does best, has yielded to the wrecker's ball, supplanted by the high-tech and perhaps too-sanitary United Center. The crowds of fervent Bulls and Blackhawks fans who once rocked the rafters in the noisy barn on Madison seem more subdued—although no less enthusiastic.

Michael Jordan, who once owned Chicago Stadium, left the team—and returned; changed his number—then changed it back again. Through it all, MJ still pretty much owns Chicago, and the restaurant that bears his name draws big crowds.

The Loop, while still relatively empty after business hours, is not as dark, deserted, and potentially dangerous in the evening as it once was. Although far from revitalized, the Loop is in the throes of a renaissance, to which the made-over Bismarck Hotel contributes with a stylish art deco piano lounge and big-band ballroom dancing. And the stretch of Clark

Street, just north of the Chicago River, not too long ago blighted by seedy strip joints and peep shows, is emerging as a hot restaurant area—as is the westerly stretch of Randolph Street that is home to Chicago's produce market.

Some hotels have disappeared. Sadly, the classy Mayfair Regent is gone. Others have made welcome comebacks—including the refurbished Whitehall, and the made-over and renamed Radisson (formerly the Sheraton Plaza), with its rooftop pool. Anchoring the Loop along the Chicago River, the new Stouffer Renaissance—with 565 well-appointed rooms, Mediterranean dining at romantic Cuisines, and proximity to the Chicago Theater and Marshall Field's flagship store—is a newcomer that is making its mark (and another vital sign of the Loop's resuscitation). Also along the river, the monolithic, 1,200-room Sheraton Chicago Hotel & Towers arrived with acres of new meeting space and a worthy addition to Chicago's dining scene with its Streeterville Grille & Bar.

There's plenty of new shopping action, too, along the "Magnificent Mile," with glittery stores (that some decry as too garish and a blemish on the Avenue's staid historic image). These include the cutting-edge Nike Town and Sony stores, a new tri-level F.A.O. Schwarz with a giant animated teddy bear waving to passersby, a Filene's Basement (that actually is upstairs) that gives an upscale look to bargains, a big new Victoria's Secret store that flourishes fanciful lace along Mag Mile, and a pair of huge book/music emporia, complete with lounging space and food and beverage service.

Chicago's volatile restaurant scene continues its frequent openings and closings, as it enters the Age of Trattoria with domination by Italian restaurants. Spain also exerts strong influence on the culinary scene as tapas bars flourish—along with new spots for Cajun and Creole cooking and southern specialties. A good sign for those who enjoy dining alfresco is the putting to rest of a silly city ordinance that stifled the spread of sidewalk cafés. Now there are more than ever.

But we're talking secrets here. For example, do you know an Italian restaurant in Chicago where the waiters sing opera? Or another where the owner does? How about a restaurant where you can have an elegant dinner and place a bet—and a spot where you can enjoy a hearty breakfast buffet and learn *how* to bet?

Or where to discover hidden Victorian rowhouses, and an Aussie shop where you can buy a didgeridoo and a Violet Crumble chocolate bar? How about a music festival with a Mozart theme, and an eatery where the most sought-after table is perched atop an elevator shaft? Or a restaurant where you can watch flamenco dancing—and another where you can learn Latin dancing? And saloons where you can hit baseballs and roll bocce balls, bars where you can listen to jazz, poetry, and violin music? Or shops where you can buy an authentic Chicago parking meter or soak in a hot tub?

This sampling of distinctive and intriguing attractions summarizes what this book is all about—showing off all of the "bests" that Chicago has to offer. Not just the classic things and places (although, of course, they are included here, usually presented in a new way), but also the unique, the offbeat, and the irreverent—in short, a fascinating collection of things to do and places to see in and around the Windy City, including restaurants, hotels, shopping, entertainment, sports (to watch and participate in), museums and theaters, parks and gardens, cultural diversions, and ethnic diversity.

The ethnicity of Chicago's neighborhoods is a major part of its charm. This book will help you discover a German village, a Lithuanian neighborhood, a Vietnamese enclave, and a historic Swedish community with a delicatessen visited by Sweden's Queen Sylvia and where they still sweep the sidewalks ceremonially. You'll learn the best stops for Italian ice, Greek olives, upscale Polish dining, and country cooking. You'll uncover the best bets for soul food—and soul music—and top spots to taste British grub, Cuban black bean soup, Russian borscht, and Jewish latkes smothered with apple sauce and sour cream. Check, too, for Kansas City-style barbecue and Texas- and Cincinnati-style chili. And sample cuisine from India and Ireland, Jamaica and Japan, California and China. You'll learn where to find the juiciest hamburgers, served indoors and out, both in the city and in the suburbs—plus the tastiest perch and best crayfish.

We introduce you to the full gamut of action from canoeing foaming white water to floating lazily down a stream in an inner tube. You'll learn where to ride a balloon and a helicopter, where to jump from a plane, scale the world's largest indoor climbing wall, play golf surrounded by skyscrapers, escape through a phone booth, and search for gangsters and ghosts.

We also take you celebrity spotting. To hotels where movie stars stay, a suite where authors stay, another where a hit movie was made (and even a rundown motel where nonsuperstar rock groups stay), as well as to sports bars where you might run into their celebrity owners. We steer you to a club where Tony Bennett and Liza Minnelli arrive unannounced, and to hangouts of syndicated columnist Mike Royko. We'll even show you a cemetery that famous Chicagoans are dying to get into.

A tour of hidden Chicago focuses on a restored prairie tucked away amid the high rises, and a delightful garden with trees and waterfalls on the roof of one. There's an office building with 16 floors of jewelers and another with a coffee shop offering the best Cajun and Creole cooking north of New Orleans. There's a gem of a historic building showing feature movies weekly—for free—and housing a studio where you can read a TV newscast and take home an "audition tape." Then there's the hotel with a beautiful Art Deco swimming pool where movie Tarzan Johnny Weismuller swam laps and TV's *Untouchables* was filmed—and another with Japanese suites with a traditional tatami-mat sleeping room, deep soak tub, and private rock garden. Close to glitzy Michigan Avenue is a vest-pocket park ideal for walking, running, and jogging.

These contrasts—and many more—are what make Chicago such a vibrant and exciting travel destination. And this book shines its whimsical spotlight on all of the diverse facets of this city with big shoulders, a friendly smile, and a warm heart.

As you may have guessed, this is not your standard guidebook. Think of us as a well-informed friend—the kind you wish you had in every city you visit. Wouldn't it be great to have a friendly native Chicagoan steer you to all of the worthwhile (and even unusual) sites, while avoiding the overrated or past-their-prime spots? Wouldn't it be fun to learn the real inside gossip and fascinating history about the sights you're seeing? We've set out to do just that—and more. Thorough chapter selections and a comprehensive index make this a practical book to use—but the innovative suggestions make it fun and (we think you'll come to agree) indispensable to use.

Looking for historic sights? You'll find the expected here, often examined in a new light . . . the landmark Water Tower and the Field Museum . . . but we also introduce you to the unexpected. We take you to a museum for history, Sunday brunch, and Gershwin, and to another for world-class art and Chicago-style jazz—and on a journey down all three branches of the Chicago River for a fish's eye view at Chicago's famous (and little-known) architecture.

Bringing the kids along? We direct you to an entire chapter of attractions keyed especially to families visiting Chicago, from out of town or from out in the suburbs. (Check out an old-time saloon with wandering magicians.) Ditto for lovers—and honeymooners—with the special selections in our "Romantic" chapter. And for when you venture beyond Chicago, we've even got you covered there. Head for our "Best of the 'Burbs (and Beyond)" chapter for insights on some special places in the suburbs and in nearby Illinois, Indiana, Michigan, and Wisconsin, such as a shop full of *Wizard of Oz* memorabilia that is visited by some of the midgets who appeared as Munchkins in the movie, and where to play 18 holes of golf without using clubs.

This is a book to browse through, perhaps chuckling at some of the folly enclosed within (such as a card shop called He Who Eats Mud, a no-nonsense tavern sign proclaiming "No Corona, no foolish drinks, limited dancing, no substitutions," and how Mike Ditka claimed that frugal Chicago Bears' owner, the late George Halas, threw nickels around "like manhole covers"). But it is also intended as a solid reference guide—we let you know not just what's out there, but why it's worth a visit. And, while this book strives to be a good, lively read, full of fun as well as fact, it also is a completely practical volume, giving full addresses and phone numbers for attractions, so you'll have all of the information you need close at hand.

This book is intended as a resource for the first-time visitor and the Chicago-area resident alike. We help the first-timer find the unexpected treasures that can literally make a vacation. As for veteran travelers, we'd be hard-pressed to believe that anyone (even an immensely curious native Chicagoan) has journeyed to all of the nearly 600 sites we've surveyed in this book. This means, of course, that we can help seasoned visitors get even more out of a trip to Chicago by helping them discover hidden gems that may have escaped them on previous trips or by pointing out new worthwhile restaurants or attractions that have opened since they last visited.

Let's face it—it *can* be hard work having a great vacation, or even a stimulating weekend in the city or night out on the town. We've attempted to take some of the work out of your play time by tracking down everything you might want to do in and around Chicago—including things you didn't *know* you wanted to do, but *will* after reading about them!

So, what this book offers is both the famous and the should-be-famous . . . both the expensive and the inexpensive (and even the free!). But, overall and most importantly, it offers a unique and entertaining perspective on one of the most diverse, friendly, and fascinating destinations in the United States. To say the least, our perspective (with equal touches of history and humor) is much like Chicago itself: you are not likely to find anything like it anywhere else.

CHICAGO BASICS

Getting Around

Among the world's major cities, Chicago is one of the easiest in which to get around. Its basic-grid street layout, its flat topography, and its location along a gentle curve of Lake Michigan shoreline combine to make Chicago's geography generally much less confusing than other cities of comparable size.

A few basic rules of orientation are all that you need to get around safely and simply. First and foremost, the lake is always east. Keeping that fact in mind can make it elementary (when along the lakeshore or just inland, where many of the city's most popular sites are located) to determine in which direction you are headed.

Another helpful bit of knowledge is the method of street and address numbering. The intersection of State and Madison Streets (once known as the "World's Busiest Corner" for its hectic foot and vehicle traffic) is the baseline from which city streets are numbered (as well as those in many bordering suburbs). State Street is the east-west baseline, meaning (for example) that Halsted Street, which is 800 West, is roughly eight blocks west of State. Similarly, Madison Street is the numbering starting point for north-south streets; Division Street is 1200 North, making it 12 blocks north of Madison.

You should also remember that all north-south streets in the entire city and all of the east-west streets north of Madison have names (rather than numbers); for the most part, east-west streets beginning south of 12th Street/Roosevelt Road are numbered (although some South Side streets have both names and numbers—such as 12th Street/Roosevelt Road, 22nd Street/Cermak Road, 39th Street/Pershing Road, and 55th Street/Garfield Boulevard).

There are also a number of major diagonal streets that angle northwest through the North and Northwest Sides (such as Broadway, Clark Street, Lincoln Avenue, Milwaukee Avenue, Clybourn Avenue, and Elston Avenue) or southwest through the South and Southwest Sides (such as Vincennes Avenue, Archer Avenue, and Ogden Avenue).

For the sake of generalities, the city's basic division units are as follows: The Loop (named for an old street-car turnaround, not the elevated train line that circles downtown, as is commonly thought) is the city's downtown area and its principal business district; its loose boundaries are the Chicago River on the north, Congress Street/Eisenhower Expressway (Interstate 290) on the south, Halsted Street on the west and Lake Michigan on the east. The Near North Side contains the shopping and sightseeing treasures of North Michigan Avenue (the Magnificent Mile) and roughly stretches north from the river to North Avenue and west from the lake to LaSalle Street. The Near South Side is home to a number of museums and historic sites and stretches south of Congress to 12th Street/Roosevelt Road and west of the lake to the Dan Ryan Expressway (Interstate 90/94). The slice of the lakeshore from North Avenue north to the suburb of Evanston and west to approximately Western Avenue is the North Side; the wide area west of Western Avenue and north of North Avenue is loosely called the Northwest Side. Directly west of the Loop, from Halsted to the city's western limits, and from Lake Street on the north to 12th Street/Roosevelt Road on the south, is the West Side. South of 12th Street/Roosevelt Road, from the city's southern and western boundaries east to approximately Western Avenue, is the Southwest Side; south of 12th Street/Roosevelt Road, to the city's southern and southeastern boundaries and from Western Avenue to the lakeshore, is the sprawling South Side (further segmented into the Southeast Side closer to the lake).

Visitors should also be aware that the terms "South Side," "North Side," and "West Side" are occasionally (if somewhat inexactly) used to describe any part of the city south, north, or west of the Loop, respectively.

Ethnic Neighborhoods at a Glance

No other American city (except perhaps New York) reflects the depth of ethnic diversity that Chicago does. From the Irish who came as laborers and stayed as political leaders to the Polish who outnumber the population of all but the largest cities in Poland to the Third World emigrés settling in neighborhoods abandoned by previous groups, Chicago is a fascinating melting pot of peoples and cultures. Following are brief overviews of some of these ethnic groups and the areas they inhabit.

Irish: Although the Irish are scattered all over the city, the Near Southwest Side neighborhoods of Canaryville and (especially) Bridgeport are the seat of Irish power and culture in Chicago. Bridgeport is where Mayor Richard M. Daley grew up and where his father, the late Mayor Richard J. Daley, lived for years.

Italian: Though many feared this neighborhood just southwest of the Loop would die when it was truncated for the erection of the University of Illinois-Chicago campus in the 1960s, a lively scene of shops and restaurants still flourishes along Taylor Street.

Polish: As with the Irish, Poles have spread throughout the city, especially on the Northwest and Southwest sides. But a heavy concentration of Polish-run businesses can still be found along and just off North Milwaukee Avenue, especially from Division Street north to Irving Park Road.

Lithuanian: The Southwest Side neighborhood of Marquette Park is home to a Lithuanian community of more than 100,000 residents. Lithuanian Court Plaza (a renamed section of 69th Street) has a variety of ethnic restaurants, groceries, and other shops.

Swedish: The North Side neighborhood of Andersonville, along Clark Street north of Foster Avenue, is home to Swedish bakeries, delis, shops, bars, and a Swedish-American museum.

Vietnamese: Mostly concentrated on a short stretch of Argyle Street on the North Side (between Sheridan Road and Broadway), the neighborhood of Little Saigon offers highly regarded restaurants, markets, shops, and a Vietnam War museum run by an American veteran.

Chinese: The long-standing Chinatown directly southwest of the Loop (centered around Wentworth Avenue) is a compact, colorful area of restaurants, shops, and homes, many featuring distinctly Oriental architecture or decorative touches. Street signs are in both English and Chinese characters.

Korean: On the Northwest Side, along Lawrence Avenue, generally west of Western Avenue, is a fairly recently established Korean neighborhood, boasting a congregation of Korean shops, markets, and churches.

Indian: Along Devon Street, west of Western Avenue, near the city's northern limits, is a row of Indian eateries, clothing shops, and video-rental stores serving the area's Indian and Pakistani population.

Greek: Known for dining (which seems universally popular and is relatively inexpensive) and lively nightlife, Greektown is concentrated along Halsted Street, immediately north of Van Buren Street, just west of the Loop. As in other big cities, a wide variety of Greek-run coffee shops and corner restaurants are spread throughout Chicago.

African-American: The South Side (with the exception of the Southeast Side) and the West Side are home to a large African-American population. Most historic or heritage-oriented sites (such as the DuSable Museum) are located on the South Side.

Czechoslovakian/Bohemian: Cermak Road/22nd Street, on the western edge of the city, entering the suburbs of Berwyn and Cicero, is an area of basic bungalows and hearty Czech/Bohemian dining. A major annual festival celebrates its ethnicity and includes a houby (mushroom) hunt.

Hispanic: The Pilsen/Little Village area, on the Near Southwest Side, boasts a largely Mexican community. The Northwest Side neighborhood of Logan Square, centered around Logan Boulevard (at Kedzie Avenue and Wrightwood Avenue), is a more gentrified area, with a still-large Mexican and Puerto Rican population.

Ukrainian: A small Ukrainian neighborhood is centered around a pair of neighborhood museums and two massive, doomed churches near Chicago Avenue and Western Avenue on the Near Northwest Side.

Jewish: Although some Hasidic Jews still congregate on the far North Side (in a neighborhood around Peterson Avenue, west of California Street) and also run the diamond marts on the "Jeweler's Row" of Wabash Avenue in the Loop, most Jewish residents have become assimilated. Many Jewish families live in the northern suburbs of Skokie, Evanston, Lincolnwood, and Highland Park.

Transportation

Chicago's integrated public transportation system, known as the CTA (Chicago Transit Authority), is one of the largest in the world. Consisting of rapid-transit trains (known as the "El," for elevated train— which also runs underground in the subways downtown) and buses, the CTA covers all neighborhoods of the city. It also runs regularly to O'Hare International and Midway airports and even ventures into a number of bordering suburbs.

Two subway lines run under the Loop: The line under State Street basically serves the South Side and the North Side along the lakeshore to Evanston; the line under Dearborn Street heads northwest to O'Hare and south, then west, along the Eisenhower Expressway. A number of overhead elevated lines from the north, south, and west converge and circle the Loop.

Bus lines are typically named for the streets they principally run on (though some run established routes on a number of streets); the termination of the run is stated on the sign giving the name and route number on the top front of the bus. In general, both north-south and east-west bus routes are spaced every four to six blocks apart. Corner signs designate bus stops, and include information on the route(s) that stop there, ultimate destinations, and hours/days of operation.

Current fare is $1.50 both for rapid transit trains and buses and 30 cents for a transfer that allows up to two more trips in a two-hour span on any bus or train line *other* than the one on which you purchased the transfer. Tokens (available in rolls of 10 for $13.50 at rapid transit stations, currency exchanges, banks, and other locations) are good for one fare on any bus or train at any time (making them the best short-term bargain); month-long passes ($88) are good for unlimited rides in a given calendar month; buses accept dollar bills as well as coins. It's a good idea to have exact change on hand. There are reduced fares for seniors, students, and children.

The suburban commuter-train system is known as Metra and serves a wide variety of outlying city neighborhoods and suburbs in all directions. Trains heading straight south or southeast into Indiana depart from the Randolph Street Station just off Michigan Avenue; trains bound for the north, northwest, west, and southwest depart from Union Station and Northwestern Station, blocks apart along the river, on the western edge of downtown. (Amtrak, the national passenger rail service, also departs from Union Station.)

For any CTA or Metra schedule or route information, you can call the Regional Transportation Authority (RTA) Travel Center at 312/836-7000 (the RTA oversees both the CTA and Metra).

Currency

The basic units of U.S. currency are dollars ($) and cents (¢), with the proportion being 100 cents to one dollar. U.S. currency consist of both metal coins and paper bills. The denominations of the coins are as follows: 1 cent, a copper-colored coin called a penny or a cent; 5 cents, a silver-colored coin called a nickel; 10 cents, a silver-colored coin called a dime; 25 cents, a silver-colored coin called a quarter (short for quarter of a dollar); 50 cents, a silver-colored coin called a half-dollar (rarely used); and a silver-colored dollar coin (rarely used). The coins increase in size with value, with the exception of the dime, which is the smallest coin (i.e., smaller than the penny).

U.S. paper currency is all one size, printed with dark green and black ink, in the following amounts: $1, $2 (rarely used), $5, $10, $20, $50, and $100 (larger denominations exist, but are no longer actively printed and are used almost exclusively by banks).

Government

The city of Chicago is under the separate jurisdictions (for separate needs) of four different governing bodies—in (somewhat) ascending order. These are The City of Chicago, Cook County, the State of

Illinois, and the U.S. Government. Basically and briefly, these bodies govern and control the following: The City of Chicago provides basic city services (police and fire protection, refuse pickup, etc.). It also provides low-income housing for needy residents, and maintains the city's public "infrastructure" (i.e., streets, parks, etc.). Cook County levies taxes on goods and services, runs the local court system, maintains public hospitals, and runs the county-wide jail. The State of Illinois collects statewide taxes, issues drivers' licenses, pays unemployment benefits and public aid to disadvantaged residents, and generally protects and promotes the general interests of all the individual entities (i.e., counties and cities) within the state. The U.S. Government collects income taxes, maintains the armed forces, delivers the mail, regulates commerce, sets and investigates standards for food quality and worker safety, and generally maintains the welfare of the citizens of the entire country.

The following are the general information numbers for the local offices of these government entities: City of Chicago, 312/744-5000; Cook County, 312/443-5500; State of Illinois, 312/793-3500; U.S. Government, 312/353-4242. The following selected government agencies may be of particular interest to foreign visitors: U.S. Customs Service, district office, 312/353-6100; O'Hare Airport Passenger Information, 312/686-2131; O'Hare Cargo Information, 708/860-0024; Immigration and Naturalization Service, 312/353-7334; U.S. State Department, Diplomatic Security Service, 312/353-6163; Office of Foreign Missions, 312/353-5762. Other city, county, state, and federal agencies are listed in a blue-paged section in the front of the local White Pages telephone directory.

Holidays

The following are holidays universally affecting government services and almost all businesses:

January 1—New Year's Day

The last Monday in May—Memorial Day

July 4—Independence Day*

The first Monday in September—Labor Day

The fourth Thursday in November—
Thanksgiving

December 25—Christmas

---

* Often observed on a Monday preceding or following this date.

The following are holidays affecting most government services and some businesses:

January 15—Martin Luther King, Jr.'s Birthday*

A Monday in February—President's Day**

The Friday before Easter—Good Friday

Easter Sunday (date ranges from March to April)

October 12—Columbus Day*

The second Monday in November—Veterans Day (formerly Armistice Day)

The Friday following Thanksgiving

Christmas Eve (or any Friday or Monday directly preceding or following Christmas)

December 31—New Year's Eve

The following are holidays (or special event days) worth noting, but having little or no effect on government services or businesses:

February 14—Valentine's Day

March 17—St. Patrick's Day

The second Sunday in May—Mother's Day

June 1—Flag Day

The third Sunday in June—Father's Day

October 31—Halloween

The first Tuesday following the first Monday in November—Election Day***

The following are widely celebrated Jewish religious holidays or holiday periods which may affect some businesses:

Late March–mid-April—Passover

Late September–mid-October—Rosh Hashannah (the Jewish New Year)

One week after Rosh Hashannah—Yom Kippur

Mid-December–late December—Hannukah

---

* Often observed on the Monday preceding or following this date.

** Observed on a Monday, usually between February 12 (Abraham Lincoln's Birthday) and February 22 (George Washington's Birthday).

*** City primary (interparty) and general election days are held in certain years during late February and early April, respectively.

Weather

Chicago's weather is both legendary and somewhat exaggerated. Yes, it can get extremely hot (witness the "killer heat wave" of 1995) and bitterly cold—but there are plenty of comfortable days in between. As for the nickname "Windy City," the truth is that Chicago is not even in the top ten of windiest U.S. cities. (In fact, the phrase sprang not from any breezy weather conditions, but in response to the bombastic, long-winded tendencies of city politicians of a previous era.) The city's average mean temperatures are 27°F (–3°C) in winter (Dec.–Mar.); 49°F (9°C) in spring (Mar.–June); 73°F (23°C) in summer (June–Sept.); and 54°F (12°C) in fall (Sept.–Dec.). January and February are usually the coldest months (with howling wind-chill factors often lowering the actual temperature); July and August are usually the hottest; April and October can be rainy. Chicago is definitely a four-season town, and visitors should be prepared to dress according to the likely weather of the season of their visit. And they should remember the old saw (which has a ring of truth) about the abrupt changeability of Chicago's weather: If you don't like the weather, stick around for an hour or two.

The proximity of Lake Michigan has a moderating effect on Chicago's weather. In summer, the lakeshore can be as much as 10 degrees cooler than areas away from the lake, including O'Hare, where the city's official temperatures are recorded. In winter, the reverse can be true, with neighborhoods on the immediate lakefront enjoying a few extra degrees of moderation.

Tipping

The following suggestions will provide a general guide for tipping in Chicago. Of course, the final arbiters for tipping are both the level of service received (as contrasted with the level expected) and personal preference. In all but the most extreme cases, undertipping (or no tipping in some situations) in Chicago is not as likely to bring the icy stares or rude comments that the same behavior may engender in, for example, New York. In general, Chicago is a polite, friendly town, and service personnel work hard for their gratuities and appreciate them when given.

Waitstaff: 15%–20% of the total bill (before tax) is the standard amount. (Automatic gratuities are often added for large groups; read the bill carefully before giving what might be an *additional* tip.)

Maitre D's or Sommeliers: Generally considered optional. Only in the top-of-the-line, fanciest restaurants do maitre d's expect to get tipped merely for showing you to a table. However, if a special service is performed, such as obtaining a "better" table or delivering a gift during dinner, $10–$20 is acceptable. The same generally holds true for sommeliers—a tip is not expected except in the finest restaurants or for special service (and then, perhaps $5–$10).

Bartenders or Bar Waitstaff: Optional, but usually greatly appreciated. For bar service, leaving some loose change is acceptable; perhaps more for special, custom-ordered drinks if skillfully prepared. For table service, $1–$2 per round (for a group) is suggested to reward good and attentive service.

Hotel Personnel: $1 per bag for luggage transfer; $2 per day for maid service (on long stays); 10% for room service (but check bill to ensure that gratuity has not already been added); 15%–20% for concierge who makes special arrangements, such as hard-to-get theater tickets or restaurant reservations.

Transportation: Taxis—round up to the next dollar or half-dollar for low fares/short trips (i.e., $3.00 for a $2.80 fare); approximately 10% for high fares/long trips. Limousine: 10%–15%. For luggage, add $1 per bag—only if handled.

Miscellaneous Service Personnel: 10%–15% (depending on the service given and/or special instructions followed) is suggested for barbers, beauticians, manicurists, masseurs, shoe shines, etc.

Calendar of Events

(Dates/periods approximate)

Early January—Chicago Boat, Sports & RV Show, McCormick Place

Late January/Early February—Sport Fishing, Travel & Outdoor Show, O'Hare Exposition Center

Late January/Early February—Chinese New Year's Parade, Wentworth & Cermak

February—Black History Month (various city-wide events)

Mid-February—Chicago Auto Show, McCormick Place

Mid-February—Virginia Slims Tennis Tournament, UIC Pavilion

March 17—St. Patrick's Day Parade, Dearborn Street

Late March—Volvo of Chicago Tennis Tournament, UIC Pavilion

April–September/October—Professional baseball season, home games at Comiskey Park (White Sox) and Wrigley Field (Cubs)

Early April—Antiques Show, O'Hare Exposition Center

Early–mid-May—Chicago International Art Expo, Navy Pier

Early June—Chicago Gospel Festival, Grant Park

Early–mid-June—Chicago Blues Festival, Grant Park

Early–mid-June—Old Town Art Fair, North Avenue/Wells Street neighborhood

Mid-June–early September—Ravinia Festival (outdoor concerts) Ravinia Park, Highland Park

Late June–early July—Taste of Chicago food fest, Grant Park

July 4 (or eve of)—Independence Day Concert & Fireworks, Grant Park

Mid-July—Chicago Air & Water Show, lakefront

Late July—Chicago-Mackinac Island Yacht Race, Monroe Harbor

Early–mid-August—Gold Coast Art Fair, River North area

Early–mid-August—Venetian Night Boat Parade, Monroe Harbor

Late August–early September—Chicago Jazz Festival, Grant Park

Late August–early September—International Festival of Racing/Arlington Million, Arlington International Racecourse, Arlington Heights

Labor Day—Chicago Federation of Labor Parade, Dearborn Street

September–December/January—Professional football season, home games at Soldier Field (Bears)

Mid-September–January/February—Lyric Opera season, Civic Opera Center

Late September–mid-June—Chicago Symphony Orchestra season, Orchestra Hall

October–April—Professional hockey season, home games at the United Center (Blackhawks)

Columbus Day—Columbus Day Parade, Dearborn Street

Mid-October—Chicago International Antiques Show, Navy Pier

Mid-late October—Chicago International Film Festival, various theaters

Late October—Chicago Marathon, begins downtown

November–April—Professional basketball season, home games at the United Center (Bulls)

Late November–early January—Christmas Around the World Festival, Museum of Science & Industry

Late November—Lighting of official city Christmas tree, Daley Center Plaza

Late November—Christmas Parade, Michigan Avenue

December—*A Christmas Carol*, Goodman Theatre

December—*The Nutcracker*, Arie Crown Theatre

Mid-December—Do-It-Yourself "Messiah," Orchestra Hall

Emergency

For any emergency police, fire, or ambulance calls, dial 911 from any phone (free at pay phones). For police non-emergencies, call 312/744-4000. For fire or ambulance non-emergencies, call 312/744-4770.

Driving and Parking Tips

Driving in Chicago is neither the near-impossibility that it is in New York nor the near-necessity that it is in Los Angeles. Here, as in most major cities, the two main driving worries are traffic jams and parking. Heavy rush-hour use clogs the interstate highways (and other primary roads) in and out of the city each morning and evening. And drivers unwilling to pay parking-lot rates (ranging from $5 to $20 per day) jockey for the available downtown street spaces every morning. A few pointers can make dealing with these hassles a little easier.

First, if possible, travel into and out of the city during off hours (to avoid the 7–9:30 A.M. and 3:30–7 P.M. crushes). Second, check ahead as to whether your hotel (or the shops, restaurants, attractions you are patronizing) offers any parking deals or discounts; many will give you a validation on your parking receipt discounting the cost of parking in a lot. Third, when necessity forces the use of pay lots or garages, check for the availability of "early-bird" rates (typically, for parking periods *beginning* before 9 A.M.); if such early timing fits your schedule, these rates can save you money. Fourth, if you must park on the street, either downtown or in the neighborhoods (especially on the space-conscious North Side) and you are unable to find a legal spot (and we are *not* recommending illegal parking), it can be important to remember the differences between illegal parking that can earn you a parking ticket and that which can cause your car to be towed away: Cars parked near fire hydrants and the ends of the block may be ticketed; cars parked near bus stops (marked with a sign) or blocking intersections, private driveways, or alleys may be towed.

General driving rules to remember: Drive on the right side of the road and pass on the left (when safety and signage allow); speed limits are 55 miles per hour (approx. 90 kilometers per hour) on highways and 55–65 mph on interstates, 45 mph (approx. 70 kph)—but lowered in winter—on Lake Shore Drive (a limited-access highway along Lake Michigan), and 30 mph (approx. 50 kph) on city streets; for now no cars are allowed on State Street downtown, between Lake Street and Congress Parkway (it has been turned into a pedestrian- and bus-only open-air mall, but will soon be reopened to auto traffic).

Banking

Typical banking hours are weekdays from 8 or 9 A.M. until 5 or 6 P.M., with limited hours (perhaps from 9 A.M. until noon or 3 P.M.) on Saturdays. Most banks have automatic teller machines (ATMs) available for 24-hour deposits and withdrawals; ATMs can also be found in many other locations, such as shopping centers, office buildings, and 24-hour convenience stores.

Telephones

Telephones are relatively easy to use, both in Chicago and throughout the rest of the United States. Area codes may be a little more confusing, simply because huge demand has depleted the supply of phone numbers within existing area codes, creating the need for additional area codes. As a result, many numbers within Chicago and its suburbs have been, are being, or will be assigned new area codes. When the changeover is accomplished by early 1997, the area will be served by five area codes instead of two.

Essentially, the city core will retain the 312 area code and many suburbs to the south will continue to use the 708 area code. A newly created 847 area code will be assigned to the northwest quadrant of metropolitan Chicago, and a new 630 code to the west and southwest suburbs (effective August 1996). Finally, a new 773 code will be assigned to parts of the city proper.

Pay phones require a 35¢ deposit (using any coin combination except pennies) for basic service; long-distance service (within the U.S.) will require up to $3.00 (in coins) for the first three minutes. Operators can assist you in placing collect, overseas, or other special calls—dial "0" (zero) to reach the operator. Hotel phones vary in method of operation and price by hotel—generally, they are more expensive than pay-phones or private-phone calls. The hotel operator can inform you as to any special tariffs for calls made from your room.

Directory assistance (to obtain published telephone numbers of individuals or businesses) can be reached by dialing "411"—this call may be free from some pay phones (but generally is not supposed to be).

Sightseeing Companies

The following companies offer sightseeing tours of Chicago and the surrounding areas: American Sightseeing, 312/427-3100; Chicago From The Lake (boat tours), 312/527-2002; Chicago Gray Line, 312/251-3107; Chicago Motor Coach Co. (using double-decker, open-top buses), 312/922-8919; Keeshin, 312/254-6400; Untouchable Tours (specializing in gangster-oriented sites), 312/881-1195; and Wendella Sightseeing Boats, 312/337-1446.

Safety Tips

As with any big U.S. city, Chicago has its share of crime (although its total per capita crime rate *is* significantly lower than those of New York, Los Angeles, Washington, D.C., and Detroit).

To minimize your chances of being victimized by criminal activities, you need to use basic common sense and an awareness of where you are. In your hotel, use lockboxes to store valuables, never leave your key unattended at the front desk, and don't announce your room number to anyone as you go out. On the streets, carry wallets in inside jacket or front trouser pockets, not hip pockets (better yet, use a money belt or a hidden, zipped compartment). Carry purses close to your body, preferably with the strap across your body. Don't carry large amounts of cash or traveler's checks with you—leave these in your hotel lockbox. Also, keep a copy of your traveler's check receipts and your passport in your hotel room or lockbox.

Chicago natives generally are friendly and helpful and usually don't mind giving directions or advice on nearby places of interest. If you wish, stop someone on the street to ask for information or directions, but beware of people who size you up and approach you uninvited, asking if you're lost or if you need anything. They *may* just be helpful Good Samaritans, but they also may be trying to gain your confidence to con you or otherwise victimize you.

The Loop is always safe during the day (although pickpockets and purse-snatchers, while not prevalent, have been known to work any area at any time) and is well-lit and mostly safe (if a bit abandoned once offices close) at night. In general, avoid any street that seems less well-lit than the one you are on and avoid traversing alleys behind streets. Some areas of the South, West, and Near Northwest Sides can be risky to travel alone at night; if in a car, keep your doors locked, and don't roll down your windows for anyone except a properly uniformed or otherwise identified police officer.

On the CTA, be watchful for people jostling you from the front or rear as you get on or off a bus or train; they may be trying to distract you while an accomplice tries to pick your pocket or snatch your purse. If riding a CTA train after dark, stand on the platform near other people and sit in the car with the conductor (who opens the doors and announces the stops). When riding buses at night, sit near the front, on the right side of the bus, in view of the driver.

Of course, in the unfortunate event of being threatened with force (whether a weapon is visible or not—and *especially* if one is), stay calm; give up the wallet, purse, or jewelry that the attacker wants; and don't cause a commotion. After the attacker has fled, immediately contact the police. In general, stay alert and be smart—maximized preparation can help minimize the chances of trouble.

DINING

Best meatloaf served by wiseacre waiters

Ed Debevic's

It's hard to imagine that in trendy River North a restaurant serving home-style food such as meatloaf and mashed potatoes with gravy would be a success. But Ed Debevic's, a 1950s-theme diner, has been a hit from the day it opened back in 1984. The formula may work because kids, who know all about diners from *Happy Days* and *American Graffiti*, are anxious to sample the "real thing," and their parents, anxious to relive those good old days, are willing drag-alongs. Ed's is as authentic as you can get. The theatrical waitstaff are wise-cracking, gum-snapping throwbacks to the innocent, fun-lovin' 1950s, who seldom step out of character. The exterior has green and white ceramic tiles and hand-painted mottos. Inside is a veritable museum of 1950s artifacts—old Coke bottles, advertising signs for products such as Green River soda, and signs promoting a root-beer concoction called Black Cow and noting that the "chili speaks for itself." Stainless steel counters and tables and "oldies" blaring from speakers complete the illusion. You'll find American favorites such as burgers and casseroles, pot roast, wet fries (with gravy), cheese fries, and sandwiches that include hot turkey and BLT. The fountain serves up old-fashioned thick malts; dessert selections include fruit and cream pies, such as apple, banana, coconut, and Ed's celebrated Oreo cookie pie. Always crowded, it's best to go during non-peak hours. As a sign proclaims: "If you think you have a reservation, you're in the wrong place."

Ed Debevic's, 640 N Wells St, Chicago, IL 60610, 312/664-1707. Mon–Thu 11 am–10 pm, Fri & Sat 11 am–11:30 pm, Sun 11:30 am–10 pm.

Best lunches served by oldest waiters

The Berghoff

Sometimes it seems as though the elderly, brusque waiters have been around almost as long as this venerable Loop restaurant. That, of course, is impossible, because the oak-paneled, old-world saloon and eatery has been in continuous operation since just before the turn of the century. German dishes are solid—schnitzel, sauerbraten, wurst platters, and gschnaetzlets (veal stew)—along with terrific red cabbage, German fries, and buttered egg noodles, plus nonpareil creamed spinach. Steaks and chops are also reliable and there is surprisingly good seafood, including halibut, broiled whitefish, and a decent rendition of bouillabaisse as a Friday lunch special. If you prefer a sandwich, the piled-high corned-beef sandwich is tops. Good bets for desserts—all homemade—are apple strudel and bread pudding. After repeal of Prohibition, The Berghoff was granted liquor license No. 1 in Chicago, so it is no surprise that it brews its own beer (as well as root beer) and offers a connoisseur's collection of smooth, private-stock bourbons.

The Berghoff, 17 W Adams St, Chicago, IL 60603, 312/427-3170. Mon–Thu 11 am–9 pm, Fri 11 am–9:30 pm, Sat 11 am–10 pm.

Best southern-style biscuits

Wishbone Restaurants

The original Wishbone, a corner café in a yet-to-be-gentrified area of the near west side, remains a popular and cheery spot for breakfast, with fresh-looking cream-colored walls and teal-colored ceiling and ductwork. There are fresh flowers on the tables and colorful wall art featuring chickens. But, with only ten tables plus some counter space, it can get crowded. "Who wants coffee? Raise your hands," says a harried waitress. It's that sort of place. Cuisine is a mix of Southern and Southwestern. Specials include Kentucky scrambled eggs (with corn and onion and topped with bacon) and red eggs (with corn tortillas, black beans, cheese, chili ancho sauce, and cilantro salsa). Homemade biscuits are served with country gravy with generous chunks of sausage. Sides include corn muffins, cheese grits, and home fries. Now Wishbone has spread out, and patrons can, too. Opening a second, much larger restaurant in a former tire store near Oprah Winfrey's Harpo Studios—its cinder-block walls decorated with colorful folk art—Wishbone has created a nice spot for lunch and dinner (with outside dining). Here you can enjoy the likes of spicy shrimp étoufée, crawfish cakes, and pan-fried chicken with sides of black beans. Soups and gumbos are thick, corn bread is light and airy and made with a little cheese and onion, spinach is sautéed simply in a hot pan with lemon and seasonings, and rhubarb-strawberry pie has just the right degree of tartness. The new location features a bar and a cafeteria.

Wishbone Restaurant, 1800 W Grand Ave, Chicago, IL 60622, 312/829-3597. Sun–Tue 6 am–3 pm, Wed–Sat 6 am–9 pm; 101 W Washington St, Chicago, IL 60606, 312/850-2663. Mon 7 am–3 pm, Tue–Thu 7 am–10 pm, Fri 7 am–11 pm, Sat 8 am–11 pm, Sun 8 am–2:30 pm.

Best mom's-style meatloaf (depending on your mom)

Kinzie Street Chophouse

If you plan a weekday lunch here, be sure to make reservations. Across the street from the Merchandise Mart, this eatery draws a major crowd, with people eating in and at the bar as well as in the dining room. Ambience is basic stucco, enlivened by scores of caricatures of sports and entertainment celebrities. Film critic Gene Siskel is a patron, as are a number of Chicago Bears players—who undoubtedly come for the protein offered by the steak and chops that are star attractions on the menu. These include cuts of prime aged beef and prime rib as well as blackened double-cut lamb chops, stuffed veal chop with sun-dried tomato pesto, and a surf-and-turf combination. But there is also comfort food, such as meatloaf and chicken pot pie. Meatloaf comes with wild-mushroom gravy and satisfyingly lumpy mashed potatoes flavored with bacon and leeks. Herb-crusted salmon with mustard sauce is another standout, as is a creative selection of pastas, including duck ravioli with sun-dried cherry sauce and wild mushroom ravioli with brown-butter sage. Barbecue aficionados will find baby back ribs, chicken, and applewood-smoked pork chops. Sides include bacon-scallion "smashed" potatoes, spinach and mushrooms, and asparagus—served cold with vinaigrette or hot with Hollandaise. Save room for a rich chocolate mousse cake or a mountainous hunk of apple pie.

Kinzie Street Chophouse, 400 N Wells St, Chicago, IL 60610, 312/822-0191. Mon–Thu 11 am–10 pm, Fri & Sat 11 am–11 pm, Sun 4–9 pm.

Best Door County-style fish boil

My Place For?

This is perhaps the only restaurant in town with a name that asks a question—the answer to which quickly becomes apparent. Although the menu also offers steak, chicken, lamb, and other entrées, this is definitely a place for seafood, sometimes Oriental style, often with a Greek accent. Tender grilled or blackened mahi mahi or swordfish are moist, flavorful, and among the best of their type offered in the city. The bountiful Greek seafood soup—brimming with fish, squid, shrimp, scallops, lobster, and vegetables in a spicy tomato-based broth—is a meal in itself. And to see how Greeks fare at Wisconsin-style fish cookery, visit during the warm weather months, when My Place For? offers an indoors version of a Door County-style fish boil, featuring whitefish steaks and red potatoes. To make sure there is no doubt as to its specialty, the restaurant redecorated in 1995, introducing a nautical theme.

My Place For?, 7545 N Clark St, Chicago, IL 60626, 312/262-5767. Mon–Thu 4:30–9:30 pm, Fri & Sat 4:30 pm–12:30 am, Sun 3:30–9:30 pm.

Best pot roast in the most romantic setting

Gypsy

Sunshine steams in through arch-topped floor-to-ceiling windows. Two dining rooms are designed around massive, flame-colored pillars. The walls are alive with vibrant paintings of gypsy musicians. The soft strains of a jazz piano drift out onto the street. This is the warm, romantic ambience of a contemporary restaurant—one that offers, among many Mediterranean-influenced dishes, that all-American classic, pot roast (lean sirloin, braised tender and grilled and served in portobello mushroom broth). The food here is creatively conceived, superbly prepared and presented, and reasonably priced—most entrées coming in under $12. Try white bean chili with cornbread or tender chicken—roasted and seasoned with garlic and herbs or grilled with wild mushroom and mustard sauce. Innovative pasta choices include roasted garlic and brie ravioli with shrimp, spicy Portuguese clam linguine, and gorgonzola tortellinis featuring spicy Italian sausage, shrimp, onions, and mushrooms. Entrée salads feature grilled chicken Caesar, and a nice selection of sandwiches includes turkey brushetta, smoked salmon crostini, and grilled vegetables with brie. Desserts at Gypsy are definitely in the "must try" category—especially homemade cheesecake, classic French profiteroles served with vanilla ice cream and chocolate sauce, and terrapin tart, made with pecans, almonds, caramel, and chocolate.

Gypsy, 215 E Ohio St, Chicago, IL 60611, 312/644-9779. Lunch Mon–Fri & Sun 11:30 am–2:30 pm; dinner Mon–Thu 5:30–9:30 pm, Fri & Sat 5:30–11 pm, Sun 5:30–9 pm.

Best Swedish discovery since Vikings found America

Svea

Thin Swedish pancakes served with tart lingonberry sauce are popular breakfast fare with the weekend hordes that truck over to this small storefront restaurant that has been an Andersonville fixture for 25 years. On Saturdays, Svea sells 200 servings of pancakes, while Sundays are a full house for the 40-seat restaurant from 7 am until late afternoon. "We believe our secret pancake recipe is the greatest discovery since the Vikings found America," quips owner Kurt Mathiasson, who is sort of the unofficial mayor of Andersonville, founder in 1976 of the Swedish-American Museum Center. Although he has lived in the United States since 1963, the native of Göteborg (a Chicago sister city) still speaks with a Swedish accent as thick as pea soup. Svea also serves sweet brown beans, limpa bread, potato sausage, Swedish meatballs, salt pork, and *panbiff med lok*—a sort of fried hamburger smothered in onions. Svea uses old family recipes to make its own pickled herring, pickled beets, and sweet-and-sour cucumber salad. On Thursdays, according to Swedish tradition, you're certain to find thick yellow pea soup on the menu. "Young men in Sweden doing their military service look forward to Thursdays," says Mathiasson, "because they know they'll get pea soup." "Viking breakfasts" are predictably hearty. They feature eggs, *falukorv* sausage, and potatoes that are first boiled, then cut up and fried—plus two pancakes.

Svea, 5236 N Clark St, Chicago, IL 60640, 312/334-9619. Daily 7 am–4 pm.

More great Swedish pancakes—and cinnamon rolls to die for

Ann Sather

Although this is a full-service restaurant, to many Chicagoans Ann Sather means breakfast—in particular, sweet, thin Swedish pancakes served with slightly tart lingonberries—with a side of Swedish meatballs or mild potato sausage. Potato pancakes also are good, and there is a wide variety of three-egg omelettes. Now that the restaurant has a liquor license, the Sunday brunch crowd can enjoy Mimosas and bloody Marys with their corned beef and eggs and eggs Florentine. Brunch choices also include three types of Benedict: traditional, with smoked salmon, and with crabcake. Lunch and dinner feature such hearty fare as roast loin of pork, chopped beef steak, panfried chicken livers, and a Swedish "sampler" of roast duck with lingonberry glaze, meatballs, potato sausage, deliciously light dumplings, sauerkraut, and brown beans. Sather's cinnamon rolls are legendary—satisfyingly gooey and buttery soft. They accompany meals (along with carrot and banana-walnut bread), and you can buy them to go. The original restaurant is on Belmont Avenue, whereas this location occupies a gabled, white-fronted building in the heart of Swedish Andersonville. Small window panes are prettily decorated with ruffled balloon curtains; a series of paintings relates a Swedish fairy tale. Fresh flowers are on every table; candles are lighted in the evening. Free parking is available with validation. In winter, hot spiced wine and glogg are offered.

Ann Sather, 5207 N Clark St, Chicago, IL 60640, 312/271-6677. Sun–Thu 7 am–9 pm, Fri & Sat 7 am–10 pm.

Biggest German pancakes

Richard Walker's

In the mood for pancakes? This is the place. In the mood for big pancakes? Try the Deutsch Delight. It's light and fluffy, oven-baked on the premises, sprinkled with powdered sugar and lemon juice—and made in a *15-inch pan*. It's so big that it spills off the plate. It's hollow inside, ideal for spooning in fresh fruit, and it's big enough to feed two or more. The most popular choice, though, is the apple pancakes, filled with apples sliced fresh every day. Three-egg omelettes are light and airy, good with thick-cut bacon. Regular buttermilk pancakes can be gussied up with a variety of toppings. For those who like their pancakes in the evening—and who have dining partners who don't—Walker's introduced in 1995 a new dinner menu featuring the likes of spicy chicken wings, steak fajitas, char-broiled chicken, Caesar steak and Caesar chicken salads, and broccoli and shrimp linguine.

Richard Walker's, 1300 N Roselle Rd, Schaumburg, IL 60195, 847/882-1100. Sun–Thu 7 am–9 pm, Fri & Sat 7 am–10 pm.

Best omelette made with double-yolk eggs

Lou Mitchell's

For a breakfast in the city—especially, a leisurely weekend breakfast—don't miss this Chicago institution. Lou Mitchell's uses double-yolk eggs, serves doorstep-size slices of Greek toast, and offers 16 tempting airy omelette combinations (try broccoli and Old English cheddar). Egg dishes arrive in still-sizzling skillets. Many of the other offerings—meltaway pancakes, Belgian waffles, and golden French toast served with cooked fruit—have their own camp followers. For some, it's enough to order freshly squeezed juice, a pecan roll or homemade Danish, and a great brew of coffee (the latter is what the restaurant brags about). Saturdays are busy, often with a line stretching outdoors, with Lou on hand, as is his custom, to hand boxes of Milk Duds to waiting female patrons—plus a shot of coffee to any takers. It's possible to get seated quickly if you don't mind a counter seat.

Lou Mitchell's, 563 W Jackson Blvd, Chicago, IL 60606, 312/939-3111. Mon–Fri 5:30 am–4:00 pm, Sat 5:30 am–2:30 pm.

Best breakfast at the airport

Andiamo, O'Hare Hilton

Although the world's busiest airport has upgraded its food service, the quality and variety is still far less than one would hope for. If you find yourself at O'Hare with time for a leisurely breakfast, it is worth walking through a connecting corridor to this oasis in the O'Hare Hilton. Select from a bountiful buffet, or order à la carte from such selections as fluffy buttermilk pancakes with blueberries, apples, or bananas; smoked salmon; eggs Benedict; and well-made hash with poached eggs. The vast, creative menu includes macadamia nut waffles, cinnamon-swirl French toast, steak and eggs, and a Japanese-style breakfast with miso soup, salted salmon, poached egg, steamed rice, spinach with bonito, seaweed, pickled relish, and green tea. More suited to American palates are egg sandwiches—made with croissants or muffins—or as a folded western omelette on a kaiser roll. A vegetarian egg beater omelette is made with spinach, mushrooms, scallions, fresh basil, and oil-free marinara sauce. An all-you-can-eat buffet is a good value (priced under $10) and includes juices, fresh fruits, yogurt, cereal, pastries, scrambled eggs, an assortment of breakfast meats, and seasoned potatoes, plus blueberry pancakes and coffee. For the traveler, the pleasant, relaxed atmosphere of this restaurant, with its bold black and white tiles and a decor featuring bright floral arrangements and posters of advertising campaigns from the early 1900s, is a welcome change from frenetic O'Hare (and also a good spot to consider for lunch and dinner). An adjoining bar and grill, Sports Edition, has 19 satellite-connected televisions and features such sporting memorabilia as a bleacher seat from the original Comiskey Park, a New York Yankees Wall of Fame, and hundreds of signed photographs of sports stars.

Andiamo, O'Hare Hilton, 312/686-8000. Daily 6 am–11 pm.

Best Vienna All-Beef hot dog

Byron's

The original location of this mecca for hot dog lovers is a cramped and barely functional hut on Irving Park Road, just west of Sheridan Road and in the shadow of the Howard El line. Workers are packed behind the counter and customers eat at picnic benches in the parking lot or, in cold weather, in their cars. With (nonexistent) ambience like this, you know the food had better be good. And it is: succulent steamed (or char-broiled) Vienna All-Beef hot dogs, served up with all the Chicago-style trimmings—mustard, fluorescent green relish, chopped onion, half a sliced tomato, shredded lettuce, green pepper, hot peppers, and a dash of celery salt. (Chicago hot dog purists spurn ketchup, but you can get it nonetheless.) For more ambience but the same food, try Byron's other three locations.

Byron's, 1017 W Irving Park Rd, Chicago, IL 60613, 312/281-7474. Sun–Thu 10:30 am–midnight, Fri & Sat 10:30 am–1 am. Also at 1701 W Lawrence, Chicago, IL 60640, 312/271-0900; 6016 N Clark St, Chicago, IL 60660, 312/973-5000; and 850 W North Ave, Chicago, IL 60622, 312/266-3355.

Poshest Polish place

Mareva's

It's axiomatic that, if it's Polish, you'll find pierogis! But if you equate Polish cuisine only with storefront, family-run "ethnic" restaurants, you'll need to think again. This is upscale Polish, and, among three kinds of pierogis on the menu is a variation filled with lobster. Noted as one of the nation's top Eastern European restaurants, its lavish interior, with brass chandeliers, etched glass, and lively Slavic melodies played on a grand piano or by a strolling violinist, evokes aristocratic pre-war Poland. Start with tricolored borscht or, perfect in summer, cold peach soup. Or perhaps steak tartare, or one of those traditional pierogis with a nontraditional filling (the lobster version comes with a sauce that blends sour cream, cognac, and saffron). Entrées include salmon and shrimp with a raspberry-champagne sauce and a number of innovative veal and seafood choices. *Zrazy* is center-cut beef tenderloin stuffed with minced veal, mushrooms, and onions, on a bed of cracked buckwheat with mushroom sauce. A must-try dessert is *chrusty*—in effect, cruellers, deep-fried dough dusted with powdered sugar.

Mareva's, 1250 N Milwaukee Ave, Chicago, IL 60622, 312/227-4000. Mon–Fri 11 am–midnight, Sat & Sun 4 pm–midnight.

Best restaurant where you eat the plate, too

Mama Desta's Red Sea Restaurant

Sharing is the thing at this Ethiopian eatery, preferably with companions you're comfortable with, since there are no utensils. A combination plate offers a sampling of the main menu categories— lamb, poultry, beef, and vegetables. Mounds of each are set on a huge platter covered with thin pancakes, with extra pancakes on the side. Simply break off a piece of pancake and use it as a scoop. Finish by eating the host pancakes, by that time soaked with juices and flavors. Many entrées, including tasty lamb stew, are seasoned by berbere sauce, made with hot peppers. If fiery dishes are your preference, order the "hot combo." A popular vegetable entrée is ground roasted yellow split peas cooked with peppers, onions, garlic, and ginger. A half-dozen beef entrées include *zilzil tibs*, beef strips broiled with a savory combination of peppers, onions, and spices. Beer is a good companion drink, with domestic brands available, plus Club from Ghana and Mamba from the Ivory Coast. The ambience is dark and romantic, with bamboo-covered walls, a jungle of plants in the storefront window, straw tables in the bar, and flickering lamps on tables.

Mama Desta's Red Sea Restaurant, 3216 N Clark St, Chicago, IL 60657, 312/935-7561. Tue–Sat 11:30 am–11:30 pm, Mon 4:30–10:30 pm, Sun 11:30 am–10:30 pm.

Tastiest Thai tofu

Star of Siam

Thai restaurants have sprouted in Chicago like rice in a paddy. All of them provide budget dining; many are storefront locations. An exception is the Star of Siam. The food is authentic, reliable, and cheap, while the ambience is hi-tech (exposed bricks and beams, plum-painted ductwork), suitable for business as well as social get-togethers and the fashionable choice of many Chicago media celebrities. It features polished wooden tables, low benches carpeted in gray with green and white striped cushions, and glittery Thai embroidery as wall art. Satay, spring rolls, spicy golden-fried shrimp cakes, and cucumber salad are recommended starters. From a long and varied list of entrées, try chicken delight (with cashews, pea pods, bell peppers, and straw mushrooms), mild curried chicken, and hot and spicy steamed curried fish.

Star of Siam, 11 E Illinois St, Chicago, IL 60611, 312/670-0100. Sun–Thu 11 am–9:30 pm, Fri & Sat 11 am–10:30 pm.

Best clay oven cookery

Klay Oven

You might expect to find Ali Baba in a kitchen that specializes in tandoor cooking, which involves using ovens shaped like the huge jars that hid Ali from the 40 thieves. A charcoal fire at the base heats the smooth clay sides for breadmaking, while chicken and seafood are roasted in the pit. You also can order clay-oven–cooked lamb and steaks. Other specialties are stir-fried dishes prepared in a *karhai*, a cast-iron wok. Try a combination of shrimps cooked with onions, green peppers, garlic, and tomatoes—or a traditional lamb curry from Punjab in North India. Appetizers include pastry triangles stuffed with peas, potatoes, ginger, coriander, and dried mango powder. For dessert, sample mango-melba ice cream. The visually light and bright dining room is filled with Indian art—hand-painted silks, textiles dotted with semi-precious stones, batiks, and colorful three-dimensional silk embroidery on velvet.

Klay Oven, 414 N Orleans, Chicago, IL 60610, 312/
527-3999. Lunch Tue–Fri 11:30 am–2 pm, dinner Sun
& Tue–Thu 5:30–10:30 pm, Fri & Sat 5:30–11:30 pm.

Poshest place for Persian cookery

Reza's Restaurant

This neighborhood Persian restaurant is better looking than you might expect. Bare brick walls are
adorned with attractive Iranian prints, floors are
hardwood, tables are lacquered wood with vases of
fresh pink carnations. Despite its gentrified appearance, it also has a club-like atmosphere, with many
of Chicago's Iranian community socializing there.
Food is reminiscent of Greek cuisine—for example,
dolmeh, grape leaves stuffed with meat, vegetables,
lentils, yellow peas, and a delicately seasoned tomato sauce. As with Greek food, prices are reasonable. Beef kabobs are good, as is *fessenjan*, a
sweet-and-sour stew of Cornish hen with walnuts.
Characterizing the menu are yogurt-based appetizers and various char-broiled combinations—shrimp,
chicken, scallops, filet mignon, and vegetables—
served with a choice of Persian dill rice or white rice.
(This Andersonville restaurant is the original location; a larger branch has opened downtown at 432
W Ontario St, 312/664-4500, at a location that is
tough on restaurants—two earlier tenants failed.)

Reza's Restaurant, 5255 N Clark St, Chicago, IL
60640, 312/561-1898. Daily 11 am–midnight.

Best restaurant to conduct business over breakfast

Les Célébrités

If you're planning to clinch a contract over juice and
eggs, the Hotel Nikko's acclaimed river-view restaurant may help set the tone. You'll even find pens and
pads on the tables. Breakfasts are marvelous, with
an ambrosial version of corned beef hash and such
unusual creations as shirred eggs with wild-game
sausage and white cheddar cheese and a spinach
and cheese omelette with sun-dried tomato pesto.
Decorated in whites and off-whites accented by a
green couch and carpeting, this dining room is elegantly appointed with chairs upholstered in soft
floral patterns and sideboards dominated by massive white vases. For starters, don't miss baked apple
served with tart cherries, pecans, and cinnamon
cream. Then maybe try gingered flapjacks with blueberries or on apple-smoked salmon omelette with
sour cream. Or you may opt for homemade French
toast or a version of eggs Benedict that features a

smoked pork loin. Add freshly squeezed juice and good Kona coffee and you have the makings of a memorable meal—and perhaps a memorable business deal.

Les Célébrités, Hotel Nikko, 320 N Dearborn St, Chicago, IL 60610, 312/744-1900. Mon–Thu 6:30 am–10:30 pm, Fri–Sun am–11 pm.

Best restaurant to conduct business over lunch

La Strada Ristorante

This is a restaurant to impress a client—particularly if you're into expense-account lunches. It is upscale and elegant, with both food and prices to match (although fixed-price lunches can make you a hero with your accountant, too). It has rust-colored walls, booths with stained-glass partitions, and starchy-white napery. The pastas, prepared tableside, are superb—standards such as fettucini Alfredo and meat-filled tortellini with prosciutto are as good as you'd expect. Standouts among entrées are saltimbocca Romano (thin veal with sage, prosciutto, and wine) and pollo scarpariello (sautéed chicken chunks full of garlic and rosemary flavor). Appetizers include baked clams, oysters in a light tomato, wine, and herb sauce, carpaccio, and bresaola (mountain dried beef with lemon and oil). A simple dessert list includes tiramisu, lemon sorbet, chocolate mousse, and zabaglione. Pasta may be half-ordered as appetizers; daily luncheon specials include one each fish, chicken, veal, and pasta dish. The fixed-price luncheons at this Italian favorite are priced under $15 and include appetizer (grilled vegetables, minestrone), entrée (sautéed mahi-mahi with ginger leek sauce, veal tips), and dessert (apple walnut tart, white chocolate bread pudding).

La Strada Ristorante, 151 N Michigan, Chicago, IL 60601, 312/565-2200. Mon–Thu 11:30 am–10 pm, Fri 11:30 am–11 pm, Sat 5–11 pm.

Best restaurant to conduct business over dinner

Gene & Georgetti's

For more than 50 years, this restaurant in the now-trendy River North area has been serving up thick, satisfying aged steaks (plus a variety of Italian and seafood entrées and a huge and famous "garbage salad") to a mostly business-meal, expense-account crowd. Some maintain these are the finest steaks in town, and it's hard to dispute it. Its decor is reminiscent of a casual yet classic men's club—dark

wood paneling, red and white tablecloths, and napery. . . . All are housed in a more-than-100-year-
old building which was built from salvaged material
from the 1871 fire. This is a classic Chicago steak
joint that attracts a mixture of locals (including a
certain level of prominent politicians and
newspeople) and out-of-towners. A big spot for big
eaters to swing that big deal. Doesn't attract many
families or young singles.

Gene & Georgetti's, 500 N Franklin St, Chicago, IL
60610, 312/527-3718. Mon–Sat 11 am–midnight.

Biggest steak & lobster

The Palm

This is a place for carnivores. There are serious
steaks (dry-aged prime beef) at serious prices, and
huge lobsters (weighing in at five pounds or more)
which, judging from the number of patrons shame-
lessly adorned with bibs, seem to be almost as
popular. The noise level is high, and the atmosphere
is casual, with brass-railed booths, every square
inch of wall space covered with more than 1,000
caricatures of comic-book characters and famous
(and not-so-famous) clientele, and sawdust on the
floor. (*Note:* This restaurant is planning a move to
Swissôtel in spring 1996, and while the menu is
expected to stay the same, the ambience may
change.) The steaks are immense (and good) and
there also are lamb, pork, and veal chops, plus some
Italian veal entrées—but best to stick to meat plain
and simple, particularly the crusty-on-the-outside,
tender-on-the-inside steaks. Salads, vegetables,
potatoes (hash browns and cottage fries both are
excellent), and sweet-tasting onion rings all are à la
carte. At lunch, you can eat considerably cheaper if
you order a hamburger or a steak sandwich.

The Palm (relocating to the Swissôtel, 323 E Wacker
Dr, Chicago, IL 60601), 312/944-0135. Mon–Fri 11:30
am–10:30 pm, Sat 5–10:30 pm.

Best old-style steak house that's new

The Saloon

No matter how they like their steaks cooked, most
people seem to like their steak *houses* warm and
cheerful. The Saloon fits the bill, with the warm,
cheery glow of soft lighting off mahogany paneling
and rich leather. Walls are stenciled earth tones with
parchment sconces, the ceiling painted with Native
American murals, the inlaid wood floor a contrast
of mahogany and blond wood. This stuffy-but-
unpretentious steak house, where you are likely to
be offered shrimp de jonge in the accent of "da

Bears" offers high-quality steaks—prime cuts of marbled beef that has been dry-aged for the optimum 17–21 days and then prepared to order. These steaks should please the most fastidious of carnivores. Cuts range from a 20-ounce porterhouse to a 10-ounce New York strip or an 8-ounce filet mignon. If you enjoy potatoes with your meal, try bacon-scallion mashed potatoes or a crispy potato cake. Don't overlook the pork chop—among the best in town—prepared in the restaurant's own smoker. Rounding out the menu are ribs, free-range poultry, salmon, and salads. House cocktail specialties include Bloody Bulls (with beef bouillon) and optional anchovy/blue cheese-stuffed martini olives.

The Saloon, 200 E Chestnut, Chicago, IL 60611, 312/280-5454. Mon–Sat 11 am–midnight, Sun 11 am–10 pm.

Best bet for soup and salad

Houston's

If you've a mind for just a bowl of soup—or a bowl of soup and a salad—Houston's does both extremely well, and offers them in combination. Soups vary day to day and include cheese soup topped with chopped tomatoes and jalapeno peppers, baked-potato soup, capped generously with shredded cheese and bacon, red beans and rice soup thick with andouille sausage, creamy mushroom artichoke soup, tortilla soup, and chili. Salads, including Caesar and club, are well made. Light, yet satisfying enough to serve as a luncheon entrée, is a combination of sliced grilled chicken, chopped greens, and julienne tortilla strips, tossed with honey lime vinaigrette and garnished with a light peanut sauce. The unusual menu features couscous as an accompaniment to hamburgers, a number of chicken dishes that include roasted chicken with black beans, and thick banana milkshakes. The dark, clubby restaurant has subdued lighting, an open black-and-white–tile serving area, and seating almost exclusively in high-back burgundy booths.

Houston's, 616 N Rush St, Chicago, IL 60611, 312/649-1121. Mon–Thu 11 am–10 pm, Fri 11 am–11 pm, Sat 11:30 am–11 pm, Sun 11;30 am–10 pm.

Best Italian restaurant with singing waiters

Primavera Ristorante

Here's a restaurant that's spacious and gracious. With magnificent marble, imported china, and exquisite Italian cuisine, Primavera is a pure delight to the eye and the palate. If the decor (which includes a 49-foot mural of scenes from a classical Italian garden) reminds you of being at the opera, well, in a sense, you are. Twenty-five talented artists comprise the Primavera Singers, who perform vocal selections as well as wait on tables. These are not "wannabes," but young professionals with impressive theatrical credentials. Eight members of the company perform on any given evening, happy to do requests, from opera, operetta, or Broadway musicals. Patrons' birthdays are heralded with an adaptation of the "Hallelujah Chorus" from Handel's *Messiah* (with "happy birthdays" substituting for the "hallelujahs"), while "Sorrento" is delivered inevitably, but with panache. As for the food, you'll want to begin your meal with an antipasto salad, including thinly sliced meats, cheeses, peppers, and other traditional Italian garnishes. Entrées include superbly cooked fettucini, linguine, and other pasta dishes, imaginative fresh seafood creations, and excellent steaks. This is a great place to let romance flourish.

Primavera Ristorante, Fairmont Hotel, 200 N Columbus Dr (at Grant Park), Chicago, IL 60601, 312/565-6655. Breakfast Mon–Sun 6–11:30 am; lunch Mon–Sun 11:30 am–2:30 pm; dinner Mon–Fri 6–11 pm, Sat & Sun 5:30–11 pm.

Best Italian restaurant with singing owner

Monastero's Ristorante

When he's not overseeing the bustling kitchen of his family-owned and -operated Italian restaurant, Joe Monastero has been known to regale his patrons with renditions of traditional Italian or operatic music. And, at other times, it's likely to be some of the most talented and promising opera students in the area offering up an aria or two. This cycle of performance reaches its peak each February and March, when these young singers compete for cash prizes and a trip to an opera seminar in Italy. (Many of Joe's "graduates" go on to sing and work at Primavera—see separate listing—or perform with area opera companies.) The cuisine at Monastero's is a good match with the classical entertainment provided—a cross-section of northern and southern Italian favorites, with a heavy concentration on veal dishes (such as osso buco and the very popular veal parmigiana) and homemade pastas (including manicotti and lasagna). Oven-broiled whitefish seasoned with garlic and olive oil is a popular seafood selection. The restaurant presents a wholesome, casual family atmosphere.

Monastero's Ristorante, 3935 W Devon Ave,
Chicago, IL 60659, 312/588-2515. Lunch Tue–Fri
11 am–2 pm, dinner Tue–Sun 4–10 pm.

Best Italian restaurant to sing about

I Tre Merli

Its name means "the three blackbirds," and the song
this authentic northern Italian restaurant sings is
one of excellence—from start to finish. This Midwest
addition to what now is a quartet of restaurants
(Genoa, Manhattan, and South Beach, Miami) occupies attractive quarters in River North, with exposed
brick walls, wood ceiling, and a cozy dining loft at
the rear. First courses include grilled sea scallops
with cannellini beans and fried leeks, fresh lobster
and avocado salad, and three different carpaccios
(seared tuna, salmon, and beef). Pasta courses feature veal ravioli with fresh sage butter; hollow spaghetti with fresh fennel, sardines, and parmesan
cheese; and not-to-be-missed lobster-filled ravioli.
Meat and fish main courses include sliced sirloin
steak with fresh rosemary, double filet of beef with
Barolo wine sauce and roasted shallots, clams
sautéed with garlic and tomatoes, and tenderly
prepared grilled sea bass served with fried artichokes—a specialty of the Italian Riviera that produces an incredibly delicate entrée (one that
delighted a dining companion who doesn't care for
most fish dishes). Finish with superb pear and
walnut tart. In trattoria tradition, the restaurant
carries its own private-label wine created by vine-
yards in Piemonte, Italy—available by the bottle,
glass, or to take home. An outdoor garden has
additional seating for 85 persons. For a simpler
meal, hot focaccia sandwiches are available in combinations that include tomatoes, fresh mozzarella,
prosciutto, fontina, goat cheese, and Italian bacon.
I Tre Merli, 316 W Erie St, Chicago, IL 60610, 312/
266-3100. Mon–Thu 11:30 am–midnight, Fri & Sat
11:30 am–1 am, Sun 5 pm–midnight.

Best Italian ice

Mario's Italian Lemonade

It's a matter of neighborhood semantics along Taylor
Street as to whether you call this refreshing confec-
tion Italian ice or Italian lemonade. Certainly, the
former is more descriptive, since this stand offers
more than a dozen different flavors, including the
original lemon, tart and revivifying. Painted red,
white, and green, this wooden stand is tucked in
front of a brownstone alongside a gourmet coffee

shop and just a little east of the fashionable New Rosebud Café. But Mario's—and Italian ice—is an institution in this neighborhood. Basically, it is crushed ice with a fruit flavoring added, served in a paper cup—your basic slushy, but with a lineage dating back centuries to the time that Arab traders introduced sorbet to Sicily. Mario's also sells nuts and seeds.

Mario's Italian Lemonade, 1070 W Taylor St, Chicago, IL 60607. Open seasonally.

Best Italian ice (North)

Tom and Wendee's Homemade Italian Ice

Street food doesn't have to be heavy or greasy or loaded with calories. Italian ice is ideal for a low-cal lift on a hot summer's day or a sultry evening. It's perfect when you go out to dinner and summon the willpower to wave away the dessert cart. Opened by two former advertising sales executives, Tom Manderscheid and Wendee Cardinal, this shop offers a tempting array of flavors of this low-cal, cholesterol-free treat. Fruit flavors include such combinations as banana-strawberry and orange-tangerine. There's also black cherry, refreshing watermelon, and the traditional lemon flavor. The taste is rich because the owners use fresh fruit instead of flavoring mixes. Chocalaholics may be surprised to find a chocolate-flavored Italian ice so dark in color and rich in flavor that it could almost be ice cream. Other tempting combinations include chocolate-almond and chocolate-walnut. This also is a spot to stop for your orange juice or for a refreshing float made with Italian ice.

Tom and Wendee's Homemade Italian Ice, 1136 W Armitage Ave, Chicago, IL 60614, 312/327-2885. Daily noon–10 pm.

Best Italian muffaletta sandwich

Club Creole

When food fanciers visit New Orleans, they likely will schedule a stop at Central Grocery or one of the other Italian delis across from the French Market. Their objective is a muffaletta sandwich—a large circular loaf filled with layers of olive salad, meat, cheese, and sausage (a half sandwich is plenty for one person). In Chicago, this diner-like eatery serves a passable likeness. For those who enjoy hot food and cold beer, this is the spot for a lunch or dinner Big Easy-style. There's gumbo, jambalaya, étouffée, Cajun fries, and Blackened Voodoo lager. The New Orleans ambience features bold black and white tile, jazz posters, framed Louisiana lottery tickets, whimsical watercolors of New Orleans drinks, and foot-tapping zydeco music piped in constantly. Try a po'-boy sandwich filled with spicy andouille sausage or softshell crab, catfish with mustard sauce, or Creole crab cakes with Cajun slaw. For starters there are oysters, spicy calamari, or Cajun popcorn shrimp—tiny crustaceans with a big bite. Sides include such standards as "durty rice," red beans and rice, and sweet-potato fries. Desserts run to the likes of pecan, praline, and sweet-potato pie. Potables include Dixie and Rattlesnake beer and such Crescent City concoctions as hurricanes and sazaracs. Popular is a Cajun martini made with pepper-flavored vodka and served with a habanera pepper and olive. As the large sign in the restaurant says, "Laissez les bon temps roulee!" (Let the good times roll!).

Club Creole, 226 W Kinzie St, 312/222-0300. Mon–Fri 11 am–11 pm, Sat 5–11 pm.

Best Italian cooking by owner's mom

Tarantino's

Here's an Italian restaurant where the sepia pictures decorating the walls *really are* the old-country grand-parents. In fact, here you're likely to be greeted by the owner's mother, Grace Tarantino, now close to 80 years old. Mama T sometimes arrives early at the restaurant to prepare pans of lasagna and batches of her acclaimed marinara and meat sauces. Start with an order of calamari—as tender as you'll find anywhere—with a light breading or, perhaps, stuffed artichokes, moist and tender. Be sure to sample the warm, chunky marinara sauce that is served on every table as a dip for crusty bread. A menu standout is Mama T's homemade lasagna, along with her baked eggplant parmigiana. Pastas are prepared *al dente* and include well-made standards such as linguine with clam sauce, fettucine Alfredo, fettucine primavera, and artichoke-filled raviolini. Chicken dishes include vesuvio, marsala, and rose-mary, while a veal specialty is *limona* (with a lemon demi-glace, served with angel hair alioli and sautéed spinach). *Giambotta* is the traditional dish of grilled Italian sausage with peppers, onions, and roasted potatoes. Finish with cheesecake or an exceptional version of tiramisu. John Tarantino (known as the proprietor of Jim n' Johnny's) has converted—with a big assist from Mama T—this warm, storefront space, with exposed bricks, attractive woodwork, and walls lined with wine bottles into a popular Lincoln Park eatery.

Tarantino's, 1112 W Armitage, Chicago, IL 60614, 312/871-2929. Mon–Thu 11:30 am–10 pm, Fri & Sat 11:30 am–11 pm, Sun 5–10 pm.

Best green noodles al forno

Club Lago

Amid the fashionable galleries, boutiques, and bistros of River North, this friendly corner tavern is a holdover from the not-too-distant days when this was a dilapidated warehouse district. It is warm and friendly, with a few booths in the bar and a back dining room. It has been run by the same family since it opened in 1952, and at lunchtime it is packed with regulars who frequent Club Lago month in, month out. "Since River North took off, we've been doing a bigger dinner business," says owner Francesco Nardini, "and we get a really big crowd on gallery opening nights." The prices, however, remain incredibly modest, and new residents and gallery owners have discovered the restaurant's wonderful green noodles baked *al forno* (in the oven) with a generous topping of cheese—a combination of fontina and sweet cheeses that, Nardini says, "is kind of a secret." The kitchen also does well with such standards as fettucine Alfredo and veal piccante (which may be special-ordered if not on the menu as a daily special).

Club Lago, 331 W Superior St, Chicago, IL 60610, 312/337-9444. Mon–Fri 11:30 am–8 pm, Sat 11:30 am–3 pm.

Best neighborhood Italian restaurant with plastic grapes—and real celebs

Slicker Sam's

This is a noisy, fun neighborhood Italian restaurant with plastic grapes hanging from the ceiling and autographed celebrity photos on the wall—Frank Sinatra, Jerry Vale, and various local sports heroes. Sam's has a strong local following—but celebs, such as Jim Belushi, also occasionally drop by. The menu is chalked on a blackboard and features many Italian standards. Linguine with white clam sauce is a standout. Beer and chianti by the pitcher, great stuffed artichokes with a garlicky bread stuffing that is moist but firm, and Dungeness crab—among the best in the city—are good reasons to visit Slicker Sam's. Other popular menu choices include garlic shrimp and baked clams. Try an order of tomato bread, juicy and flavorful with plenty of mozzarella.

Slicker Sam's, 1911 Rice St, Melrose Park, IL 60160, 708/344-3660. Tue–Sat 11 am–10:30 pm, Sun 3–10 pm.

Best Italian food & theater

Scoozi!

Rich Melman's version of a venerable Italian trattoria is the antithesis of stuffy. It's totally fun—the kind of place where sharing food, even with strangers at neighboring tables, is perfectly acceptable. A garage in its former life, this cavernous barn of a place, studiously stylish with walls of bare bricks and stucco, is capable of seating more than 400 (but even so, there often is a two-hour wait). Scoozi! is as much theater as it is food, from the giant plaster tomato suspended over the entrance to a strolling, costumed accordion player to tape recordings of conversations in Italian in the rest rooms and waiters who act and sound as though they are auditioning for *The Godfather, Part V*. But the food is excellent. Try pizza topped with sweet, caramelized onions and gorgonzola—or topped with prosciutto, portobello mushrooms, fontina cheese, and truffle oil; a Caesar salad topped with spicy fried calamari; sautéed potatoes with artichokes; and a mound of fried, batter-dipped slivers of zucchini with sage. Pastas include fettuccine with wild mushrooms in a mushroom herbed broth and spaghetti with shrimp, scallops, and calamari in a spicy tomato sauce. Scoozi! is crowded and noisy, but lots of fun.

Scoozi!, 410 W Huron St, Chicago, IL 60610, 312/943-5900. Lunch Mon–Fri 11:30 am–2 pm; dinner Mon–Thu 5–10:30 pm, Fri–Sat 5–11:30 pm, Sun 5–9 pm.

Best upscale all-you-can-eat Italian buffet

Trattoria No. 10

Just a half-block south of Daley Plaza, this upscale northern Italian restaurant is a popular business lunch spot. A somber green storefront opens onto a curved stairway with murals of Mediterranean-style buildings. One floor down are a casual yet elegant dining room and a long, mirrored bar, full of intimate nooks created by stucco archways. Bold turquoise and earth-tone floor tiles contrast with delicate lace curtains. From 5 to 8 pm the bar offers an all-you-can-eat buffet with antipasto, shrimp, three kinds of salad, pasta, chicken in a piquant tomato sauce, and toasted bread with a tasty blend of Parmesan cheese and prosciutto. Cost is $5, with a $3 drink minimum. The signature dish is ravioli, five different kinds in full and half portions. A top choice is black pasta ravioli with shrimp, garlic, and onion confit and a saffron butter sauce. Other fillings for these delicious handmade ravioli include a four-cheese blend, butternut squash, wild mushrooms, and homemade Italian sausage.

Trattoria No. 10, 10 N Dearborn St, Chicago, IL 60602, 312/984-1718. Lunch Mon–Thu 11:30 am–2 pm; dinner Mon–Thu 5:30–9 pm, Sat 5:30–10 pm.

Neighborhood Italian restaurant most favored by visiting celebs

New Rosebud Café

Like the single word whispered by the dying Citizen Kane, this Rosebud is a bit of an enigma. To wit: How did a neighborhood Italian joint become one of the hottest restaurants in town, attracting both the local cognoscenti and a steady stream of Hollywood types, such as Michelle Pfeiffer, Sean Connery, and Gene Hackman? The answer can be summed up in two words: good food. The restaurant serves up bountiful dishes of delicately cooked and sauced pasta, a variety of tempting veal dishes, and, the acclaimed king of the Rosebud's kitchen, chicken Vesuvio, moist and garlicky, with roasted potatoes and an added complement of peas. Appetizers are pleasing, and desserts are standard Italian-restaurant fare (though the cannoli is rendered nicely). Just keep spooning your excellent linguine carbonara and try not to stare at Robert DeNiro, seated a few tables over.

New Rosebud Café, 1500 W Taylor St, Chicago, IL 60607, 312/942-1117. Lunch Mon–Fri 11 am–3 pm; dinner Mon–Thu 5–11 pm, Fri & Sat 5 pm–midnight.

Best Italian food atop an elevator shaft

Vivo

Among the glitterati who gather at this trendy restaurant, the most requested seating is a solitary table poised atop a bricked-in elevator shaft. Often booked weeks ahead, it is a favorite of such celebrities such as Madonna, Phil Donahue, and Michelle Pfeiffer. Tucked away in a century-old warehouse in Chicago's wholesale produce market (an area slowly becoming gentrified and now known fancifully as the "old market district"), this multiregional Italian restaurant is as pleasing to the eye as it is to the palate. Handsome brick walls are decorated with stacked wine bottles. The high ceiling with exposed ductwork is painted black. Slabs of marble form bar tops and provide a table for prettily displayed antipasto resting atop colorful cans of tomatoes. Modernistic metal chairs were designed by one of the owners, Jerry Kleiner. Start with grilled portobello mushrooms or

a salad of watercress, tomatoes, blue cheese, fresh
pear, and toasted walnuts—followed by a pasta
course of linguine with mussels or rigatoni with
sausage, sun-dried tomatoes, and goat cheese.
Entrées include grilled sea bass, veal medallions
with artichokes, and grilled chicken breast with fresh
rosemary. An upstairs bar has bare brick walls
painted iridescent green, purple, red, and gold. The
full menu is served at eight outdoor tables. Robert
DeNiro and Harrison Ford are among celebrity visitors; talk-show host Jerry Springer is a regular.

Vivo, 838 W Randolph, Chicago, IL 60607, 312/733-
3379. Mon–Thu 11:30 am–10 pm, Fri 11:30 am–
midnight, Sat 5:30 pm–midnight, Sun 5:30–10 pm.

Best-hidden Italian restaurant in hardest-to-hide building

Mia Torre

Located in the heart of the Loop (on the restaurant
level of the Sears Tower), this Levy group restaurant
is a popular business lunch spot—and a good discovery for a quiet, well-prepared, but not-too-expen-
sive dinner after the commuting hordes have fled to
the suburbs. It also is a decent choice for a pre-
theater dinner. Visiting this colorful, open restaurant is like being in a piazza in Italy. The dining room
is flanked by a faux-brick wall with window boxes
and a view into a groceteria. Tables in the "piazza"
are metal with colorful mosaic tops; floors blend
granite and tile. Bright-colored banners hanging from
the ceiling are patterned after those that celebrate
the famous "Palio" horserace run each summer in
Siena. Food, prepared at an open-display kitchen,
includes a selection of wafer-thin pizzas featuring a
triangular pizza with mozzarella, sliced tomato,
pancetta, and basil, and another with a sun-dried
tomato crust with caramelized onions and thyme.
Specialties include: a salad of grilled portobello
mushrooms with field greens, olive oil, and lemon;
air-dried beef with artichoke and arugula salad; and
rotisserie chicken with roasted red and green peppers and potatoes. Pasta selections include ricotta-
and-spinach–filled ravioli in a cream cheese sauce
grantinéed with red pepper puree and pasta quills
with pancetta, onions, tomatoes, and spicy peppers.
An assortment of sandwiches made with herbed
focaccia bread are perfect for lunch or a simple
dinner.

Mia Torre, Sears Tower, 233 S Wacker Drive,
Chicago, IL 60606, 312/474-1350. Mon–Fri 11 am–
8 pm.

Best Italian spot to honor thy wine jug

Pazzo's Pizza & Pasta Kitchen

One of the commendable features about dining at this Italian eatery tucked away in the NBC Tower is that it places a jug of house wine on every table, with patrons invited to help themselves on the honor system (only $2.50 a glass). Another lure is price: just about everything on the menu is under $10. Then there's ambience. With etched glass, hardwood banquettes, hand-painted faux marble walls, and *trompe l'oeil* clouds drifting across the ceiling, this spot is pretty beyond expectations at these bargain prices. And the food is pretty good, too. House specialties include black-and-white–striped ravioli served on top of mixed peppers and tomato-garlic sauce, lime chicken salad on a bed of pan-fried cappellini, and a towering cup of polenta stuffed with pesto and eggplant. Standards such as linguine with clam sauce are available; portions are large and sharing encouraged. Italian-style sandwiches include sausage and peppers; a selection of salads and more than a dozen combinations of California-style wood-fired pizza round out the menu. As dessert, try a gelato or chocolate raspberry, but skip the tiramisu—it is made off premises and is far too dry.

Pazzo's Pizza & Pasta Kitchen, 455 N Cityfront Plaza, Chicago, IL 60601, 312/329-0775 (and two suburban locations). Mon–Thu 11 am–10 pm, Fri & Sat 11 am–11 pm, Sun 4–10 pm.

Best Italian country restaurant in the most improbable setting

Tucci Benucch

Ultra-thin, blistery-crust pizzas along with the wacky, movie-set decor are the big attractions at this Bloomies' building eatery. It doesn't take long to recognize the Lettuce Entertain You show-biz touch! The place is decked out to resemble an Italian country home, complete with sepia-toned photos of the "owners," wooden floors, rafters with hanging baskets, mismatched chairs, and waiters in peasant costumes. Spilling out onto the fifth-floor mall is a small "outdoor" area where you can dine or simply sip a glass of house red or an imported Italian beer and watch the shoppers go buy. Toppings for the slim pizzas include eggplant, spinach, bacon, sun-dried and fresh tomatoes, smoked chicken, Italian olives, asiago cheese, onion, and red peppers. Start with baked mushrooms or baked cheese bread (made with four cheeses) and follow with herbed, garlicky roast chicken. Pasta choices are basic—spaghetti, fettuccine, pasta shells, and angel hair—and other standards include veal piccata and chicken parmesan. Other menu selections feature baked minestrone, the Italian sandwich of the day, and desserts that include tiramisu with chocolate sauce and strawberry-rhubarb crumble. When it's offered, don't miss sampling the Tuscan white bean soup with sausage.

Tucci Benucch, 900 N Michigan Ave, Chicago, IL 60611, 312/266-2500. Mon–Thu 11:30 am–10 pm, Fri & Sat 11:30 am–11 pm, Sun noon–9 pm.

Best underpriced Italian lunch spot
Danilo's

In the early 1990s, this family restaurant, which has been around since 1969, moved from a somewhat seedy location on West Grand Avenue to a higher-rent district closer to trendy River North (and just a little north of Greektown). In an era of fashionable trattorias, this old-style Italian restaurant continues to satisfy with simple, well-prepared, unpretentious food. Antipasto may be ordered for two or more and is more than enough for two to share. Pastas are well-made standards—ravioli, tortellini, gnocchi, and mostaccioli served with meat or marinara sauce, and a stand-out version of linguine with white clam sauce. A dish not on the printed menu, but well worth requesting (usually they'll prepare it to order for lunch or dinner), is linguine with broccoli and shrimp in a garlicky light marinara sauce. Lunches are a good buy (selections include half-and-half portions of pasta) and include a crisp salad—the blue cheese dressing has a generous amount of cheese crumbled on top. Standard Italian desserts include Italian ice and tiramisu.

Danilo's, 464 N Halsted St, Chicago, IL 60622, 312/421-0218. Tue–Fri 11 am–11 pm, Sat 3:30–11 pm.

Most elegant Italian lunch spot
Avanzare

High ceilings and leaded-glass chandeliers above a nicely appointed, cavernous room; light pouring in through large windows—this is a truly stylish spot to enjoy choice northern Italian cuisine. Open with polenta or a fine antipasto selection. Top picks here include well-executed pasta dishes—such as butternut squash ravioli with walnuts and prosciutto and half-moon pasta with goat cheese, mustard greens, and portobello broth—as well as fresh seafood entrées; grilled veal chop, sautéed chicken breast, and grilled filet of beef with garlic mashed potatoes and white truffle butter also are favorites. Try one of Avanzare's delightful homemade desserts, such as tiramisu, ricotta cheesecake, and especially its flavorful ice cream. This stylish and perennially popular restaurant attracts large crowds for both lunch and dinner. When the weather is favorable, a sidewalk café is a fine spot for lingering over a cappucino and dessert.

Avanzare, 161 E Huron St, Chicago, IL 60611, 312/337-8056. Lunch Mon–Fri 11:30 am–2 pm; dinner Mon–Thu 5:30–10 pm, Fri & Sat 5–11 pm, Sun 5–9:30 pm.

Most elegant Italian dinner spot

Spiaggia

This dressy post-modern restaurant exudes style, with black marble columns (six different marbles were custom-made in Italy), pink Art Deco wall lights and huge picture windows looking out onto the ribbon of traffic on Lake Shore Drive. There's a murmur of subdued conversation, music from the piano bar, and exquisite food. Start with mussels steamed with white beans in a garlic tomato broth or a shared pizza—hot from a wood-burning oven and topped with such creations as wild mushrooms, prosciutto, parsley, garlic, and a blend of provolone and Romano cheeses. Chef Paul Bartolotta's pasta dishes are out of the ordinary, too, such as black pasta with scallops, red pepper, cream, and caviar; entrées include splendid grilled veal chop with fresh sage, grilled fish on escarole, roasted rosemary-flavored chicken, and simple-but-blameless grilled sirloin with olive oil and lemon. Desserts are special, especially tiramisu, crème brûlée tart with kiln-dried cherries, and pear poached in white wine with pinenut brittle, caramel-lemon sorbetto, and cranberry sauce. Many wines are available by the glass.

Spiaggia, 980 N Michigan Ave, Chicago, IL 60611, 312/280-2750. Mon–Thu 11:30 am–9:30 pm, Fri & Sat 10:30 am–10:30 pm, Sun 5:30–9 pm.

Most inelegant Italian lunch spot

Mr. Beef on Orleans

The wall of fame tells the story—rave reviews and autographed photos of celebrity patrons, such as Jay Leno, Jim Belushi, and members of the local media. They—and your taste buds—announce that this is the place for Italian beef sandwiches. Spicy-sweet, thinly sliced meat, swimming in flavorful gravy, is packed into a chewy roll and topped with your choice of sweet or hot peppers. Vying for popularity is the Italian sausage sandwich. Spicy sausage is char-broiled over a flaming grill. During the lunchtime crunch, customers in line for counter service pack into a tiny room with chipped white paneling; sit-down patrons enter a door marked "Elegant Dining Room" to the former patio, now inelegantly enclosed, with seating at two huge picnic tables. If you can't decide between beef or sausage, order a combo. Accompaniments include fries, shakes, and root beer. In a perfunctory nod to lighter dining, Mr. Beef added a grilled chicken sandwich which, if you must, is extremely flavorful.

Mr. Beef on Orleans, 777 N Orleans, Chicago, IL 60610, 312/337-8500. Mon–Fri 7 am–5 pm, Sat 10 am–2 pm.

Little sister of the most elegant Italian dinner spot

Café Spiaggia

Next door to the elegant Spiaggia (see previous listing), this "little sister" also is stylish, although more casual and not as pricey. A narrow, winding layout creates romantic nooks with views of Michigan Avenue; gray marble tables, green velour seats, and posters of Italian resorts add panache. You'll feel comfortable here in a sweater—or a silk suit. Start with a thin, blistery pizza—perhaps a blend of duck sausage, sage, and goat cheese—and then select from a large selection of creative pastas, maybe a seafood blend of spaghettini with scallops, clams, mussels, calamari, and tomatoes, flavored with garlic, olive oil, wine, and herbs and baked in parchment. An Italian standard, osso buco—a pair of marrow-filled veal shanks flavorfully braised with lemon zest and sage—is well prepared. Tiramisu is a standout dessert. Plenty big enough to share, it comes nestled against fresh raspberries on a plate artfully streaked with chocolate.

Café Spiaggia, 980 N Michigan Ave, Chicago, IL 60611, 312/280-2764. Mon–Thu 11:30 am–9:30 pm, Fri & Sat 11:30 am–10:30 pm, Sun noon–9 pm.

Most elegant Italian grazing spot

Tucci Milan

This is a trattoria built for grazing. A loft-style interior with abstract art, salmon-colored ductwork, and butcher paper on the tables makes it pleasant to linger over a tumblerful of house red. And the menu, with a big selection of appetizers, salads, and ultra-thin–crust pizzas—plus some creative pastas—makes sharing ideal. There are nine pizzas (including two without cheese), with crispy, paper-thin crust and inventive topping combinations such as prosciutto-pepper-smoked mozzarella, pancetta-spinach-onion-goat cheese, and wild mushrooms-garlic-Fontina cheese. Salads have the same flair—grilled chicken with organic greens and balsamic vinaigrette; fresh grilled tuna, with avocado, peppers, and capers; and spinach with radicchio, cannellini beans, roasted peppers, and a warm pancetta dressing. Lasagna is a specialty—with fillings ranging from spinach to wild mushrooms to roasted duck. A sampler plate allows the tasting of three different kinds of lasagna. Desserts are rich and perfect for multiple forks—for example, chocolate hazelnut torte.

Tucci Milan, 6 W Hubbard St, Chicago, IL 60610, 312/222-0044. Mon–Thu 11:30 am–10 pm, Fri 11:30 am–11 pm, Sat noon–11 pm, Sun 5–9 pm.

Best bet for contemporary *and* classic Italian cooking

Vivere

The Italian Village has staying power. Its colorful restaurants have been a Loop landmark for close to 70 years, bringing an authentic touch of Italy long before the trattoria was a glint in the eye of any Chicago restaurateur. Those who remember the Florentine Room, opened in 1961, will find it made over and renamed in its new life as the chic Vivere, complete with "post-industrial Baroque" decor. There are leaded-glass windows, handblown glass light fixtures, sculptured wrought iron, marble and granite, bold draperies, and handmade lace. Start with duck-filled crêpes with parmesan cream sauce, wild mushroom soufflé with onion-thyme cream sauce, or seared sea scallops. An unusual appetizer is a Napoleon of baked layers of polenta, sausage, and portobello mushrooms. Creative pastas include pumpkin-filled tortelli with almonds and parmesan and black pasta with shrimp, potatoes, fresh tomatoes, and pesto sauce. Entrées include quail with black truffle sauce and sweet potato polenta; veal tenderloin with mushroom sauce; herb-grilled lamb chop; and steak flavored with lemon, oregano, and pepper. Dessert choices include banana mousse and pear bread pudding with cinnamon crème anglaise. Vivere's wine cellar has been acclaimed as one of the best in the city.

Vivere, 71 W Monroe St, Chicago, IL 60603, 312/332-7005. Lunch Mon–Fri 11:30 am–2:30 pm; dinner Mon–Thu 5–10 pm, Fri & Sat 5–11 pm.

Trendiest trattoria to be seen at a sidewalk table

Bice

It's pronounced "BEECH-ay," and although it may not be *as* new or *as* trendy any more, it remains one of the "happening" dining spots. This northern Italian restaurant is the bambino in a family chain of eateries with branches in Milan and New York. Inside, the decor is comfortable and bright; the restaurant's Art Deco look is somewhat reminiscent of a dining salon of a transatlantic liner from the golden age of steamships. And the menu brings to mind the inventive cuisine of the restaurant's home in Italy: an extensive selection of tempting antipasti (including prosciutto with roasted peppers and mozzarella cheese and grilled eggplant with salmon and sun-dried tomatoes); entrées such as roasted rack of veal with plum tomatoes, linguine with fresh baby clams, grilled swordfish with Italian vegetables; and an extensive selection of *gelato* and other Italian desserts. To really enjoy the leisurely dining experience of Bice—and Chicago's breezy weather—take a seat at the restaurant's sidewalk café and watch the city pass you by as you dine in unquestioned style. Or don those smoky shades, try for that studied "casual" look, sip an appropriate Campari and soda, and allow yourself to "be seen."

Bice, 158 E Ontario St, Chicago, IL 60611, 312/664-1471. Sun–Thu 11:30 am–10:30 pm, Fri & Sat 11:30 am–11:30 pm, Sun noon–10 pm.

Best French restaurant a little farther out

Carlos'

Adapting their menu to what they describe as "contemporary French," Carlos and Debbie Nieto have kept their long-favored restaurant among the top tier of area French dining (with the kitchen now under the helm of chef Jacky Pluton of Lyon). A six-course degustation offers a fine reflection of the menu, including: terrine of smoked and fresh salmon with oyster and curry vinaigrette; fricassee of veal sweetbreads with wild mushroom sauce; and herb-crusted lamb chop sautéed with Napoleon of lamb loin, mint, peppercorn sauce, and cream of garlic. Or order à la carte, beginning, perhaps, with escargot ragout with red wine sauce and potatoes or a warm squab salad with arugula and fresh figs. Then move on to striped bass sautéed with black olives, eggplant cake, and carrot juice—or roasted guinea fowl with fava beans and foie gras sauce. Carlos' finishes fine meals with an excellent assortment on the dessert cart (just looking seems as though it might pad the waistline). Choose from flaky-fresh pastries (fruit tarts are especially good), silky-smooth crème brûlée, and the "Symphony of Chocolate"; even Carlos' between-course sorbets are noticeably above-average. The extensive wine list includes a decent number of available-by-the-glass selections, which can help hold down the tab (which can easily exceed $150 for two—but worth it here).

Carlos', 429 Temple Ave, Highland Park, IL 60035, 847/432-0770. Two dinner seatings nightly by reservation. First seating: Mon, Wed–Sun 5:30–6:30 pm. Second seating: Sun, Mon, Wed, Thu 8–8:30 pm; Fri & Sat 9–9:30 pm.

Chicest *Parisien*-style café at which to be seen

Un Grand Café

On the shortish stretch of Lincoln Park's swankiest residential street sits this charming French-style bistro (located in the tony Belden-Stratford apartment hotel, as is Ambria—see separate listings). The muted, comfortable atmosphere (café-style tables, poster-decorated walls, fresh-cut flowers, gleaming brass and tiles) adds to the casual enjoyment of the restaurant's bistro fare—grilled fresh seafood, roast chicken, game. Steak frites is a favorite here (with crisp little fries accompanying the nicely done meat), as is a sweet onion soup. Popular appetizers include a variety of fresh pâtés and specially made duck or rabbit sausage. A selection of fresh-fruit tarts leads the parade of tempting desserts. All in all, this café provides a nice, satisfying dining experience—and you never know who you'll see or be seen by.

Un Grand Café, 2300 N Lincoln Park West, Chicago, IL 60614, 312/348-8886. Mon–Thu 6–10:30 pm, Fri & Sat 6–11:30 pm, Sun 5–9:30 pm.

Best French restaurant way out in the sticks (North)

Le Vichyssois

Chef Bernard Cretier's classic French restaurant (which looks more like an old-fashioned roadhouse) is a good 50-mile trek from downtown Chicago, but a legion of devotees consider the trip more than worthwhile, and the rustic, timbered restaurant has good staying power. Excellent appetizers include pâtés that are textbook-perfect, a very popular lobster-clam bisque, and, as you might expect (given the restaurant's name), a definitive vichyssoise (potato and leek soup, available hot or cold). Entrées—roast duck, stuffed quail, veal kidneys with mustard sauce, shrimp with lobster sauce, and seasonal seafood—are expertly prepared and accompanied by just-right sauces. A heavy-on-the-French-side wine list and a tempting array of homemade desserts (which rotate frequently) round out the dining experience at this intriguing outpost. If you crave rich, fulfilling dining of this sort, the trip to northwest suburban McHenry County might well be thought of as a pilgrimage.

Le Vichyssois, 220 W IL 120, Lakemoor, IL 60050, 815/385-8221. Wed–Sat 5:30–10 pm, Sun 4:30–10 pm.

Best French restaurant way out in the sticks (South)

The Cottage

Discerning Chicago restaurant-goers held their collective breaths in 1990 when Jerry Buster closed shop for several months and went in search of R&R. Since the mid-1970s, this highly touted restaurant in an improbable blue-collar location has been a culinary beacon in the south suburbs. Forget about the mismatched silverware and the odds-and-ends chairs. The country-French decor is done in green and peach, providing a bright dining area to sample such offerings as honeyed, tomato-glazed ribs; black tiger shrimp with pasta and proscuitto; an incredibly tender pork cutlet; and steak with a green peppercorn cream sauce. Starters include delicious pumpkin soup. It's tough advice to follow, but go easy on the sourdough bread that comes with a chunky spread of chopped black olives, capers, and sun-dried tomatoes—especially if you plan to save room for a dessert such as raspberry cake or a chocolaholic's fix that blends a triple-threat mousse with chocolate buttercream and raspberry sauce.

The Cottage, 525 Torrence Ave, Calumet City, IL 60409, 708/891-3900. Lunch Mon–Fri 11:30 am–2 pm, dinner Mon–Sat 5–10 pm, Sun 4–8 pm.

Best taste of Provence

Cassis

It's hard to imagine a prettier spot than this southern French bistro appended to the Radisson Hotel, just a block east of North Michigan Avenue. Decorated in earth tones designed to evoke the feel of Provençe, it features bold terra cotta tile floors complemented by walls glazed to a buttery yellow.

Accessories include wheat-colored chiffon drapes; handblown glass light fixtures; sheaves of wheat tucked into sconces; and fresh and dried flowers, including sunflowers and lavender, displayed in tiny decorative vases. One end of the room is dominated by a display of 16 massive urns. Stand-out hors d'oeuvres include iron skillet–roasted mussels, codfish cakes, duck leg confit with curried lentils, and oven-roasted portobello mushrooms with pistou sauce. Follow with a main course as simple as steak frites or roast chicken or try a typical dish of the Mediterranean region, such as bouillabaisse, veal saltimbocca, lamb-and-Swiss-chard ravioli, and ratatouille-and-goat-cheese–filled cannelloni. Sides include garlic potato cakes, macaroni with wild mushrooms, and fennel gratin. Don't overlook Cassis as an elegant breakfast spot (open early because of its association with the hotel), with selections such as Belgian cornmeal waffles with fresh seasonal berries, buckwheat crêpes with caramelized bananas and crème fraiche, and eggs Benedict with applewood-smoked bacon. In warm weather, patrons spill out onto the sidewalk under gaily striped awnings and shade trees, seated on original street café chairs imported from Paris.

Cassis, 160 E Huron St, Chicago, IL 60611, 312/255-1600. Daily 6 am–midnight.

Best French restaurant to impress just about everyone

Le Français

Many claim this to be among the finest restaurants in the country. Certainly, it attracts patrons who fly into nearby Palwaukee Airport for the express purpose of dining there. Even though the celebrated Jean Banchet has moved on, the new owners, Roland and Mary Beth Liccioni, who built their reputation at the highly regarded Carlos', are maintaining the tradition. Rack of lamb, cooked medium rare and served with tiny home-grown vegetables and couscous, defines the genre; an appetizer of cold duck liver has sensuous palate and eye appeal. Between-course sorbets include an unusual Thai-style lemongrass flavor. Soups feature a smooth cream of asparagus and artichoke, a light crayfish bisque, and duck consomme with raviolis of duck, prepared en croute. A combination entrée brings together stuffed veal loin with a wild mushroom sauce and stuffed lamb loin and roast rack of lamb, au jus. Other standouts—on a menu that is outstanding—include veal sweetbreads in red wine sauce and duck with red currant sauce. Mary Beth presides over exquisite desserts—tarts, soufflé, and creations such as coconut mousse served with passion fruit and coconut sorbets, with a pineapple sauce. The wine list is, of course, superlative.

Le Français, 2695 Milwaukee Ave, Wheeling, IL 60090, 847/541-7470. Lunch Tue–Fri 11:30 am–2 pm, dinner Tue–Thu 5:30–8:30 pm, Fri & Sat seatings at 6 pm & 9:15 pm.

Best culinary journey with the lowest fares

Relish

Although "fusion" may sound like a pretentious description of food, it does describe the creative efforts of Ron Blazek, one of Chicago's bright young chefs, who offers cutting-edge concepts at moderate prices—in a totally unpretentious setting. Opened in 1991, this restaurant attracts a predominantly young professional crowd who appreciate both the food and the prices. Blazek's "playfully serious" approach to "American cooking with ethnic influences" produces such offerings as lobster and mango quesadilla and goat cheese stuffed chicken. The front room, with high, gray-painted tin ceilings and pretty dappled beige walls, is brightly decorated with eclectic art-for-sale of local artists. For warm-weather dining, there is a bricked-in courtyard. As a starter, try wild mushroom strudel or crab cakes served with a spicy blend of peppers, corn-and-chile, and cilantro aiolis. Entrées include such offerings as twice-baked lamb shank with mustard-basil crust, sweet-and-sour tandoori-style duck on lentils with yogurt-orange and cucumber slaw, and grilled salmon and leek with a spicy "voodoo sauce" served with shrimp spring roll. A not-to-be-missed dessert is the sour cream and apple tart with caramel ice cream—the apple slices firm, the pastry light and flavorful. Other favorites include blood orange upside down cake with Grand Marnier ice cream and blueberry and port cobbler with lemon ice cream. A three-course "prime time dinner" priced around $20 is ideal pre-theater fare for those making the curtain at the nearby Steppenwolf and Royal George.

Relish, 2044 N Halsted St, Chicago, IL 60614, 312/868-9034. Tue–Thu 5:15–10 pm, Fri & Sat 5:15–11 pm, Sun 5:15–9 pm.

Savviest dining with future superchefs

CHIC Café

Eating at CHIC Café (the name is an acronym for Cooking & Hospitality Institute of Chicago) is like catching a future Robert DeNiro at summer stock. You're likely to have a meal prepared by one of tomorrow's culinary stars—at today's try-out prices. How about a three-course luncheon for $13, featuring such selections as gingered butternut squash soup with cinnamon crème fraiche, duck consomme with mushroom ravioli, Creole frittata with jalapeno sour cream, and mustard-encrusted pork tenderloin with hunter sauce? A five-course dinner (served Saturday only) is priced at $28. Sit-down Sunday brunch is $15. Excellent pastry chefs whip up all manner of creative desserts such as flourless chocolate cake, double-chocolate cheesecake, and milk and buttercream–filled crepes with butterscotch sauce. Alumni have gone on to such respected kitchens as The Ritz-Carlton, Four Seasons, and Everest Room. You can peek into the kitchen through a large picture window—but be sure to select a table up front with views of the Chicago skyline. While the restaurant does not have a liquor license, diners are invited to bring their own wine, which is opened without a charge for corkage.

CHIC Café, 361 Chestnut St, Chicago, IL 60610, 312/944-0882. Sun–Fri noon–1 pm; Sat noon–1 pm; dinner 7–10 pm.

Best spot for yuppie-fied good ol' boys—Texas-style

Bub City Crabshack and Bar-B-Q

Another creation of Chicago restaurant guru Rich Melman, this is the place for some lowdown, knee-slappin', foot-stompin', Southern-style food and fun. Emulating a Carolina crab house embellished with a touch of Texas (complete with mounted long horns and pig's head), this eatery serves up the kind of food that can be best described as "vittles." Appetizers such as peel-and-eat shrimp, Cajun popcorn shrimp, and crab cakes are favorites; entrées include tangy, slow-smoked barbecued ribs; brisket; chicken; country ham; and pulled pork. Try the snow crab, among the best in the city. Sides include baked beans—simple, but good—and corn on the cob. Gumbo is a menu staple, as are T-bone and skirt steaks. Condiments on the table include a variety of piquant and flavorful sauces. Next door to the restaurant is Club Bub, a Western-style bar featuring live country music nightly and a small dance floor (boots and Stetsons optional).

Bub City Crabshack and Bar-B-Que, 901 W Weed St, Chicago, IL 60622, 312/266-1200. Mon–Thu 11:30 am–10 pm, Fri & Sat 11:30 am–11 pm, Sun 4–10 pm. (Extended hours in Club Bub.)

Best spot for yuppie-fied good ol' boys—Carolinas-style

Old Carolina Crab House

Snug in a corner at the eastern end of the renovated North Pier Terminal, this casual restaurant serves up fresh seafood Southern-style: flavorful, piled high, and easy on the pocketbook—but hard on new shirts and ties (many items are juicy and messy). As you'd expect from a traditional Southern crab house (and this rendition doesn't disappoint), the decor is warm and inviting, featuring rough-wood-paneled walls embellished with photos, fishing lures, signs, and postcards. The entrance, with its simulated bait-shop look, helps create the low-country image; tables have a waterside (albeit not Atlantic) view. The all-seafood menu includes crabs (prepared in a variety of ways), clams (steamed or fried), shrimp, mussels, oysters, lobster, catfish, and other fresh finfish, plus salad and soup, including pretty good clam chowder. The dessert menu specializes in such all-American basics as pecan pie, peach cobbler, and spicy Apple Brown Betty; a kids' menu features chicken and burgers. The fun, casual atmosphere and moderate prices make this a great place for families.

Old Carolina Crab House, 435 E Illinois, Chicago, IL 60611, 312/321-8400. Mon–Thu 11:30 am–9 pm, Fri & Sat 11:30 am–10:30 pm, Sun 11:30 am–9 pm.

Best bet for Louisiana, Carolina, and other points south

Redfish

It's a tough restaurant locale, this corner at State and Kinzie just north of the Chicago River. It has seen the demise of many eateries. But this colorful restaurant, opened in 1995, may just have the right formula: a mix of barbeque, Southern, and Cajun cooking—with po'boy and pulled pork sandwiches, red beans and rice and black-eyed pea fritters. Barbecue lovers can order the Southern Sampler (brisket, ribs, and chicken) and sit back to soak up the atmosphere, sip on a Dixie beer, and listen to Dixieland jazz. This faux-Southern roadhouse features timber walls aged with numerous coats of paint, neon beer and spirit signs, distressed chairs in a kaleidoscope of colors, and such Louisiana trappings as a stuffed alligator and weather-beaten bayou boat signs. Black booths line a wall stacked with quart jugs of Tabasco sauce. Entertainment, which features Southern bands, is served up on the "front porch" of the Bayou Grocery, complete with paint-chipped windows and corrugated roof. Munch on jalapeño cornbread and buttermilk biscuits served with honey butter and order a bowl of gumbo or BBQ duck and sweet potato chowder. Other starters include roasted artichokes with cornbread-and-oyster stuffing and BBQ shrimp with jambalaya rice. Entrées range from crawfish and catfish to hickory-smoked prime rib chop and garlic-and-rosemary grilled rabbit with Georgia chow chow and spoonbread. Desserts feature peach and blackberry cobbler, banana and chocolate bread pudding, and deep-dish pecan and white chocolate tart.

Redfish, 400 N State St, Chicago, IL 60610, 312/467-1600. Mon–Fri 11 am–11 pm, Sat & Sun 5–11 pm.

Best taste of New Orleans (nearest the El tracks)

Heaven on Seven

Unofficially, this luncheonette, on the seventh floor of an office building at about the level where the El trains rattle by, is known as Heaven on Seven. And known it is. On weekdays, lunch crowds stretch out toward the elevators. Saturdays are a quieter time to sample the authentic Cajun and Creole cooking. Amid the Big Easy posters, "See you later, alligator" signs, and bayou trappings, you'll find that brothers Jimmy and George Banos produce authentic gumbo (which they also sell by the gallon to go). Tables are loaded with a battery of spicy sauces and condiments, ready to deal with such traditional favorites as red beans and rice, jambalaya, Cajun fried chicken, hoppin' John (black-eyed peas), and two-fisted po' boy sandwiches stuffed with oysters and soft-shelled crabs. On the side, you can order jalapeño cheddar corn muffins and such southern favorites as collard greens and grits. Desserts are traditional, too—key lime pie, sweet-potato pie, and bread pudding (served, of course, with a cup of New Orleans-style chicory coffee). For those with more plebian tastes, there is a regular coffee-shop menu with burgers and sandwiches; aficionados rave about the patty melt and fries and chocolate pudding that tastes like it should. *Note:* The restaurant's "Wall of Flame" has a record-breaking collection of hot sauces that is destined for inclusion in the *Guinness Book of Records.*

Garland Restaurant & Coffee Shop, 111 N Wabash Ave (7th floor), Chicago, IL 60603, 312/263-6443. Mon–Fri 6:30 am–9 pm, Sat 7 am–3 pm.

Best taste of New Orleans (nearest New Orleans)

Maple Tree Inn

Those who were saddened to hear that this popular south-suburban restaurant was relocating (leaving the pretty garden with the massive tree for which it was named), may be pleased to learn that it now occupies the century-old building in Blue Island that once housed Helen's Old Lantern. In fact, the handsome oak bar, which Helen's patrons may remember, remains. New is the Cajun and Creole cuisine that the restaurant brought with it and the Dixieland jazz and blues that are performed on the last Saturday of every month. You'll find here the staples of Louisiana-style cooking—thick, spicy gumbo; crawfish étouffé; jambalaya; hickory-buttered or barbecued shrimp; and oysters Bienville (served in combination with oysters Rockefeller and oysters with a deviled crab topping). You could start with an order of zesty stuffed crab, follow with blackened catfish or scallops, and finish in traditional New Orleans style with bread pudding accompanied by bourbon sauce. On Fridays there's a Creole version of bouillabaisse, featuring catfish, oysters, crawfish, shrimp, and blue crab. On Saturdays, the special is stuffed pork chop. Don't look for Dixie or other bottled beer—all brews are on tap, with a selection of a dozen microbrews from around the country.

Maple Tree Inn, 13301 S Old Western Ave, Blue Island, IL 60406, 708/388-3461. Tue–Sat 4–10 pm, Sun 4–8 pm.

Best old restaurant for fresh fish

Cape Cod Room

It looks like a seafood restaurant—and it has since 1933. Maitre d' Patrick Bredin hasn't been there quite that long, but long enough to become an institution, remembering patrons' names and their preferences and being willing to make special dishes not on the menu. Tucked into the lower level of The Drake, this room is dark and intimate with cheery red-and-white checkered tablecloths. There are ship models, ships in bottles, stuffed sailfish, weathered oars, and various other nautical knick-knacks, as well as a variety of copper and brass. There is a marble-topped raw bar, and a 40-year-old wooden bar carved with many famous initials (see separate listing, "Notable Potables"). There is nothing too fancy about the food—it is fresh, superbly prepared, and expensive (this definitely is an expense-account sort of place). Standards include Bookbinder's red snapper soup served with sherry on the side, chowder,

Dover sole, Maryland crab cakes, lake whitefish, and pompano en papillote. You'll find Norwegian salmon, Great Lakes sturgeon caviar, a half-dozen lobster dishes, five shrimp dishes, six styles of scallops, and a good rendition of bouillabaisse. In season, don't miss stone crabs or soft-shell crabs.

Cape Cod Room, The Drake Hotel, 140 E Walton Place, Chicago, IL 60611, 312/787-2200. Daily 11:30 am–11:30 pm.

Best dead fish and live jazz
Philander's

This restaurant, in the landmark Carleton hotel, offers a pair of dining choices: the barroom, dominated by a large oak and marble octagonal bar, where there is live jazz six nights a week; and the adjoining main dining room, club-like with wood paneling and tall, glass-framed booths. You can hear the mellow jazz at both—and dance, if you wish, on a tiny floor in the bar. Fresh seafood choices begin with a connoisseur's selection of a half-dozen types of oysters. Other starters include baked oyster dishes, New England clam chowder that is rich and thick without resorting to artificial thickeners, and black bean soup that is flavorful but over-puréed. Entrées include Dover sole, scallops, panfried catfish, grilled swordfish steaks, poached salmon with Hollandaise sauce, bouillabaisse, crab cakes, and mahi mahi—plus lamb chops, steaks, and pasta. An unusual offering is squid cutlets, tenderized by pounding, batter-dipped, and lightly sautéed. They live up to their billing as "abalone-like." The crème brûlée is exquisite. Occupying what once was the ballroom of the hotel, the restaurant has a casual, contemporary flavor—while retaining such traditional touches as amber windows and the historic photographs of turn-of-the-century Oak Park that decorate the oak-paneled walls.

Philander's, 1120 Pleasant St, Oak Park, IL 60302, 708/848-4250. Mon–Thu 4–10 pm, Fri & Sat 4–11:30 pm.

Best fried perch—way North
Mathon's

Ichthyophagists—fish eaters, that is—head for this restaurant founded by the late Mathon Kyritsis. The eccentric Greek was famous for his televised weather forecasts based on the schooling patterns of Lake Michigan perch and his frequent pilgrimages in search of the missing arm of Venus de Milo. His son, John, now runs the restaurant, a bust of Venus graces the lobby, and it remains the place to go for golden, deep-fried or sautéed perch (these days, farm-raised in Wisconsin). Smelt also are good, and you often can find soft-shell crabs on the menu. Popular dishes include friend shrimp and swordfish, broiled or blackened. New England clam chowder is served daily, and the signature dessert is custard meringue pie with a graham cracker crust. The restaurant's nautical theme includes porthole windows, blue carpeting, wood paneling, and Phil Austin watercolors. The restaurant hosts an annual show by this artist on the first Monday in November.

Mathon's, 6 E Clayton St, Waukegan, IL 60085, 847/662-3610. Tue–Thu 11 am–9 pm, Fri & Sat 11 am–10 pm, Sun noon–8 pm.

Best fried perch—way South

Phil Smidt's

Back in 1910, Phil and Marie Smidt opened a small bar and seafood grill serving perch and pike that was just hours from the water. Today, this 450-seat restaurant not far from the original serves these same specialties. Perch are covered in lightly seasoned flour and pan-fried to a golden brown in butter or margarine and served whole or boned. Sweet pike fillets arrive broiled with lemon or fried. Equally famous are Smidt's frog legs, deep-fried and crispy or lightly floured and sautéed. Rounding out the house specialties is chicken, fried or broiled. Each is available as a single or all-you-can-eat serving. You can order appetizer portions of perch and frog legs, singly and in combination, should you opt for a steak, catfish, or lobster-tail entrée. Meals include a lavish relish tray with potato salad, cottage cheese, coleslaw, beets, and kidney beans. Finish with sweet-tart gooseberry pie, baked in a flaky pastry shell and served warm à la mode or with fresh whipped cream. Although it's in Indiana (but barely), Smidt's is easy to reach via the Chicago Skyway.

Phil Smidt's, 1205 N Calumet Ave, Hammond, IN 46320, 219/659-0025. Mon–Thu 11:15 am–9 pm, Fri & Sat 11:15 am–10 pm; May–Dec Sun 2:30–7:30 pm.

Best fried perch—city clone

Bridges

If the menu looks familiar, know that one of the owners of this newcomer to the sprawling Merchandise Mart spent 14 years at Phil Smidt's in Hammond (see separate listing). And while there is no duplicating the tradition and folksy ambience of the original, Bridges certainly has the menu down. You'll find perch, fillets or whole, buttered or plain—endless platters of them if you opt for an all-you-can-eat special. And there are frog legs, sautéed or fried, and half a chicken, broiled or fried, with either all white or all dark meat. A combination plate provides an all-you-can-eat selection of perch, chicken, and frog legs. Also in keeping with its role model, Bridges serves all entrées with an assortment of relishes—cole slaw, cottage cheese, kidney bean salad, and candied beets—as well as hot fresh bread and a choice of fries or red-skin boiled potatoes. If you're not into perch or frog legs, the menu offers a decent selection of steaks plus some other fish choices and a pasta dish or two. Also replicated is Smidt's famous dessert, gooseberry pie—plus an excellent key lime pie supplied by Joe's Stone Crab of Miami Beach. This contemporary room, done in white with swaths of pink linen decorating the ceiling, a mural of Wacker Drive's eponymous bridges, and big picture windows looking out onto the street, is the antithesis of its kitschy stepfather—especially, with a keyboard musician singing Cole Porter tunes. After 6 pm there is free angle parking on the north ramp of the Merchandise Mart.

Bridges, 222 Merchandise Mart Plaza, Chicago, IL 60654, 312/828-0929. Mon–Thu 11 am–9 pm, Fri 11 am–10 pm, Sat 4–10 pm.

Savviest spot where fish boats are a'comin'

Joe's Fisheries

Tucked away in a gritty industrial neighborhood on the banks of the north branch of the Chicago River is a little fish restaurant that sends out its own fishing boats. Joe's operates two 55-foot, 70-ton commercial fishing boats that head out into Lake Michigan well before dawn five days a week, tend gill nets that are left out all night, and return with their catch of perch and chub early in the afternoon. Decorated with nautical brick-a-brac, this eatery, a combination sit-down/take-out caters to a mix of office workers, blue-collar workers, and some celebrities—such as DePaul basketball coach Joey Myers. The restaurant is known for its batter-dipped, deep-fried shrimp and for its British-style fish-and-chips. Deep-fried selections include scallops, smelt, catfish, perch, oysters, and clam strips. Steamed to order are crab, shrimp, salmon, and whitefish. Start with seafood gumbo or Boston clam chowder; try Cajun rice, fries, or potato salad on the side. Aficionados of smoked fish can choose from chubs, trout, sable, salmon, and whitefish—smoked on the premises with various fruitwoods.

Joe's Fisheries, 1438 W Cortland, Chicago, IL 60622,
312/278-8990. Sun–Thu 10 am–midnight, Fri & Sat
10 am–3 am.

Best salmon south of Alaska (and north of Chicago)

Don's Fishmarket & Tavern

This restaurant adjacent to the Skokie Howard
Johnson is almost a throwback to the 1970s, with
its faux-nautical trappings of coiled ropes, harpoons,
ship figureheads, and prints and oils of frigates and
men-o'-war. But it also is comfortable (with well-
padded booths), cheery (with a flickering fireplace in
winter), and unpretentious. And best of all, the food
is consistently good. Start with steamed littleneck
clams, calamari, mussels steamed in garlic butter
and sherry broth, or well-made crabcakes with tomato caper remoulade. Then choose from a wide
variety of fish that usually includes salmon, grouper,
swordfish, lemon sole, scrod, fresh yellowfin tuna,
monkfish, and Lake Superior whitefish. Of course,
there's lobster from the tank, lobster tails, and a
variety of dishes featuring scallops and shrimp—
some stir-fried, others with pasta. Especially recommended is grilled scampi, simply served with
seasoned breading, garlic butter, and lemon. So well
is this dish prepared that a frequent dining companion orders it almost invariably, after considering—
but eventually bypassing—other menu temptations.
Yes, you may order steak or chicken (but why would
you want to?). Although the dining room is extremely
casual, some diners prefer adjoining Don's Tavern
(which alone is open for Saturday lunch) where they
may order such items as peel-and-eat shrimp and
fish and chips—along with many items from the full
menu. The restaurant stages many fun events, with
appropriate food, such as Mardi Gras, summer grill
time, and an annual lobsterfest.

Don's Fishmarket & Tavern, 9335 Skokie Blvd,
Skokie, IL 60077, 847/677-3424. Mon–Thu 11:30 am–
10 pm, Fri 11:30 am–11 pm, Sat 5–11 pm, Sun 4–9
pm.

Best five-alarm chili

Santa Fe Café

Outside, this place looks downscale Southwestern,
with adobe-style walls and a pink-and-green paint
job. Inside, it's a bustling mix of take-out, stand-up,
and sit-down dining—the kind of place you feel
comfortable wearing an old pair of jeans, although
during the week it attracts a business-lunch crowd.

All come for the delicious, modestly priced South-western-style sandwiches. And the chili! There are several beers on tap, a friendly bartender playing his or her favorite music on the cassette player, or perhaps a ballgame on TV. Packed into the small main dining area are about a dozen tall tables that comfortably seat two (or four, if they all tuck in their elbows). Waitpersons zip orders to the kitchen via an overhead pulley-and-wire conveyance. The popular chili is served thick and is made with a tangy two-meat (pork and beef) blend that also includes beans. Almost everyone orders it with soft-melted cheddar cheese and onions. Besides excellent chili, try a barbecue beef sandwich served in a pita envelope with a side of cole slaw and baked beans. Santa Fe also does a big take-out business.

Santa Fe Café, 800 N Dearborn St, Chicago, IL 60610, 312/751-2233. Mon–Thu 11 am–11 pm, Fri & Sat 11 am–midnight, Sun noon–10 pm.

Best five-way chili west of Cincinnati

Chili Mac's

Cincinnati five-way chili in Chicago? It may sound sacrilegious, but Kevin Drewyer, who opened a pair of chili parlors featuring this specialty, explains that his wife, Magoo, hails from Cincy. "Five-way" refers to serving options: One-way is plain chili, two-way is served over spaghetti, three-way adds shredded cheese, four-way brings chopped onion, and five-way includes kidney beans. The sauce has 15 spices, including that touch of cinnamon that many claim is the secret to Cincinnati chili. Meat is drained of about 95 percent of its fat content, and seasonings are only mildly hot (with a stack of sauces for those wishing to add heat). About $5 buys a big plateful of food, ample for sharing. Perfect accompaniments are homemade cornbread—from Magoo's recipe—and cold beer. For chili purists, other options include Texas Jailhouse (aka "Texas Brown"), which has no tomato and blends three kinds of chili peppers (it is the hottest in the house, but not a real scorcher). There's also spicy vegetarian chili, a meatless blend of 10 veggies with a spicy kick, and turkey chili, featuring cilantro and peppers. The menu includes chili dogs, taco salad, and refreshing Italian ice. A popular beverage choice is a blue margarita, made with blue curacao. The Broadway location has outdoor seating.

Chili Mac's, 3152 N Broadway, Chicago, IL 60657, 312/404-2898; 851 W Armitage Ave, Chicago, IL 60614, 312/525-3232. Sun–Thu 11 am–10:30 pm, Fri & Sat 11 am–midnight.

Best deep-dish pizza

Pizzeria Uno & Pizzeria Due

Here they are—the undisputed pizza capitals of Chicago, and, perhaps, of the entire world! Well, allow for a little hometown hyperbole, but the late Ike Sewell's Pizzeria Uno is the spot where deep-dish (sometimes called pan) pizza was invented back in the 1940s. This hefty, satisfying concoction starts out with a thick (but not overly doughy) crust, then a gooey layer of cheese, your choice of toppings (sausage, green peppers, and mushrooms sound just about perfect), and finishes with a thick slather of tomatoes and tomato sauce, all baked and served in a round, oven-blackened pan. Of the two outposts in this pizza empire—colloquially referred to as simply Uno's and Due's (DOO-ays)—Uno's, the original, is considerably smaller; both are nearly always bustling.

Pizzeria Uno, 29 E Ohio St, Chicago, IL 60611, 312/321-1000. Mon–Sun 11:30 am–1 am. Pizzeria Due, 619 N Wabash Ave, Chicago, IL 60611, 312/943-2400. Sun–Thu 11:30 am–1:30 am, Fri & Sat 11 am–2 am.

Best stuffed pizza

Giordano's

Another of Chicago's famous exports to the world of cuisine is the stuffed pizza. Sometimes likened to a calzone or a regular pie, stuffed pizza features layers of crust above and below your choice of filling and cheese, usually topped off with tomatoes (and, sometimes, additional cheese). Giordano's is the city's king of stuffed pizza (and maybe the originator—the debate still rages after more than 20 years), and its flagship restaurant on Rush Street is a perfect spot to sample this unique version of pizza. Stuffings include all of the basic pizza toppings; specialties include spinach; all veggies; and the house favorite of sausage, mushrooms, onions, and green peppers. Giordano's also serves thin-crust pizza, pasta, and salads.

Giordano's, 747 N Rush St, Chicago, IL 60611, 312/951-0747. Mon–Thu 11 am–11 pm, Fri & Sat 11 am–midnight, Sun noon–midnight.

Best left coast pizza

California Pizza Kitchen

Here's a pizza palace that's thin on crust, but long on originality. Located in a rehabbed warehouse, its obligatory exposed wood beams are accented by floor-to-ceiling mirrors, black-lacquer tables, and fluorescent neon. Part of a national chain, this restaurant creates some of the most original pizza toppings in town, offering more than 20 different varieties. Slide into an inviting over-stuffed booth, and ponder such pizza exotica as tandoori chicken, duck sausage, Peking duck, Santa Fe chicken, terriyaki, B.L.T., Caribbean shrimp, and even a Hawaiian pizza featuring a pineapple-bacon combo. Each is served in only one size, approximately eight inches in diameter, which easily feeds two. Pizzas are prepared in wood-fired ovens (oak logs are used) and are cooked to a crispy consistency. Also on the menu are more than a dozen made-fresh-daily pasta dishes, including spaghetti, linguine, and penne pasta. If you opt for a salad with your entrée, consider sharing a half salad; portions are generous.

California Pizza Kitchen, 414 N Orleans Plaza, Chicago, IL 60610, 312/222-9030. Mon–Sat 11:30 am–10 pm, Sun noon–9 pm.

"Heartiest" pizza (for pizza lovers and auto-race fans)

Bacino's

It bears little resemblance to the typical pizzeria, this comfortable eatery just steps away from Michigan Avenue. It has a clubby feel, with trappings left over from a former life as a saloon—oak paneling, inlaid backlighted stained glass, a solid bar, and a working fireplace. But the menu is pure pizza parlor—mostly pizza, of both the thin-crust and stuffed variety, plus a simple salad, meatball and Italian beef sandwiches, garlic bread, and an antipasto plate. Hottest-selling item on the menu is a deep-dish pizza the mini-chain bills as "America's 1st heart healthy pizza." A blend of low-fat cheeses, spinach, fresh mushrooms, herbs, and spices, it was designed to meet American Heart Association guidelines for fat and cholesterol. It also is remarkably tasty. Of course, all of the traditional ingredients also are available on stuffed or thin-crust pizzas—sausage, onion, green peppers, pepperoni, sirloin, Canadian bacon, and sliced tomatoes. In contrast to the sophisticated ambience of this downtown restaurant, the original location on Lincoln Avenue *does* feel like a pizzeria, with sports on TV and cold beer on draft. The "Car Room," decorated with auto-racing photos and memorabilia, reflects the hobby of owner Dan Bacin, an amateur driver who has hosted Al Unser and Paul Newman at the restaurant.

Bacino's, 75 E Wacker Dr, Chicago, IL 60602, 312/
263-0070. Sun–Thu 11 am–9 pm, Fri & Sat 11 am–
10 pm. 2204 N Lincoln Ave, Chicago, IL 60614,
312/472-7400. Mon–Thu 11 am–10:30 pm, Fri & Sat
11 am–12:30 am, Sun noon–10 pm.

Best pizzettes
The Red Tomato

To get to the pizzettes—appetizer-sized pizzas—you
have to pass by the real thing. That is because this
restaurant shares an entrance with LoGalbo's Pizzeria, which sells pizza by the slice, as it has for
about 20 years. In 1990, owner Joe DiVenere opened
this small (80 seats), handsome restaurant figuring
that this gentrifying neighborhood was ready for
something more upscale. Designed as a light first
course, pizzettes have a variety of interesting toppings, such as a combo of four cheeses (mozzarella,
Gorgonzola, parmigiana, and fontinella) and a mixture of shrimp, asparagus, grilled mushrooms, onions, and sun-dried tomatoes. Other menu highlights
include black fettucini tossed with fresh salmon,
chicken Vesuvio, homemade ravioli with sage butter,
and swordfish grilled in garlic and served with lemon
butter. There is an excellent salad of roasted red
peppers, varying risottos, and top-rated desserts including homemade cannoli, tiramisu, and wonderful
ice cream—try the hazelnut flavor!

The Red Tomato, 3417 N Southport Ave, Chicago,
IL 60657, 312/472-5300. Lunch daily 11 am–2 pm;
dinner Mon–Thu 5–10 pm, Fri & Sat 5–11 pm.

Best nonfranchise hamburger
Boston Blackies

Although this is hardly an expensive eatery, you'd
never know it from the decor. It has an Art Deco feel,
and a youngish, yuppie-ish crowd. White linen tablecloths, uniformed wait staff, a giant-screen television, and plush carpeting create the perception of
an upscale "fern bar." Surprisingly though, this
restaurant keeps prices low and service and quality
high. The thick, one-pound burgers are cooked to
order and are served with fresh beefsteak tomato,
lettuce, pickle, and onion along with a huge side
order of coleslaw (there's also a choice of buns:
Kaiser roll, hamburger bun, or rye bread). Among
the popular burger toppings are grilled onion, provolone cheese, bacon, mushrooms, and melted cheddar. Other notable menu choices are the gigantic
"garbage salads," tender grilled chicken sandwiches,

and a large plate of steak fries. Ask for plenty of napkins—the burgers are juicy.

Boston Blackies, 164 E Grand Ave, Chicago, IL 60610, 312/938-8700. Mon–Sat 11:30 am–11 pm, Sun noon–10 pm.

Best burger in the burbs

Hackney's

For more than 40 years, this small restaurant chain (four branches in the north suburbs, one in the south suburbs) has built a reputation around its hamburger. The signature Hackneyburger is a half-pound of juicy, good-quality meat served on home-baked dark rye or a bun. It comes with crispy fries, cole slaw, and a plate of sliced raw onion. A popular accompaniment is a slab of crunchy fried onion curls. Other selections include salads, steaks, fresh fish, and daily specials such as corned beef. The Lake Zurich branch has warm wood paneling, a central fireplace, and an outdoor dining patio over-looking a duck pond. The original restaurant, Hackney's on Harms in Glenview, also has an al-fresco dining area.

Hackney's in Lake Zurich, 880 N Old Rand Rd, Lake Zurich, IL 60047, 708/438-2103. Mon–Thu 11:15 am–11 pm, Fri & Sat 11:15 am–midnight, Sun 11:45 am–11 pm. Hackney's on Harms, 1241 Harms Rd, Glenview, IL 60025, 847/724-5577. Mon–Thu 11 am–11 pm, Fri & Sat 11 am–11:30 pm, Sun 11 am–10 pm (and other locations).

Best burger outdoors

Moody's Pub

Burgers alfresco! That's an unbeatable all-American combo for summer, and one of the most popular venues for same is the terraced, ivy-covered patio and gardens of this North Side beer garden. En-closed by brick walls and a wrought-iron fence and shaded by venerable maples, the spacious garden seats 150. Order a stein or pitcher of beer (or a carafe of wine) while you wait for your burger. The half-pound cheeseburger, served on a bun of dark rye, char-broiled on an open grill, is lean and meaty. Garnishes include lettuce, pickle, and raw or grilled onions. Hand-cut fries are worthy accompaniments. Also tops is the eight-ounce steak sandwich, charred on the outside, pink and tender inside.

Moody's Pub, 5910 N Broadway Ave, Chicago, IL 60660, 312/275-2696. Mon–Fri 11:30 am–1 am, Sat 11:30 am–2 am, Sun noon–1 am.

Fab fries to die for

Parky's

Fries—you'll find them (under different names) in London, England; Brussels, Belgium; . . . and Berwyn, Illinois. They're the ultimate street food—portable and delicious (but watch out for the health police). And in Berwyn, they're made daily by hand from freshly peeled and cut potatoes, as they have been since 1949, at this garish orange-and-turquoise painted fast-food stand. These fries are satisfyingly firm and crisp on the outside, soft and chewy inside. "We still make fries the way McDonald's used to do it," said founder Gene Arist, demonstrating the eatery's old-fashioned, labor-intensive machines. Parky's also has tamales and fifteen-cent dill pickles—plus floats, shakes, and malts. But the fries are what you go to Parky's for. They are consistently voted "best" in Chicago's western burbs by a local newspaper.

Parky's, 7021 Roosevelt Rd, Berwyn, IL 60402, 708/788-2966. Mon–Sat 10:30 am–8 pm, Sun noon–5 pm.

Cheesiest cheddar fries

Gold Coast Dogs

No greasy, Cheez-Whiz-coated, wimpy fries these. Instead, this local mini-chain offers crisp-on-the-outside, soft-on-the-inside fingers of Idaho's finest—tasty in their own right—covered with a generous glob of cheddar, fresh from Wisconsin. These make a great snack on their own or a perfect accompaniment to one of Gold Coast's dogs (Vienna All-Beefs, of course) or sandwiches. The burgers are thick and juicy; the char chicken flame-cooked to order at a backyard barbecue. For a different—and healthy—fast-food alternative, try Gold Coast's grilled fresh swordfish sandwich. If you'd like a beer with your sandwich, carry it out to Clark Bar, a few doors north of the Clark Street Gold Coast Dogs. It's a great local spot to watch a ball game or shoot some pool, and, since they don't serve food, they don't object to carry-ins.

Gold Coast Dogs, 418 N State St, Chicago, IL 60610, 312/527-1222; 2100 N Clark St, Chicago, IL 60614, 312/327-8887. Mon–Fri 7 am–10:30 pm, Sat & Sun 10:30 am–8 pm.

Chicago's best submarine sandwich

L'Appetito

Step into this busy little grocery and you know you're not in for a franchise-style sandwich. There are piles of crusty Sicilian loaves, the aroma of fresh-ground coffee beans, a case of imported cheeses, and shelves crammed with pasta, olive oil, and such items as pesto, garlic paste, and dried tomatoes. Sandwiches are made to order at a deli counter packed with tempting Italian cold cuts and offering hot soups to go. Subs pack Genoa salami, mortadella, capicollo (lean ham), provolone, tomato, lettuce, and oil-and-vinegar dressing into 10-inch loaves. Simple but good is a newer sandwich creation that blends smoked mozzarella with a crushed olive dressing. As you exit, admire the olive-oil–can labels that serve as foyer wall art and a prettily landscaped garden-in-miniature alongside a wall with climbing ivy. In warm weather, patrons from surrounding office buildings take their sandwiches at tables set out in the tiny garden. (A second branch has opened in the courtyard level of the John Hancock Center—perhaps more comprehensively stocked, but we prefer the ambience of the original grocery store.)

L'Appetito, 30 E Huron St, Chicago, IL 60611, 312/787-9881. Mon–Sat 10 am–6:30 pm.

Best fried chicken

White Fence Farm

There's no question about what to order should you journey to this popular southwest suburban eatery. Since the 1920s, it has built its reputation on golden, succulent chicken, crisp on the outside, moist and meaty inside. Housed in a sprawling, white-frame country-like building filled with antiques, it caters to large numbers. However, its limited menu means that turnover is fast, so that waits, when encountered, aren't too painful (reservations are not taken). Accompaniments include a relish tray and sugar-dusted corn fritters. If someone in your party doesn't want chicken, alternatives are shrimp, fish, and steaks. Desserts include ice cream and frozen yogurt, but the perennially popular dessert is brandy ice. Antique collections include clocks, music boxes, and Currier and Ives prints.

White Fence Farm, Joliet Rd, Lemont, IL 60439 (off I-55 & IL 53), 708/739-1720. Tue–Sat 5–8 pm, Sun noon–7:30 pm.

Best chicken soup mom would make (if she were Jewish and could cook)

The Bagel

This is not a "pretend" deli—it's the real thing, established in 1950 and offering authentic Jewish cooking using recipes brought from the Old World

by the parents and grandparents of the owners, the
Wolf family. For whatever ails you—even if it is
simply hunger—don't miss the golden chicken broth
thick with your choice of noodles, rice, *kasha*, or
matzo balls the size of baseballs. Another good soup
choice is mish-mash, a combination of all of the
above—a great meal for two for less than $6. Other
homemade soups include split pea, navy bean, vegetable, and lima beam—plus beet borscht and a
sweet-and-sour cabbage borscht. Sandwiches are
well-packed with lean meats and include brisket,
roast sirloin, pastrami, beef tongue (pickled or
boiled), salami, and smoked turkey breast. This deli
is especially noted for its reuben, made with lean
corned beef. And when it comes to naming specialty
sandwiches, there's no New York stuff here—it's
strictly Chicago with the Lawrence & Kedzie (pastrami and corned beef) and Devon Avenue (which
adds Swiss cheese touches). Chopped liver and gefilte
fish are made to Ruth Wolf's own recipe, while the
pickled or schmaltz herring and salmon salad are
worth a try. Save room for *luckshen kugel*, a sweet
noodle pudding with cinnamon and raisins, served
warm—sometimes as a side. An extensive pastry
counter does a good take-out business with such
goodies as cheesecake, bundt cakes, strudels, and
chocolate eclairs. For a simple dessert, order rice
pudding or a baked apple. Free parking is available
half a block east on Barry.

The Bagel, 3107 N Broadway, Chicago, IL 60657,
312/477-0300. Sun–Thu 8 am–10 pm, Fri & Sat
8 am–11 pm.

Best deli run by owner's mom

Mrs. Levy's Delicatessen

There really is a Mrs. Levy and you'll find her at this
retro-deli most days (or, when she's not there greeting guests, her lifesize cutout). Eady Levy, patriarch
of the wildly successful Levy restaurant family,
presides over this deli on the mezzanine level of the
Sears Tower. It contrives standard deli ambience—
a busy, bustling, noisy spot with black-and-white
tiled floors and walls plastered with photographs of
celeb patrons (Mrs. Levy posing with the likes of
Oprah and President Clinton). Sandwiches are piled
satisfyingly high and such staples as knishes,
blintzes, and soups are made from scratch daily on
the premises. Popular soup choices include sweet-
and-sour cabbage, chicken-matzo ball, and mushroom barley. Along with such standard sandwiches
as corned beef, pastrami, beef brisket, salami, and
chopped liver, are 11 triple-decker options that

include a combination that may even appease the health police: breast of turkey, alfalfa sprouts, cucumbers, tomatoes, and green onions tossed with a low-calorie mustard-yogurt dressing, wrapped in pita bread. Desserts range from the inevitable cheesecake to peanut butter chocolate cake and assorted fruit pies, while a soda fountain dispenses delicious shakes, sundaes, and floats, as well as chocolate phosphates and black cows (root beer with vanilla ice cream).

Mrs. Levy's Delicatessen, Sears Tower mezzanine level, 233 S Wacker Dr, Chicago, IL 60606, 312/993-0530. Mon–Fri 6:30 am–3 pm.

Best deli that's an elevator ride away

Mallers Building Coffee Shop & Deli

With potato pancakes, cheese blintzes, borscht (in summer), and homemade meatloaf, this third-floor diner draws from 16 floors of jewelry shops in the historic Mallers Building (see separate listing in "Shopping"). Soups, such as barley-bean, are thick and nourishing, served with crisp matzo wafers. A cup of soup, a half corned-beef-on-rye, smeared with stone-ground horseradish mustard, and an appropriate beverage comes in under $5. There are omelettes and, for the lunchtime crowd, a series of cold plates—chopped liver, chicken, tuna, or spinach salad—plus a big selection of sandwiches ranging from roast brisket of beef and BLT to Kosher soft salami and fried perch. There are ruebens, clubs, and patty melts, and newly added pirogies and Russian stew—plus fruit pies and cheesecake, shakes and sodas (including Dr. Brown's celery soda). Windows open out onto El tracks, and the ambience is best described as Early Diner—plaid wallpaper; brown Formica, shiny booths; institutional green trim; and, incongruously, colorful Japanese lanterns and contemporary art prints.

Mallers Building Coffee Shop & Deli, 5 S Wabash Ave, Chicago, IL 60603, 312/263-7696. Mon–Fri 7 am–3 pm, Sat 8 am–2 pm.

Most self-effacing restaurant slogan

Febo

It's amusing—but untrue. Febo's self-effacing slogan, "Famous for Nothing," discounts the fact that this neighborhood Italian restaurant has been serving fine northern Italian cuisine for more than 60 years. In fact, according to owner Robert Cecchi, Febo introduced the genre to Chicago. Febo is full of rambling rooms, dark wood paneling, and tables spread with crisp, white napery. Try an order of tomato bread—soft, crunchy, and satisfyingly garlicky with a topping of parmesan cheese. Ravioli is delicious—made on the premises, as are cannoli and other desserts. A fine range of pastas is cooked to order. Febo long has been known for its Northern Italian Festa Dinner, a spread that includes appetizers, two pastas, a chicken dish, a meat dish, choice of dessert, and beverage (served family style for four or more).

Febo, 2501 S Western Ave, Chicago, IL 60608, 312/532-0839. Mon–Thu 11 am–10 pm, Fri & Sat 11 am–midnight.

Best Nouvelle cuisine (near the lake)

Ambria

To experience the breadth of Rich Melman's Lettuce Entertain You restaurant chain—in terms of both style and price—you merely need to walk the two blocks of Lincoln Park West from casual R.J. Grunts (see separate listing) to tony Ambria. This elegant establishment, repeatedly voted among the city's best, offers superbly executed nouvelle cuisine in an attractive setting, it's art nouveau architecture set off by deep-toned woods and suede banquettes. Start with roasted quail or one of the fine pâtés (foie gras in a sherry glaze with thinly sliced, sautéed apples is a consistent winner); fresh shellfish and finfish entrées are always a good bet (try grilled sea bass with tomato coulis), as are such favorites as rack of veal with capon leg (stuffed with mushroom mousse), and duck with cranberry glaze. Desserts—soufflés, pastries, mousses, etc.—are given the same exquisite attention. As you would expect, this is an expensive spot—however, the petite and grand degustation sampling menus can provide a unique dining experience while taking less of a bite out of your pocketbook.

Ambria, 2300 N Lincoln Park West, Chicago, IL 60614, 312/472-5959. Mon–Thu 6–9:30 pm, Fri & Sat 6–10:30 pm.

Best Nouvelle cuisine (near the canal)

Tallgrass

Lockport is a well-preserved 19th-century canal town, with streets made of locally quarried limestone and a historic district featuring Italianate architecture as well as a great many examples of Greek Revival, an extremely popular design in the period before the Civil War. It also is the home of this acclaimed restaurant, located in a restored limestone building, circa 1895, that started life as a tavern and boarding house. The *nouvelle cuisine* features such culinary treats as rack of lamb with gorgonzola and thyme sauces, crispy salmon with hazelnut oil, sautéed sea bass with sweet onion and bacon-cream sauce, and a combination of veal and beef tenderloin with portobello mushrooms and sliced artichokes and a lemon-artichoke cream sauce. For lighter eaters, creative and substantial salads can serve as main courses. Desserts include torte and fresh-fruit creations such as bananas with vanilla glace and caramel sauce. The Victorian decor features antique paneling, a rococo tin ceiling, and 125-year-old gas chandeliers.

Tallgrass, 1006 S State St, Lockport, IL 60441, 815/838-5566. Thu–Sun 6–9 pm.

Best taste of the Southwest

Blue Mesa

You can find hot food (the spicy kind) and cool breezes at Blue Mesa, where the Southwestern cuisine is as good as you'll find east of New Mexico, and where there is alfresco dining in a pleasant, 80-seat area in a landscaped garden. Inside, the Southwest theme is carried out with adobe walls and fireplace and regional art. Start with quesadillas, blackened shrimp with tequila butter, Santa Fe pizza, or an appetizer-sampler selection that also includes spicy, meat-stuffed empanadas. Entrée choices include blue-corn chicken enchiladas, enchiladas del Mar, Taos tacos, superb chiles rellenos, and three kinds of fajitas—shrimp, chicken, and flank steak, sautéed with bell peppers, onions, and pinto beans. Recommended desserts are flan with berry sauce, key lime pie, and chocolate adobe pie. Beverages include imported beers and well-made margaritas.

Blue Mesa, 1729 N Halsted St, Chicago, IL 60614, 312/944-5990. Mon & Tue 11:30 am–10 pm, Wed & Thu 11:30 am–10:30 pm, Fri 11:30 am–midnight, Sat 2:30 pm–midnight, Sun 11 am–10 pm.

Best Mexican restaurant on a budget

Mi Casa-Su Casa Restaurant

On the northern edge of the DePaul neighborhood, in a large white-painted brick building with colorful red shutters and ornate wrought-iron grillwork, is this Mexican restaurant started by the Gomez family in 1968. Stucco walls are adorned with Aztec art, colorful serapes cover the tables beneath protective glass, and Mexican music plays low in the background. The extensive menu includes the standards (burritos, tacos, quesadillas, etc.), but also some truly original items. Appetizers, for example, include *natice* (bite-size cups made from a flour-based, jalepeño-flavored crust filled with beans, beef, guacamole, and chorizo, topped with sour cream) and chorizo puffs (puffed pastry filled with sausage and Chihuahua cheese). Entrées include an extensive list of seafood specialties and more than a dozen Mexican-style steaks and meats. Dinner for two with a pitcher of margaritas will cost about $40.

Mi Casa-Su Casa Restaurant, 2524 N Southport, Chicago, IL 60614, 312/525-6323. Mon–Thu 4–11 pm, Fri & Sat 4 pm–1 am, Sun 11 am–10 pm.

Most authentic regional Mexican cuisine

Frontera Grill and Topolobampo

The cuisine at these adjoining Mexican restaurants is to tacos and burritos what paté is to liverwurst. They take traditional Mexican cooking and give it the flair and style normally associated with fine French or Italian cooking. Meats, chicken, and seafood are expertly grilled or roasted and are served with inventive combinations of vegetables and sauces (the chocolate-based mole sauces are especially excellent). At Frontera, try the signature tacos al carbon, the authentic Mexican precursor of Americanized fajitas; choose from hardwood-grilled steak, duck, chicken, or pork wrapped in a homemade tortilla and flavored with peppers, guacamole, and salsa. Chiles rellenos defines the genre, while a selection of lighter entrées includes homemade tortillas in black bean sauce with chorizo sausage, salsa verde, and queso fresco served with jicama salad. At Topolobampo, opt for such specials as mahi mahi, crabmeat, and rock shrimp in grilled cactus leaf, roasted pork tenderloin marinated in red chiles, or acclaimed roasted wild turkey with a *mole poblano* sauce. Frontera, with high, dark ceilings, bright Mexican art, and light oak tables and chairs is the original restaurant and doesn't accept reservations; Topolobampo is newer, pricier, and does take reservations (and Frontera patrons may order off its menu). Both are usually *extremely* crowded during peak hours. As you might expect, these high-quality restaurants are notable exceptions to the axiom of Mexican fare being relatively inexpensive. Owners Rick and Deann Bayless traveled extensively throughout Mexico to gather the authentic regional recipes featured at these restaurants. Margaritas are exceptionally well made and there is a selection of rare tequilas.

Frontera Grill and Topolobampo, 445 N Clark St, Chicago, IL 60610, 312/661-1434. Frontera Grill: Lunch Tue–Fri 11:30 am–2:30 pm, dinner Tue–Thu

5:30–10 pm, Fri & Sat 5–11 pm, brunch Sat
10:30 am–2:30 pm. Topolobampo: Lunch Tue–Fri
11:30 am–2 pm, dinner Tue–Thu 5:30–9:30 pm, Fri &
Sat 5:30–10:30 pm.

Best spin-off of the most authentic Mexican restaurant

Salpicon

Chef-owner Priscila Satkoff has the credentials to preside over one of the most authentic Mexican restaurants to hit the Chicago dining scene since the Baylesses opened the estimable Frontera Grill. She hails from Mexico City and she once worked in the Frontera kitchen. This small but airy restaurant, with high ceilings and a bold paint job in blue and yellow, is so attractive that it defies description as a storefront. Yet it seats only about 50 and, as the word spreads about its true-to-the-source cuisine, waits are becoming lengthy at prime time (but reservations *are* accepted). Adding to the colorful ambience are fluorescent green wicker chairs, hot pink tablecloths, vibrant folk art, and multihued papier-mâché fish. Although the restaurant waited many months for its liquor license, margaritas made with fresh limes reward those who waited along with the owners. As a starter, try a variation of seviche made with lobster marinated in tequila and the juice of oranges and limes and blended with onion, tomatoes, chiles, and herbs. Or *empanaditas de bacalao*, small, flaky turnovers filled with salt cod, olives, garlic, and pickled jalapeños baked and served with a creamy jalapeño sauce. Entrées are a challenge— so many sound so good. Grilled pork tenderloin is offered in a green mole sauce—or in a chipotle sauce accompanied by zucchini tamales. Fresh fish is served Vera Cruz style—in fresh tomato sauce with capers, Manzanilla olives, pickled jalapeños, and garlic. *Tip:* When they're in season and offered as a special, don't miss the garlicky soft-shell crabs. For dessert choose such traditional (and well-made) offerings as classic flan and Mexican rice pudding or a wonderfully light orange-flavored cake soaked in three milks, topped with a thin layer of meringue and served with a fresh fruit sauce.

Salpicon, 1252 N Wells, Chicago, IL 60610, 312/988-7811. Sun, Tue–Thu 5–10 pm, Fri & Sat 5–11 pm.

Best Mexican regional cuisine in weirdest setting

Hat Dance

This Melman restaurant opened back in 1988 with a splash and an odd-couple pairing of Japanese/

Mexican cuisine. The token Japanese dishes have disappeared along with a weird sign about lascivious lips, and the restaurant has settled down to offer traditional regional Mexican cuisine with a lively spirit of adventure. Start with black bean soup or a pairing of complementary-flavored soups served side by side—or choose from such unusual appetizers as smoked chicken quesadilla with cranberry mole, baked goat cheese and spring onion fundido, or tiger prawns fried tempura-style with dry chili peanut sauce and arbol chile oil. Salads include a spicy Caesar. Even the fajitas are uncommon—one version combining wild mushrooms and other vegetables, another offering duck prepared with red chili, wild mushrooms, spring onions, tomatoes, and cantaloupe-pineapple salsa. Standard fare such as tacos, enchiladas, and burritos also receive a creative spin—soft tacos, for example, can be wrapped around a mix of sea scallops, red-chili tuna, and chipotle tiger prawns. House specialties include roasted lamb shank with chorizo-potato hash and smoked bacon-white beans, and grilled pork chops with achiote smoked salsa and corn pudding. The eclectic, designer white-on-white decor of the multilevel dining room features such oddities as inverted umbrellas and glittery sombreros suspended from the ceiling, scattered palm trees with coconuts, and a giant plaster worm guaranteed to swear you off mescal.

Hat Dance, 325 W Huron St, Chicago, IL 60610, 312/649-0066. Lunch Mon–Fri 11:30 am–2 pm, Sat 11:30 am–3:30 pm; dinner Mon–Thu 5:30–10 pm, Fri 5:30–11:30 pm, Sat 5–11:30 pm, Sun 5–9 pm.

Best south-of-the-border eatery with mom's recipes

Twisted Lizard

Tucked into a north side basement, this rustic cantina blends the cuisine of Mexico, Arizona, and Texas. Stylishly decorated in Southwestern style, it features rough-hewn furniture, a gleaming copper bar, and more than 250 eponymous lizards, hand-carved in Mexico and Guatemala. Chef Sergio Sanchez, using some recipes from his family in Mexico City, adds authenticity to such standards as flautas, enchiladas, and chimichangas. Start with *caldo xochiti*, chicken soup loaded with large chunks of meat and fresh vegetables or tortilla soup, a spicy chicken-tomato based soup with strips of tortillas, topped with Chihuahua cheese. The eclectic menu also includes chicken wings with the fire of habenero, barbecued pork chops and chicken breast, and seafood fajitas (featuring shrimp and scallops).

Freshness is a keynote of this well-run eatery. The guacamole is satisfyingly chunky and flavorful; margaritas are made from fresh lime and lemon juice, rather than a sour mix. This is a pleasant spot for Sunday brunch, with a menu that includes fruits, breads, pastries, and entrées such as burritos, *huevos con chorizo* (eggs scrambled with sausage), and *caldo de huevos* (eggs simmered in a tomato-based broth, flavored with epazote, a Mexican herb). Patrons also can build their own omelettes with a choice of Mexican cheeses, salsa, mushrooms, onions, green pepper, broccoli, and tomato.

Twisted Lizard, 1964 N Sheffield, Chicago, IL 60614, 312/929-1414. Mon–Sat 11:30 am–midnight, Sun 11:30 am–10 pm.

Best bet for Mexican seafood
Su Casa

You don't need to travel to Ixtapa or Cozumel to experience the flavors of Mexican seafood. Simply head for this unpretentious little restaurant that's had its home in Chicago's Gold Coast area since 1963. The decor is pure Mexicana, with white-painted brick walls, hanging Aztec artwork, ceramic-tile tables, and a "courtyard" with shutters, a wrought-iron fence, and silk flowers. A strolling guitarist plays Mexican folk music. There's also a small bar where guests enjoy a refreshing *cerveza* (several types of Mexican beer are available), a margarita (among the best in the city—authentic hand-mixed–style, not frozen), or a fiery *sangrita*, authentically served in a small clay-pottery cup and saucer. On the menu is standard Mexican fare, such as queso fundido (melted cheese in a flour tortilla), steak ranchero, and chimichangas. Seafood dishes are excellent here—try whole red snapper, brook trout prepared in garlic and spices, or shrimp *veraciucana* in a garlic sauce. This is a great place to visit with a group (and it can be easy on the pocketbook).

Su Casa, 49 E Ontario St, Chicago, IL 60611, 312/943-4041. Mon–Thu 11:30 am–11 pm, Fri & Sat 11:30 am–12:30 pm.

Jolly good spot for roast beef and Yorkshire pudding
Lawry's The Prime Rib

Except for lunch (when a limited—but not quite as limited—menu of other entrées is available), prime rib is the only thing you can get at this broad-shouldered shrine to beef. Carved tableside from a wheeled cart, the juicy, aged beef is available in your choice of cuts; predictably, the "Chicago" cut is a hearty, bone-in portion big enough to feed a Bear (of the lineman kind). Dinners are accompanied by a light, crispy Yorkshire pudding, real mashed potatoes, and Lawry's theatrically presented spinning salad bowl (in which a salad is prepared tableside while its bowl is spun on a bed of ice). Other à la carte vegetables (creamed spinach, baked potato, etc.) are available, as are an uninspired array of desserts, almost as afterthoughts. The star here is definitely the prime rib. The setting is upscale—in an ornate former McCormick mansion—with prices to match.

Lawry's The Prime Rib, 100 E Ontario St, Chicago, IL 60611, 312/787-5000. Lunch Mon–Fri 11:30 am–2 pm; dinner Mon–Thu 5–11 pm, Fri & Sat 5 pm–midnight, Sun 3–10 pm.

Best bet for British take-away

Winston's Sausage

Expatriated Brits who want to stock their pantries with foods from home head for this specialty store across the street from Midway Airport. Winston's is a combination meat market/neighborhood store that specializes in British food. On Wednesdays, they bake Scotch meat pies and bridies (a turnover of flaky pastry filled with seasoned meat), and you usually can buy them fresh through Saturday. At other times, you'll find these items in the freezer. You'll also discover fat rounds of spicy blood pudding and fresh link sausages, made either from pork or beef. The latter, difficult to find elsewhere, are especially worth sampling. You can buy fresh Irish soda bread and survey shelves filled with such imports as custard mix, Bisto (the ubiquitous British gravy mix), Scottish shortcake, English chocolate biscuits, chunky orange marmalade, gooseberry jam studded with fruit, and British chutney, pickled onions, and black sauce.

Winston's Sausage, 4701 W 63rd St, Chicago, IL 60629, 312/767-4353. Mon–Sat 7:30 am–5:30 pm.

Largest lunchtime salad

Chicago Claim Company

Once you get by the hokey gold-miner's theme (crossbred with Hollywood-Mexican), with bare brick showing through cracked adobe walls, this Bloomies' building restaurant is a good luncheon spot. The salad bar is packed with 60 items, encompassing all of the expected ingredients, and then some. You'll find four or five different kinds of lettuce, hearts of palm, string beans, pickled herring, and a variety of pasta salads—such as tuna, salami-and-cheese, and garlic pasta. Carnivores eschew this assembled greenery in favor of the celebrated Motherlode hamburger, charbroiled to order and built with selections from a variety of mix-and-match cheeses, sauces, toppings, and breads. There is a fajitas bar and daily and dinner specials that include fresh seafood. Good dessert choices are key lime pie made with fresh Florida lime juice and ice cream cake with Oreo crumb crust.

Chicago Claim Company, 900 N Michigan Ave, Chicago, IL 60611, 312/787-5757. Mon–Thu 11:30 am–9:30 pm, Fri & Sat 11:30 am–10:30 pm, Sun 11:30 am–8:30 pm.

Best salad bar and burgers

R. J. Grunts

Back in 1971, budding restaurateur Rich Melman opened this fun eatery aimed at the "counterculture" (and, admittedly, anyone else he could entice through its doors). Back then, the funky-chic decor; bountiful portions; and punning, inside-jokey menu was a perfect match with the hip and hippie tastes. Today, the Grunts concept has been appropriated and refined in various competing restaurants (Bennigan's, Houlihan's, T.G.I. Friday's, etc.), while Melman's Lettuce Entertain You chain has grown to dominate Chicago's mid- to upper-level dining as a nationally known success story. But some things never change—and Grunts still offers huge, juicy burgers, an overflowing salad bar, a popular Sunday brunch, and a quaint aura of its bygone era, even after the passing of a quarter century. This area (overlooking Lincoln Park) may have become one of the most desirable residential spots in the city, but success, creeping gentrification, and changing tastes certainly haven't spoiled reliable ol' Grunts. Among the staples are chili and vegetarian chili, French onion soup, tuna melt, quiche, and a variety of burgers, chicken, steaks, and ribs.

R. J. Grunts, 2056 Lincoln Park West, Chicago, IL 60614, 312/929-5363. Mon–Thu 11 am–10 pm, Fri & Sat 11:30 am–11 pm, Sun 10 am–10 pm.

Best restaurant to shout "Opaa!" (because of the food)

Rodity's Restaurant

Just west of the Loop, concentrated on Halsted Street, is Chicago's lively Greektown. Rodity's, with bunches of grapes on its etched-glass windows and

rotating spits of gyros behind the bar, is arche-
typal—informal and fun. Two large dining rooms
with half-paneled, white-stuccoed walls with blue-
painted trim are decorated with framed photographs
of Greece and marquetry murals of Aegean scenes.
Start with taramasalata, a creamy, fish-roe spread
served with crusty Greek bread; calamari (batter-
fried squid); or flaming saganaki (kefalotiri cheese
fried in olive oil and soaked in brandy) ignited at your
table to yells of "Opaa!" Popular entrées are braised
and roast lamb and simple lemon chicken, along
with Greek standards such as dolmades (grape leaves
stuffed with seasoned ground beef and rice and
served with rich egg-lemon cream sauce),
spanakotiropita (cheese-spinach pie with phyllo
pastry), moussaka (layers of eggplant and spicy
ground beef and sliced potatoes), and gyros with
chopped onions and cucumber-yogurt sauce. Accompany your meal with a bottle of roditys or retsina.
Waiters, formally dressed in crisp, white shirts, black
bow ties, and black pants—many newcomers to
America—are friendly, efficient, and given to vocal-
izing a bar or two of the Greek music that provides
a constant background. Beware of Saturday evenings when it is a task to squeeze into the bar and
waits can extend up to two hours.

Rodity's Restaurant, 222 S Halsted St, Chicago, IL
60606, 312/454-0800. Sun–Thu 11 am–1 am, Fri & Sat
11 am–2 am.

Best restaurant to shout "Opaa!" (because of the food and ambience)
Pegasus Restaurant and Taverna

This relative newcomer to Greektown is unquestionably the neighborhood's most attractive taverna.
Windows, fronted by pretty flower boxes, open onto
the street. Inside, one wall is devoted to a huge
mural of the whitewashed buildings of an Aegean
village shimmering in the sun against a blameless
blue sky. Tables are set formally, starched white
cloths and napery complementing the rich wooden
furniture. Perhaps best of all is a rooftop garden with
a spectacular view of the Chicago skyline, a marvelous summertime spot for an after-work drink, alfresco dinner, or an after-dinner glass of Metaxa
Greek brandy. Pegasus handles the standards as
well as anyone along the Halsted Greek strip—spin-
ach-cheese pie, dolmathes, moussaka, and arni psito
(roast leg of lamb). House specialties include chicken
baked with lemon and oregano served with potato
riganatti (a family recipe), yuvetsaki (an individual
baked casserole of pasta and beef topped with grated

cheese), and *viayias*, a sort of Greek-style fajitas with marinated strips of chicken breast served sizzling in a skillet with onions, green peppers, tomatoes, and mushrooms, with pita bread on the side. Seafood selections include whole red snapper or sea bass, orange roughy, shrimp or swordfish kebobs, and pan-fried codfish or smelts. Predictably, desserts include baklava, the sticky-sweet honey-raisin pastry. Worth trying is a thick, smooth homemade yogurt—which can be ordered with fresh fruit and/or honey.

Pegasus Restaurant and Taverna, 130 S Halsted St, Chicago, IL 60661, 312/226-3377. Sun–Thu noon–midnight, Fri & Sat noon–1 am.

Best restaurant to shout "Opaa!" (because of the belly dancer)

Neon Greek Village

With Hellas and its troupe of belly dancers a distant memory, this handsome club is the only one in Greektown to offer full-scale live entertainment. The house band features the bouzouki (a mandolin-like traditional Greek string instrument) and Greek singers. Traditional acts include the gyrating performance of a sequined and tasseled belly dancer. Periodically, Neon Greek Village brings in shows and performers from Greece. The dining room has well-spaced tables and clean white walls decorated with vintage musical instruments and a photo gallery of legendary Greek entertainers. A corner stage is bathed by colorful spotlights. Food includes such Greek staples as taramasalata, saganaki, shish-kabob, Grecian-style chicken, and baklava. For some standard Greek fare and first-class Greek entertainment, check this spot out on a night when a major star from Greece is to appear, when the excitement is palpable among the Greek expatriates who crowd the room into the wee small hours.

Neon Greek Village, 310 S Halsted St, Chicago, IL 60661, 312/648-9800. Thu–Sun 6 pm–4 am.

Top taverna outside Greektown

Papagus Greek Taverna

With Aegean-blue awnings and café furniture, this sidewalk taverna is a bit of Greece grafted onto the red brick facade of the Embassy Suites hotel at a busy Chicago intersection. Although it was created out of whole cloth by the Lettuce Entertain You group, it has the look and feel of a rustic old-world style taverna. Inside is a pleasant spot to linger—if only with a glass of roditys and some crusty Greek

bread with creamy smooth spreads or an order of
saganaki. The well-prepared food is traditionally
Greek—but with some contemporary accents—and
offers such standards as *taramosalata* (smooth cod-
roe spread), *spanakopita, moussakas* (ground beef
and lamb layered with eggplant, squash, and potatoes), and gyros sandwiches served on pita bread.
Regional specialties include braised lamb with orzo
pasta, pork shish kabob, and a dish featuring
macaroni pasta, baby artichokes, and spinach with
a lemon cream sauce. If you're undecided about
what to order, try a sampling of *mezedes*, appetizer-
size portions, hot and cold, that are the Greek equivalent of Spain's tapas.

Papagus Greek Taverna, 620 N State St, Chicago,
IL 60610, 312/642-8450. Mon–Thu 11:30 am–10 pm,
Fri 11:30 am–midnight, Sat noon–midnight, Sun
noon–10 pm.

Best ham hocks, greens, and sweet-potato pie

Army & Lou's

This South Side favorite has become sort of upscale
soul, patronized also by diners from the North Side.
But it remains authentic, as it has been for more
than 50 years, on and off. For the uninitiated, this
is a good spot to try soul food—ham hocks, beans,
chitlins, black-eyed peas, and mustard and turnip
greens. However, don't miss the deep-fried shrimp—
huge butterfly shrimp with an incredibly light, fluffy
batter. Soups are uniformly good; a standout is
seafood gumbo, rich with shrimp and spicy Cajun
flavors. Other favorites include smoky barbecued
short ribs, fried chicken, and delicious catfish (we
once watched a diner, with obvious relish, devour an
entire serving, bones included). Few regulars skip
dessert, particularly the rich peach cobbler, bread
pudding with lemon sauce, and outstanding sweet-
potato pie. With hours now extended to include
breakfast comes an opportunity to sample catfish
and salmon coquettes with eggs and grits.

Army & Lou's, 420 E 75th St, Chicago, IL 60619,
312/483-3100. Wed–Mon 9 am–10 pm.

Most inventive Chinese restaurant

T'ang Dynasty

It is ambitiously named for an era that brought to
China the golden age of art. Nonetheless, T'ang
Dynasty does an impressive job, with beautiful

imported works of art, a tasteful decor, and exquisite food that delights the eyes as well as the palate. Its menu is largely Mandarin—but with much innovation. For a special occasion, sample beggar's hen, a Cornish hen slow-cooked in a case of clay, which seals in juices and flavor and which is cracked open ceremoniously with a mallet. The menu is huge—more than two dozen appetizer selection, for example, standouts among which are spicy Taiwan escargot, prawn fingers, vegetable dumplings, and scallion pancakes. As a main course, try scallops that are wrapped with vegetables in egg-white pancakes and then steamed—or splurge on the Peking duck, prepared to perfection. Even traditional fortune cookies are served with flair, in a miniature Chinese junk decorated with dragons and emitting a drifting cloud (formed by dry ice).

T'ang Dynasty, 100 E Walton St, Chicago, IL 60611, 312/664-8688. Sun–Thu 11:30 am–10:30 pm, Fri & Sat 11:30 am–11:30 pm.

Best dim sum—and then some

Three Happiness Restaurant

This large restaurant in the heart of Chinatown is where a great number of the local Chinese community go to eat. It's also a major attraction with visitors, the kind of place that perfectly accommodates groups of 10 or more. If you organize such a dim sum dining group, you'll be able to sample extensively from the menu. For the uninitiated, dim sum consists of small pastries, dumplings, and other appetizer-sized portions of light Chinese food; the Three Happiness version is among the best in the city. There are more than 20 options available at any one time from the dim sum cart, including dumplings stuffed with sweet-and-sour pork, steamed shrimp rolled in a thin wheat-starch wrap, stuffed bean curd rolls, spare ribs with black bean sauce, and puffy dough filled with minced pork and steamed. There's also a small menu of entrée-sized portions (which, somehow, don't seem as good as the dim sum), and a limited dessert menu that includes custard, ice cream, and coconut pudding. Dim sum dining can be economical as well as tasty, with items ranging from $1.75 to $4.25.

Three Happiness Restaurant, 2130 E Wentworth Ave, Chicago, IL 60616, 312/791-1228. Mon–Thu 10 am–11 pm, Fri & Sat 10 am–1 am, Sun 10 am–10 pm. Also at 209 W Cermak, 312/842-1964.

Best Szechwan (plus Mandarin and Hunan) cuisine closest to the Magnificent Mile

Szechwan East

This used to be all of the above *on* the Magnificent Mile. Then, in 1995, the old Szechwan House lost its lease when the building at Michigan and Ohio was demolished—but the restaurant bounced back as Szechwan East at this new location 2½ blocks east. An excellent buy—at under $10—is a 30-item luncheon buffet (Mon–Sat), which includes two soups, hot and cold appetizers, 10 or more hot entrées, including shrimp, beef, pork, fish, chicken, and vegetable dishes, a mu shu dish, desserts, tea, and fortune cookie. A sumptuous Sunday brunch, including Peking duck and half a steamed Maine lobster, is priced at $15.95. The restaurant's extensive menu includes such dishes as beef with orange peel, Hunan salmon (fillets covered with noodles with minced pork, garlic, and brown sauce), lobster Szechwan-style (sautéed in the shell in red ginger and garlic sauce), pork with Peking sauce, and smoked tea duck (marinated in five spices and slowly smoked over tea leaves and camphor wood, then deep fried). Mu shu crepes—thin Mandarin pancakes—come filled with chicken, beef, shrimp, pork, or shredded Chinese vegetables. The new quarters include comfortable booths and a glass extension built out onto the sidewalk.

Szechwan East, 340 E Ohio St, Chicago, IL 60611, 312/255-9200. Daily 11:30 am–10 pm.

Best sushi bar in the East (of Michigan Avenue)

Hatsuhana

Fans of sushi and sashimi, tempura and teriyaki, head for this perennially popular restaurant just east of Michigan Avenue. Fresh seafood (including fluke, tuna, flounder, and other traditional raw fin- and shellfish) is attractively and inventively presented—for example. In "tiger's eyes" made of broiled white squid wrapped around smoked salmon (as the pupils) and greens (as the irises). Other Hatsuhana specialties include crisp tempura, choice of fish or beef teriyaki, and broiled Maine lobster—in fact, the favored house special combines a sampling of sushi, teriyaki, and tempura, plus half a lobster, tea, and dessert. The restaurant's well-stocked sushi bar is one of the largest in the city.

Hatsuhana, 160 E Ontario St, Chicago, IL 60611,
312/280-8808. Lunch Mon–Fri 11:45 am–2 pm,
dinner Mon–Fri 5:30–10:15 pm, Sat 5–10:15 pm.

Best authentic wiener schnitzel

Golden Ox

It's as Bavarian as a cuckoo clock, and since 1921
this restaurant has served hearty German specialties. Not even neighborhood gentrification seems to
be able to supplant this remnant of the German
community that once dominated this part of the city.
Food, service, and atmosphere are as reliable as a
new Mercedes-Benz—with prices more in keeping
with a Volkswagen. Four separate dining areas,
adorned with murals, oil paintings, dark woodwork,
and various Teutonic baubles conjure images of the
old country, with staff dressed as though rehearsing
a Bavarian play. The menu includes German standards such as wurst, lamb shanks, braised ox tails,
roast duck, spaetzle, pickled vegetable relish, and
delicious liver dumpling soup. Schnitzels are a good
bet—upon request the kitchen will prepare your
wiener schnitzel à la Holstein (crowned with fried
egg, capers, and anchovies). The cuisine is heavy,
but it is worthwhile saving room for dessert—apple,
plum, and cherry strudel, rum torte, German chocolate cake, Black Forest cake, and three kinds of
cheesecake.

Golden Ox, 1578 N Clybourn Ave, Chicago, IL
60622, 312/664-0780. Mon–Sat 11 am–11:30 pm, Sun
3–9 pm.

Best authentic hackepeter and hasenpfeffer

Zum Deutschen Eck

For a night on the town, Bavarian-style, this long-
time North Side favorite fills the bill. Dining is
authentic, from hackepeter (steak tartare, served
with fresh-baked rye bread) to hasenpfeffer
(marinated rabbit meat). And the decor of half-
timbered beams, antique beer steins, ornate stained
glass, and pewter plates could have been lifted whole
from a Munich beer hall. The same holds true for
the menu, the most popular items on which are such
classics as wiener schnitzel, sauerbraten, and rou-
laden. A perfect accompaniment for this hearty fare
is a selection of around a dozen imported beers, on
tap and in bottles. A small "oompah" band entertains
on weekend evenings; sing-along sheets are dis-
tributed to patrons, adding to the rollicking fun of

a mock-Bavarian evening. Unlike many North Side establishments, this restaurant has surrounding lots offering *plenty* of free parking. *Note:* If you enjoy the boisterous entertainment but prefer to give a miss to the heavy food, a new section of the menu includes lighter choices such as vegetarian pasta, chicken dishes, and fresh seafood.

Zum Deutschen Eck, 2924 N Southport, Chicago, IL 60657, 312/525-8389. Mon–Thu 11:30 am–10:30 pm, Fri 11:30 am–12:30 am, Sat noon–12:30 am, Sun noon–10 pm.

Best hidden wurst

Kuhn's International Delicatessen

You may not find many secrets better kept than this German eatery. Tucked away in the corner of a German deli, alongside trays of herring, strings of plump sausages, and shelves of grainy German and Polish rye bread, are a handful of Formica tables and some of the most authentic and least expensive German fare you'll find. Stop by for lunch (Mon–Fri 11 am–3 pm, Sat 11 am–4 pm) and start with ham-and-potato, traditional liver-dumpling soup, or perhaps a sampling of rollmops or herring in wine. As an entrée, pick from more than a dozen different kinds of wurst, served with sauerkraut or red cabbage and potato salad, or such traditional dishes as kasseler rippchen, sauerbraten, and wiener schnitzel. There is a large selection of international beers, ranging from Dortmunder Union to Bass Ale, plus cheeses and creamy German cakes. A good take-home bet is a loaf of Bavarian-style leberkäse, a sort of liverwurst meatloaf; buy it frozen and bake it and serve it hot—it's great party fare served with crusty bread.

Kuhn's International Delicatessen, Deerbrook Mall, Waukegan Rd & Lake-Cook Rd, Deerfield, IL 60015, 847/272-4197. Mon–Fri 10 am–7 pm, Sat 9 am–7 pm, Sun 10 am–5 pm.

Tastiest tapas tasting

Café Ba-Ba-Reeba!

As Chicago's first trend-setting tapas bar, this Melman/Lettuce Entertain You version of a sprightly Madrid or Barcelona corner bar bears repetition of a story from its founding days, when the genre was virtually unknown. This would-be patron, upon hearing of Chicago's new tapas restaurant, wondered if the vice squad would shut it down. That's *tapas*, not topless, it was explained. Now, of course, this delightful Spanish-style of dining has become as pervasive as Thai food. A tempting array of *tapas frias* (cold) and *tapas calientes* (hot) features seafood (including excellent mussels and clams), chicken, and biting chorizo sausage. Ba-Ba-Reeba also offers a nicely executed *paella*, a sizzling skillet of pork, shrimp, mussels, chicken, and vegetables over saffron-tinted rice. Worth trying are the potato omelette, ratatouille, grilled squid, baked goat cheese, and beef or chicken brochettes. Head here with a group, prepared for sampling and sharing, and watch those little plates pile up in your wake. This 360-seat restaurant, done in vivid Mediterranean colors, is located on a fashionable strip of Halsted Street and offers warm-weather dining in a pleasant adjoining courtyard.

Café Ba-Ba-Reeba, 2024 N Halsted St, Chicago, IL 60614, 312/935-5000. Lunch: Tue–Fri 11:30 am–2:30 pm, Fri & Sat 11:30 am–3 pm; dinner Mon–Thu 5:30–11 pm, Fri & Sat 5:30 pm–midnight, Sun noon–10 pm.

Tastiest tapas-tasting clone

Emilio's Tapas Bar & Restaurant

Many times, the student exceeds the master. This is the case with Emilio Gervilla, one-time chef at Café Ba-Ba-Reeba, who departed to start his own tapas restaurant. That led to a flourishing mini-chain of tapas bars in the western suburbs and, more recently, a successful location in the city. All are good, but we still prefer the original in the near-west suburb of Hillside—just a short drive on the Eisenhower Expressway. Here, the restaurateur transformed a former fast-food joint in this unlikely industrial suburb into a popular restaurant that continues to attract patrons from afar. Whet the appetite with bone-dry *fino* sherry—or order a pitcher of sangria. Then choose from a long list of hot and cold tapas. These creative appetizers are ideal for a group of four or more to share. Standouts include chilled asparagus with alioli and tomato basil vinaigrette; manchego cheese, ham, and chopped fresh tomato on grilled bread; grilled squid with garlic and lemon; snails with tomato sauce and garlic mayonnaise atop croutons bathed in olive oil; sautéed wild mushrooms with sherry; and potato-onion omelette. Classic *paella* is splendid, golden, and rich with mussels, clams, chicken, and sausage. The Spanish motif, with café curtains, mosaics and murals, provides a colorful Mediterranean-like setting. In warm weather, diners spill onto an outdoor patio.

Emilio's Tapas Bar & Restaurant, 4100 W Roosevelt
Rd, Hillside, IL 60624, 708/547-7177. Mon–Thu 11:30
am–10 pm, Fri 11:30 am–11 pm, Sat 5–11 pm, Sun
4–9 pm. Also: 444 W. Fullerton Pkwy, Chicago, IL
60614, 312/327-5100.

Best bodega west of Seville
Café Iberico

Casks stuffed with wine bottles line one wall; along
the entire length of another is a mural depicting the
bullring, flamenco dancers, and folkloric groups. The
bar features colorful mosaic tile tabletops. This
authentic Spanish tapas bar, with large dining rooms
at street and lower levels—the latter with the feel of
a Spanish bodega—is a spot to eat well and inexpensively in the heart of touristy River North. Start
with Galician-style white bean soup, thick with beans
and escarole; in summer, a fine rendition of gazpacho
hits the spot. Cold tapas include a vegetarian Spanish-style omelette, fire-roasted three-color peppers,
fresh artichokes marinated in olive oil and vinegar,
and roasted veal with raspberry vinaigrette sauce.
Hot selections feature grilled sea scallops with saffron sauce, sautéed mussels with marinara sauce,
chicken brochette with caramelized onions and rice,
grilled squid with olive oil, garlic, and lemon juice,
and baked goat cheese with fresh tomato-and-basil
sauce. A fine selection of sherries range from bone-
dry *fino* (try La Ina as an aperitif) to medium-dry
manzanillas and rich cream dessert sherries. Go for
the Spanish ambience and for the prices—tapas
average around $4 each, and Iberico brings in a
hearty platter of *paella* for under $12.

Café Iberico, 739 N LaSalle St, Chicago, IL 60610,
312/573-1510. Mon–Thu 11 am–11 pm, Fri 11 am–
1:30 am, Sat noon–1:30 am, Sun noon–11 pm.

Top tapas from Catalonia
Tapas Barcelona

Now that Chicagoans have wholeheartedly embraced
the Spanish concept of tapas, as pioneered by Café
Ba-Ba-Reeba! and entrepreneurial and hard-work-
ing Emilio Gervilla with his numerous restaurants,
you might expect the whole thing would become
specialized. This 1995 entry into the tapas dining
scene emphasizes the unique cuisine of Catalonia,
a region encompassing Barcelona and the seaside
resorts of the "Costa Brava" that is dominated by
seafood and rich sauces. Catalan specialties at this
authentic—but highly fashionable—tapas bar include: poached monkfish with warm lentil salad and

saffron garlic sauce; sautéed sea scallops with picada sauce; fresh prawns in a rich garlic broth; and marinated chicken and mushrooms with shallots and cumin olive oil. This two-story restaurant is a delight to the eye, featuring a bar of wood, tile, and gleaming copper; posters and bohemian sketches imported from Barcelona; lights artistically draped in chiffon; and wooden booths covered in painted fabrics. Adding to the Catalonia ambience is a cold tapas bar encased in glass and surrounded by a mosaic mirror, hanging dried salt cod, serrano hams, and chorizo. Managing Partner Giovanni Garelli grew up in Seville, upstairs from a tapas bar that his parents owned for 40 years. He helped his mother in the kitchen and his father in the restaurant and brings many of his mother's original recipes to this stylish restaurant. There is an excellent selection of sherry—more than 30—including chilled, bone-dry *finos* as aperitifs and rich oloroso/solera for after dinner. Desserts include traditional flan as well as chocolate crèpes filled with raspberries and white chocolate mousse and sautéed bananas with pistachios, caramel sauce, and ice cream.

Tapas Barcelona, 118 W Hubbard St, Chicago, Il 60610. Mon–Sat 11 am–1 pm, Sun 4–10 pm.

Best tastes of Arizona and Asia

Nix

Those who remember the Knickerbocker Hotel as part of the former Playboy empire are acquainted with only a sliver of its history. Opened in 1927, the hotel is a landmark that has been taken over and refurbished by Regal Hotels International. Its new look includes this stunning restaurant that is good to look at and great to eat at. Sleekly decorated in black, white, and red, Nix blends the cuisines of the American Southwest and the Pacific Rim. It sounds trendy—and it is—but that term fails to speak for the delicious taste combinations produced by a talented kitchen. Standouts among the starters are prawn dumplings served with ginger dipping sauce and roasted corn and crawfish cakes with Tabasco mustard sauce and Thai basil oil. Soups include a creamy cilantro mussel soup with ancho chili preserves and lemon grass soup with prawn ravioli, straw mushrooms, and pea shoots. Entrées feature tea-smoked chicken, grouper served with noodles and spiced crawfish tails, plum-glazed venison, and Peking duck with a Southwest spin, courtesy of honey-ancho and sour plum sauce. Even plebian hamburger gets star treatment, served with Jarlsberg cheese on a roll made from pretzel dough, imbedded with chopsticks spiraled with tempura onion rings. Scrumptious desserts are produced by an in-house pastry chef.

Nix, 163 E Walton Pl, Chicago, IL 60611, 312/867-7575. Daily 6:30 am–10 pm.

Best black bean soup
Tania's Restaurant & Lounge

Start with the food and stay for the dancing—with a little pyrotechnics in between. This beautiful Latin club grew from humble beginnings when Elias Sanchez, a Cuban émigré, opened a small café at the back of his grocery store 20 years ago. Today, Tania's (named for his daughter) is a hot spot for salsa dancing. It's open into the wee small hours, so after you master the lambada, there's always time for the merengue. Its white walls are decorated with art and artifacts from about two dozen Latin-American countries, ranging from Costa Rica and Ecuador to Puerto Rico and Peru. Included are coats of arms on wooden shields, colorful sarrapas, Argentinean gaucho trappings, llama wool rugs, maps of Cuba, and parrots on a ceiling perch. The cuisine is outstanding. Sample incredibly tender giant New Zealand mussels cooked in a green garlic sauce, and *sopa de frijoles negros*, some of the best black bean soup you'll find anywhere. Try it the Spanish way, spooning first some rice, then some soup, and then some garlic sauce from the mussels . . . *Magnifico!* And so is the *paella*, the Spanish dish of rice with chicken, seafood, and a delicious saffron-flavored sauce. Finish with flan, a dessert as popular in Puerto Rico and Mexico as it is in Spain. The fireworks are produced tableside as the waiter prepares flaming Spanish coffee, with Venezuelan rum, a sprinkling of cinnamon that sparkles like a firecracker, half-and-half, whipped cream, and a cascade of flaming Kahlua.

Tania's Restaurant & Lounge, 2659 N Milwaukee Ave, Chicago, IL 60647, 312/235-7120. Mon–Tue 11 am–1 am, Wed–Sat 11 am–4 am, Sun 11 am–3:30 am.

Most exciting passport to Latin America
Mambo Grill

The colors are as vibrant as the food at this "Latin kitchen" that fuses the food of South America, Puerto Rico, Cuba, and Mexico. Decorated in midnight blue, grape, teal, and terra cotta, this colorful storefront restaurant has bold slate floors, walls decorated with hieroglyphics, and colorful geometric designs on ceilings hung with distinctive cone lights. The flavors of its pan-Hispanic fare can be complex—a blend of hot, sweet, spicy, and smoky—and the preparations intricate—or as simple as a Cuban steak sandwich, the meat thinly sliced and packed with red onions, sliced peppers, Chimichurri sauce, and Chihuahua cheese. You can make a culinary tour of Latin America by starting perhaps with a Nicaraguan corncake mixed with sausage and olives or Dominican Republic crab cakes with cilantro tartar sauce and Creole pepper salsa. For the main course, visit Guatemala for baby back ribs with spicy guava barbecue sauce and chipolte mashed potatoes. Or take a trip to Argentina for beef tenderloin basted with chimichurri—or to Veracruz, Mexico, for mahi mahi with fresh tomato, capers, and olives. However, there is such a variety of appetizers and sides that one easily could skip an entrée and make a meal, tapas-style. Desserts include flan and mango or coconut ice cream. Potables range from margaritas, sangria, and a potent Brazilian cocktail made with Cachaca and lime juice, to imported Mexican and South American beers. A Sunday brunch, where both the food and decor are guaranteed to open your eyes, includes the likes of *huevos rancheros* and avocado-tomatillo salsa and chicken Cuban chili and chicken hash with poached eggs.

Mambo Grill, 412 N Clark St, Chicago, IL 60610, 312/467-9797. Daily 11 am–1 am.

Best paella

La Paella

Tapas may be among the hottest food fads, but for some 15 years this storefront restaurant of Paco and Carmen Sanchez has served authentic Spanish food. The ambience features an attractive peach decor and massive copper chandeliers, while the menu showcases as its signature dish the restaurant's namesake paella. The *Valenciana* version of this saffron-flavored rice dish combines meats and seafood, including chicken, lamb, and mussels. The all-seafood *marinera* version is a blend of lobster, mussels, clams, shrimp, and squid. *Zarzuela* is a stew-like seafood dish with a lobster-based brandy-and-tomato sauce. Included among appetizers—tapas, if you will—are mussels, mushrooms sautéed in garlic sauce, garlicky shrimp, and *queso Manchego* (sheep's-milk cheese served with sliced apples). One of the most popular appetizers—surprisingly, perhaps—is fish cheeks sautéed in olive oil and white wine with garlic and cayenne pepper. Soups include traditional gazpacho, garlic soup (with a poached egg cooked in it), and (occasionally) lobster bisque. Flan is a good dessert choice—or you might try a fresh-fruit tart or fresh orange slices prepared in a marinade of orange peel, cloves, and Cointreau.

La Paella, 2920 N Clark St, Chicago, IL 60657, 312/528-0757. Tue–Sat 5:30–10:30 pm, Sun 5–9 pm.

Fondest fondue
Fondue Stube

Fondue restaurants have become an anachronism, almost as extinct as the leisure suit. Of the few that remain, the Fondue Stube succeeds in staying busy—and sometimes crowded—with an assist from a classical-music trio and $12 discount coupons in the Friday newspapers. Two crowded dining rooms have Italian miniature lights, framed photography, and low tables. A variety of fondue combinations—cheese, beef, chicken, seafood, and vegetables—are served with condiments (raspberry, barbecue, béarnaise, and seafood-cocktail sauces), a decent green salad, and warm garlic bread. Dark and white chocolate is offered for dessert, with cake and fruit dunkables. Sharing a fondue is a companionable meal, that also can be illuminating. Conversation from an adjoining table: "On my second date I brought him here, and that's when I discovered he can't cook."

Fondue Stube, 2717 W Peterson, Chicago, IL 60659, 312/784-2200. Mon–Thu 5–11 pm, Fri & Sat 5 pm–midnight, Sun 4–10 pm.

Best brunch in a French courtyard
Chez Colette, Hotel Sofitel

This hotel's Sunday brunch goes way beyond the expected. You serve yourself from an array of food handsomely set up in the lobby and dine in the Chez Colette, styled as a French brasserie. The ambience of the lobby is that of a French courtyard, with a *trompe-l'oeil* of painted shutters and planter boxes, a trickling fountain, and aromas from La Petit Marché bakery. A jazz group entertains the brunch crowd as it ponders the unique offerings of Chef Christian Gaborit—homemade French pâtés, sausages, and cheeses; freshly baked country breads and croissants; hearty venison and lamb stews; chicken basquaise; roast pork; and wild rice. There are omelettes made to order; French crépes; Belgian waffles; chef-carved beef, turkey, and baked ham; fresh fruits and salads; and lox and bagels. Nestled in beds of ice are jumbo shrimp and plump oysters. Champagne flows, and a pastry table brims with chocolate éclairs, fruit tarts, mousse, cream-filled Napoleons, and other temptations.

Chez Colette, Hotel Sofitel, 5550 N River Rd, Rosemont, IL 60018, 847/678-4488, Sun 10:30 am–2 pm.

Best coffee shop

Oak Tree

This coffee shop used to be a 24-hour spot, but when it moved from Rush Street to the sixth floor of the Bloomingdale's building, it pared back its hours. It did not diminish its reliable food or its loyal following of regulars, especially shoppers—on weekends, it is not uncommon to see patrons table-hopping. The Oak Tree has been preparing hearty breakfasts (served all day) and a selection of burgers, sandwiches, and salads since 1970. Notable breakfast entrées include eggs Benedict served with fried potatoes, corned-beef hash with poached eggs, custom-designed omelettes, and lox and bagels—all of which are reasonably priced. The service by mature waitresses who are as quick with coffee refills as they are with a quip or a no-nonsense greeting is extremely efficient.

Oak Tree, 900 N Michigan Ave, Chicago, IL 60611, 312/751-1988. Mon–Fri 7:30 am–8:30 pm, Sat & Sun 7:30 am–9:30 pm.

Best late night spot (upscale)

All Seasons Café

Until they trimmed back its hours, this eatery in the landscaped lobby of the Hyatt Regency Chicago was open 24 hours a day. Even so, it remains a good spot for a reliable late-night (or early morning) meal. The restaurant, elevated within the lobby's reflecting pool, features Midwest specialties. If you're looking for breakfast, there's a Wisconsin cheese omelette, made with Swiss and cheddar; farmer's omelette, filled with sausage, bacon, potato, green peppers, and fresh mushrooms; and country-fried steak with home-style gravy and eggs. Sandwiches include club, barbecued chicken breast with fried onions and potato salad, a burger with country bacon and Wisconsin cheese, and grilled fish with sun-dried tomato remoulade and new-potato salad. You can order an entrée salad featuring Milwaukee sausage, grilled salmon, or roast chicken—or a four-cheese pizza. Entrées include stuffed rainbow trout, roasted veal shank, pot roast, pheasant breast, and, the ultimate comfort food—meatloaf with mushroom gravy and mashed potatoes. Desserts feature cheese-cake, apple pie, brownies, and double-chocolate cheesecake.

All Seasons Café, Hyatt Regency Chicago, 151 E Wacker Dr, Chicago, IL 60601, 312/565-1234. Daily 6 am–midnight.

Best art deco ice cream parlor

Zephyr Ice Cream Restaurant & Café

This slightly out-of-the-way spot has expanded from a corner ice cream parlor into two adjacent estab-lishments covering the majority of a block. The Ice Cream Restaurant still occupies the corner of Wilson Avenue and Ravenswood Avenue, its neon-and-mir-rored art deco interior reminiscent of a diner or a gleaming passenger train of the 1930s. It offers a staggering array of ice cream dishes; if you don't see a combination or concoction that pleases you (hardly imaginable, but . . .), make a suggestion, and they'll create it. The huge shakes and malts (served with the metal mixing containers holding the generous overflow) are a particular favorite. The adjacent café offers a full dining menu, a bar, and an outdoor garden; the café also serves all of the ice cream delicacies available next door.

Zephyr Ice Cream Restaurant & Café, 1777 W Wilson Ave, Chicago, IL 60640, 312/728-6070. Daily 7 am–midnight.

Most authentic South Side ribs

Leon's Bar-B-Q

Leon Finney's South Side mini-chain stands slab-and-shoulders above many of the other purveyors of barbecue in town. As soon as you walk into one of these cramped, no seating (take-out only), no-decor joints, your nostrils are pleasantly assaulted by the smoky aroma of Leon's ribs sizzling in huge ovens. The big, meaty ribs, available in half or full slabs, are liberally slathered with Leon's trademark tangy sauce; hot or mild variations are available. Other menu choices include chicken (the spicy wings are popular) and hot links. Open extra late, because you never know when you're going to get a powerful hankering for some quality barbecue.

Leon's Bar-B-Q, 8251 S Cottage Grove, Chicago, IL 60619, 312/488-4556. Sun–Thu 11 am–4 pm, Fri & Sat 11 am–5 pm. Also at 1640 E 79th St, Chicago, IL 60649, 312/731-1454; and 1158 W. 59th St, Chicago, IL 60621, 312/778-7828.

Most authentic North Side ribs

Twin Anchors

For more than 50 years this Old Town landmark has been serving up ribs. Baby back ribs are meaty and tender, slow-cooked and served with a choice of two sauces. A mahogany bar stretches the length of the front dining room, which has orange Formica tables, spacious wooden booths, and wood paneling decorated with framed nautical art and sunsets. The back room is dominated by huge namesake twin anchors; the Sinatra memorial wall has photographs of Ol' Blue Eyes, a sometime patron. The menu also offers fried chicken, a couple of steaks, breaded fried shrimp, and decent half-pound burgers. There's slaw to accompany entrées and chili and onion rings on the side. Cheesecake is the only choice for dessert, in an assortment that changes daily. This brick building, faced with large brown tiles, sits on the corner of Eugenie, a street of elegantly restored brownstones.

Twin Anchors, 1655 N Sedgwick St, Chicago, IL 60614, 312/266-1616. Mon–Thu 5–11:30 pm, Fri 5 pm–12:30 am, Sat noon–12:30 am, Sun noon–10:45 pm.

Best imitation South Side ribs on the North Side

Bones

A somewhat-upscale, just-north-of-the-city suburb is not the locale you'd pick as a likely spot to find the smoky, juicy barbecued ribs that readily are found on the city's South Side. But, never fear, Rich is here—and so is Bones, another Melman/Lettuce Entertain You joint, bringing racks of flavorful ribs north (way north) of Roosevelt Road. Choose from pork or beef ribs, as well as garlic chicken, roasted brisket, skirt steak, and—as Forrest Gump's friend Bubba might say—garlic shrimp, barbecue shrimp, fried shrimp, and shrimp linguine. Other specialties include braised short ribs and pot roast served with braised vegetables and horseradish whipped potatoes, and sweet-and-sour stuffed cabbage. Whitefish and salmon are available broiled, blackened, barbecued, and mustard glazed. Sandwich selections include BBQ beef, BBQ pork, and the popular Bonesburger, topped with blue cheese and dark, crunchy Marlboro onions—all served with coleslaw and potato (including good curly fries). The decor is fun/funky, with walls covered with caricatures of local sports, media, and political figures. Expect a large and usually lively crowd.

Bones, 7110 N Lincoln Ave, Lincolnwood, IL 60645,
847/677-3350. Sun–Thu 11:30 am–10 pm, Fri & Sat
11:30 am–11:30 pm.

Best ribs by a contest winner

Robinson's No.1 Ribs

It was back in 1982 that Charlie Robinson, an ice-
cream distributor who loved to experiment with
backyard barbecue, entered the first Royko Ribfest.
The cookoff was the brainchild of Mike Royko, syndicated columnist and rib aficionado who threw down
the gauntlet to 400 backyard chefs. Charlie's smoky
ribs came out on top and the following year he
opened a tiny eatery in west suburban Oak Park,
with seating for 14 plus two picnic tables outside.
Today, Charlie owns the entire block and has expanded his restaurant to seat almost 200. Folks
head there for slabs of BBQ baby back ribs, BBQ
chicken dinners, and sandwiches that feature BBQ
pork, BBQ beef, and pork chops. Starters include rib
tips, buffalo chicken wings, and breaded zucchini
and okra. Fixin's include hickory-smoked baked
beans, cornbread, potato salad, steak fries, corn-on-
the-cob, turnip greens, and black-eyed peas.
Charlie's smoky, spicy sauce is itself a big seller.
Made from a secret blend of tomato paste, molasses,
and 17 herbs and spices, it sells to the tune of up
to four million bottles a year. Three kinds are available—the original, one with some extra heat, and a
sweet classic brown sugar sauce—plus five different
kinds of rub-in spices.

Robinson's No.1 Ribs, 940 W Madison St, Oak Park,
IL 60302, 708/383-8452. Mon–Thu 11 am–10 pm,
Fri & Sat 11 am–11 pm, Sun noon–9 pm.

Best bet for "where there's smoke, there's ribs"

Hecky's Barbecue

Hecky Powell wears as a badge of honor the fact that
his is the only restaurant in Illinois cited by the
EPA—for smoke violation. While his take-out/deliv-
ery restaurant serves up about 54,000 pounds of rib
tips a year, Powell makes no bones about its secret.
"It's the sauce," proclaims the bright yellow sign at
Hecky's neat brick storefront. In addition to the
popular rib tips, offerings include slabs of ribs; BBQ
chicken; hot pork links; BBQ turkey drumsticks;
smoked duck; and sandwiches filled with sliced
brisket or pork, sausages, chicken, and fish. For
noncarnivores, Hecky's offers fried fish and chips,
fried catfish dinners, and fried shrimp (he makes his
own breading). Sides include red beans and rice,

baked beans, greens, cole slaw, and fries. Dessert selections are sweet potato pie and peach cobbler. Don't worry about your delivery destination being too outlandish—Hecky's has supplied ribs to cabbies waiting for fares in O'Hare's long taxi line and to sailors in harbor. Hecky's also offers jars of its self-acclaimed sauce, in hot and mild versions.

Hecky's Barbecue, 1902 Green Bay Rd, Evanston, IL 60201, 847/492-1182. Mon–Thu 11 am–10 pm, Fri & Sat 11 am–midnight, Sun 2–9 pm.

Best ribs in an Italian joint

Giovanni's

The name says "Italian"; the aroma says "ribs." In fact, when Mississippi ribmeister Tommie Jack Ferguson, winner of more than 35 top national competitions for "best ribs" and "best sauce" on the professional cookoff circuit, married into the Giovanni family, they also married traditional Italian cooking with the sweet, smoky, tangy taste of southern-style barbecue. The restaurant is located on the stretch of Roosevelt Road that runs through Berwyn and that is as Italian as spaghetti Bolognese, dotted with Italian grocery stores, meat and fruit markets, and Italian ice stands. In keeping with the neighborhood—and its name—this popular local eatery serves up pasta with homemade sauce created from an old-fashioned Sicilian recipe—spaghetti, mostaccioli, ravioli, tortellini, manicotti, and lasagna. There are thin or thick crust pizzas, with homemade crust, and sides of breaded vegetables. Yes, you can get a meatball, Italian beef, or Italian sausage sandwich (available in combination, of course). And then there are those slabs of hickory-smoked award-winning baby back ribs.

Giovanni's, 6823 Roosevelt Rd, Berwyn, IL 60402, 708/795-7171. Mon–Thu 11:30 am–midnight, Fri & Sat 11:30 am–1 am, Sun noon–11 pm.

The place for steak—and the choicest cheesecake

Eli's—The Place for Steak

Virtually a landmark, this long-standing Chicago steakhouse is as popular for its famous cheesecake as it is for its primarily beef dinner entrées. Among its many regulars are Chicago media and entertainment personalities, visiting celebrities, and "old-money" Chicagoans who have come to rely on the restaurant's service and quality. Eli's isn't trendy and isn't nouvelle, doesn't offer any gimmicks and doesn't dazzle with its basic decor. Eli's does, however, consistently serve up fine cuts of beef—aged steaks and prime rib—and a near flawless version of calves' liver with onion. And that cheesecake! Pick your favorite flavor from more than a dozen, including original plain, cinnamon apple crisp, vanilla lite, lemon lite, chocolate chip, praline, amaretto, mud pie, chocolate truffle, Heath Bar, triple chocolate, and Frango mint. (Eli's cheesecake, made by their North Side baker, is also available frozen at many Chicago-area grocery stores.) Even if you pass on the steak, enjoy a wedge of cheesecake in Eli's comfortable piano lounge.

Eli's—The Place for Steak, 215 E Chicago Ave, Chicago, IL 60611, 312/642-1393. Lunch Mon–Fri 11 am–2:30 pm, dinner Sun–Thu 4–10:30 pm, Fri & Sat 4–11 pm.

Best Weight Watchers red-alert desserts

Charlie Trotter's

Mere mention of Charlie Trotter's is likely to set off red alarms at Weight Watchers' HQ. Few desserts-to-die-for are in this league. Of course, it should be mentioned that you'll find here some of the most imaginative nouvelle cuisine in the city, with multicourse degustation menus providing a perfect introduction. A coveted table in the kitchen is reserved months in advance, as Trotter's fame has spread as a cookbook author and with the opening of a restaurant in Las Vegas. But we're talking desserts. An ever-changing menu embraces such selections as warm chocolate tart with bittersweet chocolate sauce and banana fritters; hot apple tart with black truffle ice cream; pear tartlet with banana-walnut ice cream and caramel sauce; Napoleon of bittersweet chocolate, oranges, and pecans with espresso sauce; macadamia nut cake; and a combination of chocolate flan, tiny chocolate terrines, and white chocolate mousse. For total banishment from weight-control class, check out the impressive selection of dessert wines, including vintage port, Madeira, and sherry.

Charlie Trotter's, 816 W Armitage Ave, Chicago, IL 60614, 312/248-6228. Tue–Thu 5:30–9:30 pm, Fri & Sat 5:30–10 pm.

Best restaurant to impress a client

The Everest Room

The name seems to invite critics' puns—"A peak performance. The pinnacle of Chicago's culinary mountain"—but it is appropriate for what has become one of the top restaurants in town. Chef Jean Joho has delicately blended his native Alsatian cuisine with traditional French cooking to create a dining experience of exquisite tastes and understated elegance. Starters might include smoked salmon with warm oatmeal blintzes and double lamb consommé with goat cheese ravioli; entrées feature wild bass, halibut wrapped and roasted in potato with thyme, roasted duck with honey and Alsace spice cake, and saddle of venison with wild huckleberries. For a splendid sampling of Joho's inventive choices, try the degustation, a taste of several small portions of the restaurant's offerings. A representative selection (priced at $76 per person, minimum of two) includes: foie gras with potato salad, roasted red beet soup with onion confit and smoked duck, sea scallops with endive and orange butter, filet of hake with pumpernickel crust, veal medallions with wild morels and asparagus coulis, assorted cheeses. and croustillant of rhubarb and strawberries. The tables here are large and comfortable, and the view to the west (from the 40th floor) can include stunning sunsets. All in all, your client should be suitably impressed and your pocketbook considerably lighter.

The Everest Room, 440 S LaSalle St, Chicago, IL 60605, 312/663-8920. Tue–Thu 5:30–9 pm, Fri & Sat 5:30–10 pm.

Best restaurant to impress a comptroller

Nick & Tony's

The name sounds like a neighborhood spaghetti joint—and in a sense, this is just what this 1940s-style eatery is. Except that it is brand-new, faux-old, and the neighborhood is a high-rent district steps away from North Michigan Avenue. And this place, with pretty Venetian murals, vintage Italian posters, mahogany and walnut parquet floors, and bronze-and-alabaster chandeliers, leans on the elegant side of homey. In summer, an art-deco-ish 110-seat patio with Italian marble, wrought-iron furniture, and lush flower boxes, provides a cool spot for alfresco dining across from the Chicago River. Appetizers include mussels marinara, mozzarella with tomato-basil, calamari, and portobello mushrooms with fried polenta. Pasta choices provide basics such as linguine, spaghetti, lasagna, and angel hair, plus some creative offerings such as four-cheese ravioli with pancetta, pine nuts, and rossa; shell pasta with chicken, mushrooms, and pesto cream; and rotini with chicken, broccoli, and pesto rossa sauce. There's classic chicken vesuvio, eggplant parmesan, and a daily fish selection. Among a half-dozen pizza choices, try a combination of shrimp, pesto, caramelized onion, and mozzarella. With a separate take-out bakery on the premises, you know that the fresh-baked breads and desserts are going to be good. It also means this is a good spot for breakfast—beginning your day, perhaps, with a delicious pumpkin muffin or blueberry scone, with freshly squeezed orange juice and good coffee.

Nick & Tony's, 1 E Wacker Dr, Chicago, IL 60601, 312/467-9449. Mon–Fri 6 am–11 pm, Sat 5–11 pm, Sun 5–10 pm.

Best no-nonsense cuisine in most elegant surroundings

Palette's

After more than 40 years in the hospitality business (most recently at Hyatt hotels in Chicago), Heinz Kern knows what he's doing—and how to do it well. Such is the case with the restaurant he opened in 1995 in the large, airy space in Newberry Plaza formerly occupied by Arnie's. This is one of the most attractive rooms in town—its walls lined with full-panel paintings, booths in striped black-on-black, light oak floors, terra cotta pillars, large picture windows looking out onto a greenery-filled atrium. The artwork, specially commissioned, includes a huge steel sculpture of Icarus and paintings that depict the evolution of art and music. Unusual chairs have black and gold diamond-shaped backs. Heinz is an attentive host, visiting tables as pianist Dave Green in the adjoining bar plays mood music such as "Lady Be Good." Heinz is attentive to food preparation, too, believing that "execution is the key." And so it is. The pork chops look and taste as pork chops should—they are perfectly done. The menu is not especially adventurous. But everything on it seems to get its due. There is a range of steaks and chops, roasted chicken, several fish choices, and a rendition of *paella*. Start with Gorgonzola cheesecake with gazpacho relish, corn chowder with smoked chicken, or potato crab cake with spicy scallion sauce and roasted pepper coulis. Pastas include seafood linguine, cheese ravioli, and black-and-white pasta, featuring artichokes, tomatoes, garlic, and Romano cheese. After dinner, stop at the comfortable bar for a nightcap and soft music.

Palette's, 1030 N State St, Chicago, IL 60610, 312/440-5200. Lunch Mon–Fri 11:30 am–2:30 pm; dinner Mon–Thu 4:30–10 pm, Fri–Sun 4:30–11 pm.

Best jewel box of a restaurant

Toulouse on the Park

Here's the conundrum: Is this an elegant spot for dinner or a romantic late-night rendezvous for good cognac and good music? In fact, Toulouse is both—turn left for the dining room, right for the live jazz. When owner Bob Djahanguiri moved Toulouse from the location it had occupied for 25 years on a seedy stretch of Division Street, he made a quantum leap to a charming location overlooking Lincoln Park. Decorated in the grand style of Versailles, the lavish 75-seat restaurant is painted with murals of frolicking nymphs, its plush belle epoque appointments set off by glittering mirrors and crystal chandeliers, its ceiling studded with huge glass jewels. The food easily lives up to the ambience. Creative appetizers—as pleasing to look at as they are to indulge in—include risotto sprinkled with truffles and parmesan and salmon cured with Absolut, dill, cilantro, and honey mustard accompanied by cucumber granita. Entrées include roasted quails stuffed with spinach, figs, and bacon on a bed of julienne creamed leeks, and smoked duck with chestnut gnocchi, mushrooms, turnips, and rosemary jus. Finish with lemon tart, raspberry torte, and a definitive crème brûlée. To sample the menu more extensively, opt for the "Chef's Table," a nine-course sampler of smaller portions. After dinner, sip a *digestif* in the romantic cognac bar that is dressed in rich crimson and features soft jazz and the tunes of Gershwin, Berlin, and Porter performed by well-known artists.

Toulouse on the Park, 2140 N Lincoln Park W, Chicago, IL 60614, 312/665-9071. Sun–Thu 5:30–10 pm, Fri 5:00–11 pm, Sat 5:30–11 pm.

Prettiest spot for pretheater dinner

The Exchange

If you're headed for a performance at the Shubert Theater or the Civic Opera, check out this spot for early dining—or make it a destination for a quiet, leisurely dinner. Often, it seems forgotten once the LaSalle Street moguls and pols have headed home to the burbs. More's the pity, because, perched on the balcony of a hotel that is buried amid the deep canyons of the financial district, it is one of the city's prettiest—and most unusual—dining spaces. It's a time-warp locale at which to admire the gold-leaf ceiling, vaulted arches, and marble and mahogany accents of the hotel's spectacular beaux arts lobby (the hotel was built in 1928 as a private men's club). Black bean soup has long been a fixture on the menu and makes a worthy starter—as do fresh asparagus spears served with Boursin cheese or a simple Bibb salad with lemon vinaigrette. Main course selections include such standards as tournedos of beef niçoise and New Zealand rack of lamb with garlic herb crust. Veal scalloppine is enhanced by a morel mushroom sauce; shrimp and shiitake mushroom with a light cilantro sauce is served over spinach fettucine. A three-course prix fixe dinner (soup or salad, entrée, and dessert) is a good value and available nightly.

The Exchange, The Midland Hotel, 172 W Adams St, Chicago, IL 60603, 312/332-1200. Mon–Fri 11:30 am–2 pm, 5–9 pm.

Fanciest Midwest cookery

Prairie

You'll find Mom's apple pie at this classy, contemporary restaurant dedicated to the cuisine of the Midwest—but only if Mom is a culinary-school graduate. Before opening Prairie off the lobby of the Hyatt on Printers Row, chef Stephen Langlois did travel the region extensively, searching out traditional recipes, but the menu suggests considerable creative adaptation. The name and decor, with its soft earth tones, evoke the Frank Lloyd Wright Prairie School of Architecture. The menu emphasizes fresh local produce and features corn chowder, trout terrine, brandied duck-and-pheasant loaf, Lake Superior whitefish, baked sturgeon with potato-horseradish crust, fresh coho salmon served with bacon, leeks, and walnuts, honey mustard chicken, baked stuffed walleye, boneless Iowa pork chop with barbecue butter, and juicy sirloin of buffalo. Desserts include apple-and-hazelnut upside-down tart with bourbon caramel sauce, persimmon pudding, and homemade apple and sour-cream raisin pie; the wine list features Midwestern vintners.

Prairie, 500 S Dearborn St, Chicago, IL 60605, 312/663-1143. Mon–Thu 6:30 am–10 pm, Fri 6:30 am–11 pm, Sat 7 am–11 pm, Sun 7 am–10 pm.

Best eatery near Comiskey Park

Franco's Ristorante

This Bridgeport eatery, a couple of blocks from the Dan Ryan Expressway and little more than a high fly ball from the White Sox's Comiskey Park, is a neighborhood place where locals go to eat and beat cops stop off. The food is good, plentiful, and inexpensive—basic veal and pasta, standard red and white sauces, and chianti by the tumbler. The ambience is surprisingly contemporary, with gray walls, Art Deco posters, exposed ductwork, lots of glass blocks, and sleek black and gray tubular furniture. There is a handful of veal and chicken Italian standards and a good selection of pasta, dominated by linguine served with various combinations of calamari, shrimp, clams, and broccoli. A standout is linguine with a white sauce thick with minced clams; there also are primavera and carbonara versions—although the latter may not be smoky enough for some tastes. Moretti Italian beer (from Udine) is available.

Franco's Ristorante, 300 W 31st St, Chicago, IL 60616, 312/225-9566. Mon–Thu 3–10 pm, Fri & Sat 3–10:30 pm.

Best bistro for Old Orchard shoppers
Bistro Europa

Things have changed dramatically for North Shore shoppers and diners. The Old Orchard Shopping Center has been transformed into a glittering new mall (see separate listing in "Shopping") and the Tower Garden Restaurant, a nearby fixture for more than 60 years, has become a bright bistro with a flair for European cuisine. The new restaurant has retained the classic fountain and central skylight of its predecessor and has made over the rotunda-like room with peach-toned walls, hardwood and terra cotta tile floors, French posters, and accents in bright primary colors. Start with steamed mussels with lemon pepper, onion soup crusted with bubbling cheese, crab cake in champagne sauce, or the house pâté. A selection of entrée salads includes Niçoise made with seared yellow fin tuna and grilled shrimp in mango chutney on a bed of spinach. Pasta choices include tomato linguine with artichokes, asparagus, mushrooms, and broccoli with pesto sauce. As a main course, select rotisserie chicken; steak frites with shallot butter; or lamb tart with grilled eggplant, couscous, tomatoes, and garlic. Finish with homemade ice cream or baked bananas with chocolate sauce. This pan-European restaurant offers a list of international beers and a good selection of wines by the glass.

Bistro Europa, 9925 Gross Point Rd, Skokie, IL 60076, 847/673-8767. Tue–Thu 11:30 am–9 pm, Fri & Sat 11:30 am–10 pm, Sun 11:30 am–9 pm.

Best alternative to "restaurant row"
Southgate Café

North suburban Highwood is noted for its "restaurant row" and may have more notable restaurants (including the estimable Carlos'—see separate listing) per capita than any community its size. A lesser-known North Shore alternative is this pretty Lake Forest restaurant where the food is creative and the prices reasonable. Back in 1901, this National Historic Landmark building was the local firehouse with three large bays to accommodate horse-drawn fire engines. Today, the interior features handsome red-and-green Ross hunting tartan (after owner Lawrence C. Ross), and a casual main dining room with white-painted brick walls, framed botanical prints, and bare wooden tables. Starters include black bean soup topped with chunky tomato salsa and streaked with sour cream and oven-baked garlic cloves served with goat cheese and crusty bread. Entrées include center-cut pork chops, roasted salmon in herb crust, and spicy stir-fry rock shrimp. There is a good selection of sandwiches and entrée-sized salads, plus Mexican dishes that include chicken-and-vegetable quesadillas. Chocolate cake and crème brûlée are top dessert choices. The glass-enclosed Garden Room overlooks a dining patio that opens onto Market Square.

Southgate Café, 665 Forest Ave, Lake Forest, IL 60045, 708/234-8800. Sun–Thu 11 am–9 pm, Fri & Sat 11 am–10 pm.

ACCOMMODATIONS

Best deluxe hotel—old money

The Drake Hotel

Elevators with velvet benches and white-gloved operators, rooms with high ceilings, baskets of apples and oranges set out on each floor, a staff that outnumbers guests, English tea and harp music in the Palm Court, and Bookbinder's soup in the Cape Cod Room—these help give The Drake its cachet of comfort and class. Built in 1920 of Bedford limestone, with floors of Tennessee marble, the hotel exudes the feeling of old money; yet, it is warm and appealing with modern amenities (including high-tech business communications—the sort of place where at once you're as likely to run into Marshall Field as hockey star Wayne Gretzky. (Actor Paul Newman enjoys the comforts of the Cape Cod Room, while Joe Pesci likes to hang around the piano bar at the Coq d'Or Lounge—see separate listings, "Notable Potables.") There are 535 guest rooms on 10 floors, and in-room amenities that include bathrobes and daily newspapers, chocolates at turn-down, and fresh fruit. The most recent remodeling involves converting bathrooms to all marble. The Drake's location at the north end of Michigan Avenue is ideal for exploring the shops of the Magnificent Mile and the beaches of Lake Michigan. Many rooms overlook the lake and the popular playground of Oak Street

Beach. Check out a Dickens-style dinner and other events celebrating the Christmas holidays.

The Drake Hotel, 140 E Walton Place, Chicago, IL 60611, 312/787-2200.

Best deluxe hotel—new money

Four Seasons Hotel

Occupying floors 30 through 46 (with a separate street-level entrance and a 7th-floor lobby) of the 66-story 900 North Michigan Avenue building—better known as the tony home of Bloomingdale's—the Four Seasons is a crucial link in the Four Seasons Hotels chain of top-notch accommodations. (The Four Seasons-managed Ritz-Carlton is across the street at Water Tower Place—see separate listing.) The hotel, with 343 guest rooms (including 121 executive suites with separate sleeping and sitting rooms) consistently is recognized by compilers of "best" lists—and deservedly so. Its attractive common areas are lavishly appointed with marble, crystal (the hotel contains a total of 59 chandeliers), intricate woodwork, and plush carpeting. Rooms are packed with extras. These include two-line telephones (with bathroom extensions and hold button), refrigerated mini-bars, bathrobes, hair dryers, lighted makeup mirrors, and closets with skirt hangers and tie racks. There is twice-daily maid service and complimentary shoe shine and newspaper. As with the hotel itself, its Seasons restaurant also is frequently honored by critics. Try it out for brunch, when six theme buffet stations take you on a culinary world tour—from pot roast at the Midwest Station to an exotic marinated seaweed salad at the Oriental Station. Or head for the Seasons Lounge for afternoon tea (Mon–Sat 3–5 pm), featuring bone china, starched white linens, a cozy fireplace, gentle waterfall, and views of Michigan Avenue and the lakefront. Or stop by the lounge in the evening to listen to jazz piano. *Note:* Even cigar smokers are accommodated, in the hotel's clublike bar just off the lobby. The entire Four Seasons is a successful complement to its high-class surroundings.

Four Seasons Hotel, 900 N Michigan Ave (entrance at 120 E Delaware Place), Chicago, IL 60611, 312/280-8800.

Nicest place in the Loop to visit (and you *would* want to live there

Stouffer Renaissance Chicago Hotel

Here's another vital sign of the resuscitation of Chicago's Loop. When Stouffer built this 27-floor,

565-room luxury hotel in 1991, they chose a location *south* of the Chicago River. Since then, the Loop has continued its resurgence and the hotel has established itself as one of the city's best, assembling a loyal following of business and leisure travelers and collecting a raft of stars, diamonds, and other awards. Generous amenities perpetuate a pampered feeling. Every guest room provides a thick terry bathrobe, as well as hair dryers, in-room complimentary coffee, cable TV, computer data ports, delivered newspapers, and shoe shines. Rooms feature rich, dark woods and plush drapes, carpeting, and upholstery. Bay windows are perfect for looking northeast across the Chicago River and for night viewing of the illuminated Wrigley Building and Gothic Tribune Tower. Four club floors, accessible by slotting your room card into the elevator control panels, offer concierge service, private lounge, complimentary continental breakfast, evening hors d'oeuvres, and extra-large rooms. There are an indoor pool and health club, 24-hour business center, and state-of-the-art conference facilities. Across the street is the sparkling rehabbed Chicago Theater, at which the hotel blocks prime seats and offers special packages that include Broadway blockbusters such as *Kiss of the Spider Woman*. The hotel has a similar arrangement with The Art Institute of Chicago for tickets to high-demand special exhibitions. There's Mediterranean-style dining in Cuisines restaurant and café (see separate listing, "Dining"), casual dining and terrific views in the Great Street Restaurant with its spectacular atrium, and elegant afternoon tea and evening cocktails in the Lobby Court (which features live jazz and piano music).

Stouffer Renaissance Chicago Hotel, 1 W Wacker Dr, Chicago, IL 60601, 312/372-7200.

Best hotel on a grand scale (but watch for the one-armed man)

Chicago Hilton and Towers

It's hard to imagine that something this big could be so graceful. Yet this hotel, with 1,543 guest rooms, spacious ballrooms, a two-story atrium lounge, and public areas filled with shops, bars, and restaurants—virtually a city-within-a-city—is handsome on a grand scale. In the early 1980s, Hilton spent $185 million renovating and remodeling the old Conrad Hilton, originally opened as the Stevens Hotel in 1927. The result is a lavishly ornate grande dame full of glittering chandeliers, intricate gilt work, paintings and murals, and handsome marble and parquet set off by beautiful vases and tasteful furnishings. Guest rooms are richly appointed with cherrywood furnishings, and the top three floors of the tower provide as good an executive level as you'll find anywhere (complete with its own check-in). A state-of-the-art fitness center includes a lap pool, sun deck, and running track. *Trivia note:* Many scenes from the blockbuster movie, *The Fugitive,* were filmed at this hotel—especially in the Conrad Hilton Suite (see separate listing).

Chicago Hilton and Towers, 720 S Michigan Ave, Chicago, IL 60605, 312/922-4400.

Best new convention hotel

Sheraton Chicago Hotel & Towers

When it debuted in 1992, this monolith sprawling along the north bank of the Chicago River across from the NBC Tower provided a barometer of Chicago's economic growth and of the nation's hard times. The new hotel brought to the city acres of new convention space—and it attracted thousands of job seekers who lined up outside on a cold winter morning in the hope of filling one of the new openings. The 1,200-room, $180 million property was the largest convention and business hotel to be built in Chicago in 14 years, boasting the midwest's largest ballroom as part of its 120,000 square feet of meeting and exhibition space. Adjacent to a riverfront esplanade, the 34-story hotel includes 54 suites and 96 luxury tower rooms among its guest accommodations, all featuring marble vanities and baths, coffee makers, safes, and state-of-the-art communication equipment including in-room voice mail—plus complimentary newspaper delivered every morning. This massive 1.2-million square foot property is packed with entertainment, recreation, and dining options, ranging from piano and sports bar to full health club and indoor pool with outdoor sundeck. A business center offers full secretarial services. Among the hotel's five restaurants and lounges, the Streeterville Grille & Bar quickly acquired a reputation as a destination restaurant for a mix of hearty steaks and chops and fresh-grilled seafood with light Italian accents. (A veal chop on the bone, for example, takes on a flaky lemon-parmesan cheese crust; lamp chops are served with rosemary butter; chilled carrot soup is thick and sweet; and bay sturgeon is accentuated with fresh fennel marmalade). If you tend to pass up meat entrées as prosaic, change your strategy here! This window-lined, street-level restaurant is housed in a circular room ringed with ficus trees.

Sheraton Chicago Hotel & Towers, 301 E North Water St, Chicago, IL 60611, 312/464-1000.

Best hotel for business

Swissôtel

Not unexpectedly, there's a European-business flavor to this largest hotel in the Swissôtel chain. About 45 percent of the guests and more than 20 percent of the staff are Europeans. Thirty-four function rooms of various sizes include small conference rooms paneled in rich cherrywood and furnished with comfortable leather chairs. The 60-seat, tiered William Tell Theatre has state-of-the-art audiovisual facilities and the capability of providing simultaneous translation in five languages. A business center offers soundproof telephone booths, stock market quotation board, newswire, business library, a wide range of business equipment, and secretarial support staff. The 630-room hotel, a modernistic triangle of glass, offers spectacular views of the city, river, and lake. The view is especially spectacular from the well-equipped Penthouse Health Spa on the 43rd floor. Some rooms overlook the Florida-style island green featured on an adjoining nine-hole golf course, the Illinois Center Golf Course and Driving Range (see separate listing, "Sports (Participant)"). The hotel can provide guaranteed tee times or reserve a session on the driving range. On the lower level, Café Suisse and the Garden Café offer European-style meals (including breakfasts with a variety of breads, meats, cheeses, and sausages). Swiss-trained bakers at the adjoining Konditorei produce fresh-baked breads and pastries—buy a loaf of crack-crust Swiss bread or an apple strudel to take home.

Swissôtel, 323 E Wacker Dr at Illinois Ctr, Chicago, IL 60601, 312/565-0565.

Handiest hotel in the heart of the financial district

Midland Hotel

There's free taxi service by a chauffeur-driven authentic English-style cab, complimentary buffet breakfast, free daily newspaper, and complimentary evening cocktail—what more could a corporate traveler ask of a hotel? Well, there's location, and in this respect, the Midland is ideal, situated in the heart of Chicago's business and financial district. This mid-priced hotel offers 257 guestrooms, four of which are luxurious suites. Built in 1929, this hotel completed a major renovation, adding art deco design features to its original beaux arts grandeur. Rooms are large and tastefully decorated. In-house restaurants are The Exchange (see separate listing in "Dining"), serving Continental cuisine in a formal atmosphere, and The Ticker Tape Bar & Grill, serving a combination of American, French, and Italian fare in a casual environment (look for reproductions of the stunning paintings—including a life-size self-portrait—of Tamara de Lampeka, who epitomized the Art Deco movement in Paris in the 1920s). There's also a sundry store, beauty salon, and barber shop on the premises, plus a fitness center and business center.

Midland Hotel, 172 W Adams St, Chicago, IL 60603, 312/332-1200.

Favorite hotel for celebrities (or those who just want to be treated like one)
The Ritz-Carlton

Starting with its light-flooded, greenhouse-style lobby on the 12th floor of the high-rise building connected to the Water Tower Place shopping center, this hotel stands both literally and figuratively head and shoulders above many hotels in town. (In 1995, *Conde Nast Traveler* readers voted it "Best Hotel in the United States"—a recent $17 million renovation was aimed at keeping it up to par.) Its 431 rooms offer luxurious lodging, with such standard amenities as king-sized beds, hair dryers, and double-line phones; spacious, attractive suites boast additional plush furnishings, including chairs and sofas. The Ritz-Carlton—along with, most notably, the Park Hyatt and the Ambassador East—attracts more than its share of visiting celebrities (movie stars, musicians, and sports figures) who appreciate the hotel's high levels of comfort, service, and discretion. The hotel's dining room offers acclaimed French fare—especially popular is a seven-course degustation menu—and one of the city's most sumptuous Sunday-brunch spreads. This hotel is part of the prestigious Four Seasons hotel group (as is the nearby Four Seasons Hotel—see separate listing). The Ritz-Carlton lobby, with its magnificent skylight, provides a restful respite from shopping forays into bustling Water Tower Place. Under a magnificent skylight, a fountain provides a lulling background, almost like the gentle roll of surf, for afternoon tea or a cocktail, with comfortable seating in sofas and easy chairs.

The Ritz-Carlton, 150 E Pearson St, Chicago, IL 60611, 312/266-1000.

Best high-tech upscale hotel
The Sutton Place Hotel

If "cocooning" at home, surrounded by entertainment gadgets and other high-tech conveniences, is your style, this modern hotel should appeal. Housed in a striking, award-winning (for architecture and interior design) building, The Sutton Place offers 246 guestrooms (including 40 deluxe suites). These are decked out with the latest complement of high-tech toys and other all-the-comforts-of-home accessories, such as a stereo TV and VCR (with 24-hour availability of movie rentals), a stereo receiver with compact disk player (and an in-room selection of CDs), a fully stocked mini-bar, three telephones (all with voice mail and one with a speakerphone), and a dedicated link for fax or computer hookup. Additionally, each room offers thick terry robes; hair dryers; and a selection of deluxe hair, skin, and bath products. The hotel's restaurant and lounge, The Brasserie Bellevue and Brasserie Bar, overlooking the hustle and bustle of Rush Street, is a stylish bistro-style restaurant. The Sutton Place Hotel is convenient to both the shopping of Michigan Avenue and Oak Street and the nightlife of Rush and Division Streets.

The Sutton Place Hotel, 21 E Bellevue Place, Chicago, IL 60611, 312/266-2100.

Suitest hotel on North Michigan

Omni Chicago Hotel

The recent trend toward suite accommodations extends to the Magnificent Mile with appropriate levels of luxury and sophistication. This hotel, occupying the 5th through 25th floors of a 40-story mixed-use complex, switched chains from Hyatt to Omni seemingly without pause. Especially catering to business travelers, it offers 347 two-room suites, sumptuously appointed in bold but not overpowering tones with polished woods and stylish upholstery; standard amenities in each suite include two telephones and a wet bar. On-site extras include a full-service concierge; a health club with indoor pool, sauna, and well-equipped workout room; and 24-hour room service. But don't expect the complimentary extras (breakfast buffet, daily cocktail party) found at other suite-only hotels—this is definitely upscale lodging that plays to a different market. (For a real splurge, a number of premier suites that go for up to $2,500 a night reflect the styles of famous architects such as Frank Lloyd Wright and Mies van der Rohe.) The hotel's Cielo restaurant (with floor-to-ceiling picture windows overlooking the always entertaining parade of Michigan Avenue) features a blend of American-Italian-Mediterranean cuisine, with some entrées prepared in wood-burning ovens. An adjoining bar offers occasional piano entertainment—sometimes by a prominent Chicago surgeon who enjoys stopping by to play. Check out the elevators and the ceiling of the restaurant; the delightfully whimsical clouds-and-sky scenes painted there are by Chicago artist Kathryn Kozan.

Omni Chicago Hotel, 676 N Michigan Ave, Chicago, IL 60611, 312/944-6664.

Loftiest lobby to get lost in

Hyatt Regency Chicago

This largest of all Hyatts is a city-within-a-city, with twin towers, more than 2,000 rooms, five restaurants, a sports bar, a deli, and a signature three-story atrium lobby. In 1995, the hotel completed a $21 million renovation of all of its guest rooms, meeting spaces, hallways, and ballrooms. The conservatory-like lobby has Italian granite floors surrounding a 4,000-square-foot reflecting pool with fountains. Dramatic landscaping includes 27-foot double-trunk palm trees, 14-foot ficus trees, seasonal plants, and prairie grasses. At night, suspended theatrical lighting provides dramatic illumination. Off the lobby is the All Seasons Café and Big, Brasserie and Bar (see separate listings, "Notable Potables"). Guest amenities include complimentary coffee and newspaper; live plants in all rooms; 24-hour room service; and bathrooms with wall mounted hair dryers, magnifying mirrors, and (a nice touch) television speakers. Some rooms have views of the Chicago River and Michigan Avenue bridge. The convenient location is equidistant to the Magnificent Mile and the Loop. The hotel offers the Camp Hyatt children's program (see separate listing in "Kids").

Hyatt Regency Chicago, 151 E Wacker Dr, Chicago, IL 60601, 312/565-1234.

Best hotel that's crazy about Chicago

Claridge Hotel

You want to know about Chicago history, landmarks, or politics? Or about the Native Americans who gave the city its name? Ask a bellhop—or the manager—at this small (172 rooms), European-style hotel, where staff attend periodic half-day seminars conducted by a historian. Or you could borrow a book from the hotel's library of volumes about Chicago and Chicagoans. It's all part of an effort by the hotel to embrace the city it serves that includes bell staff attired in Chicago pro sports uniforms and a display of pictures, formerly exhibited at the Art Institute, showing the Wrigley Building at one-hour intervals during a 24-hour period. In a residential backwater near high-energy Division and Rush Streets, the hotel is within easy walking distance of Oak Street Beach and Mag Mile shopping. The art deco rooms of this mid-range hotel are richly decorated and comfortable (three of six suites have wood-burning fireplaces), and the price includes continental breakfast, daily newspapers, health-club access, and limo service.

Claridge Hotel, 1244 N Dearborn Pkwy, Chicago, IL 60610, 312/787-4980, 800/245-1258.

Best hotel in a former printing plant (that salutes Frank Lloyd Wright)

Hyatt on Printers Row

At the south end of the Loop, fashionable Printers' Row is an area that once seemed doomed to urban blight. Printing plants that had flourished there moved away; the landmark Dearborn Street railroad station, with its distinctive clock tower, was shuttered. Then came the rehabbers, converting lofts into condos and transforming the century-old red brick and terra-cotta station into an office and retail center. Nearby, this intimate 161-room hotel was created by joining and renovating a 100-year-old printing plant and the Morton Building, built in 1896. Chameleon-like, the hotel went through various changes of ownership before settling under the Hyatt umbrella. The discreet lobby, with warm mahogany paneling, has a look inspired by Frank Lloyd Wright, with bold-pattern gray carpeting, walnut upright chairs and oak Adirondack-like chairs, and "Prairie School" lamps. Guest rooms are decorated in green with a Wright geometric design and feature attractive black lacquer furniture and heavy tapestry spreads. Every room has a VCR (bring your own tapes or ask the concierge to rent them for you) and every bathroom is equipped with TV, radio, phone, hair dryer, and scale. Executive suites are available in 1 to 4-room configurations; the luxurious presidential suite includes a sauna, dining area, and pantry. Adjoining the lobby is Prairie restaurant, also with Frank Lloyd Wright-inspired decor, specializing in Midwestern cookery (see separate listing in "Dining").

Hyatt on Printers Row, 500 S Dearborn St, Chicago, IL 60605, 312/986-1234.

Best hotel rooms nearest elevators

Fairmont Hotel

Afternoon tea with waiters in tails, cocktails with a tinkling piano, a restaurant where the wait staff performs operetta, and a bar with handsome Art

Deco murals. Opened in 1987, this neoclassic-style hotel of pink Spanish granite with bay windows and a copper roof quickly established itself as one of Chicago's most elegant. Public areas are a gallery of exquisite artwork. Each guest room has a separate dressing room with walk-in closet, mini-bar, electric shoe polisher, and oversize marble bathroom with separate shower stalls and water closets, telephone, scale, and even a mini TV. Anyone who has trudged through a maze of hotel corridors will appreciate a design feature that has no room farther than four doors away from an elevator. *TV and movie trivia:* Parent of Chicago's Fairmont is the flagship Fairmont in San Francisco, familiar to viewers of the 1980s TV series *Hotel*, filmed on location there. (Arthur Hailey's original novel and the subsequent movie were based on the Fairmont in New Orleans.)

Fairmont Hotel, 200 N Columbus Dr (at Grant Park), Chicago, IL 60601, 312/565-8000.

Best hotel for restored art deco

Hotel Inter-Continental

Until 1995, one of Chicago's prettiest and most historic hotels was suffering from a split personality. After having its distinctive facade hidden for so long behind scaffolding, the Hotel Inter-Continental finally swallowed up the former Forum and emerged as a single entity, seamless merged with a total of 844 rooms. This is a hotel well worth a tour. Usually, it is only travel writers and travel agents who are interested in touring hotels. The Hotel Inter-Continental, constructed in 1929 as the Medinah Athletic Club and meticulously restored at an initial cost of $130 million, may be the exception. In fact, the hotel provides tape-recorded self-guided tours even for nonguests. Climbing to the eighth floor, you're swept through a melange of architectural styles, from classic Italian renaissance to French Louis XVI, from medieval England to Spain and Mesopotamia. You'll discover Byzantine knights, Assyrian lions, and Celtic sconces—painted ceilings, inlays of marble, intricate bronze and brass trim, and sculptured details in terra-cotta, gold leaf, granite, and fine woods—all long hidden beneath layers of paint, wallpaper, and carpeting. Guest rooms feature light-colored fruitwoods with contrasting inlays of ebony or maple, lush Axminster carpets, and bedspreads inspired by 19th-century French toile design. Don't miss afternoon tea in The Salon, where fresh-baked raisin scones are served with thick Devonshire cream and preserves.

Hotel Inter-Continental, 505 N Michigan Ave, Chicago, IL 60611, 312/944-4100.

Best English club-style small hotel

The Tremont

When it comes to exuding exclusivity, the Tremont does it as well as any hotel in the city. Located on a quiet, tree-lined street less than a block from stylish Water Tower Place, this 15-story hotel features 127 rooms and seven one-bedroom suites. Accommodations are small, but tastefully furnished in earth-tone colors that include tan-patterned wallpaper, orange-rust carpeting, antique brass lamps, and oak-framed drawings. Directly off the lobby, a large oak-paneled guest lounge has a polished parquet floor with a large Oriental area rug and comfortable sofas and chairs pulled up in front of a huge fireplace. As with may small, elegant hotels, the Tremont doesn't skimp on service. From the complimentary shoeshine and Crabtree & Evelyn amenities to the turn-down service that includes cognac and chocolates on the pillows, this hotel has staked its claim as a premier Chicago property.

The Tremont, 100 E Chestnut St, Chicago, IL 60611, 312/751-1900.

Best comeback by a boutique hotel

The Whitehall Hotel

Traditionalists had plenty to smile about in the fall of 1994 when one of Chicago's premium small hotels made a quiet comeback. After being shuttered for several years, The Whitehall, a landmark in the heart of Chicago's fashionable shopping district, just steps from the Magnificent Mile, reopened after a multimillion-dollar renovation. Developed in 1928 as a prestigious apartment building and converted in 1972 to a European-flavored boutique hotel, the 21-story Whitehall is out to restore its former glitter with a high staff-to-guest ratio and stylish, comfortable accommodations. Modernized guest rooms and suites feature mahogany furnishings, including armoires and Chippendale desks, plus floral linen coverlets and valances and striped dust ruffles and draperies. The hotel has 221 guest rooms, including eight suites, each equipped with three multiline telephones with fax and PC capabilities. Toiletries are by Crabtree & Evelyn, terrycloth robes are provided, morning newspaper is complimentary. The hotel has a fully equipped fitness center, with exercise bikes available for in-room use. On the site of the former Whitehall Club, once one of Chicago's oldest private dining establishments, the hotel restaurant has traveled 180 degrees to become a casual European bistro featuring reasonably priced luncheons of thin-crust pizzas, salads, sandwiches, and fresh fish. It has an on-site bakery and an ambitious multicultural dinner menu featuring the likes of poppyseed ravioli with grilled scallions and herb-crusted tuna with Oriental greens, gin-flavored sauce, and julienne fried leeks. The adjoining lounge features a piano bar. Afternoon tea, served in the lobby Rose Garden Tea Room, (Tue–Sun 2:30–5 pm), features a selection of teas, tea breads, and finger sandwiches, plus scones with Devonshire cream and fruit preserves. The hotel's club-like lobby sets the theme for the hotel's English 18th-century decor with Oriental accents. In summer, a 64-seat side-walk café opens in front.

The Whitehall Hotel, 105 E Delaware Place, Chicago, IL 60611, 312/944-6300.

Best smaller deluxe hotel—near an old landmark

Park Hyatt

Overlooking the small, tree-shaded park square that is home to the historic Water Tower (and the Chicago Tourist Office), this is an elegant and very comfort-able small hotel with a European flavor for those to whom cost is not a prime consideration. Special touches include Swiss toiletries, three-times-daily maid service, and available limo service to nearby attractions. The Park Hyatt's combination of posh decor (rooms feature marble-topped rosewood fur-nishings), outstanding service, and an exquisite view of Michigan Avenue is well worth the hotel's pre-mium price. Hiding behind a somewhat nondescript facade, this elegant contemporary hotel is ideally located within steps of the famed shops, galleries, dining, and entertainment of the Magnificent Mile. In the hotel is Jaxx's restaurant, favored as one of the city's top "power breakfast" spots and also as a popular venue for Sunday brunch with champagne. The hotel's soaring two-story lobby with its plush velvet couches and crystal chandeliers is a nice spot to relax in the evening and listen to a classical pianist; the Lobby Lounge hosts a *trés romantique* daily afternoon tea (see separate listing in "Roman-tic").

Park Hyatt, 800 N Michigan Ave, Chicago, IL 60611, 312/280-2222.

Most modest European-style hotel

The Raphael

"Good things can come in small packages" is the maxim brought to mind by this small European-flavored hotel, conveniently located just a block east of the Mag Mile. Under a long green canopy, a doorman welcomes guests with a warm smile and friendly salutation. Directly through the beveled-glass doors of the 16-story brown-brick building, an intimate, two-story lobby, highlighted by huge cathedral windows, includes a sitting area with a comfortable mix of sofas and chairs. With its massive wrought-iron chandeliers, dark beams, and contrasting white stucco walls, its arches and balconies, the lobby has a distinctive Spanish look. To one side of the lobby is a small guest library; to the other, an entrance to the hotel's restaurant and bar, which features live entertainment nightly and is one of the neighborhood's most popular piano bars with a coterie of regulars, many of whom come prepared for a stint at the microphone. Two small elevators serve the hotel's spacious and bright suites and rooms, which pick up the Mediterranean theme and feature large picture windows, high ceilings, individual climate control, and ornately tiled bathrooms (which are stocked with embroidered towels). Standard amenities include a mini-bar and cable TV. As often is the case with its European counterparts, this small hotel emphasizes personal service, quality, and value. We give it high marks in all three categories.

The Raphael, 201 E Delaware, Chicago, IL 60611, 312/943-5000.

Best high ceilings in the high rent district

The Seneca

For those who prefer high ceilings to high tech, this hotel on tree-lined Chestnut Street, in the shadow of the John Hancock Center, blends residential, extended-stay, and overnight accommodations—with about 100 of its 262 rooms earmarked for the latter. High ceilings with crown moldings contrast with modern bathrooms and kitchens with microwaves and dishwashers. Amenities include a rooftop sundeck, fitness center, and in-room coffee service and voice mail. Hallways feature glittering chandeliers, artfully arched doorways, and inlaid carpeting. Each floor features a convenient washer and dryer. There's no need to walk far for excellent dining options. Located in the building are The Saloon (see separate description in "Dining"), which has become one of Chicago's premier steakhouses—and one of its cheeriest—and the *trés romantique* Grappa (see separate listing in "Romantic") with its wonderful fresh pasta and hard-to-resist desserts. Also in the building is Chalfin's, a New York-style deli with pastrami, chicken livers, lox, and other deli standards. The shopping at Water Tower Place is just across the street.

The Seneca, 200 E Chestnut St, Chicago, IL 60611, 312/787-8900.

Still the best hotel rooftop pool

Radisson Hotel & Suites Chicago

The old Sheraton Plaza enjoyed a loyal following in part because of its location, just a block east of the glittery shops of Michigan Avenue—and because of a wonderful rooftop swimming pool that almost seemed like a transplant from a Florida resort. These features remain—although just about everything else has changed, for the better, including the name. Now wearing the Radisson imprimatur and looking sleek and smart after a $7 million renovation, this hotel is a great find, stuffed with amenities (including a fitness center and voice-mail messaging) and offering such extras as complimentary coffee and iron and ironing board in all guest rooms. Although the hotel has a contemporary ambience, accommodations are comfortable almost to the point of being cozy, with 334 guest rooms, including 88 suites (some with kitchenettes). Adjoining the hotel is one of the city's prettiest restaurants, Cassis (see separate listing in "Dining"), offering an innovative interpretation of the food of Provençal. Even the hotel's location has actually *improved*—with a flourish of activity east of Michigan Avenue (and especially along St. Clair Street) as popular new restaurants, sidewalk cafés, espresso bars, and bakeries pop up like crocuses in a wintry garden.

Radisson Hotel & Suites Chicago, 160 E Huron St, Chicago, IL 60611, 312/787-2900.

Best expensive hotel suite

Conrad Hilton Suite

This suite sits like a castle atop the Chicago Hilton and Towers. Built and furnished at a cost of $1.6 million, it is yours for a mere $4,000 a night—although that includes the services of a maid, butler, and limousine, plus dinner and cocktails for 12 of your closest friends. The suite includes a grand salon with fireplace, library with a 15-foot bar, a fully equipped kitchen (as an optional extra, you can arrange to have the pantry stocked with wines, caviar, imported cheeses, and other goodies), three bedrooms, three bathrooms with jacuzzis, and two powder rooms. The suite is served by four private elevators and a heliport. The Grand Salon, filled with

Louis XVI reproduction furniture, is illuminated by four gold-and-crystal chandeliers valued at $10,000 each and has cream-colored Oriental rugs custom woven at $30,000 apiece. Four large windows with balconies offer spectacular views of the skyline and lakeshore. The suite once was a bilevel ballroom and the original French windows and some of the intricate molding remain.

Chicago Hilton and Towers, 720 S Michigan Ave, Chicago, IL 60605, 312/922-4400.

Most authentic Japanese suite
Hotel Nikko

For a taste of Japan, splurge on one of Nikko's two Japanese-style suites. Each features a traditional tatami-mat sleeping room, deep-soak tub, and a private rock garden. (At $750/night, "splurge" is the operative word.) This sleek hotel of gray granite and gray-tinted glass hugs the north bank of the Chicago River, opening onto terraced promenades and landscaped Japanese gardens. In the lobby is a rare 200-year-old screen featuring a weaving of the Nikko temple (near Tokyo), part of a half-million-dollar collection of contemporary and Oriental art and artifacts. Western-style guest rooms feature original art, large bay windows, marble baths, mini-bars, and separate dressing areas. Amenities include plush robes, turndown service, free shoe shine, and complimentary fresh coffee and morning newspaper offered in the foyer of the Celebrity Café. The hotel offers a health club with sauna and massage facilities (you can order a Japanese-style massage in your room). The Benkay restaurant has a sushi bar and six private tatami rooms (with leg wells as a concession to Western limbs) and views of the river. A business center has computers, fax machines, telex, dictating equipment, photocopier, secretarial service, and business library.

Hotel Nikko, 320 N Dearborn St, Chicago, IL 60610, 312/744-1900, 800/NIKKO-US.

"Write" suite to stay in
Omni Ambassador East Hotel

Unquestionably, this is one of the most civilized hotels in town, exuding class and comfort, from fresh flowers in the lobby and an attentive staff to 275 immaculately appointed rooms. It long has been the choice of celebrities, who like to hold forth at Booth One in the storied Pump Room (see separate listing in "Dining"). More recently, it has become the choice of publishers who dispatch authors on book promotional tours. We stayed in the so-called "author's suite" the night after Kirk Douglas had occupied it, promoting his latest literary opus. Occupying three rooms on the 16th floor, the suite has overstuffed chairs, attractive paintings and plants, and, of course, a writing desk—with a handsome leather top. Perhaps the biggest attraction is the library, filled with a few hundred or more volumes signed by the guests. The variety ranges from John K. Galbraith to Nancy Sinatra, from Edward Albee to Jimmy Breslin and Shel Silverstein. Nonliterary types can request the room, but it usually is booked months in advance, and non-VIP guests (including travel-guide authors) are subject to being bumped. But, if you do splurge and book the $369 suite, check the bookshelf for a copy of you know what.

Omni Ambassador East Hotel, 1301 N State Pkwy, Chicago, IL 60610, 312/787-7200.

Grandest hotel to become unsunk

The Bismarck Hotel

This sprawling Loop hotel, opened in 1894, rebuilt in 1924, belongs to an era of steamer trunks, genteel ladies' luncheons, and smoked-filled rooms. Its owners and managers, in the midst of ongoing rehab under the slogan "everything old is new again," are hoping it can be reborn once again as a hotel of the 1990s and beyond. It isn't there yet, but it is on its way. Floors are being spruced up one by one, its 500 rooms and suites are being refurbished, and the public spaces already are beginning to glitter the way they did when the hotel bustled 24 hours a day and local Dems took an entire floor for political wheeling and dealing. The lobby is a showcase of Art Deco, as is the adjoining Green Orchid bar/cabaret (see separate listing in "Notable Potables"). The Crown Room is striving to resuscitate its reputation for fine dining while the Walnut Room (see separate listing in "Music, Entertainment, and Non-Pub Nightlife") has revived ballroom dancing to big bands. In contrast, Gate 3½ is a big-screen sports bar with a Blackhawks hockey theme (see separate listing in "Notable Potables") that is as contemporary as the United Center, while the Palace Café is a chrome-plated retro diner decorated with suspended 78 rpm records and offering quick meals and fountain creations. A courtesy van makes shopping and sightseeing stops, and packages include sometimes-tough-to-get Blackhawks' tickets (the Wirtz family owns the hotel and hockey club). Jack Benny and Jack Dempsey stayed here; so did John Wayne and Jimmy Carter. Mayor Richard J. Daley kept the entire fourth floor as his private offices. Adjoining the hotel, the huge Palace Theater, plush with flashy gilt, filigree, and frescoes, once attracted top vaudeville acts, later first-run movies, and now is starting to attract blues and jazz, charity events, and prize fights.

The Bismarck Hotel, 171 W Randolph St, Chicago, IL 60601, 312/236-0123.

Best hotel where they leave the light on
Motel 6

Now, Motel 6's folksy spokesman Tom Bodett (he of "we'll leave the light on for you" fame) really has something to brag about. The budget chain not only opened its first property in the central part of a major city, but opened it next to trendy, see-and-be-seen Bice and only steps away from the glittering shops of the Magnificent Mile. What's more, the chain inherited and is keeping in place many of the stylish trappings of the French-owned former occupant, the Hotel Richmont. These include the gilt, lacquer, mirrors, silk, sconces, and damask of the lobby, the reproductions of impressionist paintings hung in the corridors, and a sort of faded beaux arts flavor to the guest rooms. In contrast are the lilliputian bars of chain soap and plastic cups in the bathrooms and the no-frills policy—no parking, no free coffee, no continental breakfast, and certainly no mint on the pillow. To compensate are budget prices—higher than you'll find along the highway outside of Peoria, but a bargain in this high-toned locale. Rates vary, but can dip to as low as $59 a night (plus tax), but are hiked to $79 during prime time, such as when major conventions hit town. Good news, too, for the romantics who enjoyed the Continental-style bistro that occupied the street level during the hotel's previous life. An Italian restaurant, Il Toscanaccio, has moved into the space. With doors and windows thrown open to the street, a sidewalk café, and pretty murals, it may be even more charming than its predecessor. Leave that light on!

Motel 6, 162 E Ontario St, Chicago, IL 60611, 312/787-3580.

Most news for budget hotel shoppers
Best Western Inn of Chicago

In the 1960s this was a predominantly residential hotel with a penthouse floor housing the Chicago Press Club. Although the press club has gone the way of two of the four daily newspapers that served Chicago in those days, this property makes the most of its media antecedents. Its Newsmakers restaurant, a bright, pleasant spot to eat inexpensively, has become an archive of local media, its walls adorned with more than 200 photographs and other documents related to local newspaper, magazine, radio, and television journalism. Every booth and table is decorated with reproductions of historic front pages, many from the defunct *Chicago Daily News*, with headlines chronicling the century's blockbuster news events: "A giant leap," "Paris falls," and " 'For the woman I love': Edward." The hotel offers a prime location steps from the Magnificent Mile at modest chain prices. Basic but comfortable accommodations include 358 rooms and suites with such amenities as pay movies, voice-mail message system, and room service. Penthouse suites with living areas and sliding-door access to a rooftop patio are a good buy at $250–$325. The busy lobby is bright and cheerful with access to the restaurant and adjoining sports bar. Small, creaky elevators demand a bit of patience. A White Hen Pantry convenience store is directly across the street.

Best Western Inn of Chicago, 162 E Ohio St, Chicago, IL 60611, 312/787-3100.

Best hotel for dining in

The Lenox House

Prior to a massive renovation in the mid-1980s, this building housed the somewhat seedy, residential Croyden Hotel. Today, this all-suite, moderately priced hotel is wooing travelers on extended stays (who make up approximately 40 percent of its guests). The hotel's 325 rooms range from studio to one-bedroom suites. Each is equipped with a kitchenette, coffee maker, teapot, and, for guests staying 30 days or longer, all necessary kitchen utensils. Standard amenities include a complimentary morning paper and a basket filled with morning staples such as tea, coffee, and juice; hair dryers; and complimentary privileges at a nearby health club. Although the Lenox House may not be as glamorous as many Chicago hotels, it does provide good value to guests who are willing to stretch travel budgets with some self-catered in-room meals. And the location, just a short block west of Michigan Avenue, is nonpareil. In the building is a branch of Houston's restaurant chain, warm, clubby, and a great spot for soup and salads (see separate listing in "Dining").

The Lenox House, 616 N Rush St, Chicago, IL 60611, 312/337-1000.

Closest hotel for Cubs fans

City Suites Hotel

Lots of young singles live in the bustling Lakeview East neighborhood, and when their folks visit, many stay at this comfortable, affordable neighborhood hotel that dates back to the 1920s when it catered to the nearby vaudeville houses and cabarets. Today, it is popular with baseball fans visiting nearby Wrigley Field. Offering 29 suites and 16 guest rooms, the refurbished—but still comfortably worn—hotel has a European charm (at rates around $75 for a room, $89 for a suite). The creaky elevator with its manually operated metal gate is reminiscent of a Parisian pension. Guest rooms and public spaces are decorated with photographs from the 1920s and 1930s; the lobby has a cheerful working fireplace. Suites include a sleeper sofa, armchair, and desk. Although the hotel is close to the elevated tracks, soundproof, double-insulated glass windows help keep out the noise. Rates include morning coffee and Ann Sather's celebrated cinnamon rolls (the Swedish restaurant is right next door for those wanting a fix of Swedish pancakes and lingonberries). For dinner try the romantic Bella Vista (see separate listing in "Dining"), just steps away.

City Suites Hotel, 933 W Belmont Ave, Chicago, IL 60657, 312/404-3400.

Best hotel for Sunday in the park

The Belden-Stratford

This hotel, across from the Lincoln Park Conservatory and Zoo, keeps good company. Occupying the ground floor are Ambria (see separate listing in "Dining"), consistently listed among the city's top 10 restaurants for its exemplary multinational cuisine and Art Nouveau decor, and the more casual Un Grand Café (see separate listing in "Dining")—a good bet for steak frites. Although only about 25 of its rooms are available for overnight guests, the fact that this is largely an elegant residential apartment-hotel adds to its impeccable ambience. Setting the tone is the dramatic three-story Grand Lobby crowned by a dazzling, hand-painted sky motif ceiling and featuring a gold and alabaster chandelier, Empire period furniture, brass railings, and lush bordered carpeting. The hotel has a rooftop sundeck—perfect for views of Chicago's dramatic skyline across the treetops of Lincoln Park—and a fitness center. Rooms are equipped with voice mail and coffee makers. This Lincoln Park hotel is well worth looking into—and checking into—especially for the early-morning views of the sun rising over Lake Michigan.

The Belden-Stratford, 2300 Lincoln Park W, Chicago, IL 60614, 312/281-2900.

Best bet for four-posters and cinnamon rolls

Park Brompton Hotel

This hotel isn't downtown—but nor are its prices. However, unless you have business in the Loop, this is an excellent location—especially for sightseeing. The Park Brompton is close to Lincoln Park Zoo, the Lincoln Park Conservatory, Wrigley Field, and the dining and theater of Halsted Street. You can walk to the lakefront and to busy Belmont and Broadway, and catch a bus virtually at the hotel's doorstep for a ride of 15 minutes or so to the shops of North Michigan Avenue. Rooms are a bargain at $75 a night—$89 for a suite. Located on a quiet, tree-lined street in a residential neighborhood, this new small hotel is housed in a building dating to the 1920s. The owners, who also operate City Suites Hotel (see separate listing) and Surf Hotel, are striving for the ambience of an English inn and have installed four-poster beds and tapestry furnishings. Breakfast is complimentary and includes juice, coffee, and the nonpareil cinnamon rolls of Ann Sather (see separate listing in "Dining").

Park Brompton Hotel, 528 W Brompton Place, Chicago, IL 60657, 312/404-3499.

Best hotel near O'Hare (that's closest to Paris)

Hotel Sofitel Chicago

For a taste of France, take a CTA train bound for O'Hare International Airport but get off one stop before the airport. The Hotel Sofitel has hand-painted murals and French antiques in the lobby; a bakery that turns out croissants, baguettes, and pastries fresh daily; and a shop stocked with merchandise from many of the provinces of France. The 305 guest rooms are furnished with handcrafted reproduction furniture; amenities include French toiletries by Nina Ricci and a fresh rose and French chocolate truffle at turn-down. Classic French cuisine is served at the elegant Café de Paris; try the grilled sea scallops in lemon butter sauce—or celebrate a birthday or anniversary with a toast of Armagnac (every vintage available from 1927 to 1976). More informal meals are available at the brasserie, Chez Colette. Le Club Fitness offers a sauna and rooftop indoor pool.

Hotel Sofitel Chicago, 5550 N River Rd, Rosemont, IL 60018, 847/678-4488, 800/233-5959.

Best hotel at the airport

O'Hare Hilton

It's incredible what technology can do. Here's a hotel with rooms virtually on the runway of the world's busiest airport, where you can see aircraft arriving and departing all day and night—but can't hear them. Sound-resistant windows, an insulated position in the center of five terminals, and proximity to the protected control tower, make this truly a quiet oasis. This large property (with 858 guest rooms, including 31 suites) is well suited to business travelers. In addition to coffee makers and hair dryers, rooms have two telephones with data port, voice mail, desk, and—in more than half of the rooms—fax machines. There's also a full-service business center offering copying, secretarial, and translation services. Relaxing execs can even play a round of golf—via golf-simulating video machines—at several prestigious courses. Those who remember this hotel from the late 1980s, when it was showing signs of almost two decades of wear and tear, likely will not recognize it. Bought by Hilton and closed in 1991 for total refurbishing, it reopened the following year after a $46 million renovation. The Athletic Club, new in 1995, offers free weights, nautilus, aerobic equipment, pool, sauna, jacuzzi, steam room, massage therapist, and tanning beds. Food service is available in the bright Andiamo restaurant (see separate listing in "Dining") and at Chicago's last remaining Gaslight Club—a steak house of the Playboy Club genre. For area residents with an early flight out, this is the perfect solution to getting a good night's rest while avoiding a pre-dawn commute.

O'Hare Hilton, at O'Hare Airport, Chicago, IL 60666, 312/686-8000.

Best bet for business on the North Shore (and determined Old Orchard shoppers)

Howard Johnson Hotel

Business travelers to the Chicago area with calls to make on the North Shore find good value and convenience at this comfortable HoJo in suburban Skokie (which was awarded the chain's 1995

President's Award as the top hotel in the Midwest). So do serious shoppers planning major forays into the sparkling new Old Orchard Center. Within the 136-room hotel is a 42-room executive tower designed for business travelers and offering king-sized beds, big-screen TVs, and complimentary beverages each evening in Don's Tavern. There is a 25' x 50' lap pool (with adjacent patio, exercise room, and whirlpool) and the dining convenience of the hallmark Don's Fishmarket (see separate listing in "Dining") just off the lobby. An example of the value offered is a seasonal package priced at $59 per room (permitting up to four persons to a room), that includes hot complimentary breakfast (eggs, hash browns, bacon, sausage, sweet rolls, cereals, and fruits) and complimentary local transportation. On Monday evenings there is a complimentary poolside party where manager Ed Copeland officiates as bartender. *Tip for area residents:* Annual and semiannual pool memberships are available.

Howard Johnson Hotel, 9333 Skokie Blvd, Skokie, IL 60077, 847/679-4200.

Rundown motel most favored by nonsuperstar rock groups

Spa Motel

It's ignored by most guidebooks, and its yellow pages listing simply says "Close to Downtown (which it isn't)—Reasonable Rate—Lounge," but this motel has become legendary to the small army of rock groups and performers who have bunked there. While superstar groups stay at ritzy downtown hotels, up-and-coming groups playing the club-and-college circuit favor the Spa for its reasonable rates, its relative proximity to many of the North Side and north suburban clubs, and its tacky ambience. Groups such as R.E.M., the Replacements, and other critical and popular favorites have stayed there, and it's probably only a matter of time until one of its visitors immortalizes the old place in song. Check out the Spa Lounge for stars of the future—or maybe not.

Spa Motel, 5414 N Lincoln Ave, Chicago, IL 60625, 312/561-0313.

NOTABLE POTABLES

Best bet for brogues, blarney, & ballads

Kitty O'Shea's Pub

It doesn't sound authentic, an Irish pub in a Hilton flagship hotel. But that doesn't take into account the 20 or more chefs, bartenders, and wait staff with brogues as thick as fog over the Irish Sea, recruited under an Irish government exchange program. There's Irish suds on tap—Guinness and Harp—old-country folk music, and wall art that includes classic Guinness posters, vintage photos of the auld sod, framed recipes and blessings, and a collection of shillelaghs—walking sticks to the uninitiated—carried by prominent Irish-Americans in St. Patrick's Day parades. You can order Irish liqueurs and whiskeys, including "Black Bush" (premium black label Bushmill's Irish Whiskey). The food is standard bar fare, with a few predictable "Irish" dishes such as fish and chips, shepherd's pie, and bread pudding.

Kitty O'Shea's Pub, Chicago Hilton & Towers, 720 S Michigan Ave, Chicago, IL 60605, 312/922-4400. Mon–Sun 11 am–2 am.

Best Irish pubs that are part of the St. Patrick's Day Parade

Kincade's and Kelsey's

When St. Patrick's Day rolls around (*rolls* being the operative word), Chicago's many Irish pubs also roll up the carpet, move out the furniture, and wait for celebrants to arrive from the city's famous St. Paddy's parade. Two of Lincoln Park's popular Irish bars take it a step farther—they invite patrons to be *in* the parade. Each year, the two sister-saloons join the festive parade with a banner-bedecked double-decker bus (which patrons are invited to board—there is a $10 donation). When the bus returns, the merriment continues at the two pubs, each decorated for the occasion with green shamrocks and bunting, where Harp, Bass, and Guinness flow and piled-high corned beef sandwiches and Irish coffee await. Kincade's projects an 1890s ambience with wood-paneled walls, hammered tin ceiling, and floor-to-ceiling windows looking out onto busy Armitage Avenue. Kelsey's is a long, narrow—rather upscale—pub with a mirrored wall framing a massive bar that holds a premier selection of vodka, Scotch, and cognac. A rear room holds a widely used pool table. Both pubs have many TV monitors, usually tuned to sports, scattered throughout.

Kincade's, 950 W Armitage Ave, Chicago, IL 60614, 312/348-0010. Sun–Fri 11 am–2 am, Sat 11 am–3 am; Kelsey's, 2265 N Lincoln Ave, Chicago, IL 60614, 312/348-1666. Mon–Fri 3 pm–2 am, Sat 11 am–3 am, Sun noon–2 am.

Best literary Irish pub

O'Rourke's

You might not run into many honest-to-God writers at the newest incarnation of this tavern that long has harbored the reputation as the hangout of literary types and intellectuals—particularly of hard-drinking Irish ones. Since it moved from its former marginal neighborhood on North Avenue to a flourishing theater district, its clientele is more likely to consist of actors (including movie star Brian Dennehy) than writers. But you still get the literary flavor of the old place, with the huge photos of Brendan Behan, Samuel Beckett, William Butler Yeats, and James Joyce. And, of course, there's Harp and thick, syrupy Guinness stout on tap, as well as a couple of English brews, Bass and Watney's.

O'Rourke's, 1625 N Halsted St, Chicago, IL 60614, 312/335-1806. Sun–Fri 4 pm–2 am, Sat 4 pm–3 am.

Best traditional drinkable green liquid on St. Patrick's Day

Chicago's Irish Pubs

Even some hard drinkers stay safely at home on March 17 in Chicago, scorning it as "amateurs' night." Others? Well, they wouldn't miss a St. Paddy's night on the town, and some choose to get an early start at one of the many Irish bars that by lunchtime already are full-to-overflowing. Some saloons move out most of the furniture—for safety's sake and to fit in more celebrants. Check out the Irish bars listed in this chapter and you'll find fiddlers and pipers, folk songs and drinking songs, and face-painters ready to apply shamrocks and leprechauns to any willing physiognomy. You'll find Harp and Guinness aplenty, and green-dyed beer flowing at some establishments. Among popular St. Patrick's Day saloons are Butch McGuire's, Cork & Kerry, Kelsey's, Kincade's, Kitty O'Shea's (see separate listings), and the Harp & Shamrock Club (1641 W Fullerton Ave, Chicago, IL 60614, 312/248-0123).

Best traditional, nondrinkable green liquid on St. Patrick's Day

Chicago River

Only a town as blatantly Irish as Chicago would dream of dyeing its river green on St. Patrick's Day. But that is what happens every March 17, as it has since the 1960s. The tradition came about as an accident, when city workers used green dye in an attempt to sleuth out the source of a pollutant. Thus came the idea of dumping 100 pounds of oil-based dye into the river. Unfortunately, it worked too well, and the river stayed green long after the last drunk had sobered up and the last green streamer had been swept away. Today, city crews use a biodegradable dye without that tendency to outstay its welcome. (And if you see the river the other 364 days of the year, and wonder, "But it's *already* green," you're right, it *is* green with algae—but you should see it on St. Paddy's, when it is absolutely *Kelly* green.)

Best jolly old English pub

Red Lion Pub

Englishman John Cordwell has transplanted a bit of his native land to this English-style pub. You can order an English beer or ale, choosing from more than a dozen brands, or sip on a pint of chilled

Woodpecker cider (the mildly alcoholic kind). The owners and wait staff regale anyone willing to listen with stories of the ghosts they claim haunt this former 1920s gambling hall. Decor of the dark, green-painted pub runs to such British memorabilia as a London Underground map and advertisements for Player's Navy Cut cigarettes and Rolls Royces. Out back is a beer garden and terrace, open late May–early October. Food is English-pub–style, which means it is wholesome but not great. Selections include Welsh rarebit, fish and chips, steak-and-kidney pie, shepherd's pie, Irish stew, Cornish pasties, and sausage rolls—with trifle and apple tart for dessert.

Red Lion Pub, 2446 N Lincoln Ave, Chicago, IL 60614, 312/348-2695. Daily noon–2 am.

Best Scottish pub to sample scotch

The Duke of Perth

"The idea was to create an authentic Scottish pub," says owner Colin Cameron, a former Dundee police officer who settled in Chicago in 1988. The Duke has scrubbed wooden tables and art and artifacts—grouse prints, fly rods, walking sticks—on loan (and for sale) from the Scottish antique shop of Colin's partner. Scotch whiskey is the big draw, with 74 malts from which to choose. You can pay $15 for a glass of 26-year-old Bladnoch, a lowland malt. Edradour, from the world's smallest distillery, costs $4.50. The food is mostly standard burgers, chicken, and salads with Gaelicized names, but there is an authentic Hebridean leek pie and all-you-can-eat beer-batter cod and hand-cut chips on Wednesdays and Fridays. Special events include Scotch tasting and Pipe Night, when patrons are invited to bring bagpipes.

The Duke of Perth, 2913 N Clark St, Chicago, IL 60657, 312/477-1741. Mon–Fri 11:30 am–2 am, Sat 11:30 am–3 am.

Best spot to watch your brew being brewed

Goose Island Brewery

This brewpub is all that remains of the late, la-mented 1800 North Clybourn warehouse-turned-boutique-mall, demonstrating its staying power by providing Chicago's best brewed-on-premises suds since the late 1980s. Stay in the downstairs bar overlooking the handsome copper brewing vats (used to brew about 40 styles of fresh beer annually) or move to the spacious upstairs dining room for excellent food that is far removed from standard pub fare. Beer is used as an ingredient in many dishes—a rich Cotswold cheese soup is made with stout, porter is used in mustard served with British-style sausages, and stout also is used with white chocolate to create a topping for delicious cheesecake. Either way, you'll be able to enjoy the dark wood surroundings while sampling such Goose Island specialties as Honker's Ale and Old Clybourn Porter, most served in their own special glasses. A "sampler" selection offers a group of beers in six-ounce sizes that arrive with a mat that explains what they are as well as their origins—they range from German-style wheat beer to traditional Yorkshire bitter. You'll have a tough time putting down the homemade potato chips that are light, crunchy, and not a bit greasy (the brewpub goes through about 3,000 lbs. a week). George Wendt, whose TV character "Norm" was a habitué of Cheers, sometimes visits when he is in town. Goose Island offers free tours of the brewing operation each Sunday at 3 pm. Improvements on tap (so to speak) call for the addition of a billiard room, expanded dining, and enclosed patio. *A special treat:* A monthly series of Brewmeister Dinners match a specific cuisine with appropriate beers. The four-course dinners, with many dishes featuring beer as a fundamental ingredient, revolve around such themes as Bastille Day, Oktoberfest, wild game, and the cuisine of Belgium. *Historical note:* The brewery is named for an island created in 1890 when a channel was cut into the North Branch of the Chicago River. The "island" was settled by Irish who planted cabbage patches and raised geese—hence, its name.

Goose Island Brewery, 1800 N Clybourn Ave, Chicago, IL 60614, 312/915-0071. Mon–Thu 11 am–1 am; Fri–Sat 11 am–2 am; Sun 11 am–10 pm.

Best bar where the world's your oyster

Blue Crab Lounge

Next door to Shaw's Crab House (see "Dining") is the restaurant's comfortable combination raw bar and cocktail bar. It succeeds admirably on both counts. The raw bar is heaped with fresh oysters (the origins of which rotate with the season), huge peel-and-eat shrimp (also available in a spicy version), and little-neck clams; these are served individually or in servings of six, accompanied by a piquant seafood sauce with a touch of horseradish and crusty fresh-baked bread with butter. (From 4–6:30 pm every day is "Oyster Hour," when a selected type of oyster or two are deeply discounted to $2.50 per half-dozen.) Gumbos, chowders, and other appetizers also make great after-work bites, as do selected entrées from the main restaurant's menu (especially the crab cakes). The Blue Crab offers up good beers (Anchor Steam and Samuel Adams seem to go particularly well with the raw bar offerings) and well-mixed libations.

Blue Crab Lounge, 21 E Hubbard St, Chicago, IL 60611, 312/527-2722. Mon–Thu 11:30 am–10 pm, Fri 2:30–11 pm, Sat 5–11 pm.

Best pub with classical music & classic art

John Barleycorn Memorial Pub

Long before yuppies, there was the John Barleycorn, with classical music and a nonstop slide show of art from a 5,000-slide collection. This friendly corner saloon, built in 1890, has high tin ceilings, oak paneling, and a curtained-off, three-board dart-playing area where the darts have real points and you keep score on a blackboard. Decor includes a collection of handmade ship models, dating to the late 1800s. Food features soups, salads, and a sandwich selection that includes a half-pound steakburger. Chili is served with garlic bread and topped with cheddar cheese and scallions. Holdup man John Dillinger is said to have been a patron, described as a quiet, well-dressed man who liked to buy a round. His mistake was taking in a movie at the nearby Biograph Theater.

John Barleycorn Memorial Pub, 658 W Belden Ave, Chicago, IL 60614, 312/348-8899. Daily 11 am–2 am.

Best country bar for city folk

Whiskey River

Even if you can't distinguish a two-step from a tango, this is the spot to put on a rhinestone-studded shirt, leather vest, Stetson hat, and cowboy boots—and feel completely at home. You can even pick up some free lessons on that two-step (you'll have to go elsewhere to tango). Just as country music has carved itself a solid niche on *Billboard* magazine's "Hot 100" album chart, so this cowboy honky-tonk in the trendy Webster/Clybourn Avenue corridor has forged a solid constituency of city folk ready to become cowboys (and cowgirls) for an evening. The facade, plastered with every old road sign imaginable, looks like a vintage Route 66 gas station. Inside, the decor

runs to weathered barn siding and rustic accoutre-
ments. The large dance floor is surrounded by a
split-rail fence and stand-up bar tables, and the
music is provided by live performers or a DJ in an
overhead booth. Ladies can check their purses with
the keeper of the saloon's long bar. Between dances,
you can sip a tequila or down a Lone Star beer,
nibble on free hors d'oeuvres—BBQ wings, nachos,
and veggies—or play pool or darts. On concert nights,
you might stumble across a red-hot set by old-guard
favorite Jerry Jeff Walker. But you could just as
easily find yourself settling into a mellower groove
with newer acts such as Martina McBride. Cover
charge is $3 Wednesdays and Thursdays; $4 Fridays
and Saturdays; and whatever the market will bear
when big-name acts hit the stage.

Whiskey River, 1997 N Clybourn Ave, Chicago, IL
60614, 312/528-3400. Mon–Thu 5 pm–2 am, Fri–Sat 5
pm–3 am.

Best cocktails from the 1920s

Hotel Inter-Continental Bar

In keeping with the hotel's lavishly restored art deco
grandeur, the bar off the lobby serves specialty
cocktails reminiscent of the 1920s. The Polo—named
for the elitist sport, not the explorer—blends rum
and orange and lemon juices; the Alphonse, named
after a newspaper cartoonist of the era, combines
creme de cacao, gin, and cream. The Full House
mixes yellow chartreuse, benedictine, and bitters;
the Bijou is concocted from Grand Marnier, ver-
mouth, and bitters. A wicked martini is served in a
carafe nestled in a glass bucket of ice. Ornate club
chairs have lions, eagles, and rams carved into the
armrests. Across the foyer, The Salon offers the
music of a jazz trio into the late evening hours.

Hotel Inter-Continental Bar, 505 N Michigan Ave,
Chicago, IL 60611, 312/944-4100. Mon–Sat 11 am–
12:30 am, Sun noon–12:30 am.

Best bar stocked with toys & games

Blue Frog

The games people play: They're hanging from the
ceiling, taped to the walls, and stacked in huge piles
ready for patrons to play at this whimsical bar that
has been likened to Pee-Wee Herman's rec room. The
entire ceiling is festooned with symbols of pop culture—Man From U.N.C.L.E., Patty Duke, and Truth
or Consequences games; boxing robots; a beach raft;
a toy fire truck; a chemistry set. You can order a beer
and enjoy a serious game of Monopoly or pass the

time at Chutes & Ladders. The menu (shaped like
a game board) includes char-grilled burgers, meatloaf
sandwiches, tuna melts, a vegetarian sandwich, and
"straight-from-hell" grilled-steak chili, topped off with
cheese, onions, and jalapenos. Outside is a small
patio shaded by a red-and-white awning; inside
(through a door with hundreds of tiny pink pigs in
a porthole window) are black café tables and friendly
graffiti covering the white walls. Owners Mimi and
Rose Reed used to sell pressure gauges, so don't
think this doesn't make sense.

Blue Frog, 676 N LaSalle St, Chicago, IL 60610, 312/
943-8900. Mon–Thu 11:30 am–midnight, Fri 11:30
am–1:30 am, Sat 11:30 am–2:30 am. Sun hours
vary.

Best restored corner bar

Schubas Tavern

This restored neighborhood bar, built as a Schlitz
tavern earlier this century, has a good bar menu and
a friendly ambience. In the front room, which has
high, restored tin ceilings, a youngish crowd bellies
up to an oak-and-mahogany bar, keeping an eye on
TV sports and ordering Harp, Guinness, Bass,
Samuel Adams, Double Diamond, Anchor Steam,
and Leinenkugel's beer on tap. In the back dining
room, with blonde oak half-paneling and tables and
a vaulted ceiling, a slightly older crowd concentrates
on dining. There are burgers, cheddar cheese fries,
BLTs, chili, tuna melts, and barbecue back ribs,
with cheesecake and pie for dessert. Stop here, too,
for a country breakfast with grits and ham steak, or
eggs Benedict or Florentine. Check for a full schedule of jazz, folk, and rock music performed on a
small back stage.

Schubas Tavern, 3159 N Southport Ave, Chicago, IL
60657, 312/525-2508. Sun–Fri 9 am–2 am, Sat 9 am–
3 am.

Best bar for cognac & coffee

Big, Brasserie and Bar

To top off an evening in style, step up to this marble-
topped bar, casually rest a foot on its polished brass
rail, and, with as much aplomb as possible, order
a snifter of A.E. Dor Vielles Reserve Grande Champagne Cognac Louis Phillipe 1840, lot #5. It was
distilled before the Civil War, and this particular
nightcap will set you back $275 for one and one-half
ounces. For the same price you also could order a
rare grappa or a 30-year-old single-malt Scotch. This
glass-enclosed bar displays its costly inventory on

a dramatic floor-to-ceiling back bar, accessible by movable brass ladders. It carries 87 varieties of single-malt Scotch, 46 types of brandy, 115 armagnacs, 164 cordials and liqueurs (including artichoke, mango, and watermelon flavors), 34 types of schnapps (such as butterscotch, peanut brittle, and grapefruit), and 100 beers. A brass-accented coffee station features 32 fresh-ground varieties, including cappuccino and espresso. Bartenders are moonlighting musicians and practice "flair" bartending, a combination of mixing, flipping, and pouring drinks (à la the Tom Cruise movie *Cocktail*); there is both impromptu and scheduled entertainment.

Big, Brasserie and Bar, Hyatt Regency Chicago, 151 E Wacker Dr, Chicago, IL 60601, 312/565-1234.

Best beer garden
Cork & Kerry

When summer finally arrives in Chicago, residents and visitors like to sip and sup in the great outdoors. The huge beer garden of this far South Side establishment is a great place to enjoy a libation or two under the summer sky. The garden, along the side and in back of the building, is a sprawling 3,500 square feet and is made up of varying levels of deck with old street-paving bricks as steps and ramps. The garden is nicely landscaped, with flowers, plants, and shade trees; authentic old Chicago lampposts provide light. Located in the solidly middle-class Beverly neighborhood (just north of the city's southern limits), the Cork & Kerry attracts a mixed and friendly crowd; single women usually feel comfortable here alone or in groups. Check out the decor around Christmastime—the bar's elaborate miniature holiday scenes are perennial winners of a neighborhood decorating contest. *A nomenclature note:* The bar's name may sound particularly Irish, but the bar isn't really; it's more of an "Irish/Chicago" type of place, in the manner of Butch McGuire's (of which this appears to be a larger, less-yuppified version).

Cork & Kerry, 106145 Western Ave, Chicago, IL 60643, 312/445-2675. Mon–Fri 2 pm–2 am, Sat noon–2 am, Sun 2 pm–midnight.

Best "killer" margaritas
El Jardin

This sprawling, lively cantina (with several entrances over nearly a full block, an adjacent small café, and two outdoor gardens) is a great place to head with a group, particularly after a Cubs game. (El Jardin is a few blocks south of Wrigley Field.) Dine here on a variety of Mexican specialties, or just order a bunch of terrific appetizers (good chips and salsa, great quesadillas)—but, whatever you do, definitely partake in the restaurant's excellent margaritas. Available by the fishbowl-sized glass or by the pitcher, these are real, mixed concoctions, not frozen, convenient store-style slushies. Sweet and salty and satisfying, these drinks can definitely creep up on you. I once saw a group of couples get chip-throwing silly after quickly downing a few pitchers of El Jardin's potent margaritas. Olé!

El Jardin, 3335 N Clark, Chicago, IL 60657, 312/528-6775. Sun & Mon 10:30 am–10 pm, Tue–Thu 10:30 am–10:30 pm, Fri & Sat 10:30 am–midnight (longer hours in summer).

Wickedest martini

Cape Cod Room Bar

Even though many consider the extra-dry, oh-so-potent martini an anachronism in this age of wine coolers and "light" just about everything, this cocktail still has its adherents. And it is appropriate that many head for the Cape Cod Room at The Drake Hotel to partake of one of the best-made martinis extant. This traditional pampering seafood house (where maitre d' Patrick Bredin is himself an institution) is a stalwart at Chicago's old-money luxury hotel. The bar in the Cape Cod Room, installed in 1933, also is a landmark in its own right. It is scarred with graffiti carved by the famous, including Marilyn Monroe, Joe DiMaggio, Jack Benny, and Vince Lombardi. Patrons caused a furor when management tried to replace the landmark bar. The Executive Martini is made with 4 ounces of gin, served with a swirler, and priced at $6.50. (The bartenders here also lend their expertise to creating a traditional Manhattan.)

Cape Cod Room Bar, The Drake Hotel, 140 E Walton Pl, Chicago, IL 60611, 312/787-2200. Daily noon–11 pm.

Best bar after you've passed the bar

Clark Street Bar & Grill

Walk into this bar around cocktail hour and say "Hi, Counselor," and half the patrons are likely to look up to greet you. Located in the LaSalle Bank Building, this is the quintessential Chicago attorneys' hangout. An old-style saloon with lots of glass, wood, and chrome and nostalgic photos of old-time Chicago prominents and street scenes, it has private booths ideal for discussing the latest brief. Even if you're not interested in becoming better acquainted—professionally or privately—with lawyers, this is a good spot for free edibles. Those who drop in after work can take advantage of a wide array of free hors d'oeuvres that include chicken wings, turkey nuggets, meatballs, pizza, stuffed tomatoes with rice, and a large cheese tray. Every Thursday there is a popular taco bar.

Clark Street Bar & Grill, 130 S Clark St, Chicago, IL 60603, 312/558-8950. Mon–Fri 7 am–7:30 pm.

Definitive singles bar

Butch McGuire's

First, a geography primer for the uninitiated: What often is referred to as "Rush Street" (meaning the entertainment district, not the street itself) is actually located primarily on Division Street, west of State Street. That said, two more words will suffice for the "meet market" singles bars on Division—don't bother. Those determined to go anyway should at least choose Butch McGuire's, the "original" singles bar (since 1961) and pretty much a cut above others on the street. The bar's Irish/Chicago decor is warm and interesting, and the crowd is usually lively and friendly (i.e., single women, you will likely be "hit on"; single men, you will likely be scrutinized). McGuire's lays claim to the creation of the Harvey Wallbanger, a feat that seems to recede in relevance with each passing year.

Butch McGuire's, 20 W Division St, Chicago, IL 60610, 312/337-9080. Mon–Fri 10 am–4 am, Sat 9:30 am–5 am, Sun 9:30 am–4 am.

Most entertaining piano bar

Coq d'Or Lounge

When he's visiting Chicago, actor Joe Pesci may be found hanging around here. It is his favorite piano bar—as it is with the many regulars who admire Buddy Charles, Chicago's legendary piano-bar virtuoso. After almost two decades at the long-since-shuttered Acorn-On-Oak, Charles found a new home—as did his considerable following—at The Drake Hotel. This dark, warm bar, with its soft lighting, club-like paneling, and red upholstery, is a perfect spot for Charles, as he goes through his repertoire of jazz, pop, ragtime, and show tunes—with a smidgen of rock 'n' roll thrown in. In his inimitable style, Charles intersperses songs with a nonstop monologue about great performers of jazz and swing, the history of music in Chicago, tributes to his idol, Fats Waller, and various musical trivia.

Most piano-bar musicians play and sing. Charles *performs*—as happy with Noel Coward and Cole Porter as he is with Duke Ellington and Louis Armstrong. Catch him Tue–Sat 9 pm–2 am. *Note to whiskey aficionados:* The bar is known for its collection of small-batch bourbons.

Coq d'Or Lounge, The Drake Hotel, 140 E Walton Pl, Chicago, IL 60611, 312/787-2200. Mon–Sat 11 am–2 am, Sun 11 am–midnight.

Funkiest piano bar

Joann

If by chance you haven't been to this funky saloon in the decade since the development of River North put its Wells Street location in the high-rent district, you're in for a real jolt of déjà vu. It looks as though the entire place was transplanted, unchanged, to this appropriately seedy block of Clark Street. There's even gravelly voiced Louie Jacobone at the piano in front of the long mirror and nude paintings, passing the microphone to patrons gathered around the piano bar eagerly perusing numbered song books. There's the same marquee-style sign out front and the same weird decorations inside—bordello-red wallpaper, long shiny red bar, old-movie stills, a collection of vintage family portraits that look as though they were bought in a job lot, lewd slogans, and cheap glass chandeliers. But for friendly bar staff and a chance to belt out "Misty," this is the place. There are a few electronic game machines up front and free parking in the nearby Cosmopolitan Bank lot.

Joann, 751 N Clark St, Chicago, IL 60610, 312/337-1005. Tue–Fri 7 pm–2 am, Sat 8 pm–3 am.

Best poetry bar

The Green Mill

"All Roads Lead to Uptown," read ads for this legendary cocktail lounge. And Broadway leads to the door of this well-worn art deco club. It once played regular host to "Scarface" Al Capone, though today it is better known for its late-night jazz sets (especially the all-star jam sessions offered most Saturday nights). But on Sunday nights, the focus swings from music to words, as the Green Mill hosts a series of weekly poetic prize fights known as the Uptown Poetry Slam. A Slam is far from the sedate, ladies-preservation-society type of atmosphere you might picture when you hear the words "poetry reading." Instead, streetwise poets, young and old alike, read their hard-fought, gritty works in series of one-on-one competitions, with audience reaction determining the winner. Long-time host and neo-beat poet Marc Smith instructs the evening's judges to award scores ranging from ten to "negative infinity." New blood is always welcome—but leave any "Roses are red" stuff at home, unless you want to be laughed off the stage. There's a $5 cover charge on Slam nights.

The Green Mill, 4802 N Broadway, Chicago, IL 60640, 312/878-5552. Mon–Fri noon–4 am, Sat noon–5 am, Sun 11 am–4 am. Uptown Poetry Slam: Sun 7–10 pm.

Best sports bar—Cubs

Harry Caray's

If you're near Wrigley Field, before or after a game, there are plenty of interesting neighborhood joints (with varying degrees of baseball devotion) surrounding the old ballyard, such as Murphy's Bleachers, Jimmy & Tai's, the Cubby Bear, and even the hyper all-sports bar of Sluggers. But slightly farther afield (and no less devoted to the Cubbies) is veteran announcer Harry Caray's bar and restaurant. Stop in here for the extensive collection of uniforms, helmets, bats, baseball cards, and other memorabilia, a cold Budweiser (Harry Caray's brand), a game on the tube, and some surprisingly good Italian fare. (Especially recommended: Appetizers of crispy calamari and deep-fried ravioli.) And, unlike in some celebrity-owned spots in town, Harry can often be found here during baseball season, working the crowd and toasting his favorite team with his favorite brew. (P.S. Harry's famous catch phrase, "Holy Cow," doubles as the restaurant's phone number—check it out. P.P.S. Don't miss sampling made-on-the-premises, thick-cut potato chips.)

Harry Caray's, 33 W Kinzie St, Chicago, IL 60610, 312/465-9269. Mon–Thu 11:30 am–10:30 pm, Fri 11:30 am–midnight, Sat noon–midnight, Sun noon–10:30 pm.

Best sports bar—Bulls

Michael Jordan's Restaurant

Even from a distance, it is readily apparent that this is Michael's place. Towering over the roof of the restaurant is a giant billboard showing MJ as he was meant to be seen—suspended gracefully in space with a basketball, not a baseball, close at hand. Even when No. 23 took a year off to flirt with a baseball career, the billboard remained as a symbol of what might have been—and what still may be. Now that Jordan has returned to lead the Bulls, his River North restaurant and bar truly is the place to watch the team in action. In the bar, a $350,000, 20x6-foot video wall offers state-of-the-art sports coverage (and allows up to three different projections at once). A three-tier "skybox" area offers prime viewing of the video wall. You can dig into some decent meatloaf or macaroni and cheese (both made from wife Juanita's recipes), check out the souvenir stand stocked with more than 200 items, and view Air Jordan memorabilia that includes his jerseys (including one of the blue North Carolina jerseys from his collegiate days), championship rings, and *Sports Illustrated* cover. You may even catch a glimpse of the man himself (he's known to stop by two or three times a week when the team is in town). But be prepared to wait for a table if you come to eat; though the restaurant is cavernous (with 175 seats—the entire complex accommodates 600), it attracts thousands of fans as hungry for celebrity as they are for food. Steaks and chicken are good entrée choices—and don't miss fried green tomatoes as an appetizer. *A fun tip:* If you call ahead, you'll hear the voice of Jordan himself guiding you through the voice mail.

Michael Jordan's Restaurant, 500 N LaSalle St, Chicago, IL 60610, 312/644-DUNK. Bar (lunch, dinner, snacks) Sun–Thu 11 am–11 pm, Fri & Sat 11 am–12:30 am.

Best sports bar—Blackhawks

Gate 3 ½, The Bismarck Hotel

You won't usually find the Chicago Blackhawks on free television, but you will find all of Chicago's pro hockey team's home and away games on multiple large-screen television sets at this sports bar. This popular Loop watering hole is unabashedly NHL territory—not surprisingly inasmuch as the Wirtzes own the Bismarck Hotel *and* the Blackhawks. Tables resemble giant hockey pucks, and the bar's main area is replete with a simulated "rink" floor, complete with blue lines and enclosed by plexiglass safety walls. The saloon is decorated with Blackhawks' memorabilia, and staring down on the imbibers are the Blackhawks faithful—fans depicted in a 45x6-foot photograph taken during the Hawks' last home game at the old Chicago Stadium. Although there's not usually a quiet spot to be found, you can retreat to relative privacy by claiming the table in the penalty box. Full bar service includes domestic and imported beers. Fountain drinks (floats, malts, and shakes) also are available. You can order the inevitable "Blackhawk burger"—or meatloaf, chili, prime rib, grilled chicken breast, Caesar salad, and bar food such as jalapeno poppers filled with cheddar cheese, Cajun popcorn shrimp with spicy remoulade sauce, and spicy chicken wings.

Gate 3½, The Bismarck Hotel, 171 W Randolph St, Chicago, IL 60601, 312/236-0123. Mon–Fri 11 am–1 am, Sat & Sun noon–1 am.

Best sports bar—Bears

Knuckles

The southwest corner of the Hyatt Regency Chicago's main lobby used to hold an intimate comedy club, part of the Catch A Rising Star chain. In fact, a friend recalls sitting not five feet from the stage when Jerry Seinfeld sizzled through a killer set just before his TV show became a big hit. Today, however, the biggest hits you'll see here will be on one of several TVs showing the Monsters of the Midway as they punish opposing quarterbacks and wide receivers at Soldier Field and other NFL stadiums. Knuckles, developed jointly by Hyatt and the Chicago Bears, is a cozy spot to catch Dave Wannstedt's team, as well as many other professional and college games. During a break in the action, check out the autographed pictures, posters, jerseys, and memorabilia from Bears greats such as Walter Payton and Jim McMahon. Or try your hand at a game of billiards, electronic darts, or "Pop-a-Shot" basketball. To liven things up when "Da Bears" are resting up between victories, Knuckles hosts Margarita Mondays and regular Sports Trivia Nights. After a few hot dogs and brewskies, you might even find yourself singing "Bear Down, Chicago Bears." "Iron Mike" Ditka would be proud.

Knuckles, at the Hyatt Regency Chicago, 151 E Wacker Dr, Chicago, IL 60611, 312/565-1234. Open Mon–Fri 5:30 pm–midnight, Sat & Sun 11 am–midnight.

Best sports bar—boccie

J.C.'s Pub

Imported Italian beer, dishes of pasta swimming in rich red sauce homemade from an old family recipe, and the clack of wooden boccie balls striking each other. It doesn't get much more Neapolitan than this popular pub/eatery in southwest suburban Crestwood. J.C.'s has four boccie courts, set in an attractive beer garden. No need to call ahead for a reservation to play—simply add your name to the list, and when your turn comes, play for up to 45 minutes. Played on a court of sand, boccie originated about 100 years ago in Turin in the Piedmont region of Italy. It's similar to lawn bowling or maybe shuffleboard; the object is to bring your ball to rest closest to the smaller ball, known as the "jack." The first team to score 15 points wins. Among the most popular pasta dishes at J.C.'s are spaghetti, mostaccioli, meat-filled ravioli, and chicken and sausage parmesan. The sausage, too, is homemade, and every meal is accompanied by big loaves of garlic bread baked twice daily. Made-from-scratch soups include sausage tortellini, corn crab chowder, and cream of wild rice. Thin-crust pizza is made with fresh ingredients in the restaurant's own kitchen. This is a lively, crowded spot, ideal for a good time with a bunch of good friends. *Secret sauce ingredient:* In the it-may-not-sound-good-but-it-sure-tastes-good department, the restaurant makes its acclaimed red sauce from an old family recipe that uses neck bones.

J.C.'s Pub, 13101 S Cicero Ave, Crestwood, IL 60445, 708/388-7755. Mon–Thu 11 am–2 am, Fri & Sat 11 am–3 am, Sun 4 pm–1 am.

Best sign in bar window

Sterch's

The block of Lincoln Avenue containing this bar is an eclectic one, to say the least. A pioneer of Chicago's French restaurants, The Bakery, used to be just south, and nearby establishments range from the industrial dance club of Esoteria to the rowdy frat party of The Big Nasty. But amid all this sits Sterch's, the closest thing the block has to an unpretentious "neighborhood bar," with softball trophies behind the bar and interesting people in front of it. Darts; pinball; a wide variety of beers; and a casual, comfortable atmosphere for conversation are the main attractions here. The semilegendary window sign, which appeared during the yuppie-frenzy that overtook the area around the bar in the early '80s, perfectly sums up the bar's take-no-guff attitude: "No Corona, no foolish drinks, limited dancing; no substitutions."

Sterch's, 2238 N Lincoln Ave, Chicago, IL 60614, 312/281-2653. Sun–Fri 3:30 pm–2 am, Sat 3:30 pm–3 am.

Best gay and lesbian bars

Chicago is home to a vibrant gay and lesbian scene, mostly centered around North Halsted Street, from (approximately) Belmont Avenue (3200 North) to

Addison Street (3600 North), in the New Town area
(also dubbed "Boys Town"). The bars here are mostly
aimed at gay men—although some are also fre-
quented by lesbians. Most notable among the Halsted
bars are Roscoe's (3354), The Men's Room (3359),
Bucks (3439), Christopher Street (3458), and Little
Jim's (3501). Two very popular gay dance clubs are
Carol's Speakeasy (1355 N Wells) and Berlin (954 W
Belmont—also a favorite with a decadent and out-
there nongay crowd). Among lesbian bars, Lost and
Found (3058 W Irving Park Road) is a long-estab-
lished, low-key spot, and Paris Dance (1122 W
Montrose Street) is a lively, upscale dance club. The
entire scene is fairly close-knit—patrons and em-
ployees of the above-listed nightspots can direct
interested parties to other, less-publicized gay and
lesbian bars and clubs.

Best bar to keep you on track

The Winner's Circle

This off-track betting emporium gets classier as you
work your way higher. At street-level, there's the
hustle-bustle of hard-core punters, waving form
sheets and betting tickets, the voice of a track
announcer booming from overhead television
screens. Ride the escalators to the top floor and
you'll find the same action in infinitely more sedate
surroundings. The floors and bar are dark green
marble; half-paneled walls are decorated with racing
prints. Nobody is shouting or elbowing. Dining room
tables have white linen and individual TV monitors.
The food is surprisingly good and reasonably priced
(although unsuccessful wagering can result in a
costly lunch or dinner, even if you bet at the $2
window). Lunches run to soup, sandwiches, three
salads, and fettucini. Dinner selections include
steak, prime rib, baby-back ribs, pork chops, and
chicken breast sautéed in parmesan. Racing is tele-
cast from all the Chicago-area tracks, with featured
races simulcast from out of state.

The Winner's Circle, 177 N State St, Chicago, IL
60601, 312/419-8787. Mon–Thu 11:30 am–10 pm, Fri–
Sat 11:30 am–midnight, Sun hours vary.

Best billiard parlor—upscale

Lucky's

You're not likely to bump into Paul Newman or Tom
Cruise at this upscale poolhall (housed on the first
floor of a renovated brick factory once occupied by
Schwinn Bicycle), but nor will you find hovering
clouds of smoke, a dirty tile floor, and fast-talking
hustlers. This contemporary River North billiard

hall/restaurant is one of the most elegant in the city, featuring 13 reconditioned pool tables, two bars, a dance floor, and a full restaurant serving such unexpected-in-a-pool-hall delicacies as grilled lamb sausage and rabbit stew. To participate in the classic clash of stripes and solids here, it will cost you $12 per hour Fridays through Sundays and $10 per hour during the week.

Lucky's, 213 W Institute Place, Chicago, IL 60610, 312/751-7777. Tue–Fri 5 pm–4 am. Sat 8 pm–4 am.

Best bar to shoot pool—downscale

Grant's Tavern

Although not a necessarily "downscale" bar (on the contrary—it's been spruced up, inside and out), this Halsted Street establishment is a comfortable and fun bar that happens to have a well-worn, popular pool table in its backroom. Pick up a drink from the bar, mark your name on the "wait board" in the back, and pass the time by watching your potential opponents run the table or by playing a few frames on the ancient shuffle bowling game. Grant's also offers good munchies (mini-burgers, nachos, etc.) from a tiny kitchen off the pool room, a comfortable summertime back patio, and a great jukebox. While sitting at the bar, look up at the black ceiling above the canopy of wood beams; ask your bartender how they got all those dollar bills to stick up there.

Grant's Tavern, 2138 N Halsted St, Chicago, IL 60614, 312/348-3665. Mon–Thu 4 pm–2 am, Fri 11 am–2 am, Sat 11 am–3 am, Sun 11 am–10 pm.

Best bar to play shuffle bowling

The Lodge Tavern

This bar is on Division Street, so it's definitely of a piece with the sardine-crowded singles bars lining that famous/infamous street. That said, it's also a bit more party-minded and rollicking, while neighboring bars may be predatory and snobbish. One of the bar's focal points is the well-worn shuffle bowling (also called table bowling) game, in which a weighted metal puck is slid along a flat alley at sensors that "knock down" pins suspended from above. Silly, maybe—but fun, fairly easy to play, and a good way to meet new people or to pass the time with those you're with. The Lodge sponsors a hotly contested shuffle bowling tournament each year. It also has a decent selection of rock on the jukebox and usually a game on the tube.

The Lodge Tavern, 21 W Division St, Chicago, IL 60610, 312/642-4406. Mon–Thu 2 pm–4 am, Fri–Sun 2 pm–4 am.

Best college bar—University of Chicago

Jimmy's Woodlawn Tap

"The bar is old, the decor is old—*I'm* old," said 80-something Jimmy Wilson, friendly raconteur and owner of this Hyde Park landmark, which has been serving U. of C. students and famous visitors—such as Saul Bellow and Dylan Thomas—since 1948. Starting in a single room, Jimmy's has expanded over the years into three adjacent stores. The "old" decor is that of a classic Chicago tavern: wood-and-mirrored back bar, beer signs, a full complement of books for reading material and argument-settling—and, since this is U. of C. territory, these books include the complete works of Shakespeare, a full encyclopedia, and a Latin dictionary. "I welcome the university students. They love this place—it's like a home away from home for them," Jimmy said. "Years later, they come back, and say, 'Jimmy, nothing has changed'—except the prices," he adds with a laugh. You can usually find Jimmy presiding over his kingdom seven days a week, during the late-afternoon, early-evening hours.

Jimmy's Woodlawn Tap, 1172 E 55th St, Chicago, IL 60615, 312/643-5516. Daily 11 am–2 am.

Best college bar—DePaul

Kelly's Pub

Located in the shadow of the Howard El tracks (its garden seating is directly beneath where the trains rumble overhead), this longtime neighborhood bar has become in recent years a popular hangout for students attending nearby DePaul University. They head here for inexpensive draft beers; basic bar food; good tunes on the jukebox; and, especially on weekend nights, the young, rowdy exuberance of their fellow DePaul classmates. This popular collegiate watering hole opens before lunchtime for those who may have been burning the midnight oil (or perhaps those burning the candle at both ends).

Kelly's Pub, 949 W Webster Ave, Chicago, IL 60614, 312/281-0656. Sun–Fri 11 am–2 am, Sat 11 am–3 am.

Best college bar—Loyola

Cheers Café Chicago

Everybody might not know your name here, but you'll certainly recognize the name of this bar (which actually predates the classic TV sitcom by a few years). This friendly, local hangout on the city's Far North Side doesn't sport the typical Chicago bar look (dark wood, mirrored back bar, real or simulated pressed-tin ceiling), favoring more of a crisp, art deco appearance. Drawing a diverse crowd of students from nearby Loyola University and local residents, Cheers offers an above-average selection of bar food (half-pound burgers, Cajun chicken, barbecued ribs, etc.), sports on four ten-foot screens, and four buck-a-game pool tables in the basement. One of Cheers' highlights is its wide sidewalk café (one of the largest in the city); from May through the end of September, this is a comfortable, casual place to relax and watch the busy parade of Sheridan Road pass by.

Cheers Café Chicago, 6600 N Sheridan Rd, Chicago, IL 60626, 312/338-8960. Mon–Fri 5 pm–2 am, Sat 5 pm–3 am; also some earlier opening times & Sun hours in summer.

Best frat-party-style bar

The Big Nasty

Those interested in reliving those carefree days at good ol' Tappa Kegga Brew—or to see what they may have missed by not pledging a fraternity or sorority—might head to this ramshackle, rollicking bar on Lincoln Avenue. The crowd is young and you may feel a bit out of place if you're over, say, 25. But, then, it's all a matter of attitude. You won't have to agonize too long over your choice of libation—the bar serves only beer and "Jell-O shots," paper cups filled with fruity gelatin cubes made with vodka instead of water. And you may not want to dress up or worry too much about your hair, because the other thing sold here is cans of Silly String—by the end of the night most of the crowd is covered with the (easily removable) neon strands of the stuff.

The Big Nasty, 2242 N Lincoln Ave, Chicago, IL 60614, 312/404-1535. Thu & Fri 8 pm–2 am, Sat 8 pm–3 am.

Best neighborhood of bars and clubs

Lincoln Avenue and Halsted Street

This really is a "no contest." The crowded, noisy, pick-up bars of the Rush and Division area mostly are without personality. Ontario Street is up-and-coming, but is better known for dining than for pure nightlife. The unquestionable choice for the best night-time odysseys are the busy Lincoln Park thoroughfares of North Lincoln Avenue and North Halsted Street. From friendly neighborhood joints (Sterch's, Grant's Tavern) to live-music spots (Lounge Ax, the Halsted Street blues clubs) to dance clubs (especially Esoteria), these two streets have enough interesting and close-to-each-other sites to make them perfect for a night of casual pub-and-club-hopping. Halsted and Lincoln conveniently intersect at Fullerton Avenue, in an area with a motherlode of bars, clubs, shops, theaters, and restaurants.

N Lincoln Avenue and N Halsted Street, north of W Armitage Avenue (2000 North) to approximately W Wrightwood Street (2600 North).

Best bet for suds and spuds

Mashed Potato Club

Oprah may have started Chicago's mashed-potatoes mania (with horseradish-spiked dish at now-closed Eccentric), but this Wrigleyville saloon perpetuates it, featuring 104 different toppings for potatoes. These range from asparagus, black beans, zucchini, and homemade beef gravy to water chestnuts, goat cheese, and crab. Offbeat selections include jelly beans and M&Ms, which owner Greg Kovach says patrons order as dessert on sweet potatoes. "We go through 5 pounds of jelly beans every week," says Kovach. The restaurant also uses close to 200,000 pounds of red potatoes a year. They are mashed, skin on, the old-fashioned way, by hand with a wooden paddle in 50-pound batches. The wait for one of the sixty-two seats in the high-ceiling dining room can run up to two hours on Saturday evenings. The decor is a funky blend of psychedelic colors, paint-splashed designer table cloths, and tasteful black-and-white photographs of nudes. "We also stress the 'circuses' of dining," says Kovach. "We are eclectic, eccentric, and erotic."

Mashed Potato Club, 3912 N Clark St, Chicago, IL 60613, 312/871-4062. Sun–Thu 5–10:30 pm, Fri 5 pm–3 am, Sat 5 pm–1:30 am.

Best buys on appetizers and beer by the yard

Primavera Ristorante Bar

A lively hotel bar, big-screen TV for watching sports, and a great buy on hors d'oeuvres and beer—these form a winning combination that make this an ideal cocktail-hour meeting spot (the bar is big enough that the TV need not be intrusive). For a buck you get five jumbo shrimp, clams, or oysters with cocktail sauce. An individual-size pepperoni pizza is also $1. Wash them down with a half-yard of beer (Bud or Bass on draft), served in the traditional bulb-based glass supported by a wooden stand. It costs $4 and holds the equivalent of about two bottles, A full yard, which stands really tall on the bar, is $6. There's also a limited menu from the kitchen of the adjoining Primavera Restaurant (see separate listing, "Dining"). *Souvenir suggestion:* Yard glasses are for sale in the bar.

Primavera Ristorante Bar (Fairmont Hotel), 200 N Columbus Dr, Chicago, IL 60601, 312/565-6655. Mon–Sun 11 am–12 am.

Best bar to find greasy hamburgers & Mike Royko

Billy Goat Tavern

Success hasn't spoiled Billy Goat's. Although curious tourists and suburbanites drop by to see the underground "chizburger, chizburger, chizburger" joint of *Saturday Night Live* fame, essentially it remains the haunt of reporters, press operators in hats fashioned from newspapers, late-night drunks, and, occasionally, Mike Royko. Ribeye sandwiches are a good buy, and "chizburgers," cooked to order on a spattering griddle, are satisfyingly greasy. A framed collection of yellowing newspaper stories chronicle Chicago sports, newspapering, and the life and times of the late "Billy Goat" Siannis, the original proprietor. Legend has it Siannis placed a curse on the Cubs when he and his mascot goat were ejected from Wrigley Field during the 1945 World Series, which the Cubs promptly lost. Even though present owner Sam Siannis says he has removed the curse, the Cubs and their fans are still awaiting a return to the series. Somewhere, an old Greek and his goat probably are smiling.

Billy Goat Tavern, 430 N Michigan Ave (lower level), Chicago, IL 60611, 312/222-1525. Mon–Fri 7 am–2 am, Sat 11 am–3 am, Sun 11 am–2 am.

Best martinis for staying upright

Café Gordon

In an era of the Internet and Hootie and the Blowfish, of fusion food and filtered water, there's the martini. This drink of the twenties and the fifties is enjoying a remarkable renaissance that puts it up there with the return of cigar smoking and big bands. On Thursday evenings, this bar adjacent to the Tremont Hotel hosts Café Martini Club. Alongside the bar, triangular glasses nest in a bed of ice, surrounded by a colorful array of lemons, limes, and oranges and backed by a phalanx of vodka bottles—presaging a menu offering 14 different kinds of martinis. Dubbed "weenie tinis" and priced at a modest $3.50, they weigh in at 1 1/2 ounces each—a good size for sampling (and staying upright). The 007, bone-dry Kettel One vodka—shaken, not stirred—arrives freezer-cold, with a thin film of ice, like the surface of a lake on the point of freezing. Other choices pair vodka with campari, sambuca, and Godiva liquor (for the Choco Tini), and also feature gin, cognac, and whiskey. The Kurant Affair is made with Absolut Kurant, fresh raspberries, and lime. Edibles include artichoke fritters with béarnaise sauce, fried calamari with cilantro dipping sauce, crab cakes with braised bok choy and whole-grain mustard, and mussels steamed in red wine.

Café Gordon, 100 E Chestnut St, Chicago, IL 60611, 312/280-2100. Sun–Thu 7 am–10:30 pm, Fri & Sat 7 am–midnight.

Best neighborhood bar where there's no beer on tap

Gino's North

Walk into this cozy Edgewater Beach tavern and pizza parlor just steps east of the Granville El stop, and you'll find yourself transported right back to 1941, when the place was built. Nothing has changed here in the intervening five-plus decades; not the two-tiered art deco ceiling, not the sinuously curved cherrywood bar, not the four cozy tables tucked along the west wall, and not the five-foot marble statue behind the bar (a beautiful woman from antiquity likely as not to have a Bulls cap perched on her head). Well, okay, a few things have changed over the years. In the mid-1980s, the place shifted its menu from steaks and chops to delectable home-made pizzas and sandwiches and underwent a name change (from the Snow Drop). In the early 1990s, Gino's underwent a change in ownership as well. Proprietors Paul and Georgia (call her George) Wenger serve up hand-tossed, 10" pizzas for between $5 and $6 and Old Style and Budweiser for a mere $1.75 a pop. Speaking of pop, that's the only thing you can get on tap here; Gino's is strictly a bottles and cans, shot-and-a-beer establishment. Patrons include students from nearby Loyola, old-timers from this far North Side neighborhood, and many regulars from the nearby Artists-in-Residence apartment complex. This is about as friendly a bar as you'll find in the city; if George doesn't know your name when you walk in, she'll have it locked into memory by the time you finish your first round.

Gino's North, 1111 W Granville St, Chicago, IL 60660, 312/465-1616. Tue–Sun 2 pm–midnight.

Best bar to meet yuppies

Glascott's

We don't mean to be hard on this popular Lincoln Park watering hole. It's just that this spot seems to attract the highest concentration of topsider-and-jeans-wearing, BMW-driving, condo-owning, Corona-with-lime-swilling yupsters in the entire city. It's a nice-enough-looking bar, with always a game on the tube or an oldie on the jukebox. But if you were on an urban safari, trying to bag the species *Northsidus Annoyingus Conspicuous-Consumerus*, this would be your happy hunting ground. Often densely crowded, especially Thursday through Sunday nights—it seems to do a land-office business—which is only fitting, since it's owned by (and named after) a leading Lincoln Park real estate consultant and landowner.

Glascott's, 2158 N Halsted St, Chicago, IL 60614, 312/281-1205, Mon–Fri 11 am–2 am, Fri 11 am–3 am, Sun noon–2 am.

Best bar to grin & bear it

Grizzly's Lodge

The first thing you'll notice about Grizzly's is the giant wooden hand suspended above the front door, pushing out of a checked sleeve and pointing the way inside. The second thing you'll notice are the bears. Three of them patrol a waterfall on an outside mural; another appears on a sign above the entrance, clenching a salmon in its teeth; yet another, this one a wooden cut-out, stands before the log-cabin facade holding a placard that says, "Your table is waiting." Inside, the bear theme continues—a chainsaw-sculpted bruin wearing dark sunglasses holds menus, a bearskin rug hangs on one wall. Hunting paraphernalia is arrayed around the varnished-wood bar and the dining area of about 20 small tables. There's so much kitsch to look at—including a full-size canoe suspended above the island bar, a huge hanging pocket knife, a veritable thicket of horns on every wall, and a handsome tin ceiling—you might not notice the ten TVs. But you should concentrate on the fresh wild game that is Grizzly's trademark. From simple Plains fare, such as buffalo burgers and thick elk steaks, to duck sausage, venison goulash, and wild boar chops, there's plenty to tempt the carnivore. Others can nibble on seafood, fish, pasta, and salads. Wash it all down with one of Grizzly's signature drinks, such as the Beam Bear Trap (aka Lynchburg Lemonade) or Hair of the Bear (Long Island Iced Tea) and you'll be ready for hibernation.

Grizzly's Lodge, 3832 N Lincoln Ave, Chicago, IL 60657, 312/281-5112. Open daily 11 am–2 am. Beer garden open May–Sept Sun–Thu until 11 pm, Fri & Sat until midnight.

Best self-proclaimed bar for "discerning weirdos"

The Northside

Once upon a time, one of the best bars in the city was a small, eclectic bar called the Northside, located under the El tracks on Webster Avenue in Lincoln Park. Today, The Northside isn't as far north—it has been transplanted to the Bucktown neighborhood, bringing with it artifacts of the old place (parts of the wood-and-mirror back bar, the former outside door—now inside—with the old 939 address on it). And, say those who followed its move or have discovered it since, it's still a great, casual hangout. The new place has a long, narrow front room with exposed brick and rotating artworks, plus a back room for pool or live music and an attractive outdoor garden area complete with boccie court. As ever, the scene is complemented by a variety of taped music (ranging from the Talking Heads to Miles Davis to Philip Glass, depending on who's behind the bar). A new menu of affordable fresh-made sandwiches, soups, salads, and other specials is a continuation of the bar's popular Sunday brunch. Overall, a very successful transplant.

The Northside, 1635 N Damen, Chicago, IL 60647, 312/384-3555. Daily 11 am–2 am.

Best seedy dive for late-night rock 'n' roll

The Lakeview Lounge

Every Thursday through Saturday night from 10 pm all the way to 4 or 5 am, three rock 'n' roll veterans who call themselves Night Watch (and who range in age from about late '20s to mid-'50s) pump out a never-ending stream of pop and country-tinged hits from the 1950s, 1960s, and 1970s from a stage that is improbably set right behind the bar, between the liquor bottles. A stripped-down combo featuring a bass player, guitarist, and drummer (and a friendly owner/bartender who chimes in occasionally on tambourine), Night Watch entertains a motley crew of Uptown denizens looking for a little bit of no-cover fun before heading home to their fleabag apartments. This is the kind of place you could charitably refer to as a "bucket of blood," but the mood of the customers is generally jovial and the band is both a rip-roaring hoot (especially on such cover-band staples as "Viva Las Vegas") and sometimes something of a musical revelation (especially on their superb Santana numbers). Best of all, you can play "stump the band" by dropping a few bucks in the tip jar and hollering out the name of an obscure golden oldie; chances are, these guys will know it well enough to nail it cold. Remember the scene from *The Blues Brothers* when Elwood Blues tells the crowd at Bob's Country Bunker, "You don't have to go home, but you can't stay here"? Well, The Lakeview Lounge is the perfect bar to head to when every other self-respecting tavern has shown you the door.

The Lakeview Lounge, 5110 N Broadway Ave, Chicago, IL 60660, 312/769-0994. Live music Thu–Fri, 10 pm–4 am, Sat 10 pm–5 am.

MUSIC, ENTERTAINMENT, & NONPUB NIGHTLIFE

Best big bands for ballroom buffs

Walnut Room, The Bismarck Hotel

How's your tango, foxtrot, and cha-cha? If they're rusty—or even nonexistent—it doesn't really matter. You can fake it and still have fun at this restored showroom where "everything old is new again." On selected Friday nights big band ballroom dancing returns to the Oak Room, where couples can enjoy dinner and/or drinks and dance the night away on a 1,200-square-foot terrazzo dance floor beneath glittering chandeliers imported from Berlin in 1926. The bands of Jimmy Dorsey, Count Basie, and Stanley Paul are among those that play this room, which attracts a crowd that includes a surprising number of X-ers along with the fleet-footed silver-haired couples seen tripping the light fantastic. Frequent requests include Glenn Miller's "String of Pearls," Hoagy Carmichael's "Stardust," and "Chattanooga Choo Choo," usually with harmonizing by the band's featured vocalists.

Walnut Room, The Bismarck Hotel, 171 W Randolph St, Chicago, IL 60601, 312/236-0123.

Fieriest flamenco dancing

La Perla

In the heart of Madrid, the Café de Chinitas offers a combination of good food and fiery flamenco dancing. In the heart of Illinois, there also is such a café, where the food has the magic of the Mediterranean and the dancing, accompanied by the clacking of castanets, the clapping of hands, and the staccato beat of tapping heels, is pure Spain. In western suburban Hillside, where expatriate Spaniard Emilio Gervilla opened his wonderful tapas restaurant, Emilio's (see separate listing in "Dining"), this energetic and creative restaurateur has opened another eatery offering a colorful blend of food and entertainment from around the Mediterranean shores. Once a month, on a Thursday evening, there are performances by authentic Spanish flamenco dancers and the spellbinding, soul-stirring instrumentation of a flamenco guitarist. Also once a month, on a Wednesday, the restaurant presents Argentinean tango dancers—and *every* week on Fridays and Saturdays there is entertainment by a jazz trio or jazz pianist. Those who go for the food will find a range of Emilio's acclaimed tapas: hot varieties that include mussels baked with a curry tomato glaze; roasted eggplant with fresh herbs, goat cheese, and basil; and cold tapas such as dolmades (Greek-style grape leaves stuffed with lamb, Spanish sausage, tomato, and red pepper); and humus, the famous dish of North Africa—a chick-pea purée with olive oil and lemon served with flat bread. Entrées include some extraordinary pizzas (including a Moroccan version) and casserole Marseilles—Emilio's variation of bouillabaisse that blends shrimp, scallops, clams, oysters, fish, and vegetables in a tomato-saffron broth.

La Perla, 2135 S Wolf Rd, Hillside, IL 60162, 708/449-1070. Mon–Thu 11:30 am–10 pm, Fri 11:30 am–midnight, Sat 5 pm–midnight, Sun 5–9 pm.

Best cabaret for movie ghosts

Green Orchid Room, The Bismarck Hotel

It's a bar like something out of a 1940s movie. You walk up a short flight of stairs from the art deco lobby, through etched-glass doors guarded by a pair of six-foot, gleaming metal ornaments resembling abstract palm trees, and you half expect to see tough-talking Alan Ladd, gangster-boss George Raft, and Veronica Lake of the peek-a-boo hairdo. You *will* find a subdued atmosphere with soft lighting and mellow music. Low-key cabaret-style entertainment is provided by a jazz trio or a piano-playing chanteuse rendering nostalgic numbers such as "Pennies from Heaven," "The Nearness of You," and "Bewitched,

Bothered, and Bewildered." Decor of this intimate room is a tony match of deep emerald and light green, colors picked up in the styling of roomy booths along one wall, each with a miniature green-shaded table light. In the center of the room, candles flicker on small tables covered with white linen and attended by art deco chairs with wooden bucket backs. Along one wall is an ornate wooden back bar retrieved from a tavern in southern Wisconsin. Full bar service and a light menu is offered.

Green Orchid Room, The Bismarck Hotel, 171 W Randolph St, Chicago, IL 60601, 312/236-0123. Hours vary seasonally.

Smallest big-time night club
The Gold Star Sardine Bar

It is aptly named, this stylish club in the handsome old Furniture Mart. It is tiny, and when it gets packed, as it does on weekends, you practically have to shoulder your way in and stand elbow-to-elbow. But it does attract the stars. Tony Bennett showed up unannounced one night when I was there, and the wall of fame outside lists dozens of Gold Star alumni, including Liza Minnelli, Bobby Short, Woody Herman, and Buddy Rich. Count Basie once played a set with a 16-piece band and almost literally brought the house down. Celebrities aside, it is worth going to listen to the sweet, mellow voice of classically trained Patricia Barber, a long-time regular, as she feelingly turns out a modern-jazz classic or some George Gershwin or Cole Porter. She's been the in-house singer-pianist since 1984 and performs on Tuesdays, usually accompanied by bass and drums. Count Basie's "Shining Stockings" is her most requested number. Food runs mostly to soups, salads, and sandwiches, including White Castle sliders—accompanied by a wide-ranging list of champagne. Near the door is a quote from the *New York Times:* "Easily the best cabaret in America." This small, intimate room is primarily a serious *listening* place—with burly men ready to shush—and possibly eject—those who insist on competing with the entertainment.

The Gold Star Sardine Bar, 680 N Lake Shore Dr, Chicago, IL 60611, 312/664-4215. Mon–Fri noon–2 am, Sat 7 pm–3 am.

Classiest club for music, conversation, and dining
Yvette

This club hits the mark on all three above-mentioned considerations. Music? Most certainly, courtesy of its trademark dual pianos. Conversation?

Sure—especially over drinks, espresso, or cappuccino, perhaps while idly doodling on the paper table coverings with a selection of provided crayons. Food? Definitely. Yvette serves a terrific bistro-style menu of appetizers (excellent gravlax, homemade pâté, and salads) and simple yet elegant and nicely achieved entrées. Try the tender sautéed veal medallions, with shallots and mushroom sauce and served over angel hair pasta or any of the menu's fresh fish dishes. Yvette is a perfect place to linger among the gentle strains of Gershwin, Porter, or Berlin on the piano while sharing a dessert or a coffee.

Yvette, 1206 N State St, Chicago, IL 60610, 312/280-1700. Mon–Thu 5 pm–midnight, Fri & Sat 5 pm–2 am, Sun 11:30 am–4 pm, 5 pm–midnight.

Best jazz cellar
The Bulls

If you've a mind to listen to modern jazz in a club with a modest $5 cover charge (Monday through Thursday), then you'll definitely want to visit this long-established jazz cellar. For more than 30 years, this Lincoln Park hot spot has been the stage for many Chicago musicians. More than a few nationally and internationally known artists got their first break here. Inside this dark, cavernous club are stuccoed walls (which enhance acoustics) and a small elevated stage looking onto a scattering of small tables. Although modern mainstream and some traditional jazz are the emphasis here, other types of groups, such as the Reginald T. McCants Ensemble, Symbia, and the Ken Chaney Xperience play on occasion. There's a pretty good sound system, and don't be surprised if a local radio station is conducting a live broadcast from the locale. Drinks are a little pricey, so those on tight budgets will need to sip slowly. For a good seat, it's essential to go early.

The Bulls, 1916 N Lincoln Park West, Chicago, IL 60614, 312/337-3000. Daily 8 pm–4 am (music starts at 9:30 pm).

Best jazz club where Satchmo's drummer sits in
Andy's

Over the years, Andy's has blossomed from a blue/white collar saloon into a renowned jazz club, although it remains a friendly, neighborhood place. Its "Jazz at Five" program (weekdays 5–8:30 pm) makes it a great after-work spot to relax with a drink and some good music. With walls covered with photographs of jazz luminaries and banners from Chicago

Jazz Festivals past (many festival performers appear on Andy's stage), this big, shabby saloon looks like a warehouse that rehabbers didn't get to yet. But the cozy darkness, bright neon signs and Tiffany-style lamps, red oilcloths on worn tables, and pure high C notes from a lead trumpet can transport you to the Mississippi Delta. You can order up some potato skins, a surprisingly good thin-crust pizza, and a variety of sandwiches. Each weekday evening features its own particular players—Mondays through Wednesdays, for example, the talented John Barry Quintet performs. Guest musicians often sit in— sometimes including octogenarian Barrett Deems, drummer for the late Louis Armstrong's All Stars.

Andy's, 11 E Hubbard St, Chicago, IL 60611, 312/ 642-6805. Mon–Thu 11:30 am–midnight, Fri 11:30 am–1:15 am, Sat 6:30 pm–1 am.

Best avant-garde jazz club

Weeds

This, in the best possible connotation of the word, is a dive: small, cramped, dark, with a decor that can be best described as chaotic (posters, artwork, objects hanging from the ceiling). Aficionados hang out to hear heartfelt, eclectic music—maybe garage-band rock one night, maybe acoustic folk another. At other times, it may be experimental jazz—such as an understated yet powerful version of the jazz classic "A Night in Tunisia" that we heard a spare trio (whose drummer was the teenage son of the bass player) perform here one time. Everyone can feel welcome at Weeds (from suits to jeans), but it most decidedly is *not* for everyone.

Weeds, 1555 N Dayton, Chicago, IL 60622, 312/943- 7815. Mon–Fri 3:30 pm–2 am, Sat 3:30 pm–3 am.

Noisiest Dixieland jazz spot

Dick's Last Resort

This waterside restaurant and bar was the first to open in the rehabbed North Pier complex and drew big crowds. Although the converted red-brick warehouse since has filled up with bars, restaurants, shops, and museums, providing new diversions for its fun-seeking patrons, Dick's seems as crowded— and as noisy—as ever. Probably it is because the big buckets of ribs are as satisfying as they are messy and the brand of Dixieland jazz—the likes of Jim Clark's Jazz People and Frank Jackson's Jazz Entertainers—is as entertaining as it is loud. The chairs are mismatched, the tables are battered, and the wiseacre waiters must have studied at Ed Debevic's. But this is a fun spot. The beer is cold and the food is good and plentiful, including chicken, pork chops, catfish, frog legs, crab legs, and shrimp. Look for Dick's funny, cartoony ads—which sum up the joint's attitude perfectly—in the *Reader* or in the Friday weekend preview sections of Chicago's two dailies. And don't miss Dick's Sunday Gospel Brunch—it's a revelation.

Dick's Last Resort, North Pier, 435 E Illinois St, Chicago, IL 60611, 312/836-7870. Mon–Thu 11 am–2 am, Fri 11 am–4 am, Sat 10:30 am–3 am, Sun 10:30 am–1 am.

Best live music club—jazz

Joe Segal's Jazz Showcase

A sometimes quirky but always important figure, Joe Segal has been a legendary presence on the city's jazz scene since the late 1940s. His once-wandering club (now comfortably ensconced in the Blackstone Hotel) consistently plays host to the biggest names in jazz music, including out-of-town acts that rarely play the city's other clubs (with the exception of the much small Gold Star Sardine Bar—see separate listing). The Jazz Showcase especially jumps during August—which it celebrates as Charlie Parker Month (featuring music and musicians associated with the late "Bird")—and during the city's Jazz Festival (late August–early September), when many of the performers stop by after their sets in nearby Grant Park for late-night jam sessions. *A curious fact:* This is the only nonsmoking jazz club in the city (and, perhaps, the only one *anywhere*).

Joe Segal's Jazz Showcase, Blackstone Hotel, 636 S Michigan Ave, Chicago, IL 60615, 312/427-4846. Hours and days vary; often closed for weeks at a time (especially in winter).

Best live music club—folk

Old Town School of Folk Music

Not quite a club, but more than a school—this is a versatile landmark in the world of folk music and the focal point of folk activity in Chicago. The remodeled-in-1989 building houses a main concert hall, a variety of other performance spaces and classrooms, and even a museum and music store. Fans can see big and up-and-coming acts in folk and other traditional music forms—and they can also sign up for classes in guitar, banjo, fiddle, and other musical instruments. If folk music is your passion, this is a comfortable hangout to meet like-minded enthusiasts.

Old Town School of Folk Music, 909 W Armitage Ave, Chicago, IL 60614, 312/525-7793. Days & hours vary with schedule.

Best live music club—alternative/punk

Metro

If you're not into Gershwin or Rachmaninoff, here's a spot in town where you can see such bands as Nine Inch Nails or Veruca Salt or PJ Harvey. Just wait until dark, put on your black clothes and your I-don't-care-about-anything face, and head up Clark Street, just past Wrigley Field, to this music-and-dance club. On the multiple levels of this yin/yang, ornate/run-down building, you can find loud live music; sweaty dance floors; and a dark, atmospheric bar. Attracts a mixed crowd, including true music-lovers and just-in-it-for-the-look poseurs, city-dwellers (out in force every night) and suburbanites (found more typically on the weekends), and young punkers and grizzled scene veterans.

Metro, 3730 N Clark St, Chicago, IL 60613, 312/549-3604. Bar open Sun–Fri 9:30 pm–4 am, Sat 9:30 pm–5 am; showtimes and dates vary with acts.

Grungiest live-music club

The Double Door

Although adherents of such grunge-rock Meccas as Lincoln Park's Lounge Ax (2438 N Lincoln Ave) and Wrigleyville's Metro (see separate listing) will argue that their hangouts have more history behind them, the new Double Door is located just south of the very epicenter of Chicago hip—the intersection of North, Damen, and Milwaukee avenues, which comprises the heart of Wicker Park. This working-class Polish and Hispanic neighborhood has been transformed in recent years into a Generation X playground replete with bookstores, coffee shops, record stores, bars, and restaurants catering to the twentysomething crowd. The Double Door, located on the site of a seedy liquor store of the same name, books local, American, and British bands that hope to follow in the hit-making footsteps of such popular Chicago acts as Liz Phair, Urge Overkill, and Smashing Pumpkins. A midsize venue, the Double Door specializes in the kind of high-decibel, rough-and-tumble concert experiences guaranteed to give migraines to anyone old enough to remember Watergate.

The Double Door, 1572 N Milwaukee Ave, Chicago, IL 60647, 312/489-3160. Thu–Fri 8 pm–2 am; Sat 8 pm–3 am; Sun 8 pm–2 am.

Best live music theater—soul

The New Regal Theatre

This lavishly remodeled (at a cost of several million dollars) theater continues a rich heritage and presents some of the top acts in soul, rhythm-and-blues, and popular black music. Named for the South Side's former grandiose Regal Theatre (which played host to such stars as Sammy Davis, Jr., Duke Ellington, Louis Armstrong, and Nat "King" Cole from 1928 to 1973), the New Regal was created out of the old Avalon Theatre, a classic movie palace dating from 1927, retaining the Avalon's ornate lobby design and intricate mosaics. Today, this restored theater is carrying on the tradition of the original Regal, bringing top-name acts and other special presentations to the South Side. Among the personalities that have appeared at the New Regal are Gladys Knight and the Pips, Natalie Cole, Patti Labelle, and B.B. King, as well as performances by the Dance Theater of Harlem and of *Sarafina!* the acclaimed musical about South Africa.

The New Regal Theatre, 1645 E 79th St, Chicago, IL 60649, 312/721-9230.

Best live music clubs—blues

B.L.U.E.S. & Kingston Mines

These twin poles of the mighty Chicago blues scene sit across Halsted Street from each other. Neither is exactly pristine (although, between the two of them, Kingston Mines wins the award for unabashed grunginess), and both usually end up being suffocatingly crowded on weekend nights. But, that's what the blues are all about. Both places offer live music seven nights a week, with the performers being a good mix of national stars (admittedly a relative word in the world of blues) and local bands. Come early (for a hard-to-get seat), stay late (time will likely seem to fly), pound a few liquid-replacing cold brews, and just groove along with the band, knowing that, at that very moment, you are within the few-hundred-foot Ground Zero of the worldwide blues scene.

B.L.U.E.S., 2519 N Halsted St, Chicago, IL 60614, 312/528-1012. Sun–Fri 8 pm–4 am, Sat 8 pm–5 am.
Kingston Mines, 2548 N Halsted St, Chicago, IL 60614, 312/477-4646. Sun–Fri 8 pm–4 am, Sat 8 pm–5 am.

Best live music spot to have a (bowling) ball

Fireside Bowl

Playing host to a young, mostly suburban crowd on concert nights, the Fireside is an extremely likable, surprisingly low-key music venue that just happens to double as an old bowling alley. Although its West Side Bucktown surroundings are on the shabby side, the Fireside is a safe place to hear the latest home-grown alternative rock bands. And nobody seems to mind that several members of the audience invariably try to pile up strikes and spares while the bands play on a small stage at the west end of the spacious room. Cover charges vary, but they're usually only a couple of bucks; the drinks are cheap as well. You might have to wait a while to rent shoes while the beleagured counter man dashes into the adjacent bar to fill orders, but considering the low cost of a night at the Fireside, it's easy to overlook such minor inconveniences. (Plus, at $1.50 per line and $1 for shoe rental, this is a great bowling bargain even when there's no band playing.)

Fireside Bowl, 2646 W Fullerton Ave, Chicago, IL 60647, 312/486-2700. Mon–Sun 7:30 pm–2 am.

Best blues club run by a Chicago blues legend

Buddy Guy's Legends

Just south of the Loop, at the corner of Eighth Street and Wabash Avenue, sits the home of another blues icon, Buddy Guy. Housed in side-by-side former storefronts, Legends is spacious, clean, and offers good sight lines to a raised stage. This may seem to break the mold of the usually grungy Chicago blues club—but, as ever, the proof is in the playing, and Legends attracts a variety of fine local and national acts. Extra added bonus—the presence (when he's in town) of the club's namesake, whom Eric Clapton once called the finest blues guitarist he'd ever heard. And, when Buddy's around, you never know when his rock-blues pals, such as Clapton or members of the Rolling Stones, might show up to jam with him.

Buddy Guy's Legends, 754 W Wabash Ave, Chicago, IL 60605, 312/427-0333. Sun–Fri 4 pm–2 am, Sat 4 pm–3 am.

Best "Harlem comes to the South Side" club

The Cotton Club

Stylish, hot (as in "cool"), and often packed, this semirecreation of the classic Harlem nightclub is one of the places to see and be seen on the South Side. It attracts a professional crowd of mostly "Buppies" (Black Urban Professionals) from across the city and nearby suburbs. They flock here both for jumping live jazz music and thumping disco dancing—in separate rooms (although there can be some mildly disturbing sound crossover when the disco is particularly loud and the jazz a bit more subtle). Check out the photos of performers who graced the club's Big Apple namesake during the "Harlem Renaissance" of the 1920s. Patrons here like to dress to the nines—you'll want to, as well.

The Cotton Club, 1710 S Michigan Ave, Chicago, IL 60616, 312/341-9787. Sun–Thu 5 pm–2 am, Fri 5 pm–4 am, Sat 8 pm–5 am.

Rousingest reggae club

Wild Hare & Singing Armadillo Frog Sanctuary

There are basically two ways to get to Jamaica from Chicago. One is by hopping a plane from O'Hare—the other (cheaper, but admittedly more temporary) way is to visit a little bit of it at this club just south of Wrigley Field. At the Wild Hare, you'll find live reggae seven nights a week from both local and national bands, cold Red Stripe beer (direct from the islands), and a copious variety of rum-and-fruit-juice drinks. Not much dancing space . . . but everyone crowds into it when the seductive reggae beat takes over. Across the street is Exedus II, the city's other primary reggae club. (P.S. A third way to get a taste—quite literally—of Jamaica is dinner at the Caribbean Delight (see separate listing, "Dining") run by Jamaican expatriate Irene Daley.

Wild Hare & Singing Armadillo Frog Sanctuary, 3530 N Clark St, Chicago, IL 60657, 312/327-4273. Sun–Fri 8 pm–2 am, Sat 8 pm–3 am.

Best club where both the food and music are "hot"

Bossa Nova

You say you *are* the two it takes to tango, and that you're ready to samba or dance to a reggae beat? You'll find it all at this hip club, which, like its namesake dance, blends the music and rhythms of South America and their African roots—and then takes it all several steps further. "Global" is the term owners Roger Greenfield and Ted Kasemir like to hang on their highly successful club, which features jazz, salsa, big band, reggae, or samba and offers cuisine that has Mediterranean, Spanish, Pan-Asian, and Caribbean influences. The beat begins at the club's elevated bandstand weekdays at 8 pm, Fridays and Saturdays at 10 pm. In this setting, tapas are ideal edibles—try pan-roasted venison medallions served with black-eyed pea chili and crisp corn tortillas; wok-seared prawns with grilled polenta and charred tomato salsa; or seared beef tenderloin with chipotle hazelnut sauce, root vegetable chips, and salsa. Entrées include the likes of boneless chicken breast, grilled lamb tostada, mahi mahi, and spiced pork tenderloin. Potables include Jamaican Red Stripe and Brazilian Xingu Black beer, and a range of potent cocktails including the "Martini From Hell" (with the heat of scotch bonnet chili peppers) and the eponymous Bossa Nova (a blend of overproof rums aged Brazilian-style with pineapple and orange juices—and with a limit of two per person). The ambience is as eclectic as the food and music—a mix of rustic and contemporary industrial design, with pinspot lighting, gilded mirrors, mahogany antebellum shutters, leather banquettes, and heavy velvet draping—all in warm earth tones.

Bossa Nova, 1960 N Clybourn Ave, Chicago, IL 60614, 312/248-4800. Mon–Wed 5:30–10:30 pm, Thu 5:30–11:30 pm, Fri & Sat 5:30 pm–1:30 am.

Best café where they don't serve food

B Side Café

Come to this Lincoln Park club with an appetite for dance and you won't be disappointed; the B Side serves up platter after platter of red-hot "house" and hip-hop music in a space that formerly catered to hard rockers as the Avalon. Completely restyled both physically and attitudinally, the B Side rarely starts jumping before midnight, making it a candidate for a last stop on a Chicago club-hopping tour. After arriving through sensually arched doorways and hallways decked out in corrugated aluminum, hip young patrons make a splash on the large, polished-wood dance floor while more sedate night owls take in the show from the many comfortable overstuffed chairs set up along the walls. The club boasts an eclectic mix of live music and DJs, so you might want to call ahead to find out what type of groove you're in for on any given night.

B Side Café, 959 W Belmont Ave, Chicago, IL 60657, 312/472-3020. Wed–Fri 10 pm–2 am, Sat 10 pm–3 am.

Best club to see (and be) Elvis
Vinyl

If Elvis really was seen, it most probably was at this restaurant/nightclub that features what may be the most entertaining Sunday brunch in the city. From 10 am to 3 pm, the North Clybourn eatery is transformed into Graceland North as a couple of Elvis impersonators drape their scarves over unsuspecting diners while the King's music plays in the background and his movies run on a big-screen TV. Everywhere you turn, you'll be reminded of Big E, as Vinyl is a shrine of ticky-tacky Elvis busts and the like. Laminated 8" x 10"s of the King serve as placemats; even ashtrays have Elvis's picture. Gum-chewing waiters with cigarette packs tucked into T-shirt sleeves serve such libations as the Pink Cadillac and Bloody Priscilla. Brunch is served à la carte from the menu, with items ranging from $2.50 to $6.25. Pancakes are good (with bottles of pure maple syrup on the tables), as is Italian ham. But true Elvis fans will want to order the peanut butter and jelly French toast. Elvis fanatics will want to dress up like the King (they'll receive a free meal for their trouble)— even youngsters arrive in Elvis garb. Open every night for dinner, Vinyl features eclectic cuisine, where a Mexican selection of black bean and plantain empanadas with créme fraiche coexists alongside crab cake with celery root remoulade sauce and duck liver pâté with pistachio chutney. Live bands appear Wednesday and Thursday (Wednesday is Samba Bamba night) and DJs spin dance music Wednesday through Saturday. Stop by and hang out in the front bar or upstairs lounge, or stay for dinner (reservations are recommended on weekends).

Vinyl, 1615 N Clybourn Ave, Chicago, IL 60614, 312/587-8469. Sun 10 am–3 pm and 5:30–11 pm; Mon–Wed 5:30–11 pm; Thu 5:30 pm–midnight; Fri–Sat 5:30–1 am.

Most neighborly rock 'n' roll club
Cubby Bear Lounge

In the shadow of Wrigley Field, just kitty-corner from the old ballyard, sits this somewhat-split-personality club. During baseball season, an eclectic group of Cubs fans (from cigar-chomping, Old Style-drinkers to the college-sweatshirt crowd) have a few cold ones before or after the team's day games. But at night, rock 'n' rollers and other neighborhood dwellers head there for cheap and loud music (a good mix of local bands and cultish national acts), a comfortable atmosphere, and a variety of inexpensive munchies.

The bands can vary from hard-core punk to straight-ahead pop music to the occasional jazz or reggae combo; check ahead if you have very definite tastes. Those who remember the bar as a dark, dingy place will find that renovations have spruced it up a bit—without glossing over the joint's worn and tattered ambience.

Cubby Bear Lounge, 1059 W Addison St, Chicago, IL 60613, 312/327-1662. Sun–Fri 5 pm–2 am, Sat 5 pm–3 am; also usually open before and after Cubs home games during baseball season.

Best live music—stadiums
The Rosemont Horizon

Its birth was troubled (the half-finished frame collapsed, killing a number of workers), and its sound is often suspicious at best (and downright muddy at worst), but this big barn near O'Hare International Airport attracts the big-name acts and is the metro area's primary concert venue. (Did we say "near" the airport? A major flight path rumbles directly over the stadium, but the music—*usually*—drowns out the sound of the planes.) The Horizon's schedule offers mostly rock events, with some country and soul music. In addition to concerts, the multipurpose stadium hosts wrestling matches, "monster truck" events, and annual circus visits (the Moscow Circus, in our book, is tops). Each fall and winter, the CBA basketball Chicago Rockets and the International Hockey League Chicago Wolves play their home games at the Horizon.

The Rosemont Horizon, 6920 N Mannheim Rd, Rosemont, IL 60018. 847/635-6601.

Best live music—open air
World Music Theatre

For open-air rock and pop music (with a smattering of jazz, classical, and country music thrown in for good measure), the World offers the best of many worlds. With better acoustics than its north suburban predecessor, the late Poplar Creek Music Theater, and greater seating capacity than any other outdoor music pavilion and performance venue in North America, the World rocks hard. Located southwest of Chicago near I-80, the venue hosts the biggest of the big-name acts that play the area during the summer. With a mix of fixed pavilion seating and first-come, first-serve lawn spaces, the World accommodates 27,000 music lovers. A busy summer schedule includes the likes of Anita Baker, Fleetwood Mac, Black Sabbath, Van Halen, Chicago, Steve

Miller, The Beach Boys, and—yes!—the Mighty
Morphin Power Rangers. (Note to aging rock fans: A
community-imposed noise curfew ensures that you'll
be snug in your bed well before the cows come
home.)

World Music Theatre, Ridgeland Ave and Flossmoor
Rd, Tinley Park, IL 60477, 708/614-1616. Season runs
from late May through September.

Best live symphonic music hall
Orchestra Hall

Home to the Chicago Symphony Orchestra (see
separate listing) since 1905, Orchestra Hall has long
been a Michigan Avenue landmark and the unofficial
(yet undisputed) capital of classical music in Chicago. When the CSO isn't in residence here, Orchestra Hall plays host to touring orchestras, smaller
classical groups, choruses, and special concerts by
"name" performers in classical music. A popular
annual event is December's "Do-It-Yourself Messiah,"
when the hall is packed with amateur singers, who
enthusiastically belt out Handel's classic music to
the accompaniment of an orchestral ensemble. The
hall's sound is impeccable, and the sight lines, even
from the nosebleed seats, are mostly above average.
Trivia note: The hall's full (but rarely used) name is
Theodore Thomas Orchestra Hall; it was named after
the CSO's founder.

Orchestra Hall, 220 S Michigan Ave, Chicago, IL
60604, 312/435-6666.

Arguably the best orchestra in the world
The Chicago Symphony Orchestra

Quick quiz: Who has received the most Grammies,
the highest award for recorded music? It isn't Barbra
Streisand or Pavarotti, or even the Beatles and the
Rolling Stones combined. The answer is Sir Georg
Solti, whose 28 Grammies (mostly acquired with the
Chicago Symphony Orchestra) tops them all. The
1990–1991 season marked both the CSO's 100th
anniversary and Sir Georg's last year as music director (he continues as an occasional guest conductor). In the wake of his 20-plus-years with the CSO,
Sir Georg left the orchestra even stronger and more
highly regarded than it was when he began. This is
not only one of the top recording and touring orchestras in the world, but also the highly treasured
crowning jewel of cultural Chicago. Whatever the
scheduled program, a CSO performance (at Orchestra Hall—see separate listing) is one of the best

entertainments in town. The orchestra's current music director, the respected pianist and conductor Daniel Barenboim, delivers more of the same.

The Chicago Symphony Orchestra, Orchestra Hall, 220 S Michigan Ave, Chicago, IL 60604, 312/435-6666. Season runs from approximately late September through mid-June.

Best place to hear the fat lady sing

Lyric Opera of Chicago

Controversial public-utilities executive Samuel Insull built Commonwealth Edison into a powerhouse—literally and figuratively. In the 1930s, he ran afoul of the public and the law and was thrice tried—and acquitted—on fraud and other charges following the collapse of his holding company. Insull's most lasting legacy may be the massive 45-story skyscraper he built in 1929, which houses what is internationally acclaimed as one of the world's best opera companies. The Italian government long ago recognized Lyric's importance by making a precedent-shattering grant-across-the-seas, and since has conferred one of its highest decorations on Lyric's world-admired General Director, Ardis Krainik. Throughout the subscription season, the Lyric regularly produces opera with international big-name, big-voice stars such as Placido Domingo and Kiri Te Kanawa. In addition to classical grand opera, the Lyric also produces experimental works, such as Frank Galati's avant-garde staging of Dominick Argento's opera The Voyage of Edgar Allan Poe. In 1985, Lyric introduced projected English titles on an over-the-stage screen. The handsome art deco interior is rich with elaborate ornamentation in red and gold. Outside, the masks of tragedy and comedy are carved in the ornate terra-cotta above the imposing colonnaded entrance.

The Lyric Opera of Chicago, Civic Opera House, 20 N Wacker Dr, Chicago, IL 60606, 312/332-2244. Season runs from approximately September through February.

Trendiest dance spot

Shelter

Long lines outside of a former warehouse, doormen playing club-god ("You, you, and you, go ahead; sorry, sir, members only tonight."), and a cavernous room of smoke, lasers, mirrored balls, and even lava lamps. Yes, one of the first examples in Chicago of an oh-so-hip, who-do-you-know?, too-cool-for-its-own-good type of New York dance club is still going

strong after several years as *the* place to be. The
music is loud (mostly dance-pop, alternative rock,
and beat-heavy "house" music), the decor is dark,
and the people strive to be "beautiful." Wear black;
brush up on your attitude; and prepare to dance,
pose, see, and be seen. If you're an inveterate club-
hopper, you'll probably love Shelter; if you're not,
you may be amused to discover what all the fuss is
about. Cover varies.

Shelter, 564 W Fulton St, Chicago, IL 60606, 312/
648-5500. Thu & Fri 9 pm–4 am, Sat 9 pm–5 am.

Best dance spot under the palms

Yvette's Wintergarden

Don't tell Harry Connick, Jr., that Chicago's Loop is
comatose after hours. Coaxed to the piano bar at
this stylish bistro, the entertainer lingered to play
for two hours. It is located in a postmodern 65-story
granite-and-glass skyscraper—in the atrium, where
palm trees soar 50 feet and a waterfall cascades. It
attracts Lyric Opera goers with pre-performance dinners and late-evening diners with its comfortable
ambience. There's dancing to a combo and a con-
vivial piano bar where you may catch sight of celebrity patrons. Not too long ago the heart of downtown
Chicago was dark and dangerous after business
hours. "When I opened this restaurant in 1990, I
knew I was taking a gamble, but I had faith in the
Loop," says Bob Djahanguiri, who pioneered the
bistro concept in Chicago when he opened the elegant Yvette on State Street. Today, as the Loop
sheds its sepulchral image, Yvette's Wintergarden
flourishes as a business lunch spot and supper club.

Yvette's Wintergarden, 311 S Wacker Dr, Chicago,
IL 60606, 312/408-1242. Mon–Thu 11:30 am–10:30
pm, Fri 11:30 am–11:30 pm, Sat 5–11:30 pm.

Most traditional celebrity dance spot

The Pump Room

It's not a dance spot, per se, but on weekends people
do like to get up to dance to a three-piece band. It's
probably because the Pump Room has such an aura
of stardom. Humphrey Bogart and Lauren Bacall
had their wedding breakfast here. Frank Sinatra has
been a regular (when he's in town) for about 40
years, and stars such as Clark Gable, Cary Grant,
and Katherine Hepburn were visitors—as was Queen
Elizabeth II. The room opened in 1938, and during
the era of coast-to-coast train travel, stars would
detrain in Chicago expressly for the purpose of being
wined, dined, and seen in the Pump Room's famous

Booth One. The room's celebrity following is chronicled in a fascinating gallery of photographs adorning the foyer. American cuisine features prime rib, double-cut lamb chops, and crispy roasted duck and desserts such as strawberries Romanoff and lemon meringue pie.

Pump Room (Omni Ambassador East Hotel), 1301 N State Pkwy, Chicago, IL 60610, 312/266-0360. Mon–Thu 7 am–9:45 pm, Fri & Sat 7 am–11:45 pm, Sun 7 am–9:45 pm.

Most popular spot for dancing, billiards, & assorted sports

Excalibur

Previously the Limelight nightclub, this sprawling, castle-like building (that in yet another former life housed the Chicago Historical Society), constructed of huge bricks and incorporating lion statues to greet patrons at the door, now houses one of Chicago's nouvelle-hip clubs. Often-long lines and overpriced drinks do little to inhibit the club's popularity when weekends roll around. Inside is a combination amusement arcade–dance club. Upstairs patrons immerse themselves in pulsating dancing on a large, perpetually crowded dance floor. On the main level is more dancing—and some listening to live performances. The basement offers refuge from the pervasive heat, with billiards and video games. People-watching is good sport. The parade ranges from a younger crowd clad in black to tentative business execs arriving straight from office or convention hotel (with every conceivable mix in between). Comely waitresses wander the floor offering buckshots of some indescribable liquid, while patrons play electronic trivia with hand-held controls as they view overhead monitors. Excalibur is a giant, not-so-adult playgound—but at least provides an interesting contrast to some of the tamer Chicago clubs of this large size.

Excalibur, 632 N Dearborn St, Chicago, IL 60610, 312/266-1944. Mon–Fri 4 pm–4 am, Sat 4 pm–5 am, Sun 4 pm–4 am.

Tiniest dance spot really a restaurant

Gordon

One of the most sophisticated restaurants and innovative kitchens in town also is a nice spot to dance the night away or listen to soothing late-night jazz. On Fridays from 8 pm until midnight and Saturdays from 9 pm to 1 am, a jazz combo (the Nancy Keppel Duo is a regular) plays music for listening and dancing. You can order light—perhaps simply dessert and champagne. Or half portions of all standard menu items are available at half price plus $1. The wine list includes 15 French champagnes. The flourless chocolate cake with bittersweet chocolate mousse has been served at the restaurant since 1976 and defines the genre. Interesting appetizers include smoked salmon twist served on a potato pancake with four caviars, seafood and lobster egg roll with seaweed salad, and simple-but-well-prepared artichoke fritters with Béarnaise. If you dine earlier, there is live piano music nightly (6–10 pm).

Gordon, 500 N Clark St, Chicago, IL 60610, 312/467-9780. Mon–Thu 11:30 am–9:30 pm, Fri 11:30 am–12:30 am, Sat 5:30 pm–12:30 am, Sun 11 am–9:30 pm. Brunch Sun 11 am–2 pm. Lunch Mon–Fri 11:30 am–2 pm. Dinner Sun–Thu 5:30–9:30 pm; Fri, Sat 5:30–midnight.

Best new wave dance club (that looks like a street)

Neo

After entering a long, narrow alley off Clark Street in the Lincoln Park neighborhood, you walk through a door and suddenly find yourself—on Lower Wacker Drive? Actually, it's a dance club fashioned to resemble the cement-gray-and-river-green roadway beneath the Loop. This long-time club is one of the twin peaks (with Exit) of the city's punk-new wave subculture. The latest, loudest music from the U.S. and the U.K. gets played, packing the dance floor. Service at the bar can be spotty (it's hard to catch a bartender's ear when the decibels are pumping), but dancing, not drinking, is the main pursuit anyway. Doesn't really start hopping until late, when throngs descend after 2 am bars and clubs close. *Fashion note to the uninitiated:* Wear lots of black.

Neo, 2350 N Clark St, Chicago, IL 60614, 312/528-2622. Sun–Thu 9 pm–4 am, Fri 6 pm–4 am, Sat 6 pm–5 am.

Best place to boogie while sampling the nation's top micro-brews

U.S. Beer Co.

This odd-shaped corner bar in the up-and-coming North Clybourn corridor was known as the Triangle from 1933 to 1995 and was known locally for its right-angle pool table. However, in 1995 the owners renamed the joint, got rid of the table, and became the hottest spot in the city to sample micro-brewed beers from around the United States. More than living up to its name, the U.S. Beer Co. serves up an ever-changing menu of more than 140 micro-brews, including 24 on tap. After sampling suds from the likes of Austin's Celis White or the popular Pyramid and Sierra Nevada lines, you can dance to live music Thursday through Sunday. Bands range from pop cover acts to local alternative rockers, with a little bit of everything hitting the stage on Sunday open-mike nights. Call ahead for a schedule.

U.S. Beer Co., 1801 N Clybourn Ave, Chicago, IL 60614, 312/871-7799. Sun–Fri 11 am–2 am, Sat 11 am–3 am.

Best gift of gabfests

TV Talk Shows

Television talk shows have become the talk of the town. New York has Dave Letterman, California has Jay Leno, and Chicago is home to the irrepressible Oprah Winfrey—plus a whole lot of wannabes. Since Oprah carved her niche in Chicago and throughout the nation with her popular daytime talk show, the airwaves have become crowded—good news for anyone wanting free tickets to join a talk-show audience. Oprah established her own studio called Harpo (that's Oprah spelled backwards) on the city's near west side and tickets to tapings of her show are the toughest to come by. Other options are Jenny Jones and Jerry Springer, who both tape their programs in the NBC Tower (which also offers 50-minute tours of its radio and TV studios; $5), and Mort Downey, Jr., who tapes at Orbis Studios (call for times and procedures for obtaining tickets).

The Downey Show, Orbis Studios, 100 S Sangamon Ave, 312/595-2960; Jenny Jones, NBC Tower, 454 N Columbus Dr, 312/836-9485; Jerry Springer, NBC Tower, 312/321-5350; Oprah Winfrey, Harpo Studios, 1058 W Washington St, 312/591-9222.

Best free long-running concert series

"Under the Picasso" Concerts

Back in 1992, the city ordered a giant birthday cake to celebrate the 25th birthday of the once-controversial sculpture created by Pablo Picasso. It seems that Chicagoans have come to accept—if not love—this abstract pile of steel that has become the city's unofficial symbol. The cake was lagniappe to those who head for the Richard J. Daley Center Plaza for its "Under the Picasso" program of concerts and

other activities. Presented at noon each weekday
year 'round, this free entertainment is held literally
in the shadow of the 50-foot-high untitled Cor-Ten
steel sculpture. When the weather turns, the concerts move into the Daley Center lobby. In a typical
month, this eclectic program regaled lunchtime
brown-baggers with a jazz trio, contemporary Brazilian music; a preview of a new musical; a flamenco
guitarist; a musical variety program by senior citizens; African dance; contemporary piano; a competition for street musicians; a Latin American music
festival; and performers from Puerto Rico, Mexico,
and Nigeria. There have been a children's choir celebrating Rosh Hashanah, the Jewish New Year, and
a weekly farmers' market. Changing art exhibits are
held in the Daley Center in conjunction with other
events.

"Under the Picasso" concerts, Richard J. Daley
Civic Center Plaza, Washington St between
Dearborn & Clark sts, Chicago, IL 60601, 312/346-
3278.

Choicest campus carillon concerts
Rockefeller Memorial Chapel

For a pleasant outing, explore leafy Hyde Park/
Kenwood and enjoy a carillon concert at a splendid
neo-Gothic chapel. The tree-lined streets and ivy-
covered towers of the University of
Chicago, along with rich swaths of parkland, give
this southeast corner of the city a dignified air,
reminiscent of one of Europe's great university towns.
When it was settled in the 1850s, Hyde Park became
Chicago's first suburb. Carillon concerts are given
at the Rockefeller Memorial Chapel on the East Campus. Designed by Bertram G. Goodhue, the architect
of the Empire State Building, this monumental neo-
Gothic chapel was built between 1926 and 1928.
Faced with Indiana limestone, it is embellished with
elaborate carvings, sculpture, and inscriptions. The
chapel's 207-foot tower houses what was, at the time
it was built, the world's second largest carillon, with
72 bells weighing a total of 220 tons. Tours of the
carillon are offered prior to concerts (phone for
schedule). In a neighborhood where town and gown
merge to create a stimulating intellectual environment, there is a wide-ranging calendar of events.
These include orchestral concerts hosted by the
chapel, including performances of Handel's *Messiah*.

Rockefeller Memorial Chapel, 5850 S Woodlawn
Ave, Chicago, IL 60637, 312/702-2100.

Best comedy club

Zanies

The presence of this longtime club, just a block south of Second City (see separate listing), makes Wells Street a great destination for laughs. The country's top stand-up acts (many direct from the late-night comedy pinnacles of *The Tonight Show* and *The Late Show with David Letterman*) regularly perform here, in the usually conducive atmosphere of a 100-seat club with a two-drink minimum. Famous comedy clubs such as the Improv have opened johnny-come-lately branches in Chicago in recent years, but Zanies remains a stalwart favorite in town for a night of comedy. Beware of sitting up front—audience members in the first two rows can be fair game for ridicule (or otherwise picking-on) from some comedians.

Zanies, 1548 N Wells St, Chicago, IL 60610, 312/337-4027. Days and hours vary with performance schedule; usually open Tue–Sun.

Best improvisational comedy

Second City

It wouldn't be too far-fetched to say that contemporary comedy (as seen at the hundreds of comedy clubs that have sprung up around the country and on late-night television) was born at this legendary club. Such disparate comedic talents as Shelly Berman, Mike Nichols and Elaine May, Joan Rivers, John Belushi, and Bill Murray trod the boards here, performing in Second City's semiannual "reviews"—shows of vignettes and skits which originate in improvisational rehearsals and are written solely by the ever-changing cast members. After almost 35 years, audiences still flock to these reviews for entertaining comedy and a chance to perhaps see future superstars. After regular performances of the scheduled review, a free-admission improv "jam session" takes place, often attracting visiting comedy stars or Second City alums (such as Jim Belushi, Betty Thomas, and George Wendt). Also at this Piper's Alley location is the Second City ETC—sort of the Second City junior-varsity squad, which also performs comedic reviews. *Adjacent entertainment:* Also in this complex is a three-screen movie theater and a long-runing interactive play, "Tony 'n' Tina's Wedding" (at which the entire audience are guests at a hokey parody of a New York-style Italian wedding).

Second City (and Second City ETC), 1616 N Wells St, Chicago, IL 60614, 312/337-3992. Tue–Sun, show times vary.

Best club with a silver screen

Brew & View at the Vic Theatre

You may have seen this Lincoln Park theater on TV
serving as the backdrop for cable stand-up comedy
specials, but that doesn't do justice to the hilarious
good time patrons seem to have on evenings when
this nightclub is transformed into a boozy movie
theater. Barring a concert or other special performance, the Brew & View screens a double-feature
of second-run thrillers or comedies every night of the
week—with a cult classic midnight flick (*Dazed &
Confused* is a perennial favorite) thrown in for no
extra charge Thursday, Friday, and Saturday nights.
Admission is $3 (and you have to be at least 18 to
get in), but that's only half the story; there's a special
deal on concessions and drinks every night. For
instance, on Tuesdays, Fridays, and Saturdays,
buying a $7 "Brew & View cup" allows you to drink
your fill of tap beer and well drinks all night long.
This policy leads to minor rowdiness, but beefy,
roaming ushers keep the shenanegins well under
control. Patrons on the lower level stake out tables
off the dance floor for chatting, smoking, drinking,
and inhaling greasy slices of pizza. Romantic types
and viewers with keen balance often choose to camp
out in the ultra-steep balcony section, which lies just
steps away from its own upstairs bar. Movie schedules vary day by day, so be sure to call in advance.

Brew & View at the Vic Theatre, 3145 N Sheffield
Ave, Chicago, IL 60657, 312/618-8439.

Best first-run movie theater

McClurg Court Theatre

In this day and age of duplex, multiplex, and octoplex
(and beyond) theaters, it's hard to find a great
uncramped spot to enjoy a *real* motion picture. Of
course, it doesn't really matter whether you see the
next *Friday the 13th* sequel in a shoebox or not, but
for the interesting and complicated works of compel-
ling directors such as Martin Scorsese and Francis
Coppola, you want a big-screened, comfortable theater—you want the huge, 70mm Dolby sound-
equipped main screen at McClurg Court. Hard to
believe, but this spacious theater was once even
larger before two additional, smaller theaters were
carved out of the old space. Unfortunately, you're
not as likely to see deserving works by lesser-known
(or just less commercial) filmmakers on the main
screen. But anytime a movie you want to see is
playing at the McClurg, it's worth a call to see

whether it's on the biggest screen. And, if it is, it's worth a special trip to see a movie the way it ought to be seen.

McClurg Court Theatre, 330 E Ohio St, Chicago, IL 60611, 312/642-0723.

Best independent movie theater

The Music Box

The only first-run independent movie house left in Chicago, this Wrigleyville landmark has delivered top-flight escapism on and off over the years since it first opened the day after the stock market crash of 1929. An old-fashioned marquee blurbs first-run, limited-showing "arty" and foreign films, midnight shows, and classic cartoon festivals. Arrive a few minutes early to take in the panoramic vista of clouds and a starry night sky stretching across the ceiling of the 750-seat main theater. A fine example of Moorish movie-palace architecture, the Music Box also features a 100-seat theater dedicated to documentaries. In addition to the first-run "art film" fare offered in the main theater since 1983, the Music Box packs in the crowds for its eclectic weekend matinee series and the cult classics it screens at midnight each Friday and Saturday. Be warned: Admission prices are as high as those at the multiplexes—unless you purchase a bargain, five-ticket pass for $25. An organist entertains between shows. (When the Chicago International Film Festival comes to town every November, many festival screenings are on the Dolby-stereo-equipped screen of this well-maintained old-time movie palace). *Snacking tip:* The candy counter carries a selection of munchables far superior to usual movie-theater fare.

The Music Box, 3733 N Southport Ave, Chicago, IL 60613, 312/871-6604.

Best small movie theater

The Fine Arts Theatres

The four small theaters in this complex were created in space formerly occupied by old stage theaters and are comfortable, nonsterile places to see good movies. Bookings tend to run to the more artistic domestic releases (by directors such as Woody Allen, Spike Lee, and Jim Jarmusch) and popular foreign offerings, with many area-exclusive showings. The theaters are on the ground floor of the historic Fine Arts Building (next door to the landmark Auditorium Building on South Michigan Avenue), longtime home to musicians, artists, and various businesses serving them. The maxim lettered above the building's interior entrances sums up the general philosophy here: "All Passes, Art Alone Endures."

The Fine Arts Theatres, 418 S Michigan Ave, Chicago, IL 60605, 312/939-3700.

Best remaining drive-in movie theater
The Cascade Drive-In Theater

They don't make 'em like this anymore, and more's the pity. This outdoor movie theater is a fine piece of Americana that has thrived in suburban West Chicago for more than 25 years. Here's where you'll find features starring 30-foot-high versions of the latest Hollywood icons such as Harrison Ford and Winona Ryder. And during intermissions are those time-warp snack-bar trailers that invite you to sample a soft drink, popcorn, and a foot-long hot dog right from the steamer. Nostalgia buffs also will enjoy the bargain admission price of $5 for the Cascade's first-run double (and often triple) features. Of course, this place doesn't just cater to young lovers—youngsters are welcome here with mom and dad (there's even free candy at the ticket booth). Season runs spring through fall. Movies start at dusk, seven nights a week. The fastest route to the Cascade from downtown Chicago: Take I-290 (the Eisenhower Expressway) to Route 59; head north about five miles to North Avenue; turn right, then keep your eyes peeled for Clint Eastwood, Meryl Streep, or whomever looming visible on the south side of the road.

The Cascade Drive-In, North Ave east of Route 59, West Chicago, IL, 630/231-3150.

Best bet for free movies
Chicago Cultural Center

There's no popcorn, but the movies are free—as are a variety of other cultural programs—at the hand-some Chicago Cultural Center. You can attend a seminar on being a savvy traveler, dance to the big band sound, enjoy a piano concert, and see a movie classic. After 94 years as the city's central library, this exquisite beaux arts building, full of rare marble, mosaics, and bronze, now showcases one of the most comprehensive programs of free arts in the country. On practically every day of the year visitors can attend free programs and exhibitions covering a wide range of the performing, visual, and literary arts. Included are music, dance, theater, films, concerts, lectures, and workshops. Influenced by the 1893 World's Columbian Exposition, this originally was designed as two buildings. This is evidenced by the separate feel of its entrances; at Randolph Street, pairs of Doric columns convey a Greek influence; at Washington Street, three bronze-framed doors enhance a Roman design. Regularly scheduled tours guide visitors up a grand staircase of white Italian marble to admire lush mosaics in colored glass, marble, and mother-of-pearl, and, from Tiffany, lamps, windows, and a dome believed to be the world's largest. Offerings at the monthly "Nostalgia at Noon" free concert series range from traditional jazz and Latin American rhythms to Greek dancing and bluegrass music with an Appalachian dance caller.

Chicago Cultural Center, 78 E Washington St, Chicago, IL 60601, 312/744-6630.

Worst place to see a movie if your name is John Dillinger

Biograph Theatre

It's July 22 in the hot summer of 1934, and a fugitive bank robber named John Dillinger decides to take in a movie (specifically, *Manhattan Melodrama*) at the "Ice-Cooled" (as a banner proclaims) Biograph Theatre. Unfortunately, he didn't go stag—and his date, the so-called "Lady in Red," sold him out to the FBI, who shot and killed Dillinger in the alley just south of the theater. (The 1970s movie *Dillinger* has the alley on the wrong side of the Biograph.) Today, Big John would hardly recognize the place—it's been remodeled and split into one main and two smaller theaters, but the old "Ice-Cooled" banner has been known to show up outside on some steamy summer nights. Movies shown at the Biograph are a mix of commercial releases and occasional "arty" or foreign films. Overall, a comfortable, modern movie house, with more than a touch of history underscored by the flapper mannequin in the box office out front.

Biograph Theatre, 2433 N Lincoln Ave, Chicago, IL 60614, 312/348-4123.

MUSEUMS, GALLERIES, THEATERS & OTHER SITES

Shortest jet flight (in lowest-flying 727)

Museum of Science and Industry

While old favorites such as a descent into a recreated coal mine and a tour of a captured German U-Boat remain big draws, there is plenty that is new—and exciting as well as educational—at Chicago's most popular tourist attraction. Opened in 1995, "AIDS: The War Within," presents straightforward scientific information about the immune system, HIV, and AIDS. In keeping with the museum's goal of providing unique environments for learning, this exhibit places the visitor within a mysterious "invasion" site reminiscent of a sci-fi scene. Another interactive exhibit features flight simulators and large-scale recreations of U.S. Navy ships. "Navy: Technology at Sea" allows a walk-through of the "hangar deck" of aircraft carrier USS *George Washington*, where an actual A-7A Corsair II jet fighter is displayed. The exhibit also includes the full-scale interior of a nuclear attack submarine and the high-tech combat information center of a destroyer. "Take Flight" is an exhibit featuring an actual, 133-foot-long United Airlines 727, which comes to life five times daily in a seven-minute simulated flight from San Francisco to Chicago, during which wings, lights, and landing gear are fully operational. If you do much of your traveling on the Internet, you may be interested in "Imaging: The Tools of Science," a look at how computer-based imaging technology is utilized in science, law enforcement, entertainment, and medicine (play brain surgeon and diagnose a patient's tumor and eradicate it using computer-aided radiosurgery). Other perennial favorites include hatching baby chicks and the Henry Crown Space Center, displaying an actual NASA space capsule, a full-size model of the Apollo lunar lander, moon rocks, and space suits. Here, too, is the Omnimax Theater, a six-story wrap-around movie theater showing adventure and exploration films, and such pop-culture offerings as a Rolling Stones' concert. *Best ticket buy:* Save by getting a combination ticket that will admit you to the museum and an Omnimax performance.

Museum of Science and Industry, 57th St and Lake Shore Dr, Chicago, IL 60637, 312/684-1414. Memorial Day–Labor Day Sat–Thu 9:30 am–5:30 pm, Fri 9:30 am–7 pm; Labor Day–Memorial Day Mon–Fri 9:30 am–4 pm, Sat & Sun 9:30 am–5:30 pm. General admission: $6 adults, $5 seniors, $2.50 children 5–12; combinations available.

Fastest time machine to ancient Egypt
Field Museum of Natural History

The dramatic "Inside Ancient Egypt" exhibit, built at a cost of $2.2 million, uncovers the mysteries of ancient Egypt. It is the only place outside of Egypt where you can enter and explore a life-size mastabatomb complex. The three-level, painstakingly reconstructed tomb of Unis-ankh, son of the pharaoh King Unis, is constructed around the museum's original tomb chambers, excavated and transported from Egypt in 1908. After touring the upper levels of the tomb, visitors descend a 35-foot burial shaft to view two tomb chambers dating back to about 2400 BC. The exhibit includes the original 14,000-pound limestone false door, reconstructed antechambers, storage rooms, burial chambers, and a courtyard that includes special lighting to simulate a sun-drenched desert terrain. The exhibit contains more than 1,400 priceless artifacts spanning Egyptian civilization from 500 B.C. to A.D. 300, including 23 mummies, a working canal and marsh exhibit, the nearly 4,000-year-old royal boat of the Pharaoh King Sen-worset III, a shrine to the cat goddess Bastet, and a recreated Egyptian marketplace. The museum's better known exhibits include prehistoric mammals, North American birds, an Indian totem-pole collection, and "Sizes," which depicts the scale of things in the natural world. *For dinosaur enthusiasts:* A trio of exhibits are sure to entice fans of triceratops and other prehistoric creatures: "DNA to Dinosaurs," an overview of evolution; "Teeth, Tusks, and Tar Pits," a history of life on earth; and "Brachiosaurus: The Largest Mounted Dinosaur in the World." (The museum also schedules a "Family Overnight" program, where kids and adults bed down in the museum and participate in various workshops and events, such as a flashlight tour of the Egypt exhibit—see separate listing in "Kids.")

Field Museum of Natural History, Roosevelt Rd & Lake Shore Drive, Chicago, IL 60605, 312/922-9410. Daily 9 am–5 pm, $5 adults, $3 seniors, $3 children 2–17 (maximum admission $16 per family).

Best spot east of Hollywood to see stars

The Adler Planetarium

The stars you'll see here are not necessarily household names—for example, Sirius, Betelgeuse, and Rigel. The Adler was built in 1930 (the same year the planet Pluto was discovered) as one of the first modern planetariums in the country. Today, it offers an extensive collection of astronomical instruments, some NASA artifacts, and exhibits examining and comparing the planets of our Solar System. An exhibit installed in 1995 looks at the very heart of astronomy by allowing visitors to decode the language of light by engaging them in simple, hands-on experiments using many of the same tools astronomers use. In contrast, another permanent exhibit opened in 1995 looks at the early tools of astronomy—sundials, astrolabes, armillary spheres, and others from Adler's world-renowned collection of early scientific instruments. But the highlight of a visit is the Sky Show, wherein the stunning splendor of the night sky (unlike in Chicago, a sky not rendered opaque by city lights) is displayed on a dome ceiling by a Zeiss Mark VI planetarium projector—which itself looks like a barbell-shaped object from outer space. The show also details other wonders of the universe—meteors, comets, black holes, nebulae, and the like. Stop at the museum shop for a wide variety of space-related items, from prisms and planet mugs to telescopes, videos, and books for the amateur astronomer. Or take a class on such subjects as telescope making or "Stargazing in Cyberspace" (a hands-on evening with computers connected to the Internet in Adler's new Cyberspace Learning Center). Or simply go for the view of the city skyline across the lake from the planetarium (which sits on a promontory jutting out into the water) that is nearly as stunning as the Sky Show—especially at night.

The Adler Planetarium, 1300 S Lake Shore Dr, Chicago, IL 60605, 312/922-STAR. Sat–Thu (and hols) 9 am–5 pm, Fri 9 am–9 pm. $4 adults, $2 seniors, children.

Best place for a whale of a time

Oceanarium, John G. Shedd Aquarium

Whales, dolphins, and sea otters have arrived at Chicago's lakefront, with the first addition to this venerable aquarium in more than 60 years. Opened in 1991, the marble-clad, low-profile, 170,000-square-foot Oceanarium is the world's largest indoor marine-mammal pavilion, doubling the size of the existing aquarium (which was already the world's largest). Built on 1.8 acres of reclaimed former lake bed, this newest pavilion has five exhibition pools. Highlight of the Oceanarium is the Pacific Northwest Coastal Habitats, which contain 400 feet of nature trails in an environment of sloping rockwork, flowing streams, and Pacific vegetation. The trails wind around four cold-saltwater habitats, home to beluga whales, false killer whales, Pacific white-sided dolphins. harbor seals, and Alaskan sea otters. A shallow tide pool contains starfish, sea anemones, clams, mussels, and crabs. The Oceanarium complex also contains a 60,000-gallon penguin habitat, a 3,600-square-foot special exhibit gallery featuring changing exhibits, a 277-seat auditorium, a library, gift shop, and a cafeteria. *Feeding frenzy:* The residents of the Oceanarium devour 256 pounds of restaurant-grade seafood daily. *Note:* Because the Oceanarium is an extremely popular attraction, advance ticket purchase is highly recommended.

John G. Shedd Aquarium, 1200 S Lake Shore Dr, Chicago, IL 60605, 312/939-2438. Mon–Fri 9 am–5 pm, Sat & Sun 9 am–6 pm. $8 adults, $6 children 6–17 and senior citizens (with ID), free, children under 6 years of age. Special discount on Thu.

Best tribute to Addams' family

Jane Addams Hull House Museum

It's hard to imagine that the neighborhood occupied by the sterile gray concrete slabs of the University of Illinois Chicago campus once was a noisy, smelly slum. New immigrants—Jews, Italians, Bohemians—tramped unpaved streets and alleys, crowded into unsanitary tenements, and labored in appalling factories. So it was in 1889 when Jane Addams and her associate Ellen Gates Starr rented rooms in an Italianate mansion built when the area was a pleasant residential suburb. They opened the first neighborhood settlement house in the United States, giving aid and succor to the poor and disadvantaged, struggling to improve living and working conditions, and championing child-labor laws to protect children who often put in 12-hour days in sweatshops. Addams' work for social reform earned her the Nobel Peace Prize in 1931. Meanwhile, Hull House had grown to a complex of buildings that included a dining hall, residences, classrooms, a music school, and an art gallery. When the university campus was built in the 1960s, most of these buildings were razed. As a tribute to the work of Addams and her colleagues, the original house and dining hall remain. They house a fascinating museum detailing Addams and her colleagues' work and chronicling the history of the once-teeming, ethnically rich neighborhood.

Jane Addams Hull House Museum, 800 S Halsted St, Chicago, IL 60607, 312/413-5353. Mon–Fri 10 am–4 pm, Sun noon–5 pm.

Best bet for mastering the masters
Art Institute Highlight Tour

Ranking among the world's top art museums, The Art Institute displays human creativity ranging over 40 centuries. Sometimes this excess of riches can be a little overwhelming—especially to the first-time visitor—and a nice introduction is a Collection Highlight Tour offered daily at 2 pm (plus a special kids' tour at 1 pm on Saturdays). These free tours last from 45 minutes to one hour and concentrate on a half-dozen or so major works. Usually included are Georges Seurat's "A Sunday Afternoon on the Island of La Grande Jatte," Gustave Caillebotte's "Paris, A Rainy Day," Edward Hopper's "Nighthawks," and Grant Wood's "American Gothic." Tours vary with each particular staff lecturer, and discussion is invited. On the first Saturday of each month, tours also are conducted in Spanish. On Tuesdays, admission to the museum is free.

The Art Institute of Chicago, S Michigan Ave at E Adams St, Chicago, IL 60603, 312/443-3600. Mon, Wed, Thu, Fri 10:30 am–4:30 pm, Tue 10:30 am–8 pm, Sat 10 am–5 pm, Sun & hols noon–5 pm. $6.50 adults, $3.25 children, students, seniors.

Best design-in-miniature
Thorne Miniature Rooms at The Art Institute

So perfect in detail are the miniature rooms in this collection that you almost expect to see Lilliputian figures inhabiting them. The miniature clock in the

Massachusetts drawing room actually keeps time, the rug in the Late Jacobean Drawing Room is a hand-woven antique, and the tray of the copper tea set in the Cape Cod Living Room is crafted from an American copper penny. Although no human figures are represented, the illusion of someone's presence is created with miniature objects—an open book, a ball of yarn, a teacup. There are 31 European and 37 American rooms-in-miniature, built by top artisans to a $1/12$ scale. Mrs. James Ward Thorne began collecting miniatures as a girl and later developed the idea of using miniature rooms to provide a history of interior design. Rooms date from 1500 to 1940, with most representing the 18th century. After closing for four years for meticulous conservation after close to 50 years' wear and tear, the rooms reopened in 1989 in a new horseshoe-shaped gallery.

Thorne Miniature Rooms at The Art Institute, N Michigan Ave at E Adams St, Chicago, IL 60603, 312/443-3600.

Smartest spot to get smart about art

David and Alfred Smart Museum of Art

Tucked away on the University of Chicago campus, this often-overlooked fine arts museum contains works by Rembrandt, Rodin, and Matisse, Frank Lloyd Wright and Tiffany. Its collections, started in the 1890s, contain more than 7,000 objects spanning five millennia. Works are from diverse cultures in a variety of media. There is modern sculpture by Degas, Matisse, Moore, and Rodin, and expressionist watercolors by Grosz, Heckel, and Nolde. A collection of old-master prints includes the work of Rembrandt, Delacroix, and Dürer. There are ancient Chinese bronzes, modern Japanese ceramics, and paintings by Daubigny, Gérôme, San Gilliam, Childe Hassam, Rothko, and Suzanne Valadon. Important holdings: a collection of ancient Greek vases, including a rare example by Euphronios; medieval sculpture from the French Romanesque Church of Cluny III; and old-master paintings and sculptures that include a Renaissance reliquary made for Pope Paul III. Frank Lloyd Wright's distinctive design is represented by furniture from world-famous Robie House (see separate listing). The museum, launched through a major gift by the Smart Family Foundation, is named after the founders and publishers of *Esquire* magazine. Special exhibits range from Chinese porcelain to Aboriginal art. Pleasant courtyards contain sculptures.

David and Alfred Smart Museum of Art, 5550 S Greenwood Ave, Chicago, IL 60637, 312/702-0200. Tue–Fri 10 am–4 pm, Sat & Sun noon–6 pm.

Best place to ponder Pablo

Picasso Sculpture

This huge, whimsical-looking piece of art has become such an indelible part of Chicago that it's odd to recall the uproar that surrounded its unveiling back in 1967. "What in the world is that?" went the confused cry back then: A woman? A dog? A big waste of city money? Only Pablo knew for sure, and he never told. But time has a way of breaking down old barriers and calming ruffled feathers. Today, the untitled work is referred to casually and proudly as "the Picasso" and has become—along with the Water Tower—an unofficial symbol of the city. Time has flown—the Picasso has already been a part of Chicago longer than Richard J. Daley was mayor. And we'd like to think that both Pablo and The Boss would approve of children scampering around the sculpture's base and sliding down its short incline: modern art as playground equipment. *Entertainment note:* Check out the "Under the Picasso" lunchtime concert series held at the plaza year-round (see separate listing in "Music").

Picasso Sculpture, Richard J. Daley Center Plaza, Dearborn St & Randolph St, Chicago IL 60601.

Best of the rest public art

Self-guided Sculpture Tour

Not only is Chicago an architectural textbook with excellent examples of classical styles by master builders—"frozen music," as architecture has delightfully been termed—but the city also is endowed with a wealth of public art. Distinctive works of art in such diverse media as glass, wood, steel, paint, film, neon, fiber, and ceramic have been installed at more than 50 sites. Sprinkled throughout the city are the works of such as Calder, Chagall, Miro, Moore, Noguchi, Taft, and, of course, Picasso. Conduct your own self-guided tour. Pick up a copy of the Chicago Office of Fine Arts' *Loop Sculpture Guide*, a handsomely produced, pocket-size booklet that highlights 30 works (and lists an additional 34 "nearby" sculptures) and includes a foldout map, detailed descriptions, and photographs. A free companion volume, *Chicago Public Art Locations*, has listings of artworks (including hanging art at libraries) at locations throughout the metropolitan area.

Public Art Program, Department of Cultural Affairs, 78 E Washington St, Chicago, IL 60601, 312/744-7487.

Most art galleries in a ten-block area
River North

What once was a grimy industrial and warehouse district dubbed "Smokey Hollow" has been transformed into the supercharged piece of real estate known as River North. Crammed into about ten square blocks (bounded by the Chicago River on the west and south, State Street on the East and Chicago Avenue on the north) are 35–40 retailers, around 40 restaurants, 20 fast-food places, 20 antiques dealers, and approximately 70 galleries. River North, now widely acknowledged as an important art center, claims that it is second only to Manhattan with its proliferation of galleries. It is sometimes whimsically referred to as "SuHu," a contraction of two street names (Superior and Huron) and a take-off of New York's SoHo. On nights of multiple openings, when as many as two dozen galleries simultaneously hold receptions to launch new exhibits, the district attracts up to 10,000 art lovers who wander from gallery to gallery, suitably provisioned with wine-to-go. Pick up a free copy of *Chicago Gallery News* (phone 312/649-0064), a handy guide to galleries and openings (along Michigan Avenue as well as in River North).

River North Association, 229 W Illinois St, Suite 4W, Chicago, IL 60610. 312/645-1047.

Best gallery showcasing contemporary artists
Phyllis Kind Gallery

Step into this gallery to find a wide variety of contemporary works from national and international artists (including many Chicago artists), that range from well-known to little-known to just-starting-out. Phyllis Kind, art lover and gallery owner for more than 25 years, holds monthly exhibitions in the main exhibition room of her River North gallery, displaying contemporary artworks by single artists and groups of artists. Previous exhibits have included the works of such well-known artists as Ed Paschke and Roger Brown. A smaller gallery features paintings, prints, and sculpture from lesser-known artists. Because the gallery frequently features the work of emerging artists, collectors with an eye to discovery and patronage (and bargains) may be able to scout out tomorrow's masterpieces. Phyllis Kind also owns a gallery in New York City.

Phyllis Kind Gallery, 313 W Superior St, Chicago, IL 60610, 312/642-6302. Tue–Sat 10 am–5:30 pm.

Best street art fest
Gold Coast Art Fair

Every summer, for one weekend in August, the area on and around Rush Street, just north of Chicago Avenue, becomes a teeming open-air bazaar of art. Wandering the blocked-off streets of the Gold Coast Art Fair, you can find artworks of varying types and styles, from artists of varying abilities. These typically can include delicate watercolors, bold oil paintings, pottery, wood-carvings, and a usually interesting array of wearable art, such as handcrafted jewelry or specially designed T-shirts or sweatshirts. The proximity of bars and restaurants in this neighborhood (the western edge of the Gold Coast), makes this a fun fair to stroll, stopping for libations or a snack. (There has been talk of moving the fair off Rush Street—the location may change in coming years.) Other city art fairs of note include the 57th Street Art Fair in Hyde Park, the city's oldest art fair (dating from 1947), in early June: and the Old Town Art Fair (centered around Lincoln Park West and Menomonee Street in this attractive, compact neighborhood) in mid-June.

Gold Coast Art Fair, around N Rush St (100 E) and E Chicago Ave (800 N). Early-mid-August.

Most major Mexican art
The Mexican Fine Arts Center Museum

This often-overlooked museum is the only one in the Midwest devoted to the works of Mexican and Latin American artists. Three galleries each host changing exhibits. The main gallery showcases the work of some of Mexico's most famous artists, including Orozco and Siqueiros (noted for the "Mexican Mural Renaissance" of the 1920s, 1930s, and 1940s, bringing Mexican art to the eyes of the world) and features five exhibitions annually. The smaller West Gallery features six exhibitions per year and includes an auditorium where concerts and dance are performed. A third gallery concentrates on solo exhibitions by emerging artists and mounts nine exhibitions each year. The museum gift shop carries books and folk art imported from Mexico and Latin America (and does a big business with local folk-art collectors). The museum also offers guided tours and sponsors an outreach program that introduces visual arts to students.

The Mexican Fine Arts Center Museum, 1852 W 19th St, Chicago, IL 60603, 312/738-1503. Tue–Sun 10 am–5 pm. Free admission.

Most major American art

Terra Museum of American Art

Tucked away along glamorous North Michigan Avenue, this museum houses one of the world's foremost collections of American art. It is manageable, small enough to be toured in two or three hours—or, better yet, in a leisurely afternoon after a hectic morning of shopping. It's spacious, airy, and modern. In design, this museum is reminiscent of Frank Lloyd Wright's controversial Guggenheim in New York. Take a freight-like elevator to the fourth floor, and then descend a winding walkway, exploring gallery by gallery, with glimpses of busy Michigan Avenue along the way. Spanning more than two centuries of American art, you'll find works by Sargent and Stella, Whistler and Wyeth, among a collection of more than 800 works that includes many of the country's finest examples of American Impressionism. Masterpieces include Morse's "Gallery of the Louvre" and Bingham's "Jolly Flatboatmen No.2." The museum attracts major traveling exhibits—such as "Winslow Homer in Gloucester." A gift shop sells reproductions in the form of posters and notecards as well as tote bags and books. Admission is free on the first Sunday of the month.

Terra Museum of American Art, 666 N Michigan Ave, Chicago, IL 60611, 312/664-3939. Tue noon–8 pm. Wed–Sat 10 am–5 pm, Sun noon–5 pm. $4 adults, $2 seniors, free students & under 12.

Most avant-garde art museum

Museum of Contemporary Art

Modern art supplants martial arts when the Museum of Contemporary Art moves into its gleaming new building on a two-acre site formerly occupied by the Chicago Avenue National Guard Armory. (Grand opening is scheduled for July 1996; meanwhile, the MCA continues to occupy the former bakery where it began life in 1967.) The 147,000-square-foot new facility, the first U.S. project of noted Berlin architect Josef Paul Kleihues, will quadruple exhibit space and include a one-acre sculpture garden overlooking Lake Michigan. What remains unchanged is MCA's reputation to present the finest and most provocative contemporary visual and related arts—painting, sculpture, photography, video, dance, music, and performance. Emphasizing the tremendous variety of MCA's programs have been exhibits focusing on Alan Hockney's colorful opera set designs, the photography of Robert Mapplethorpe, the monumental work of ten contemporary Japanese sculptors, an Andy Warhol one-man show, a celebration of pioneering modernist architect Mies van der Rohe, and the legendary collection of George Costakis (featured in "Art of the Avant-Garde in Russia"). The new building will include a full-service restaurant and a museum store with an extensive selection of art books, magazines, and other literature, as well as an eclectic selection of one-of-a-kind gifts including many handmade items. Set in an urban canyon between Michigan Avenue and the historic Water Tower on one side and Lake Michigan on the other, the limestone-and-aluminum building will occupy one of the city's most desirable locations. A selection of works from MCA's permanent collection will be showcased in four vaulted, naturally lit galleries on the top floor, each containing 2,500 square feet of space.

Museum of Contemporary Art, 237 E Ontario St, Chicago, IL 60611, 312/280-5161. Tue–Sat 10 am–5 pm, Sun noon–5 pm. $5 admission, $2.50 seniors and students; free on Tue.

Best of the clix pix

The Museum of Contemporary Photography

In appropriately sleek and contemporary galleries, you'll find some of the world's best contemporary photography. In 1988, this became only the second photography museum in the country to receive accreditation from the American Association of Museums. A permanent collection of more than 3,500 photographs focuses on contemporary American photography produced since the publication of Robert Frank's *Americans* in 1959. The museum's Midwest Photographers Project offers the opportunity to view in a print-study room recent works on loan from regional photographers. The scope of the museum's full calendar of first-class and often-provocative exhibits includes such diverse subjects as space photography, little-league baseball, and contemporary Russian photography. Special programs include lectures and a big Photographic Print Fair that brings together galleries and dealers from around the country.

The Museum of Contemporary Photography, Columbia College Chicago, 600 S Michigan Ave, Chicago, IL 60605, 312/663-5554. Sept–May Mon–Fri 10 am–5 pm, Sat noon–5 pm; June & July Mon–Fri 10 am–4 pm, Sat noon–4 pm. Free.

Best black history museum

DuSable Museum of African-American History

Long before Mississippi migrants trekked north in search of freedom and a better life, a black man played a prominent role in Chicago's history. In 1779, Jean Baptiste Point du Sable, a well-educated son of a French father and black mother, established Chicago's first commercial enterprise, a trading post, which he later developed into a prosperous farm. The museum that bears his name is a storehouse of art, artifacts, documents, and memorabilia relating to the history of African-American people in the United States. It traces their history and their contributions in the arts, technology, and culture. A collection of 56 paintings illustrates blacks in early Illinois, and a series of murals by Eugene Eda depicts blacks and whites who have contributed significantly to African-American history. The museum has among its holdings a massive mahogany hand-carved mural, by Robert Witt Ames, depicting 400 years of African-American experience, and offers a large display of sculptures, masks, carvings, and fabrics from West Africa. The museum, which started life as a Chicago Park District fieldhouse, is a mix of art and history—which doesn't neglect such aspects as lynchings and the KKK, slave ships, photos of returning infantrymen from WW II with medals for gallantry and of Henry O. Flipper, the first black graduate of West Point, as well as a montage of stereotyping and insulting commercial products (such as "Little Black Sambo" books and games and sheet music for "My Sugar Coated Chocolate Boy"). A gift shop carries books, jewelry, fabrics, carvings, prints, and folk art crafted by African, Caribbean, and African-American artisans. A lively calendar of events includes history courses, crafts, workshops, concerts, festivals, and an annual book fair.

DuSable Museum of African-American History, 740 E 56th Pl, Chicago, IL 60637. 312/947-0600. Mon–Wed, Fri & Sat 10 am–5 pm, Thu 10 am–6 pm, Sun noon–5 pm. $3 adults, $1 children under 13; free on Sat.

Best museum to go on an archaeological dig

Spertus Museum of Judaica

Gently sifting through the sand, you strike something solid. Carefully, you dig deeper, brushing centuries of debris away from the item. Could it be a delicately carved figurine, a pottery vessel, or maybe even a glittering piece of historic jewelry? Such are the treasures and the learning experience to be found at the Artifact Center at this uncommon museum. Especially geared for children and families to explore together, the Artifact Center also provides insight into the ways of life found in the Middle East and Mediterranean areas more than two millennia ago. Other items on display in the rest of the museum can range from the inspiring to the heartbreaking. Among the former: Jewish religious objects such as ancient Torahs, Passover plates, Hannukah lamps, and artifacts associated with the time-honored rites of circumcision and bar mitzvah. And the latter: The heart-rending Zell Holocaust Memorial with artifacts and photographs that bear grim testimony to man's inhumanity—where confiscated personal items found at Auschwitz contrast with swastika arm bands and steel helmets as reminders of this reign of terror. Between these extremes are displays, exhibits, artifacts, and artworks illuminating and celebrating the Jewish experience throughout history. Has a large permanent collection (which is rotated); also hosts special exhibitions.

Spertus Museum of Judaica, 618 S Michigan Ave, Chicago, IL 60605, 312/322-1747. Sun–Thu 10 am–5 pm, Fri 10 am–3 pm. $4 adults, $2 seniors & students; free on Fri.

Best museum of Swedish culture
Swedish-American Museum Center

On Saturday mornings a bell-ringer makes his rounds of Andersonville shops as storekeepers ceremonially sweep the sidewalks with corn brooms. For although other ethnic groups have moved in, Andersonville (see separate listing, "Dining," "Shopping"), centered around a few blocks of Clark Street, north of Foster Avenue, remains the country's most concentrated Swedish community outside of Lindsborg, Kansas. There are Swedish delis, restaurants, a bakery (see separate listings), and annual events such as Midsommarfest and the December Festival of Lights. This attractive museum, with white-painted brick walls, occupies the former Lind hardware store, which sold supplies to carpenters, 25 percent of them Swedes, rebuilding Chicago after the Great Fire of 1871. It tells the story of Swedish immigration to America; at one time, every sixth Swede left the homeland for America. There's the recreated drawing room of a well-to-do immigrant family, and a farm kitchen with a straw-filled wooden sofa that doubled as a bed for the hired man, and displays of the kitchen implements and tools that many immigrants brought with them. Special exhibits feature prominent Swedish-Americans such as Charles A. Lindbergh, Jr., Knute Rockne, Civil War naval architect John Ericsson, Andersonville native Gloria Swanson, and nurseryman Pere Peterson, who planted many of the trees in Lincoln Park. A museum shop sells Dala horses, recipe books, wood crafts, tapes, cards, and T-shirts.

Swedish-American Museum Center, 5211 N Clark St, Chicago, IL 60640, 312/728-8111. Mon–Fri 11 am–4 pm, Sat 11 am–3 pm. $2 adults, $1 senior, 50 cents children under 12.

Best museum of Polish culture
Polish Museum of America

If you know little about Ignacy Jan Paderewsky, you can correct that oversight with a visit to what is claimed to be America's oldest ethnic museum. Paderewsky was a world-class pianist, composer, and one-time prime minister of Poland. The museum displays paintings of the legendary Polish statesman, along with many of his personal effects, and a reconstruction of his bedroom at the Buckingham Hotel in New York City, where he was exiled during World War II. Chicago contains a Polish community said to be second in size only to Warsaw, and this museum celebrates its heritage, honoring Generals Polaski and Kosciuszko, who helped fight for American freedom, composer Chopin, astronomer Copernicus, scientist Sklodowska-Curie, painter Wyspianski, and Shakespearean actor Modjeska. Displays include a massive stained-glass window designed for the New York 1939 World's Fair, Polish War Relief posters, and large collections of costumes and art. Special events include concerts and theater. A gift shop carries folk crafts, puppets, and dolls.

Polish Museum of America, 984 N Milwaukee Ave, Chicago, IL 60622, 312/384-3352. Daily 11 am–4 pm. Donation suggested.

Best museum of Lithuanian culture
Balzekas Museum of Lithuanian Culture

There's a serious side and a whimsical side to this museum that chronicles the history and culture of the tiny Baltic state. Politically, you'll get an understanding of Lithuania's struggle for self-rule. Culturally, you can attend weaving demonstrations, learn the ancient art of scratch-carving Easter eggs, and take youngsters to the Children's Gallery, where they can dress up in medieval costumes and enjoy hands-on activities at the recreation of a 19th-century farmstead. The museum has special exhibits, such as a show of Lithuanian-American performing-arts posters, and a full calendar of events such as piano concerts, folk-art demonstrations (including the making of Christmas ornaments over several weekends beginning late November), lectures, work-shops, and movies in both Lithuanian and English. Permanent exhibits include antique weapons, ar-mor, textiles, dolls, folk art, rare maps and prints, and colorful displays of Lithuanian costumes. A gift shop has dolls, crystal, leather goods, amber jewelry, wood carvings, textiles, books, and records.

Balzekas Museum of Lithuanian Culture, 6500 S Pulaski Rd, Chicago, IL 60629, 312/582-6500. Sat–Thu 10 am–4 pm, Fri 10 am–8 pm.

Best museum of Ukrainian culture

Ukrainian National Museum

Located in new quarters in the heart of the Near Northwest Side neighborhood of Ukrainian Village (centered around Chicago Avenue and Western Avenue), this museum celebrates and preserves the history and heritage of the Ukraine. Displayed here are tapestries, crafts, costumes, decorative items (such as ceramics, woodworking. and embroidery), and other historical objects relating to this region, the history of which reaches back more than 3,000 years before the birth of Christ. Especially interest-ing is the collection of decorated "Easter eggs" (the development of which in the Ukraine long predates the existence of Easter). Museum volunteer Olha Kalymon (a septuagenarian full of excitement about the museum and her native culture) explained it this way: Since it was believed that birds flew near the sun, the yellow in their eggs was thought to be material from the sun god. Thus, the blessed eggs were inscribed with symbols (triangles, stars, lines, flowers, animals, etc.) representing good wishes, and were given as gifts. Most of the area's 25,000 resi-dents of Ukrainian descent live in the neighborhood surrounding this cultural landmark.

Ukrainian National Museum, 721 N Oakley Blvd, Chicago, IL 60612, 312/421-8020. Thu–Sun 11 am–4 pm. Donations suggested for adults.

Best misnamed museum

Oriental Institute Museum

This misnamed museum also may be one of the most overlooked. More's the pity, because it houses a major collection of Middle Eastern antiquities. The name "Oriental" is misleading, chosen before the terms "Near East" and "Middle East" were coined. Adding to its identity problems, the museum is located out of the mainstream, tucked away amid the Gothic architecture and tree-lined streets of the University of Chicago campus. You'll find Egyptian mummies, a fragment of the Dead Sea Scrolls, and a 16-foot-high red quartzite statue of the famous boy-king Tutankhamen. There's an archway built from 2,500-year-old bricks from Nebuchadnezzar's Babylon; gold jewelry that belonged to Persian kings; tiny, intricately carved amulets; and a 40-ton Assyrian winged bull from a king's palace. Collections cover cultures dating from approximately 7,000 years ago to the tenth century of our era, with art and artifacts from Egypt, Mesopotamia, Anatolia, Iran, and Syria/Palestine. Special programs include Sunday afternoon films, special lunchtime tours for adults, and a children's program that includes such delightfully named events as "Food and Fun from Long Ago" and "The Bull With Five Legs." A colorful gift shop, The Suq, has a bazaar-like array of jewelry, sculpture, and metalwork, including copies of museum originals and ever-popular Egyptian mummy beads. *Note:* The museum is currently undergoing renovation. Call before planning a visit.

Oriental Institute Museum, University of Chicago, 1155 E 58th St, Chicago, IL 60637, 312/702-9521. Tue & Thu–Sat 10 am–4 pm, Wed 10 am–8:30 pm; Sun noon–4 pm. Free.

Best place to try out as a TV anchor
Museum of Broadcast Communications

If your fantasy is to anchor the news, phone for a reservation and head for this unique museum. Then, slip on an "MBC" blazer, slide into an anchor chair at the NewsCenter, and read the news from the Tele-PrompTer as corresponding footage rolls. The result is a 15-minute newscast, complete with opening music, credits, and actual commercials. For $19.95, you can purchase a copy. But doing a newscast is only part of the fun at this museum, where memories come tumbling out almost as soon as you step in— such as a recreation of the vault where the lovable penny-pincher Jack Benny hoarded his wealth, and the overstuffed closet of Fibber McGee (complete with the original crash sound effects used on the show as stuff cascaded out). The museum preserves tapes of television and radio broadcasts past. Choose your favorite old TV show with the help of a user-friendly computer; then play it in an individual booth. Displays include broadcasting artifacts, such as vintage radio and television sets—black and white models with polished cabinetry designed as pieces of furniture—the camera used for the first Kennedy-Nixon debate, and ventriloquist Edgar Bergen's Charlie McCarthy and Mortimer Snerd dummies (unlikely as radio seems as a medium for ventriloquism—think about it!—"Murphy Brown's" real-life father did make it big). A gift shop—appropriately called "Commercial Break"—carries a variety of broadcast-related souvenirs.

Museum of Broadcast Communications, Chicago Cultural Center, 78 E Washington St, Chicago, IL 60602, 312/987-1500. Mon–Sat 10 am–4:30 pm, Sun noon–5 pm. Free.

Best place to give peace a chance

The Peace Museum

It's a sad commentary on humankind that this museum attracts only about 20,000 visitors a year. Many museums display guns, swords, and other instruments of war; this unique museum is dedicated to the cause of peace and to human and civil rights. The museum presents four major exhibitions annually and has a permanent collection ranging from 19th-century antiwar prints to a John Lennon guitar. It has developed exhibits on a range of topics, including the life of Dr. Martin Luther King, Jr., the role of popular music in efforts for social change, the effect of war toys on children, and artwork created by Japanese atomic-bomb survivors. An annual summer exhibit, "Drive-by Peace," provides a hands-on lesson in peacefully solving conflicts and envisioning a new neighborhood, home, school, and world. A 20-week program of art, poetry, essay-writing, and role-playing channels kids' imaginations and energies away from violence and conflict.

The Peace Museum, 314 W Institute Pl, Chicago, IL 60610, 312/440-1860. Tue–Sat 11 am–5 pm. $3.50 adults, $2 children, seniors, students.

Best bet for Civil War buffs

The Chicago Historical Society

This museum preserves the varied and fascinating history of "The City That Works," from its humble beginnings as a marshy Indian settlement and canoe portage between the Great Lakes and the Mississippi River to its present as one of the world's top cities. In addition to photography, artifacts, and displays focusing on Chicago, the museum also features a particularly heavy concentration of Civil War items, especially in its acclaimed permanent exhibit, "A House Divided: America in the Age of Lincoln." Located in 3,600 square feet of gallery space on the museum's second floor, this exhibit features such Civil War artifacts as the bed Lincoln died in, the table at which Lee surrendered to Grant at Appomattox, and the table and chair at which Lincoln signed the Emancipation Proclamation. The museum's bookstore stocks a wide variety of Chicago, Civil War, and Lincoln books, posters, photographs, and other related gift items. The Big Shoulders Cafe (see separate listing in "Dining") offers light dining, soft live music, and a romantic ambience.

The Chicago Historical Society, 1601 N Clark St, Chicago, IL 60614, 312/642-4600. Mon–Sat 9:30 am– 4:30 pm, Sun noon–5 pm. $3 adults, $2 students & seniors, $1 children; free on Mon.

Best museum for seeing triple

Museum of Holography

You're probably carrying around in your wallet a sample of this new-wave artform—the hologram on your bank credit card is one of its practical applications, as a hard-to-forge security device. The three-dimensional effect of a hologram is created by a split laser beam, and this museum has four galleries of holograph artworks, plus a gift counter where, for as little as $5, you can buy a hologram suitable for framing, plus an array of holographic earrings, pendants, watches, money clips, and other 3-D baubles. As you wander the galleries, the effects are intriguing—and can be startling: A cheeky kid pokes out his tongue, a cute puppy reaches out an engaging paw, haunting eyes follow you across the room, a great white shark lunges. Museum founder Loren Billings says that "holography and its mutations will be as important to mankind as the printing press."

Museum of Holography, 1134 W Washington Blvd, Chicago, IL 60607, 312/226-1007, Wed–Sun 12:30–5 pm. $2.50 adults.

Most books and maps

The Newberry Library

When the Great Chicago Fire of 1871 blazed through the city, the residence of one Mahlon D. Ogden was the only house in its path to survive. So notes a plaque on the site now occupied by the Newberry Library. Time eventually took care of Ogden's wooden mansion, replaced in 1892 by this monumental Spanish Romanesque building. Facing a park in Washington Square, its dark granite walls are clad with ivy and encompassed by black iron railings and shade trees. Free and open to the public, the Newberry is one of the world's great independent research and education centers in the humanities. It houses 1.5 million books, five million manuscripts, and 75,000 maps. It offers seminars on such topics as blues music, bookbinding, and Irish poetry. Lectures and classes cover such subjects as "The Beer

Barons of Milwaukee" and "The Culture of Democracy in China." There are reading rooms, a bookstore, and changing exhibits. The Newberry offers guided tours, stages concert series and a mammoth book fair, and is a noted center for genealogical research. At an annual holiday bazaar, shoppers can browse merchandise from 40 of the Chicago area's museum stores, cultural centers, and other non-profit gift shops. The event also offers food and entertainment.

The Newberry Library, 60 W Walton St, Chicago, IL 60610, 312/943-9090. Tue–Thu 10 am–6 pm, Fri & Sat 9 am–5 pm.

Best all-around dance troupe

Hubbard Street Dance Company

Formed in 1977 by four dancers with a dream of fusing traditional dance with modern elements, today this eclectic company stands at the pinnacle of the local dance scene and has earned a lofty reputation around the world. Hubbard Street's large troupe of dancers most often combine jazz and ballet dancing techniques, blazing a trail with its established repertory as well as a constantly evolving assortment of new, specially commissioned works. The company's high standards and prominent standing in its field usually guarantee above-average performances. Hubbard Street presents dance productions at various venues throughout the year, most notably including the Civic Opera House.

Hubbard Street Dance Company, 2185 N Wabash Ave, Chicago, IL 60604, 312/663-0853.

Cheapest (and breeziest) front-row theater seats

Theater on the Lake

On a summer's evening, when there's a freshening breeze off the lake, this theater is a pleasant (and inexpensive) spot to enjoy plays and musicals. Operated by the Chicago Park District in partnership with professional theater companies, Theater on the Lake is housed in a screened-pavilion built in 1920 as a sanatorium and later used as a USO Center. Although screens enable moderating breezes to blow through, they also preclude the use of air-conditioning. As a result, patrons can get uncomfortably sticky when the air is still and humid. Nonetheless, this lakeside venue does offer quality non-equity theater—shows such as *Applause, Harvey, Evita, Into the Woods, The Cemetery Club,* and *Driving Miss Daisy.* And even when the weather is not right, the price certainly is. All tickets are one price, under

$5—less for a season subscription—and can be reserved by phone for individual performances. Even during sellouts, it often is possible to get seats, since unclaimed tickets go on sale 45 minutes before curtain time. Founded in 1952, this summer community theater offers 380 seats surrounding its central stage. *Tip for free admissions:* Each season, the theater recruits volunteer ushers—adults and teens—who are able to see productions free of charge.

Theater on the Lake, Fullerton Pkwy at Lake Shore Dr, Chicago, IL 60614, 312/742-7771.

Historic theater where the building may be better than the performances (but not always)

Chicago Theatre

It has suffered some criticism in recent times, this exquisitely restored historic theater, from those who charge that it books in some second-rate talent. This, however, is changing—with the staging of Broadway blockbusters such as *Kiss of the Spiderwoman* (with Chita Rivera) and *Joseph and the Amazing Technicolor Dreamcoat* (with Donny Osmond in the lead role). Built as a go-for-baroque movie palace in 1921, this ornate theater was opened by silent-screen master of pantomime Buster Keaton and offered a lively blend of screen and stage. Among famous performers to tread its boards were Jack Benny, Sid Caesar, Will Rogers, Al Jolson, and Sophie Tucker. In its some 75 years, the Chicago Theatre has seen a variety of highs and lows, from its regal term as the flagship for the old Balaban and Katz movie chain to its dilapidated, shuttered years in the early 1980s. Happily, the story did not end up with a wrecker's ball. Instead, the old theater was extensively restored and reopened in 1986—a baroque wonder with glittering chandeliers, Tiffany stained glass, a sweeping grand staircase, and a facade of ornamental terra-cotta. Restoration cost about $4 million. Today, the theater hosts a range of performers from superstars (such as Frank Sinatra, David Copperfield, and Liza Minnelli) to up-and-coming rock or soul acts and sometimes-tired touring companies of revival musicals. But, even if a particular show isn't worth the price of admission, the grandeur of the theater can help make up for it . . . a little, anyway.

Chicago Theatre, 175 N State St, Chicago, IL 60601, 312/902-1500.

Historic theater where the performances are usually reliable

Goodman Theatre Mainstage and Studio

Nestled up against the famous Art Institute of Chicago, this theater, founded as an amateur theater group in the late 1920s (which metamorphosed into a professional company in the 1950s), has grown into Chicago's leading "establishment" theater. Among its revivals of theater classics such as Eugene O'Neill's *The Iceman Cometh* and Thornton Wilder's *The Skin of Our Teeth* (plus the occasional musical), the Goodman often offers new or adapted works as daring and breathtaking as those found at Steppenwolf (indeed, these two theater powerhouses have been known to collaborate on the occasional project). This theater attracts big name lead actors, such as Dustin Hoffman and Brian Dennehy. The Goodman is also home to the 100-seat Studio, where experimental and student works are performed. (The Goodman presents a popular annual Christmas-season run of *A Christmas Carol*—see separate listing in "Kids".) *Seating note:* Seats in the Mainstage provide ample legroom and good sight lines; rows are configured without a central aisle.

Goodman Theatre Mainstage and Studio, 200 S Columbus Dr, Chicago, IL 60603, 312/443-3800.

Best of the best in Chicago theater

Steppenwolf Theatre

Chicago's local theater scene is one of the hottest and most interesting in the country. And the leading light in this near-Golden Age is Steppenwolf Theatre, the risk-taking, consistently excellent ensemble company that produces some of the finest theater in the United States. Steppenwolf's productions range from stagings of works by today's leading playwrights (including Sam Shepard, Lanford Wilson, and David Hare) to unique literary adaptations (such as *The Grapes of Wrath*, which later played on Broadway) to revivals of theater classics; the common denominator is high-quality works, usually with at least an edge of experimentation. Many ensemble members have gone on to Hollywood and TV success, such as John Malkovich (*Dangerous Liaisons*), Laurie Metcalf (*Roseanne*), and Gary Sinise (*Forrest Gump*)—but most still return nearly every season to help produce or star in the group's shows. In 1991, a new theater, rehearsal, and office complex supplanted the group's longtime headquarters (which was farther north on Halsted Street).

Steppenwolf Theatre, 1650 N Halsted St, Chicago, IL 60614, 312/335-1650.

Best theater-ticket bargains

Hot Tix Booths

If you enjoy the theater and you like to hunt bargains, head for the Hot Tix booth—preferably *before* it opens, because it is strictly first come, first served. Operated by the League of Chicago Theaters, it offers half-price day-of-performance tickets to more than 100 member theaters. Availability varies with time of year and day of week—demand is high during fall and early spring, particularly on weekends. Choices may run to as many as a dozen shows, or perhaps as few as three or four—with 20 about tops. There are no phone orders, so you (or a proxy) must show up in person. But you do save 50 percent! There are additional booths at the Lake Theatre, Oak Park and in Evanston (1616 Sherman Road). Also operated by the League (but subject to lapses in service) is Curtain Call (312/977-1755), a recorded listing of what's currently playing, recited by category.

Hot Tix, 108 N State St, Chicago, IL 60603; Chicago Place, 700 N Michigan Ave (6th floor), Chicago, IL 60611 (and suburban locations). Mon–Fri 10 am–7 pm, Sat 10 am–6 pm, Sun noon–4 pm.

SPORTS (SPECTATOR)

Perhaps the best-loved stadium in sports

Wrigley Field

Sure, the Boston Garden had its handsome parquet floor and Fenway Park has the Green Monster of a left field wall. But, even with the installation of lights in 1988 (a moment of silence for the passing of tradition, please), this brick-and-ivy home of the storied Chicago Cubs is still the closest thing to a shrine you'll find in the world of professional sports. This is especially true when gravelly voiced sportscaster Harry Caray leads the crowd in the traditional singing of "Take Me Out to the Ballgame" during the seventh-inning stretch. Since 1914, the boys of summer have been cavorting in Wrigley's emerald field—usually playing under natural lighting (progress notwithstanding, more than three-quarters of home games are still played during the day). And, from Tinkers-to-Evers-to-Chance to Ernie Banks and Billy Williams to Ryne Sandberg, Andre Dawson, and Mark Grace, Chicago has loved its Cubbies. Today, coveted bleacher seats are sold out in advance (except when fans are soured by a strike), making them harder to come by, but any seat here is worth a day at the ol' ballpark. Let time slip by with a cold one, a hot dog, and the most American of all pastimes. Sing it again, Harry!

Wrigley Field, 1060 W Addison St, Chicago, IL
60613, 312/281-5050. Season runs from
approximately early to mid-April to late
September–early October.

One of the newest stadiums in sports

The New Comiskey Park

Gone is Charles Comiskey's famed 80-year-old
"Baseball Palace of the World," where the Chicago
White Sox hosted American League superstars from
Babe Ruth to José Canseco. But, with the passing
of the old comes the birth of the new . . . and the
gleaming, $150-million-dollar New Comiskey Park
more than makes up for the loss. The new park,
which opened on April 19, 1991, and ushered in a
new era of baseball-only parks, combines classic
elements (such as the White Sox's famous exploding
scoreboard) with modern conveniences, including
escalators, additional washrooms, expanded concession areas (maintaining Comiskey's tradition of offering top-notch ballpark food), and Automatic Teller
Machines on each level. Other innovations at the
park include a speed-pitch machine allowing fans to
match their fastballs against major-league baseball's
best, instant photo booths that produce baseball
card–style photos, and a Hall of Fame that includes
"Shoeless" Joe Jackson's original contract. All in all,
a very suitable playground for Chicago's "other"
baseball team which itself boasts a glorious tradition
and a core of fanatic supporters. True Sox fans will
tell you their minions are more knowledgeable, real
baseball fans than those "yupsters" that flock to that
certain North Side park. Luckily, the city is more
than big enough for both Sox and Cubs supporters,
who dream of that elusive-since-1906 "Subway
Series" (the last of which, South Siders will proudly
point out, was won by the Sox). *Historical note:* The
Sox have been playing ball on the South Side since
shortly after the turn of the century (the St. Paul
Saints, founded in 1893, became the Chicago White
Stockings in 1900).

The New Comiskey Park, 333 W 35th St, Chicago,
IL 60616, 312/924-1000. Season runs from approximately early April to early October.

The house that Jordan built

The United Center

Constructed in 1994 just across the street from the
former site of the beloved Madhouse on Madison
(aka Chicago Stadium, a fixture since 1929), the
United Center is a beautifully modern facility with

cushy seats and TV monitors for courtside fans, as well as 216 suites (the old building had no sky boxes). While it lacks the charm—and the foundation-rocking noise levels—of the stadium, it has quickly become one of the most popular stops on any tourist's Chicago itinerary, thanks to the life-size bronze statue of one Michael Jeffery Jordan out front. Its futuristic technology includes an eight-sided color video scoreboard that has replay capabilities, displays comprehensive statistics, and is said to be one of the most sophisticated in any arena in the world. Amenities of the building complex, which covers 45 acres, include eight escalators and nine elevators (the old building had none of either) and 50 rest rooms (versus 16 in the old building). Already this building, which seats 21,500 for basketball, has a quirky history: Jordan's number was retired here, but he said he'd never play here, and then he did play here with a new number (45), until he decided to break the jinx of the new building by un-retiring No. 23. Whew! Selected as the host building for the 1996 Democratic National Convention, the United Center was given the thankless task of persuading the world to forget about all that unpleasant news footage of violent confrontations in the streets between police and protestors during the 1968 fiasco.

The United Center, 1901 W Madison St, Chicago, IL 60612, 312/455-4500. Bulls season runs approximately November to April.

Hottest spot for cold steel on ice

The United Center

Unquestionably, Chicago is not quite the hockey town that it is the baseball, football, and basketball town—especially since the glory days of the 1960s when "Golden Jet" Bobby Hull and the irrepressible Stan Makita were the toast of the town (and still remain popular celebrities in a city that reveres its sports icons). Waning popularity is partly due to the fact that Bill Wirtz, owner of the Chicago Blackhawks, has for years refused to televise the team's home games locally, even during sellouts, even during the Stanley Cup playoffs. Even as the underexposed, fifth-most-popular Chicago professional sports team, however, the Blackhawks used to sell out all 18,000 seats at the old stadium for every home game, and they've continued that tradition by filling all 20,500 seats sold for hockey in the United Center. And while Blackhawks fans might not be legion, they are among the most rabid sports fans on this or any other planet, always ready to scream and shout during power plays and fights and always with a ready supply of headgear to toss onto the ice should a Hawk notch a three-goal "hat trick." The pandemonium that is a Hawks game begins with the first organ notes of "The Star-Spangled Banner," over which it is customary to scream, not sing.

The United Center, 1901 W Madison St, Chicago, IL 60612, 312/455-4500. Blackhawks season runs from approximately October to April.

Coolest spot for the monsters of the midway

Soldier Field

Halas. Grange. Luckman. Ditka. Sayers. Butkus. Payton. Singletary. Ditka again. McMahon. The Fridge. Such is the glorious history (ancient and recent) of the Chicago Bears, charter team of the NFL. And at least as of this writing (a move to a domed stadium and/or a move to the suburbs are perennial topics of discussion), they play their bruising, defense-and-run-oriented brand of football in Soldier Field. Subject to the idiosyncrasies of weather blowing in off Lake Michigan, this breezy lakefront stadium can be unbelievably pleasant—such as on a warm, sunny Sunday in late fall. And it can be undeniably harsh—such as on a frigid Sunday in December that causes fans to bundle up their outsides and fortify their insides. It also can be unpredictable—such as when a thick fog blew in during a playoff game against Philadelphia (in 1988) when fans behind the goals could barely see the goal posts, let alone action on the field. From the championships of the 1930s and 1940s to the swaggering and bragging 1985 team that won Super Bowl XX, Chicago has loved its Bears with a devotion bordering (sometimes—such as in the lean, Payton-only years) on the incomprehensible. Since its construction in 1924, Soldier Field has been host to a variety of other sporting and musical events, ranging from the famous Dempsey-Tunney "long count" heavyweight fight in 1927, concerts by such groups as The Grateful Dead, and the opening ceremonies of the 1994 World Cup soccer games. But it is as the home of the city's "Monsters of the Midway" that Chicagoans best know this old stadium. At least, that is until the team moves to a new suburban stadium after 1999.

Soldier Field, 425 E McFetridge Dr, Chicago, IL 60605, 708/295-6600. Bears season runs approximately September through December.

Tamest spot to watch wildcats— no more

Dyche Stadium, Northwestern University

What a difference a season makes. Although hitting the books is still more important at Northwestern University than hitting the quarterback, the university suddenly found itself with a football team. Not only did it confound the experts in 1995 by putting together a 9–1 season and winning the Big 10 title, but also by earning a ticket to the Rose Bowl. This was the team's first trip to Pasadena (or to any postseason bowl) since January 1949, following the last time they triumphed in the Big 10 conference, in 1948. Prior to that, NU had last won the Big 10 title in 1936. All of which explains why for so long Wildcats football fans had the most apologetic college cheer among followers of gridiron fortunes: "Our SAT scores were higher than yours!" Of course, that chant is still pretty much valid. Academic standards are high at NU. In fact, even as the Wildcats were set to celebrate "The Dream Season" in early December 1995, Rose Bowl fever was officially "put on hold" and players were not permitted to grant media interviews, to allow almost two weeks to prepare for semester exams. Meanwhile, tickets to the Rose Bowl (and presumably to future games at Dyche Stadium) have become more rare than a dumb NU grad, and souvenir stores around campus were hard pressed to keep enough Wildcat T-shirts, caps, mugs, and other mementoes in stock.

Dyche Stadium, Northwestern University, Evanston, IL 60208, 847/491-7070. Season generally runs from early September through late November.

Best bet to bet the millions

Arlington International Race Course

On July 31, 1985, a massive fire ended the life of the old, somewhat seedy Arlington Race Track. However, this tragedy made possible the rebirth of the new, state-of-the-art Arlington International Race Course. A combination of high-tech communications (featuring more than 700 closed-circuit monitors), innovative architecture (open-air and enclosed spectator viewing areas, plus a variety of cafeterias, restaurants, and bars), and immaculately kept grounds make this course among the best and most highly regarded in the world. Look for the giant bronze statue of the track's most famous champion horse, John Henry. Arlington is home to one of the richest events in racing, the annual Arlington Million. This exciting race attracts an international field of three-year-old thoroughbreds and is broadcast (and wagered on) around the world. This sleek and sparkling-clean incarnation of the Arlington course is a fun destination for devoted horse-players and families alike. And convenient, too, with a Metra train to take you right to the door. *Political note:* At press time, this racetrack was seeking political relief from competition from the new breed of casino riverboats that it claims is diminishing attendance (having been refused permission to open its own "riverboat" casino on a pond at the track). *Family outing:* "Breakfast at Arlington" is a special free program beginning on Saturdays at 7 am that includes a demonstration race, a tour via tram of the backstretch and barn area, and a Q&A with a featured trainer and jockey hosted by the track announcer (with questions answered about reading form charts, wagering, etc.). A buffet breakfast is offered at $7.95.

Arlington International Race Course, Arlington Heights, IL 60006, 847/255-4300. Season generally runs from mid-May through mid-October.

Best bets for (considerably) less than a million

The Chicago area's other race tracks toil in the impressive shadow of the gleaming newer Arlington International Race Course (see separate listing). And although these may be a little worn and dingy, they can provide thoroughbred- or harness-racing action when the big track is closed—or isn't convenient. Each year, all of the area tracks bid on different schedules of thoroughbred and harness action—and, as you might guess, Arlington is pretty much able to dictate what it wants—meaning that the type, season, and length of schedule can vary widely from year to year. However, in general, Maywood Park offers harness racing, Sportsman's Park and Balmoral Park mix a short schedule of thoroughbreds with mostly harness, and Hawthorne Race Course usually balances separate thoroughbred and harness schedules. Sportsman's and Hawthorne are adjacent in Cicero, just southwest of the Chicago city limits; Maywood is in the suburb of Maywood, west of the city, just beyond Oak Park; and Balmoral is located in the far south suburb of Crete.

Sportsman's Park, 3301 S Laramie St, Cicero, IL 60650, 708/652-2812. Hawthorne Race Course, 3501 S Laramie St, Cicero, IL 60650, 708/780-3700. Maywood Park, 8600 W North Ave, Maywood, IL 60153, 708/343-4800. Balmoral Park, Hwy. IL 1 & Elms Court Ln, Crete, IL 60417, 708/672-7544. Seasons vary.

Best inside track to auto racing

Sante Fe Speedway

While Chicago may not be a big town for motorsports (rush hours on the Dan Ryan and Kennedy expressways notwithstanding), this family-owned and -operated track has been providing a varied schedule of racing (and other automotive-themed events) since the early 1950s. Located approximately 20 miles southwest of the Loop, Sante Fe Speedway offers a weekly calendar of NASCAR-sanctioned stock car races on its clay quarter-mile and half-mile tracks. (Clay-track racing isn't as flat-out fast as stock-car racing on asphalt, but it can be more exciting, as participants jockey for position on sloping curves that come up every few seconds as they speed around the track.) Other events at this site (the only spot for complete motorsports in the immediate area) include monster-truck meets, demolition derbies, and midget-car races. The track often sponsors special nights for organized groups (Scouts, Indian Guides, etc.). Santa Fe Speedway usually offers at least three events each week.

Sante Fe Speedway, 9100 S Wolf Rd, Hinsdale, IL 60521, 708/839-1050. Late May–mid-Sept. $8 adults, $2 children under 12 (admission higher for some events).

Nearest place to go to the dogs

Wisconsin Greyhound Racing

"It's great that we now have greyhound racing," said the man from Wisconsin, "but where will they find small enough jockeys?" It's an old joke, but, until 1990, most people in Wisconsin didn't know that much about the sport. Then, in the wake of new legislation, the state's first two greyhound parks were opened, both conveniently accessible to the huge Chicago market of potential punters. Both are state-of-the-art facilities with banks of TV monitors, bars, food courts, snack counters, and upscale clubhouse facilities (with color monitors at every table). Wagering is similar to horse-racing, with win, place, show, quinella, perfecta, trifecta, and daily double betting options. There are evening races and matinees, with post times every 12 minutes, and year-round racing at one or the other of the two tracks. Accompanied children under 12 are permitted to matinees—but be sure to warn them not to hang around with the jockeys.

Dairyland Greyhound Park, PO Box 459, Kenosha, WI 53141, 414/657-8200, 800/233-3357. Geneva Lakes Kennel Club, PO Box 650, Delavan, WI 53115, 414/728-8000, 800/477-4552.

Best place to yawn at a cricket match

Wells Field

Wickets in the Windy City? Expatriated Brits and curious Chicagoans head for the Northwestern University campus for action on the cricket pitches at Wells Field and James Park. This British sport—complete with tea breaks and players dressed in immaculate whites—pits local squads against visiting teams composed of British Commonwealth expatriates (St. Louis, for example, fields all-India, all-Jamaica, and all-England elevens). In England, where the rules of the game were developed in the 1740s, an inning can last all day and a game may stretch to five days. In Chicago, they manage to fit the game into a single afternoon. Matches are played on Saturday and Sunday afternoons from early June through late September. Spectators are welcome and there is no admission fee. It may be confusing to Cubs fans, but it is a pleasant, civilized way to spend an afternoon. Tea, anyone?

Wells Field, Central St & Ashland Ave, Evanston, IL 60201 (adjacent to Dyche Stadium); James Park, Oakton & Dodge sts, Evanston, IL 60201. Info: Northwestern University Intramural Sports Dept, 847/491-5240; Evanston & Skokie Cricket Clubs, PO Box 605. Evanston, IL 60602.

Most proper place to preen at a polo match

Polo & Equestrian Club of Oak Brook

For the price of an $8 grandstand seat, you become a jet-setter for an afternoon and catch the action of a few chukkers of polo as you sip a tall Pimm's suitably garnished with cucumber. Matches are played on Sundays (beginning at 1 pm mid-June to mid-September). The action is fast and exciting and the competition vigorous as two teams of four mallet-wielding riders each attempt to drive a 4½-ounce ball into the opponent's goal. A well-trained polo pony is able to wheel quickly and is capable of fast acceleration and quick stops, following the ebb and flow of the game almost without guidance. However, the coordination between horse and rider is a joy to watch. Concession stands provide a variety of food and drink. After the matches, spectators are invited to meet the players in The Players' Club Pavilion and dine and dance until dusk.

Polo & Equestrian Club of Oak Brook, 1000 Oak Brook Rd, Oak Brook, IL 60521, 708/990-2394.

SPORTS (PARTICIPANT)

Most convenient golf courses (close in)

Chicago Park District Courses

To play golf in Chicago doesn't necessarily mean forking out fat greens fees—not for those who play the Chicago Park District's six urban courses. Costs are low, tee times may be reserved, and there are even two driving ranges and a miniature golf course. These courses can be scenic, too, as evidenced by the links at Lake Shore Drive and Waveland Avenue—formerly known as "Waveland" and renamed to honor former judge Sydney A. Marovitz. Even discounting Park District hyperbole describing the course as "reminiscent of the setting of Pebble Beach," this *is* an undeniably pretty setting along the breezy lakefront, with views of sailboats cutting across Lake Michigan and of Chicago's spectacular skyline. This 3,290-yard, par 36 course has tight greens and well-placed sand and water hazards (48 bunkers represent states in the Union when the course was built). Each hole was modeled after one of the most challenging on courses throughout the country. Another lakeside links is Jackson, at 63rd Street and Lake Shore Drive, the only Park District 18-hole course. The newest course, the Robert A. Black (2045 West Pratt Avenue), has a 2,600-yard, par 33 layout designed by the architects who created tournament-sanctioned Kemper Lakes.

Chicago Park District, 425 E McFetridge Dr,
Chicago, IL 60605, 312/294-2200; 312/747-2200 for
golf info. Fees vary by site, season, and day.

Most challenging golf course (farther out)
Cog Hill Golf & Country Club

Although it is something that is not widely known,
suburban Chicago boasts an impressive array of
high-quality golf courses. (In fact, one southwest
suburb—Orland Park—claims the largest per capita
concentration of golf courses in the country.) This
country club, approximately 45 minutes southwest
of downtown, is one of the best year-round sites for
golf that allows public use (with reservations). Cog
Hill offers four 18-hole courses, a driving range, and
complete pro shop and rental equipment;
"Dubsdread," its championship course, was ranked
by *Golf Digest* magazine among the Top 100 courses
in the United States. You never know who might be
trying out the course in the foursome behind you.
As of this writing, Cog Hill is a semipermanent host
site for the Midwest's most prestigious golf tournament, the Western Open, and is being considered as
host of the U.S. Open, and will stage the U.S.
Amateur tournament in 1997.

Cog Hill Golf & Country Club, 119th St & Archer
Ave, Lemont, IL 60439, 630/257-5872. Fees vary by
season and day.

Best golf a chip shot from downtown
Illinois Center Golf Course and Driving Range

What happens when a building boom goes bust and
plans for a massive office building are put on the
back burner? You build a golf course in its place!
This is what happened in 1994 when this 9-hole, par
3 golf course opened on 31 acres of prime downtown
real estate, just a chip shot or two off busy Michigan
Avenue and a few blocks from the heart of the financial district. Designed by famous golf-course
architects Dye Designs International, the course
includes the trademark Dye island green. The course
has a practice green, teaching pros, and a double-
deck, 40-slot driving range lighted for after-dark
practice and covered, heated driving stalls for colder
weather. A clubhouse offers a pro shop, indoor golf
learning center (with swing analyzers and video
equipment for personal tapings), locker rooms, and
a bar and grill. Memberships are available. Adjacent
Swissôtel, a popular business venue (see separate
listing in "Accommodations") offers golfing guests

reserved tee times (often a rare commodity) and also driving range reservations. These are obtainable through the concierge desk (which sports a golf flag and pole). Also, groups meeting at the hotel may book golf tee times through the hotel's sales department.

Illinois Center Golf Course and Driving Range, 221 N Columbus Dr, Chicago, IL 60601, 312/616-1146. Daily 6:30 am–8:30 pm.

Best all-around recreational resource
Chicago lakefront

Lake Michigan is one of Chicago's greatest resources. With 24 miles of publicly owned lake frontage threaded with parks, fishing piers, docks, and harbors, it also is a major focus of recreation. An 18-mile trail parallels a stretch of shoreline containing five parks and some of the city's extraordinary museums and famous sights. The trail is popular with bicyclists, skaters, runners, and walkers who savor cool lake breezes as they exercise. The northern terminus of the trail is the horseshoe peninsula enclosing Montrose Harbor, where Cold War missiles, since dismantled, pointed toward the Soviet Union. At the south end of the trail, near 71st Street, the South Shore Cultural Center offers theater and jazz. Trailside sights include a colorful replica of a Haidan Indian totem pole. The original was brought to Chicago by cheese magnate J.L. Kraft and returned to British Columbia in 1985 because of its historical tribal significance. The trail passes a monument of Lincoln during the period he was described as "a tall, gawky-looking fellow." The sculpture won worldwide acclaim for Augustus Saint Gaudens, who produced numerous pieces of Chicago's public art. The trail passes Oak Street beach, one of the city's most popular—and chic—beaches. For more cerebral recreation, the concrete pavilion, just south of North Avenue beach, has four built-in chess boards. Between moves, players enjoy striking views of the skyline. Other landmarks include revitalized Navy Pier, Buckingham Fountain, and Chicago's "Big Four" museums—Adler, Field, Shedd, and Science and Industry. The Park District's bikeway map highlights 28 points of interest.

Trendiest health club
The Athletic Club

This high-tech health club is a private-membership sports facility near Illinois Center. (Arrangements with the adjacent Hyatt and Fairmont allow hotel guests temporary membership privileges.) Within the six-level atrium-style building, you'll find just about everything needed to reshape and rejuvenate the body. Included is a $1/11$th-mile indoor track; eight-lane junior Olympic swimming pool; free weights; aerobic exercise rooms; a gymnasium with basketball hoops; and a rooftop putting green, sundeck, and splash pool. Also offered is a large selection of state-of-the-art weight training machines, supervised by individual trainers. Focal point of the Sporting Club is the 110-foot polymer wood resin "Wall," the largest in the world simulating the rock climbing experience (see separate listing).

The Athletic Club, 211 N. Stetson Ave, Chicago, IL 60601, 312/616-9000. Mon–Fri 5:30 am–10 pm, Sat & Sun 8 am–8 pm.

World's highest indoor climbing wall

The Athletic Club

For climbers who enjoy pitting their skills against sheer rock face, Chicago offers nothing to match the Grand Tetons—or even the climbing challenges of Wisconsin's Devil's Lake. But it does have "Mount Chicago"—and it is available to climbers whatever the weather. So, if scaling a 110-foot rock wall with your bare hands is your idea of a lunch break, then you'll be interested in visiting this high-tech fitness center adjoining the maze of shops, restaurants, and hotels of Illinois Center. Occupying a floor-to-ceiling, seven-story atrium is the world's tallest indoor, artificial rock-climbing wall. Designed in France, the wall is actually stronger than rock, built of super-tough polymer resin anchored to steel girders. Rock climbing experience isn't a prerequisite. Novices attend a one-hour orientation class covering safety skills, equipment use, and basic climbing technique. Surprisingly, this type of climbing is very controlled and quite safe. A body harness with a rope attached to anchored carabinier fasteners prevents climbers from falling more than a couple of feet. The key to this sport is upper-body and hand strength. Embedded all the way up the wall are preformed hand grips, which climbers use along with special nonskid shoes. This is a members-only club, but temporary memberships are granted to guests of the Fairmont Hotel, which is linked to the club by underground walkway.

The Athletic Club, 211 N Stetson Ave, Chicago, IL 60601, 312/616-9000. Mon–Fri 5:30 am–10 pm, Sat & Sun 8 am–8 pm.

Best tennis courts (outdoor)

In Chicago, there are many places tennis players can indulge in their sport of preference. Among them are more than 700 Chicago Park District-run courts (which are usually free, but often include potentially long waits), as well as many nonmember tennis clubs, such as Lake Meadows Tennis Club, which features six lighted courts, and Mid-Town Tennis Club with 18 courts (see separate listing). Park District courts include Waveland Courts (with 20 courts available at $2 per day), Diversey Courts (with four courts available at $7 per hour), and Wilson Courts (with five free courts). Many of the courts operated by the Park District include lights for night play and are open 7 am–10 pm, seven days per week. *Start them out early:* Get youngsters interested in tennis with enrollment in free tennis clinics that are part of the summer sports camp program (for ages 10 to 17) offered by the Chicago Park District. Tennis camps are held at a dozen or so parks and sports centers sprinkled throughout the city.

Chicago Park District, 312/747-2200; Lake Meadows Tennis Club, 3211 E Ellis St, Chicago, IL 60616, 312/225-3373.

Best tennis courts (indoor)

Mid-Town Tennis Club

Sprawling like a huge factory along a block of West Fullerton Avenue (just west of the Lincoln Park neighborhood on the North Side), this club is one of the city's top spots for tennis. It features 18 indoor Astro-turf courts, three practice lanes with ball-hitting machines, 24 teaching pros on staff, and a well-stocked pro shop. Although it's a private club, guests of many of the city's major hotels (and members of various tennis associations or other large out-of-town tennis clubs) can use the club during weekdays and weekend evenings; inquire with the club as to availability. Highly competitive tournaments (for all levels of ability) are often scheduled.

Mid-Town Tennis Club, 2020 W Fullerton Ave, Chicago, IL 60647, 312/235-2300.

Best jogging/running paths

Lincoln Park

For a scenic, aesthetically pleasing workout, head to the paths that crisscross Lincoln Park (the park itself, rather than the bordering neighborhood of the same name), most notably between Fullerton Parkway on the north and North Avenue. The paths pass statuary (Franklin, Grant, Shakespeare, Abe himself) and landmarks (the Victorian-era Conservatory and Café Brauer), and wind around the zoo (or through it when it's open) and the park's southern lagoon. The park is almost universally safe—but prudence dictates no solo jaunts after dark. The best times to hit the trails are first thing in the morning (for relative solitude and the sunrise over the lake) or just after work (for crowds and—perhaps—chance meetings). To cross Lake Shore Drive to the cement jogging-and-bicycling strip alongside the lake, use the foot bridge just north of North Avenue or the viaduct at Fullerton.

Chicago Park District, 425 E McFetridge Dr, Chicago, IL 60605, 312/747-2200. Lincoln Park Fieldhouse, 2045 N Lincoln Park West, Chicago, IL 60614, 312/294-4750. All city parks close at 11 pm.

Most grueling guided tour of Chicago
Chicago Marathon

This annual 26.2-mile guided tour of Chicago is taken by about 10,000 sweaty people on a Sunday in late October. The swiftest complete the tour inside 2½ hours. This big-time marathon, attracting elite runners from around the globe, is a good spectator event as well as one for *fit* participants (preferably with at least six months' training). You can watch the start at Daley Plaza and walk over to catch the finish at Grant Park. There's entertainment along the route—typically by high-school bands and drill teams and by ethnic groups such as the Shannon Rovers, a mariachi band, and, as the race winds through Chinatown, a Chinese dance troupe. Disc jockeys play music at various points along the route. Highlights of past marathons include the world record time of 2:08:05 set in 1984 by Welshman Steve Jones and the 1985 2:21:21 time of Joan Benoit that set a new American record for women. There's a total of more than $250,000 in prize money. Registration fee is $25.

Best hotel pool where Tarzan swam
Hotel Inter-Continental

It doesn't take a large stretch of imagination to picture Johnny Weissmuller, Olympic gold medalist and movie Tarzan, swimming laps in this 25-meter junior Olympic-sized pool. Nor is it difficult to imagine elite visitors relaxing on woven-wicker furniture or watching from balcony seats. Located on the 14th floor, the pool was considered a feat of engineering in 1929 and the crowning jewel of the Medinah Athletic Club. With its handsome Majolica tile, ornate terra-cotta and marble Fountain of Neptune, wrought-iron scones and chandeliers, the opulent Venetian-influenced pool has been meticulously restored. Natural light floods in through aqua-toned stained-glass windows. The glass, shaped to resemble fish scales, reflects in the pool and shimmers like fish when the water is riffled. Nonguests may use the pool and a state-of-the-art health club with weight room, exercise area, and cardiovascular equipment room at a cost of $10 per visit ($85 a month, $850 annually). Change rooms, saunas, showers, and toiletries are provided. Massage services and a personal trainer by appointment. *Movie trivia:* This is where mobster Al Capone threw a flamboyant poolside party on an episode of the *Untouchables* TV show.

Hotel Inter-Continental, 505 N Michigan Ave, Chicago, IL 60611, 312/321-8830.

Best beach for watching volleyball
Oak Street Beach

Summer can seem so long-awaited and so intense in Chicago. And when the rays of the sun sufficiently warm the water and the sand, this Gold Coast beach (nestled along a curve of Lake Shore Drive and accessible via a walkway under the Drive) attracts a crowd of beautiful people, shoeless office workers on lunch breaks, and sun-lovers from across the city and outlying areas. This is a great spot for beach volleyball, both impromptu games and "officially sponsored" tournaments (usually in the shadow of giant inflatable beer cans touting said sponsors). But if even that sounds too strenuous, just kick back, relax, and enjoy the passing parade of often-exquisite barely dressed bodies. Both sexes can enjoy some low-impact ogling here, as the beautiful people flex their muscles and work on their tans. This beach gets very crowded, but the crowds thin out once the sun slips behind the skyline (long before sunset).

Oak Street Beach, Oak St & Lake Shore Dr. Memorial Day–mid-Sept, 9 am–9 pm. Chicago Park District beach info: 312/747-0832.

Best smelt fishing
Lake Michigan shoreline

When spring arrives, smelt fishers (many accompanied by groups of friends, spouses, and children) head for Lake Michigan in pre-dawn hours to set up nets to catch the ubiquitous small, finger-sized fish (which are related to salmon and trout) as they head to the shore to spawn. To say the least, this is not exactly a prime example of skill fishing—it seems that cases of beer and tailgate party-type munchies are as much a part of smelt fishing as are nets and fish-holding buckets. Most sporting-goods stores can outfit you for smelt fishing for around $30, and many groups of veteran fishers will gladly give you pointers. To join the party, set your alarm for around

2 am and head for a stretch of lakeshore; a particularly good and popular spot is just south of Navy Pier.

Best perch fishing

Montrose Harbor Pier

For close to 40 years, man and boy Marty Steadman, a Chicagoan born and bred, has been fishing Lake Michigan for perch. He remembers the "good old days" when it was easy to end up with a stringer of fat perch but also feels that after a decade or so in decline, fishing has picked up again. He's one of the diehard fishermen who head for the cement pier at Montrose Harbor, and these days he often goes with his son. When the fish are biting and the action is hot, you'll find in excess of 100 people on the pier before dawn, casting for "jumbos." There is a baithouse in the adjoining park where you can buy tackle and live bait, including minnows, various kinds of worms, and the "peelers" (crabs that have shed their shells) that many old-timers swear by. Tackle ranges from ultra-light spinning and spin-cast outfits to traditional bamboo poles, and the so-called "power lines"—actually a hand line rigged with a heavy weight and multiple hooks. Jumbo perch can weigh in at around one pound, but usually are smaller.

Montrose Harbor Pier, east of Lake Shore Dr at Wilson Ave (4400 N). Chicago Park District harbor information: 312/747-7527.

Best salmon fishing

Chicago Sportfishing Association

You don't have to travel to the Columbia River or other storied Pacific salmon-fishing locales to hook a fighting coho or hefty chinook. Pacific salmon are right here in Lake Michigan, transplanted as part of a hugely successful program to revive sportfishing in the Midwest. In fact, right off the Chicago shoreline, anglers are hauling in 20-pound salmon and trout on charter-boat excursions. Salmon are fun to catch, but don't look to a cheap dinner. Charter-boat prices start at $395 for a maximum of six persons for five hours. Included are the use of fishing tackle and expert guidance in fighting and landing your fish. Of course, there's never a guarantee of catching fish, but charter-boat skippers, with their reputation (and livelihood) on the line, will use their skills and experience to give you the best possible chance. Be prepared for an early start (on the dock before 7 am, back by noon). Charter boats operate out of most harbors in the greater Chicago area and usually belong to an association such as the one listed below.

Chicago Sportfishing Association, 3414 S Parnell St, Chicago, IL 60616, 312/922-1100.

Best spot to learn to sail

Chicago Rainbow Fleet Learn-to-Sail Program

There's clear sailing ahead for men and women in search of yachting expertise—and each other. The Chicago Park District's Rainbow Fleet learn-to-sail program is an inexpensive route to the former with a notable reputation for the latter. It is headquartered at the Burnham Harbor where, for about $85 for five one-hour lessons, you get a complete introduction to sailing that includes both classroom training and hands-on experience. In class, you'll learn basics such as detecting wind direction, the effects of being upwind and downwind, and the theory of tacking, as well as safety practices. Afloat in the protected harbor you'll learn maneuvering, balance, and techniques such as the use of a dagger board (a device used to stabilize the boat). The class is fun, and it is a great way to meet interesting people. You don't even need to know how to swim to participate (but, if you don't, it's not a bad idea to learn).

Chicago Rainbow Fleet Learn-to-Sail Program, Burnham Harbor, 1362 Lynn White Dr, Chicago, IL 60610, 312/294-2399.

Choicest canoe rentals

Chicagoland Canoe Base

To explore Chicago's waterways the way the city's first tourists, Marquette and Jolliet, did (albeit not in a birch-bark vessel), head to this Northwest Side shop specializing in canoe rentals. For around $30 per day, customers can rent various-sized canoes plus necessary accessories, such as carrying racks (for mounting canoes on cars), paddles, and personal flotation devices. The outfitter also stocks more than 700 books on watersports and a large selection of area maps. The store reports that the most popular waterways for navigation by its customers include the North Branch of the Chicago River, the Des Plaines River, the Skokie Lagoons, and the Busse Reservoir. This is the only store in the area that rents canoes; personnel there can put you in touch with various canoe clubs and groups.

Chicagoland Canoe Base, 4019 N Naragansett Av, Chicago, IL 60634, 312/777-1489. Mon–Wed, Fri & Sat 9 am–5 pm; Thu 9 am–9 pm.

Best bets for biking, skating, and paddling

Lincoln Park

Even more so than the city's other fine parks, Lincoln Park provides a variety of summertime activities. Paramount among these are fun ways to propel yourself along the paths and waterways of the park. To get your wheel's spinning, head to the bike and skate concession at Cannon Drive and Fullerton Parkway, and rent a bicycle, a pair of roller skates, or, perhaps, a pair of trendy roller blades. Skaters favor both the park's meandering paths and a short stretch of the nearby lakefront; cyclists often head farther afield along Lake Michigan—the Chicago Lakefront Bikepath extends along the lakeshore from 79th Street on the south to Ardmore Avenue on the north . . . a total of approximately 137 blocks. For a more leisurely excursion, try a paddleboat ride on the park's elongated lagoon. These two-seater boats powered by pedals are fun for adults and kids alike; personal flotation devices are provided with the rental.

Lincoln Park Bicycle & Roller-Skate Rentals, 2400 N Cannon Dr, Chicago, IL 60614. Lincoln Park Paddleboat Rentals (behind Café Brauer), 2000 N Stockton Dr, Chicago, IL 60614.

Best 16-inch softball pickup games

Oz Park

One of the quickest ways to tag yourself an out-of-towner is to watch a neighborhood softball game and ask, "But where are the fielders' gloves?" While the rest of the country seems to favor 12-inch (or even 14-inch) softball played with mitts, Chicagoans know that *real* men and women play 16-inch softball barehanded. In this spirited, bar league-type of game, this can mean more than a few jammed fingers (rarely will you find a devoted 16-inch player who also plays the piano), but, in general, it's a fun, easy-to-play game. To watch or even join in pickup games, head for Oz Park in the Lincoln Park neighborhood. This sprawling, appealing park (named for L. Frank Baum's fictional wonderland; the author once lived on an adjacent street) attracts games nearly every evening and weekend afternoon during summer. It's also near Halsted Street bars, an important consideration for most true 16-inch-softball players, who consider post-game revelry as indispensable as a burly clean-up hitter.

Oz Park, Webster Ave (2200 N) and Larrabee St (600 W) at Lincoln Ave.

Best spot to horse around

Palos Hills Riding Stables

Hidden lakes and ponds, cattail marshes, and meadows abloom with wild flowers await riders who explore on horseback the miles of bridle paths of the Cook County Forest Preserves. Tucked on the edge of more than 13,000 acres of preserve in the Southwest suburbs is the riding school owned and operated by Martha and Chris Doll, a family business for 30 years. The school provides lessons for beginners, intermediates, and advanced riders and offers Western and English styles. Lessons are conducted in outdoor fenced stables; during winter, in a heated indoor area. Experienced riders can head out to the meandering trails of the forest preserve, directly across the street from the stables. A one-hour lesson, covering the basics needed to get started, costs about $15. During summer, the school sponsors summer camp, horse-show competitions, and barbecues. Four times a year, "Horsing Around With Singles Day" offers equestrian-minded singles a day of enjoying the horses and a chance to make new friends.

Palos Hills Riding Stables, 10100 S Kean Ave, Palos Hills, IL 60465, 708/598-7718. Classes held year-round; call for current schedule.

Best shot for straight arrows

Archery Custom Shop

Whether you bow-hunt, shoot arrows for recreation, or do neither but wish to learn about either or both, this west-suburban store (just beyond the Chicago city limits) is the place to go. The Archery Custom Shop is fully stocked with more than 1,500 standard bows and crossbows, as well as a wide variety of accessories, clothing, books, and videos. The shop's upstairs is an indoor practice and competition range featuring 20 targets. General lessons and high-level professional instruction are available, as is information on area clubs (including a number of Chicago Park District practice sites), contests, and hunting outings. This shop is an approved warranty repair site for most major-manufacturer archery equipment.

Archery Custom Shop, 7240 W Madison St, Forest Park, IL 60130, 708/366-4864. Mon–Fri noon–9 pm, Sat 10 am–5 pm.

Best ice skating (outdoor)

Chicago Park District Ice Skating Rinks

For those unable to follow the sun and who don't want to hibernate, the Chicago Park District offers numerous programs and activities to help make Chicago's often bitterly cold winters more bearable. Ice skating can help warm body and spirit—you can worry later about stiffness and pain. Flooded baseball fields in Lincoln Park provide an oval-shaped rink created and maintained by the Park District (resurfaced regularly with a fresh coat of ice) for free use by the public. Near the rink is a warming house, open on weekends. Be sure to call first; availability varies according to weather conditions.

Chicago Park District, Lincoln Park at Waveland Avenue, Chicago, IL 60614, 312/742-7839.

Best ice skating (indoor)

McFetridge Sports Center

New York City has the traditional seasonal skating rink at Rockefeller Center. St. Louis has "the Great One," Wayne Gretzky, no doubt inspiring a new generation of youth to leave their skateboards behind and take up ice skating and hockey (well, maybe not). But Chicago, even with its famed ice-box winters, just isn't that big a skating town. However, if gliding on silver skates like Hans Brinker is one of your passions, you *can* skate in Chicago, even in August. This Park District facility (on the Northwest Side) offers open skating most weekend days and some weekdays; equipment rental and blade-sharpening are available. Although we can't say we've tried this (if people were meant to skate, we wouldn't have invented sidewalk salt), it sounds like a fun way to keep cool on a sweltering summer day in the city.

McFetridge Sports Center, 3843 N California Ave, Chicago, IL 60618, 312/742-7586. Open year-round; hours vary by season.

Slickest sledding

Swallow Cliff Toboggan Chutes

Back in the late 1920s and early 1930s, America's Olympic hopefuls came to this south suburban Cook County Forest Preserve to hurtle down the Alpine Ski Jump. Today, the hopefuls are youngsters with an eye to the sky, hoping for sufficient snowfall for a family outing to the Swallow Cliff toboggan chutes. Providing the thrills are six 90-foot-high concrete chutes built with a wooden deck. After trudging up

111 stairs, your toboggan flies down the 376-foot-long chute and onto a 900-foot-long swail at the bottom. You can rent a toboggan ($3 an hour) large enough to hold up to four adults. If you bring your own sled (only traditional toboggan-types are permitted), it is subject to a safety inspection. There are a warming house with a fireplace and a snack bar with coffee, hot chocolate, and a limited selection of edibles. Phone ahead (recorded information at 708/448-4417) to be sure the chutes are open.

Swallow Cliff Toboggan Chutes, Cook County Forest Preserves, Hwy 83 $1/8$-mile W of Rte 45 (La Grange Rd), Palos Hills, IL 60465, 708/366-9420.

Toughest scrums

Rugby Football

It was during a soccer game at England's Rugby School in 1823 that a schoolboy disregarded the "no hands" rule, scooped up the ball, and sprinted toward goal. This breach led to the game of rugby football, forerunner of American football. British-style rugby is popular in Chicago, with 20 clubs from the city and suburbs competing in the Chicago Area Rugby Football Union. You can watch a game (or participate in one) during spring and fall. Rugby is a contact sport, played 15 to a side, in which kicking, tackling, and lateral and backward passing are allowed. Blocking and forward passing are prohibited. Play begins from a "scrummage"—a huddle in which players of both teams attempt to kick the ball to a teammate. A touchdown, called a "try," is worth three points, five if converted by a place-kick. A drop-kick scores four points, a place-kick earns three. Spectators join in the rugby postgame tradition of repairing to a local watering hole for traditional suds and songs. Check for games and locations.

Chicago Area Rugby Football Union, P.O. Box 4033, Oak Park, IL 60303-4033, 708/879-1300.

KIDS

Best dining spot with kids—breakfast

Walker Bros. Original Pancake House

Synonymous with Sundays around the Chicago area is a visit to one of the Walker Bros. pancake houses. Kids love this classic North Shore breakfast spot because of the great and unusual pancakes. Adults love to go along because of the great oven-baked omelettes—spinach or ham with bacon and cheese are good. Pancakes include a chocolate-chip version and banana pancakes, made with fresh fruit and served with a tropical sauce made with oranges and pineapples. Of course, Walkers is famous for its apple pancakes, serving close to 1,000 a week, and for huge, fluffy German pancakes served with fruit. A junior plate offers three pancakes, a choice of meat or an egg, and a Snickers bar. The pancakes are made from a recipe that food maven the late James Beard named as among the best in the country. Other breakfast choices include pigs in a blanket— sausages wrapped in jackets of flaky pastry, a well- made eggs Benedict, and crepes featuring spinach, seafood, or imported Belgian chocolate. The ambi- ence is stunning—sunlight streams in through stained-glass and antique Tiffany leaded windows, oak paneling is accented with gleaming brass. Next door is the delightful hands-on Kohl Children's Museum (see separate listing), making a combined breakfast/museum outing a nice idea.

Walker Bros. Original Pancake House, 153 Green
Bay Rd, Wilmette, IL 60091, 708/251-6000. Sun–Thu 7
am–10:30 pm, Fri & Sat 7 am–11 pm.

Best dining spot with kids—lunch

Rock 'n' Roll McDonald's

There's nothing unusual about a McDonald's with
a drive-up window—but how about one with a restored 1960s Corvette parked in the dining room?
This McDonald's, with its rock 'n' roll theme, is the
second-busiest in the world (only after the
McDonald's in Moscow). It serves 2.5 million customers annually, many of whom are attracted as
much by the bop as by the burgers. This veritable
museum is crammed with antique dolls of Elvis,
Howdy Doody, Mickey and Minnie Mouse, and
Popeye, hundreds of movie posters, and stills of such
stars as Marilyn Monroe, Frankie Avalon, and Little
Richard. There's also a life-size display of the Beatles.
Booths are equipped with mini-jukeboxes, from
which patrons can select their favorite 1950s hits,
played free of charge. Try your hand at one of the
vintage game machines (proceeds benefit local chari-
ties), print your name on a metal medallion, or simply
browse the remarkable collection of rock 'n' roll
memorabilia. Also found here (but not at your typical
McDonald's) is an automatic teller machine and a
gift counter. Best to go during weekday mornings or
post-lunch afternoon; expect to wait up to 45 minutes on weekend nights.

Rock 'n' Roll McDonald's, 600 N Clark St, Chicago,
IL 60610, 312/664-7940. Daily 24 hours.

Best dining spot with kids—dinner

Hard Rock Café

Universally, restaurants in this popular chain (more
than a dozen worldwide) are a hit with kids. Witness
the frequent waits at most locations. Kids drag along
parents, who often are surprised by the good quality
of the basic fare—plump hamburgers, spicy chili,
chicken, and ribs. Of course, it is not the food but
the motif (and the cachet) that attracts the kids.
Adorning the walls of this circular building is a
melange of rock-music memorabilia, including gui-
tars from Motley Crüe and INXS, a guitar—"ax" in
the vernacular—one owned by superstar Mick Jagger
of the Rolling Stones, countless pictures of "rockers,"
and authentic gold records. The Hard Rock attracts
a largely out-of-town crowd, prepared to wait in line,
and willing to pay around $15 for a souvenir T-shirt,
which are almost as popular as the food.

Hard Rock Café, 63 W Ontario St, Chicago, IL
60610, 312/943-2252. Mon–Thu 11 am–11 pm, Fri 11
am–1:30 am, Sat 11 am–1 am, Sun 11:30 am–10:30
pm.

Best dining spot with kids—brunch
The Ritz-Carlton

Sometimes adults can't resist sneaking a slice of
pizza or an ant-on-a-stick from the children's Sunday brunch table. It is set up in a separate area from
the sumptuous brunch spread and is designed to
disabuse youngsters of the idea that Sunday brunch
is *bor-ring*. Kid-height tables are set with leopard-
print tablecloths topped with silver chafing dishes
filled with everything from pizza-by-the-slice and
macaroni and cheese to chicken nuggets and ants-
on-a-stick (celery filled with peanut butter and rolled
in raisins). Bowls are filled with M&Ms, fresh fruit,
and Jell-O. A stuffed animal jungle sets a backdrop
for the brunch. Meanwhile, back at the adult area
are made-to-order omelettes, piles of crab claws,
mounds of shrimp, and assorted pâtés and French
cheeses—plus brunch standards such as eggs
Benedict and Belgian waffles with shaved chocolate,
raspberries, and blackberries. A salad station includes the likes of grilled salmon with red onion
caper relish, onion tart with rissoto, and roasted
Cajun potato salad. For the health conscious, an
"alternative" station features offerings lower in fat,
cholesterol, sodium, and calories—the likes of cous
cous salad, root vegetable salad, and celery root and
apple slaw. Yes, on Sundays it is appropriate to take
along youngsters when you decide to put on the Ritz.

The Dining Room, The Ritz-Carlton, 160 E Pearson
St, Chicago, IL 60611, 312/266-1000. Sun brunch
seatings at 10:30 am and 1 pm.

Best dining spot to drive up to with kids
Superdawg Drive-In

As you head for this Far Northwest Side eatery, you
may want to explain the differences between "drive-
in" and "drive-up" dining to the kids, because this
is one of the few examples of the former remaining
in the Chicago area. Year-round (yes, even in winter),
you can pull up here, have your order taken over a
squawk-box speaker, and wait for a car-hop to deliver
your food. (Alas, since this is Chicago and not L.A.,
your car-hop won't be on roller skates.) Superdawg
offers solid, if basic drive-in food—dogs, burgers,
homemade chili and soups, steak sandwiches, fries,
malts, etc.—but the main attraction is the unique

service. (Another whimsical attraction is the huge
fiberglass he-man and girlfriend hot dog characters
complete with lit, blinking eyes towering over the
structure's roof.)

Superdawg Drive-In, 6363 N Milwaukee Ave,
Chicago, IL 60646, 312/763-0660. Sun–Thu 11 am–1
am, Fri & Sat 11 am–2 am.

Best dining spot with a side order of magic

Schulien's Restaurant and Saloon

Kids love magicians but don't always have the same
affinity for nutrition. They can get an order of both
at this old speakeasy that has been entertaining
Chicagoans with dinner-table magic since 1915.
Owner Charlie Schulien, now in his sixties, recalls
his father, Big Matt Schulien, performing magic
tricks during Prohibition. This family tradition continues in an old-style tavern with original woodwork
and leaded glass around the bar. Sleight of hand,
card tricks, and other magic are performed evenings,
beginning at about 6:30 pm, by four rotating magicians. Enjoy dinner and request that a magician stop
by your table afterwards. With the knowledge of
what's to come—and when—kids often display rare
attention to their plates. The cuisine is hearty German—
schnitzels and pork hocks, with a generous complimentary relish tray, plus ribs, thuringer, brats, and
a selection of sandwiches with appeal to youngsters.
Tough justice: Among this saloon's entertaining wall
signs is one attributed to Matt Schulien in the
1930s—"Don't you squawk if you get a tough steak.
You only got one! I've got a whole icebox full."

Schulien's Restaurant and Saloon, 2100 W Irving
Park Rd, Chicago, IL 60628, 312/478-2100. Tue–Fri
11:30 am–10 pm, Sat 4–11 pm, Sun 4–10 pm.

Best dining spot to party with your kids

Chuck E. Cheese

Whether for an elaborate kids' birthday party or just
a fun family night out, outlets of this franchised
chain of pizza parlors provide an entertaining atmosphere designed to occupy today's raised-on-TV-and-
video-games kids. Presided over by Chuck E. Cheese
("the 'E' stands for entertainment!"), a lively
audioanimatronics (à la Disneyland) mouse, these
restaurants offer not only pizza, a salad bar, hot
dogs, Italian submarines, and other sandwiches, but
also games, rides, and other diversions. Approximately twice an hour, Chuck E. and his three-piece
band regale the crowd with versions of pop hits as

well as upbeat original songs, while TV monitors show close-ups of the mechanical animals. Seating is in large booths or at long tables (which can be reserved for parties or large groups). For parents who aren't sure that they could bear so much "fun" without a diversion or two themselves, Chuck E. Cheese serves beer, wine, and wine coolers, along with soda and coffee. Expect frequent requests for funds to feed the voracious appetites of game machines; tickets are awarded for skill, redeemable for mostly junky—but kid-pleasing—prizes at a booth. (Some locations of this chain were previously known as ShowBiz Pizza Place.)

Chuck E. Cheese, 4031 W 95th St, Oak Lawn, IL 60453, 708/425-5800. Sun–Thu 10 am–10 pm, Fri & Sat 11 am–11 pm. Also 12 other Chicago-area locations.

Best hotel when traveling with children
Camp Hyatt

Family trips may become more memorable when parents and children spend time not only with each other but away from each other. The Camp Hyatt program offers this—along with an alternative to using the TV as a babysitter—with supervised programs for children ages 3 through 15. Kids take cooking classes with a hotel chef, go kite-flying, and are involved in such activities as arts and crafts, sports, sing-alongs, puppet shows, movies, museum tours, and various outings. There is a charge for the program of $4–$5/hour, $25/day, exclusive of meals. Other kid-friendly amenities include children's menus for room service and at restaurants, reduced room rates (kids free in parents' room, half price for a second room), a Kids' Frequent Stay Program (redeemable for a carrypack), the loan of games, and a check-in package that includes a free cap.

At various Hyatt hotels (see separate listings, "Accommodations").

Top tour that loops the Loop
Loop Tour Train

For anyone with any trepidation about riding Chicago's famous elevated trains (and there really is no reason to be fearful, except perhaps during nighttime and off hours), this guided tour aboard an El train provides a good introduction. It also is a good way to get a unique perspective of downtown Chicago architecture and learn something of Loop history. Held on Saturday afternoons with four different departure times (12:55, 1:35, 2:15, 2:55), the 40-minute tour makes a good family outing ($5 adults,

$2.50 children under 12). Tour guides point out such landmarks as the Chicago Board of Trade, with its distinctive rooftop statue of Ceres, the Roman goddess of grain and harvest; Marshall Field's flagship store on State Street; the new beaux-arts-style Harold Washington Library Center; and the Monadnock Building, built in 1891, an architectural treasure which, though only 16 stories tall, once was the world's tallest building and remains the highest wall-bearing structure in Chicago. The Loop train opened in 1994 in conjunction with the "'Round & About The Loop" visitor facility (which sells tour tickets) in the Chicago Cultural Center, which incorporates exhibitions, a video overview, and literature featuring public art, attractions, and landmarks in the Loop.

Chicago Cultural Center, 77 E Randolph St, Chicago, IL 60602, 312/744-2400.

Best boat for history and histrionics
Wacky Pirate Cruise

As the pirate captain growls a "Shiver me timbers, mateys," new shipmates climb aboard, in search of high adventure on the wild waters of the Chicago River and Lake Michigan. It may not be a tall-masted ship flying the feared skull-and-crossbones, but Mercury Cruiseline's Wacky Pirate Cruise is the next best thing for kids (and their parents). The one-hour cruise mixes pirate antics and songs with low-impact geography and history lessons as the cruise slips under bridges and through the Chicago lock system, offering a lakeside view of Navy Pier, the city's Water Filtration Plant, the Shedd Aquarium, and the Adler Planetarium. Junior buccaneers are issued pirate hats and a kazoo (for lively accompaniment during "Yo Ho Ho and a Bottle of Rum," and other outlaws-of-the-sea chanteys) and at cruise's end, receive a certificate commemorating their "survival" of this rugged journey. Strong rumor has it that the cruise's lively pirate host, "Buccaneer Bob," is the former Michigan Avenue bridge saxophone player, Little Howlin' Wolf.

Wacky Pirate Cruise, under Michigan Ave bridge at Michigan Ave & Wacker Dr, 312/902-1500. June–Sept Thu–Sun 10–11 am. Mailing address: Mercury Chicago's Skyline Cruiseline, PO Box 68, Palatine, IL 60078. $8 adults, $5 children under 12.

Best spots to watch the presses roll
Newspaper Tour

Chicago is a great newspaper town, with columnists such as Mike Royko and Bob Greene carrying on the traditions of Ben Hecht and Ring Lardner. Although the city is down to two major dailies, they provide a lively competitive environment. Both offer free tours—ideal to introduce cyberspace kids to the traditions of newsprint. Although the editorial offices of the *Chicago Tribune* remain in the historic Tribune Building on Michigan Avenue, printing has moved across town to the Freedom Center. Touring the five-story plant, visitors view ten offset presses that can print up to 70,000 newspapers an hour and the packaging area, where 28 million sections are inserted to create almost 400,000 newspaper bundles every week. They watch a nine-minute video about the newspaper's history and production and learn how a telecommunication satellite transmits pages to printing sites throughout the Midwest. In contrast, the *Chicago Sun-Times* is conceived, composed, and printed under one roof at its headquarters alongside the Chicago River. Forty-five-minute group tours visit the newsroom, composing room, and press room. Even those who don't take a tour can ogle the mighty presses through the glass partitions of a corridor paralleling the press room.

Chicago Tribune, Freedom Center, 777 W Chicago Ave, Chicago, IL 60610, 312/222-2116. Guided tours hourly Mon–Fri 9:30 am–3:30 pm. *Chicago Sun-Times,* 435 N Wabash Ave, Chicago, IL 60611, 312/321-2311. Tours by reservation only Mon–Fri 10:30 am.

Best bet to get in the Schwinn of things

Bicycle Museum of America

Parents, remember the Stingray bicycle from the 1960s, with its high-rise handlebars and banana seat? Grandparents, how about the Hopalong Cassidy from 1950, complete with fringes and six-gun and holster? This is a fun museum for families—with plenty of hands-on exhibits—that also offers some learning about cultural and socioeconomic history. It demonstrates how society has been transformed and modernized by changes in technology as it chronicles bicycling's broad, rich contribution to American culture. A world-class collection—you would have to go to England or Holland to find a bicycle museum of this caliber (Europe has 40 bicycle museums)—follows the history of the bicycle from 19th-century bone-rattling, filling-loosening antiques to the dazzling machines of today and tomorrow. With thousands of artifacts woven into a multimedia exhibition, it is, as curator James L. Hurd likes to say, "the King Tut's tomb of the bicycle." Here, you'll acquire such tidbits of information as the fact that Queen Victoria rode a bicycle and helped make public exercise socially acceptable; that in the 1890s Chicago had more than 100 bicycle clubs; that in 1899 there were 101 bicycle manufacturers in Chicago. Start your tour by watching a 15-minute video, "The History of the Bicycle," then view more than 140 machines, including an 1870s Ariel "penny farthing," an 1898 Sociable (a "honeymoon" tandem bike with side-by-side seating), and a shiny, red streamlined 1934 model designed to resemble a motorbike. The collection ranges from 1818 to next year's models.

Bicycle Museum of America, North Pier, 435 E Illinois St, Chicago, IL 60611, 312/222-0500. Mon–Thu 10 am–6 pm, Fri & Sat 10 am–8 pm, Sun noon–5:15 pm. $1.50 adults, $1 children & seniors.

Dandiest night with dinosaurs
Family Overnight, The Field Museum

In real life, of course, there is no Jurassic Park—at least not yet—so there's no likelihood of you and your kids being locked in overnight with dinosaurs. On the other hand, there's the Family Overnight program at the Field Museum. Held six to eight times a year, it allows children grades one to six and accompanying adults to spend the night in the museum. They are invited to bring sleeping bag, pillows, foam pads, flashlights, and anything else that will help them bed down in one of the exhibit areas—perhaps with Northwest Coast Indians and Eskimos to keep them company, or maybe with Indians before Columbus. Here is an opportunity to tour the museum after hours and to take an eerie self-guided flashlight tour of the Inside Ancient Egypt exhibit with its pharaoh's tomb, mummies, and gold baubles. Included are natural science workshops and a storytelling session. The museum provides an evening snack and continental breakfast. Groups are large, with up to 300 participants, so there typically is not a waiting list (although a similar project, for scouts and other groups, is so much in demand that its is drawn by lottery). Cost is $40 per participant ($35 for museum members). The event usually runs from 5:45 pm Saturday until 9 am Sunday.

Family Overnight, Field Museum of Natural History, Roosevelt Rd & Lake Shore Dr, Chicago, IL 60605, 312/922-9410.

Best old-time country store
The Hollywood Country Store

Norm Scaman, a compulsive collector, has stocked this 1893 building with merchandise from the early

1900s. Formerly known as the Olde Country Store, this time-warp spot was rechristened with the acquisition of a 100-year-old railroad-station sign for "Hollywood, Illinois"—a community that became known as Brookfield in 1918. Shelves here are lined with tins and boxes—tea, coffee, cocoa, Log Cabin syrup; clotheslines strung wall to wall are festooned with household goods, corsets, and long underwear. There are a potbellied stove, a display of haberdashery, and a pole with a metal grabber for retrieving items from high shelves. A prized possession is a potato-chip can marketed under the brand name Mrs. Japp. The company prudently became Jay's Potato Chips on December 8, 1941, the day following the attack on Pearl Harbor. An old post office features a brass combination mail slot, money orders from 1908, and registered mail from 1898. Scaman delights in helping youngsters exchange baseball cards (he has a 50,000-card collection) and make their careful selections at his candy counter.

The Hollywood Country Store, 8420 Brookfield Ave, Brookfield, IL 60513, 708/447-7955. Sat & Sun noon–4 pm.

Best miniature grocery store

Kohl Children's Museum

By traveling no farther than north suburban Wilmette, children can take an exotic journey to ancient Phonecia in the new Long Ago and Far Away exhibit. After a simulated voyage on a Phonecian sailing ship, they can help prepare a meal for the king, search for treasure in the mines and bargain for goods in an exotic market. Closer to home is a more familiar marketplace—a supermarket-in-miniature, where youngsters fill shopping carts with groceries; learn how to use scales and the cash registers; and learn how to shop for healthy meals in the fruit, vegetable, dairy, and meat departments. Other exhibits include part of a real Chicago El train that transports kids on a simulated tour of the city; workshops on cultural diversity and recycling; and visits from a roaming robot named Orbit. By encouraging children to do the kinds of things they enjoy doing in play, this museum provides a learning experience. In fact, unless you tell them, youngsters won't know they're busy learning—not when there is fun role-playing with clothes to dress up in and face painting, enormous bubbles to create, a sports car and motorcycle to "drive," and an array of toys to play with, from blocks and construction sets to simple computers. *Dining tip:* For big fluffy pancakes and pigs-in-blankets, stop next door at Walker Bros. Original Pancake House (see separate listing, "Dining").

Kohl Children's Museum, 165 Green Bay Rd,
Wilmette, IL 60091, 847/251-7781. Tue–Sat 10 am–5
pm, Sun noon–5 pm.

Top spot for tactile tunnels
Chicago Children's Museum

Squeals of childish delight are the norm at this
wonderful hands-on museum that really more resembles a giant playground—although learning is
the purpose behind the play. At the "hospital," young
doctors and nurses examine real x-rays, apply plaster casts, slide behind the wheel of an ambulance,
and graft onto a patient (through the magic of Velcro!)
a new heart, lung, or spleen. In a miniaturized
Chicago, youngsters can visit a scaled-down post
office and TV station and stop at the Art Institute,
where they can dress up in plumed hats, ruffles, and
baubles to imitate historical portraits. Popular attractions include a fully equipped mini-kitchen, a
bubble machine (that produces a bubble large
enough to enclose a child from head to toe), a crawl-
through tunnel of multitextured materials to test the
sense of touch, and an exhibit called Magic and
Masquerades that delves into the mystery and beauty
of West African masks and artifacts. Be sure to visit
the Recycle Arts Center and kid-friendly museum
shop. Newly relocated at Navy Pier, the museum has
expanded its hours and added new exhibits.

Chicago Children's Museum, Navy Pier, 700 E
Grand Ave, Chicago, IL 60611, 312/527-1000.
Tue–Sun 10 am–5 pm. Admission: $5.00 per person;
members and infants free; free Thu 5–8 pm.

Best bet for helping hands
The Lambs

This is a sure bet to bring joy to the faces of youngsters—while helping more than 200 mentally re-
tarded adults find meaning in their lives through
productive jobs and learning experiences. They wait
on customers and operate cash registers, providing
a learning experience for visitors, too. The Lambs
began in 1961 as a storefront pet shop. The current
pet shop, in a remodeled turn-of-the century barn,
has the largest selection of kittens and puppies in
the state. Kids love the Children's Farmyard, with
animals to pet, hayrides, and pony rides. There also
are rides on a carousel, a miniature train, and a
vintage firetruck. An 18-hole miniature golf course
has a farm theme. Lambs operates nine businesses
on its 63-acre grounds. Workers produce beautiful

silk-screened cards, stationery, T-shirts, and sweat-shirts—and bake cakes, pies, turnovers, nut breads, doughnuts, and perennially popular butter cookies. An ice cream parlor has floats and sundaes; the Country Store offers an array of jams, jellies, chocolates, old-fashioned sponge candy, and slabs of homemade fudge. Special events include Kids' Day, complete with clowns and jugglers, water-ski show, arts-and-crafts fair, three major summer concerts (country, oldies, and jazz), a Halloween Festival, and Christmas Bazaar (Santa is in residence on weekends in December). The rustic Country Inn serves lunches, dinners, and a Sunday champagne brunch.

The Lambs, Inc. I-94 at Rockland Rd (Rte 176), Libertyville, IL 60048, 847/362-4636. Daily 9:30 am–6 pm. Admission free to grounds & special events; nominal charge for rides & attractions.

Best place for a blast (virtually speaking)

Virtual World

This virtual-reality gaming center has brought a little bit of outer space to the third-floor northwest corner of Streeterville's North Pier shopping and entertainment complex (see separate listing, "Shopping"). Here, you and your children can sign up to play Red Planet, in which you will drive a race car on Mars in a real-time contest vs. other live kids and adults. More bloodthirsty customers (you know who you are) will want to pick a nickname such as Psycho or Crusher and strap into a virtual reality simulator for a bone-crushing round of Battletech. How to describe the experience. . . . Well, after viewing a warm-up video starring noted thespians Judge Reinhold and Joan Severance, you sit inside a pod not unlike the driving simulators some may remember from high school. Before you know it, you're looking through the eyes of a giant, killer robot and using your joystick to jockey around the desert and blast a bunch of other giant, killer robots (one or more of which might be guided by your children). The great equalizers of the game are that you get to keep coming back after you "die," and players are grouped together by skill level to lessen the chance that a mall hotshot will rein your first few runs. Although it's quite a thrill, the guilty aspects of this simulated space-age violence begin to sink in when, shortly after the contest ends, each player is handed a custom print-out that gives a blow-by-blow account of who killed whom (think, "Psycho vaporizes Crusher's torso with a laser-cannon blast" and you'll get the general idea). If you plan to play, stop by the center as soon as you arrive at North Pier; on busy days, your "flight" might not leave for upwards of an hour. *About price reality:* At about $10 for each ten-minute gaming experience, the prices here are as futuristic as the technology.

Virtual World, North Pier, 435 E Illinois St, Chicago, IL 60611, 312/836-5977. Mon–Thu 11 am–11 pm, Fri–Sat 10 am–1 am, Sun 10 am–11 pm.

Wildest spot in the city

Lincoln Park Zoo, Farm-In-The-Zoo, and Children's Zoo

Where to find a lion just off the lake, a penguin in the park? The answer is this urban zoo, smack dab in the middle of Lincoln Park. This compact zoo attracts large crowds of families, no matter the weather. They come for pleasant strolling, close-up views of animals, and special children's attractions. The farm, complete with barns and coops, is one of the few places where city kids can see and pet cows, lambs, and horses, and watch chicks hatch. (A note of warning—the farm can get a bit fragrant, especially during summer.) The Children's Zoo offers a variety of wild and woolly animal young to see (and sometimes pet), and special wildlife demonstrations; invariably, the handlers haul out some sort of reptile—the kids crowd around and fearlessly volunteer to touch and hold it, while their parents rapidly shrink back. Unwary parents sometimes find themselves with a squawking bird perched on their heads or a hissing (but harmless) snake wrapped around their arms—much to the amusement of their kids!

Lincoln Park Zoo, 2200 N Cannon Dr, Chicago, IL 60614, 312/742-2000. Daily 9 am–5 pm. Free.

Funnest frogs and fossils

Chicago Academy of Sciences (Children's Gallery)

You want Jurassic Park, you want dinosaurs? Take kids to this once-stuffy, once-pedantic museum that now features interactive exhibits and includes a mechanical dinosaur as part of its mission to interpret Chicago's natural history. The widely known "secret" way to get youngsters to learn is to let them follow their imaginations along whichever adventurous trail they will lead. And the Children's Gallery of this compact museum is a perfect spot to let kids' curiosities and imaginations run rampant. The gallery is a truly hands-on exhibit, offering fossils to examine (and perhaps make rubbings from), safe snakes and other reptiles to hold, puzzles to build, and giant turtle shells that kids love to wear on their backs (probably imagining that they are turtles of the Teenage Mutant Ninja variety). Seasonal activities—leaf-pressing, paper snowflake-making, etc.—are offered as well. The museum's main exhibits are also of interest to children, especially the detailed dioramas showing Chicago as it would have appeared hundreds, thousands, and even millions of years ago.

Chicago Academy of Sciences, Mail: 2060 N Clark St, Chicago, IL 60614, 312/549-0606. Museum: 435 E Illinois (Navy Pier). Daily 10 am–5 pm. $3 adults, $2 seniors and children. Tuesdays free.

Best children's theatre

The Children's Theatre Fantasy Orchard,
Wellington Theater

This theater company, which debuted in 1990, is devoted to presenting fairy tales the way they were written. Artistic Director Dana Low explains, "If the character was meant to be evil, that's the way he or she is portrayed." This, she says. helps children distinguish good from evil and "lets the children root for a hero." The company has had enormous success with its realistic fairy-tale productions, as popular with adults as they are with kids. Previous productions include Rumpelstiltskin and Little Red Riding Hood. The company puts on two productions a year (running approximately three months), with plans to add a special Christmas show. Impressive production values—utilizing high-tech lighting, creatively designed sets, and talented actors—combine with a comfortably designed theater to make this an affordable and memorable family outing.

The Children's Theatre Fantasy Orchard, Wellington Theater, 750 W Wellington, Chicago, IL 60657, 312/ 539-4211. $6 adults, $4.50 children. Performances change approximately every three months.

Best puppet show

Puppet Parlor

A former neighborhood grocery, this nondescript storefront conceals an intimate marionette theater that delights youngsters and even attracts adults unaccompanied by children. Patterned after the well-known European marionette theaters, it is the home of the National Marionette Company. This highly professional company has a complete workshop equipped to sculpt, make body parts, and sew costumes. Professional actors are used to record the parts; sets and lighting are of high quality. The 80-seat theater produces such classics as *The Wizard of Oz* and *Hansel and Gretel.* The latter, with a cast of 30 marionettes and original music by Englebert Humperdinck, creates a wonderful world of make-believe with an eerie forest, crying trees, talking crows, shimmering waterfalls, and a candy-covered castle. In the foyer, decorated with puppet likenesses of the late Yul Bryner and Maria Callas that were salvaged from Chicago's famous and long-defunct Kungsholm Theater, children can buy popcorn and pop, hand puppets and marionettes.

Puppet Parlor, 1922 W Montrose Ave, Chicago, IL 60613, 312/774-2919. Sat & Sun 2 pm. Admission $5.

Best and biggest big top
Ringling Brothers, Barnum & Bailey Circus

Every November, the United Center's winter tenants, the Bulls and Blackhawks, hit the road, turning their playground over to the elephants and lions, acrobats and clowns, and other performers of the world-renowned Ringling Brothers, Barnum & Bailey Circus. The three-ring circus's annual ten-day to two-week stand at the new stadium attracts families, school groups, and circus lovers young and old. They delight in the time-honored animal tricks, daredevil stunts, and clowning antics that are the famed circus's stock in trade; current circus highlights include high-wire motorcycling and precisely dancing and leaping horses. The Ringling Brothers circus also spends about a week and a half at the Rosemont Horizon in northwest suburban Rosemont; the Horizon has also played host to occasional visits by the excellent Moscow Circus, a more intimate, single-ring circus. (The small Shriner's Circus makes annual visits to the Near North Side's Medinah Temple.)

Ringling Brothers, Barnum & Bailey Circus, the United Center, 1901 W Madison St, Chicago, IL 60612, 312/455-4500. Also at the Rosemont Horizon, 6920 N Mannheim Rd, Rosemont, IL 60018, 847/635-6601.

Best Ice Shows
Graceful pirouettes and scripted pratfalls! Chicago's varied calendar of ice shows ranges from the antics of costumed cartoon characters to the precise artistic performances of former Olympic stars. At various times from approximately November through March, such cartoon-like shows as the *Ice Capades* and *Walt Disney's World on Ice* and such dance skating–oriented shows as the newer *Stars on Ice* and *Skating* are performed at the United Center, the UIC Pavilion,

and the Rosemont Horizon. *Ice Capades* and the Disney show are popular favorites running two to three weeks at a time; the other shows feature performances by such former Olympians as Scott Hamilton, Debi Thomas, Brian Boitano, and Katarina Witt and are generally one- or two-night special presentations. (Those who like their skating entertainment a hint more rugged—although perhaps not as winning in its ways—head to the United Center for Chicago Blackhawks hockey games!)

United Center, 1901 W Madison St, Chicago, IL 60612, 312/455-4500. University of Illinois-Chicago Pavilion, 1150 W Harrison, Chicago, IL 60607, 312/413-5700. The Rosemont Horizon, 6920 N Mannheim Rd, Rosemont, IL 60018, 847/635-6601. Schedules vary.

Nicest Nutcracker

The Nutcracker

The holidays wouldn't be the holidays without nuts—and *The Nutcracker*. This ballet, written in 1892 by Russian-born composer Peter Ilyich Tchaikovsky, is performed annually at McCormick Place's Arie Crown Theater and has become a local holiday tradition. For youngsters, this production, with its delightful toyland theme, can be the perfect introduction to ballet. Full of pageantry, this production has an elaborate set, dazzling performances, a handsome prince, an army of toy solders, and twirling ballerinas that turn into twinkling snowflakes. And, of course, the captivating music of Tchaikovsky. Holiday performances run approximately November through December, with proceeds going to charity.

Arie Crown Theater, McCormick Place, 2301 S Lake Shore Dr, Chicago, IL 60616, 312/791-6000.

Stingiest Scrooge

Christmas Carol Production

Ebenezer Scrooge, Bob Cratchit, Jacob Marley's ghost, Mr. Fezziwig, Tiny Tim, and the rest of the cast of Dickens' classic novel come to life—in a unique way—during The Goodman Theatre's perennial production of *A Christmas Carol*. This long-running production, yet another holiday tradition in a city that has so many, is the perfect spirit-lifter during the weeks before Christmas. This rendition also mirrors the city's ethnic diversity with its non-traditional casting of black, white, Hispanic, and Asian actors. It's a fun time for kids and adults alike, where you can give as well as receive joy. Members of the audience are encouraged to bring canned foods (or a small donation) to be deposited in "Sharing It" program bins (a citywide effort to collect food for the needy). Thus, one tangible response to "Bah, Humbug!" is to participate in this worthy cause. Tickets are priced at $15–$34. *Note:* It is Goodman's policy that unsold tickets for *all* shows throughout the year go on sale at the box office at 6 pm before every evening performance and at 1 pm before every matinee.

A Christmas Carol Production at The Goodman Theatre, 200 S Columbus Dr, Chicago, IL 60603, 312/443-4947. Mid-Nov–late Dec.

Best Christmas trees

"Christmas Around the World," Museum of Science and Industry

Santa Claus, Father Christmas, Saint Nicholas—tannenbaum, Christmas trees. Although the names and traditions may differ around the Christian world, the celebration of Christmas commonly evokes both an introspection and an out-giving. It is a time when, even in today's harsh society, goodwill finds a way to emerge intact. For more than half a century, the annual "Christmas Around the World" exhibit has brought smiles to the faces of onlookers, both young and old. Located on the entrance floor of the giant museum, the exhibit features 40 ethnically decorated Christmas trees (from countries around the world with such diverse cultures as Germany, Belgium, Mexico, and Great Britain), an indoor ice rink, a 40-foot hanging snowflake, Christmas window displays provided by Marshall Field's department store, a shop selling decorations, a place to buy snacks, and a Santa Claus photo concession. Children's choral groups perform ethnic holiday music and dances. The exhibit runs for five weeks, from approximately November 23 through January 1. Free with admission to the museum.

"Christmas Around the World," Museum of Science and Industry, 57th St & Lake Shore Dr, Chicago, IL 60637, 312/684-1414. Labor Day–Memorial Day Mon–Fri 9:30 am–4 pm, Sat & Sun 9:30 am–5:30 pm. $6 admission, $4 seniors, $1.50 children 5–11; free on Thu.

Swiftest swordplay

Medieval Times

Prepare to be hustled—gently perhaps, but nonetheless, hustled—to buy photographs of your group eating, drinking, cheering, etc., and to stock up with souvenirs. This can escalate the cost of an outing that is pricey to begin with (more than $100 for a family of four—for dinner and show, taxes and gratuities extra). But is it worth it? Perhaps, for a special outing, this medieval show may be worth a splurge. The swordplay, jousting, and other combat are incredibly well choreographed and realistic. The horsemanship and dressage are impressive. Small kids are thrilled by the strutting stallions and the fierce combat; teenage girls are captivated by the dashing knights (and cluster for their autographs, like medieval groupies). Everyone seems to get into the act of cheering his or her knights to victory (each guest receives a color-coded crown corresponding to his or her champion knight). Even the food is passably okay—spare ribs, whole roasted chicken, herbed potato, appetizers, soup, and cake—the menu never varies, so they should have it down pat. And, of course, fetched by serving wenches, this medieval banquet is designed as "finger food" (no utensils provided, per 11th-century setting), and kids *love* that. *Travel tip:* If you approach on I-90 (as most do), alert the kids to watch for the medieval castle, circa A.D. 1083, looming incongruously alongside the busy interstate.

Medieval Times, 2001 N Roselle Rd, Schaumburg, IL 60195 (I-90 & Roselle Rd), 847/843-3900. Sun–Thu $30.95 adults, $21.95 children, $26.95 seniors; Fri & Sat $35.95 adults, $21.95 children, $35.95 seniors. Call for showtimes.

SHOPPING

Best shopping (old-money riche)
Oak Street

In the wake of the Great Fire of 1871, when virtually every wooden structure in Chicago was destroyed, sturdy brownstone mansions were erected by Chicago's wealthy. Today, these same mansions, handsomely restored, are home to some of Chicago's most chic and expensive boutiques. This is the way shopping used to be, before the advent of high-tech atrium malls. On the short stretch of Oak Street between Michigan Avenue and Rush Street, one can wander serendipitously among close to 50 shops and boutiques. This is big-bucks country, with accented French and Italian designer names that might seem more at home on Rodeo Drive (and, indeed, many have Beverly Hills branches). Celebrity spotters may strike gold at Ultimo, the glamorous fashion boutique housed in a shop with a stylish, mottled brown marble facade, while a red-brick townhouse is the discreet home of Gianni Versace, a boutique of Italian designer apparel and accessories for men and women. Hermes carries fashionable handbags and Bottega Veneta fine Italian leather accessories, briefcases, luggage, and shoes. A white canopy fronting a white-brick building leads into the Midwest bastion of Italian couturier Giorgio Armani. This top Gold Coast shopping area includes many galleries, jewelry shops, and perfumeries. Other top stops include: Marilyn Miglin, Inc., skin care consultants; MCM, designer robes, ties, and scarves; Cote D'Or Coiffures, offering the latest fashions in hair styling; and Bang & Olufson, carrying a selection of cutting-edge electronic merchandise including audio and video equipment. Linger at a tree-shaded sidewalk table at the Ice Cream Club. Or stop for coffee at Starbucks, a cookie at Mrs. Fields, or northern Italian specialties at Spiaggia (or its more casual little sister, Cafe Spiaggia—see separate listings in "Dining"), rated among Chicago's finest.

Oak Street (1000 N), between Michigan Ave and Rush St (Most stores open Mon–Sat).

Best shopping district (nouveau riche)

Halsted-Armitage area

If there was a neighborhood called "Yuppieville" and it had a Main Street, it undoubtedly would be the stretch of Halsted Street around its intersection with Armitage Avenue. In fact, it's almost inconceivable that as recently as the late 1970s (and, in some cases, even into the early 1980s), North Halsted Street in Lincoln Park was a rundown street of liquor stores, beat-up low-rent apartments, and dingy storefronts. But the last decade and a half have seen it transformed into the upscale neighborhood's primary shopping thoroughfare, particularly in the few blocks around this intersection. Here can be found meticulously appointed stores offering designer and casual clothing, shoes, bathwares, linens and towels, housewares, and antiques. Reflecting the boom in child-bearing among the yuppies that make up this neighborhood's most conspicuous residents, there is a heavy concentration of upscale stores specializing in maternity clothing, children's shoes and clothing, and toys. Add to these Halsted's variety of nearby bars and restaurants, and you have Lincoln Park's favorite (and priciest!) shopping street. *Meet the local butcher:* The neighborhood's young professionals shop for cuts of meat, smoked sausages, and cheeses at Gepperth's Meat Market, an old-fashioned butcher shop with shingles over its windows and heavy oak doors.

Halsted St (800 W) and Armitage Ave (2000 N).

Best budget shopping district (ain't it a bitch)

Lincoln-Ashland-Belmont area

If Oak Street is hopelessly beyond the reach of your pocketbook or if you just like to save money on your purchases (and care little about designer or brand names), the shops surrounding this major North Side three-way intersection are for you. The shops here tend to be mostly cluttered, sometimes-dingy storefronts, offering bargain prices on a variety of items; typical are the several immigrant-run stores selling general merchandise ranging from pantyhose to laminated-wood Elvis Presley plaques and clocks. Shoes are big here—major chains (such as Fayva, Payless, and Thom McAn) compete for customers with discounters (most notably, our favorite-named store in this area, Shoo Bazaar). And it seems as if every other store (especially on Lincoln Avenue, south of its intersection with the other two streets) is a thrift shop, a surplus store (the Army-Navy Surplus is one of the best in the city), or an antique wholesaler. Shopping here can yield bargains, but it's definitely not for everyone.

Belmont Ave (3200 N) and Ashland Ave (1600 W) at Lincoln Ave.

Best shopping center

Water Tower Place

This may be the definitive place to browse. There's even a systematic way to accomplish it: Ride to the 7th-floor level in the centerpiece glass elevators, and browse/shop your way back down, floor-by-floor, via the escalator. This seven-story atrium, named for the nearby historic structure that survived the Great Chicago Fire of 1871, was the first shopping mall to appear on the Magnificent Mile—although "mall" is hardly the word for this gleaming, contemporary retail shopping area anchored by Marshall Field's and Lord & Taylor. The modern decor incorporates chrome, glass, and marble and features a handsome waterfall in the main entrance on the mezzanine level. There are more than 120 specialty shops, plus a multiscreen cinema, and several restaurants, including Lettuce Entertain You's appealingly versatile Food Life area and the adjoining Mity Nice Grill. Parking is available in the basement. *Shopping respite:* High above bustling Water Tower Place, the elegant, art-filled 12th-floor lobby of the Ritz-Carlton hotel offers a soothing respite from shopping. Under a magnificent skylight, a fountain provides a lulling background, almost like the gentle roll of surf, for afternoon tea or cocktails, with comfortable seating in sofas and easy chairs.

Water Tower Place, 835 N Michigan Ave, Chicago, IL 60611, 312/440-3165 (mall information telephone number).

Best mall you might miss

The Shops at the Mart

Because it is slightly west of downtown, one of Chicago's most attractive shopping malls may be missed by visitors who flock to stores along Michigan Avenue and in the central Loop. In fact, this contemporary mall is located in one of Chicago's oldest merchandising centers. Built in 1930, the art deco Merchandise Mart covers two city blocks. Hailed as "the colossus of marketplaces," this monumental landmark was built for retailer Marshall Field and later sold to Joseph P. Kennedy. Surrounded by gleaming marble, brass, and etched glass, "The Shops at the Mart" comprise more than 70 specialty shops and restaurants located on two floors. Well-known retailers include The Gap, Lerner New York, Coconuts Records, The Limited, Casual Corner, The Coach Store, The Athlete's Foot, and Crabtree & Evelyn. There is an excellent dollar store, All For One, and anchoring the mall is an attractive branch of Carson Pirie Scott. In the south lobby, murals depict exotic marketplaces throughout the ages. There is a 400-seat food court and casual dining at T.G.I. Friday's. Au Bon Pain offers French specialties at alfresco tables alongside the Chicago River. Beside the river, stone containers splash bright geraniums and the Roman-like "Hall of Fame" displays bronze busts of eight merchandising giants mounted on massive pillars.

The Shops at the Mart, 222 N Bank Dr (on the Chicago River between Wells & Orleans sts), Chicago, IL 60654, 312/527-4141. Mon–Fri 9 am–6 pm, Sat 10 am–5 pm.

Loftiest shopping spot

North Pier

Amid a trendy residential area of converted lofts and new high rises, this 85-year-old waterfront warehouse contains about 50 specialty shops and five restaurants and bars (some with outdoor dockside seating). Once the largest distribution center in the Midwest, North Pier has been artfully rehabbed, displaying exposed beams, bare-brick walls, and green-painted metal floors and winding staircases. The three-floor complex appeals to a trendy, touristy crowd, positioning itself on the cutting edge of shopping and entertainment. There are shops specializing in sheepskin sportswear, diving apparatus, holographic art, kites, and fashion sunglasses. Fun-seekers can have their caricatures drawn, buy a retired city parking meter and a T-shirt with a sunlight-activated motif, play miniature golf on an indoor course with Chicago landmarks (and a full bar), and strap on video helmets and immerse themselves in Virtuality, the ultimate video-adventure game. Restaurants include The Original A-1 with Tex-Mex food and decor to match, Old Carolina Crabhouse, serving up Southern-style seafood (see separate listings in "Dining"), Fat Tuesday (with Cajun food and daiquiris), and Tavern on the Pier (a sports bar with soups, salads, and sandwiches). Entertainment includes jazz, folk singers, sing-alongs, and loud, meat market–style music.

North Pier, 435 E Illinois St, Chicago, IL 60611, 312/836-4300. Mon–Thu 10 am–9 pm, Fri & Sat 10 am–10 pm, Sun 11 am–7 pm.

Best bargains on Boul Mich

Filene's Basement

The 800 block of Michigan Avenue across from ritzy Water Tower Place has created quite a stir. In addition to the huge Borders Bookstore and a Victoria's Secret outlet chided by its Magnificent Mile neighbors for putting up window displays more in keeping with a bordello than one of America's fanciest shopping Meccas, someone had the nerve to open—how to say it—a *discount* department store on Boul Mich. While it is true that the character of the street would be disastrously altered if a Woolworth's or Walgreens opened on every corner, the new Filene's Basement is more boon than bane to downtown shoppers. Except for the mock movie marquee above the escalator that reads, "The Big Sale, Now Showing!" it's hard to tell the difference between Filene's and many of its upscale neighbors—until you look at the price tags. Filene's two floors feature name-brand apparel at savings of 30 percent to 70 percent off regular prices (and even more on sale days). *Examples:* The men's department's offering of 100 percent silk sports shirts for $39.99, Giorgio Armani shirts from Barneys in New York reduced to $49.99 from $125, and dress shirts from Gieves & Hawkes that run as high at £80 in London's Savile Row marked down to $40. There are similar bargains on women's clothing and accessories, from designers such as Perry Ellis, Andrea Jovine, Harvé Benard and Giorgio Sant' Angelo. (Not all the merchandise normally on display at Filene's Boston flagship can be found at the Mag Mile store, however. According to a clerk claiming to be in the know, Chicago's Neiman-Marcus branch refused to let the North Michigan Filene's sell a shipment of clothing sent by Neiman's parent company.)

Filene's Basement, 830 N Michigan Ave, Chicago, IL 60611, 312/482-8918. Mon–Fri 10 am–9 pm, Sat 9 am–8 pm, Sun 11 am–7 pm.

Best place to be like Mike

Nike Town

When Bulls legend Michael Jordan made his brief foray into the world of minor-league baseball (and had so much trouble handling those "wicked, double-A curve balls," as his pal and Nike commercial co-star/director Spike Lee memorably opined), Nike Town's signature Jordan Pavilion was briefly in danger of being shrunk down due to flagging interest. Instead, Rare Air's return to basketball led Nike's Magnificent Mile mega-shoe-and-a-whole-lot-more-store to move the Jordan shrine to a bigger, more prominent space on the third floor. Featuring examples of every shoe MJ has ever worn on a field of play—plus various items of clothing and two sets of his golf clubs—the pavilion elevates commerce to an almost spiritual plane for Jordan's legions of fans. As Spike Lee's alter ego Mars Blackmon is so fond of saying in Michael's Nike commercials, "It's *got* to be the shoes." Other points of interest at what is one of the most popular stores for kids to drag parents to (or is it vice versa?) include a gallery of *Sports Illustrated* covers and life-size sculptures of athletes. Nike commercials play on a giant screen and waves wash across screens built into the floor. A regulation-size section of basketball court is flanked by a larger-than-life photograph of MJ, with the William Blake quotation: "No bird soars too high, If he soars with his own wings."

Nike Town, 669 N Michigan Ave, Chicago, IL 60611, 312/642-6363. Mon–Fri 10 am–8 pm, Sat 9:30 am–6 pm, Sun 10 am–6 pm.

Best shopping for (expensive!) women's fashions

Janis

Those for whom making a fashion statement with their wardrobe is important—and to whom a price tag ending in multiple zeros is of no concern—head for this trendy Mag Mile boutique. It carries a line of women's designer fashions for everyday and evening wear that it describes as "artistic dress." You are likely to either love it or hate it (assuming you can afford it), and considering the store has been around since 1985, we surmise that enough people love it (and can afford it). The store stocks only designer wear bearing such well-regarded labels as Caraiti, Wainewright, and Holly Harp and includes many exclusive items. Most of the inventory is constructed of woven raw silk, in a multitude of colors, with prices starting at $1,000. The store also stocks a selection of colorful handmade jewelry and accessories.

Janis, 900 N Michigan Ave, Chicago, IL 60610, 312/642-9444. Tue–Sat 10 am–7 pm, Sun 11 am–5 pm.

Preppiest casual wear

Eddie Bauer

Although its location is definitively urban—with El trains rattling by on the tracks above Wabash Avenue—this is a store evocative of outdoor adventure. You enter past rows of backpacks and money belts and showcases crammed with sunglasses, ski goggles, compasses, sports watches, and binoculars. But this also is the shop for Ivy League, preppy outfits—Oxford shirts, cable crew sweaters, and a variety of casual clothing fashioned from wool, corduroy, suede, canvas, and cotton. You'll find an enormous selection of sweaters of various weights and a large department with stylish parkas and sweatsuits. There is a counter where you can buy wool gloves, floppy felt hats, and other haberdashery. Downstairs is devoted exclusively to women's wear and to a shoe department with a range of men's and women's footwear, from sturdy hiking boots to casual moccasins.

Eddie Bauer, 123 N Wabash Ave, Chicago, IL 60602, 312/263-6005. Mon & Fri 10 am–7 pm, Tue–Thu, Sat 10 am–6 pm, Sun noon–5 pm.

Preppiest casual wear at outlet-store prices

Lands' End Outlet Stores

Some blue canvas outside and some rope-wrapped columns inside are the only concessions to a nautical theme you'll find at this Lands' End outlet store (a combination of formerly separate men's and women's shops relocated from their Elston Avenue premises). But you can sail into bargains on catalog overstocks and end-of-the season merchandise. This is the ultimate button-down shop, full of preppyish sportswear, dress shirts, dresses, and children's wear. There are minimum savings of 20 percent off original catalog prices—up to 50 percent if you're able to take advantage of weekly specials (for example, women's jeans for $6). There's a department with children's and toddlers' clothing, a small selection of shoes, and a few nonclothing items such as totes and towels. In addition to sportswear, the men's department has sports jackets, shoes, ties, and belts.

In Evanston, a Lands' End "Not Quite Perfect" store (816½ Church St) offers customer returns and imperfect merchandise beginning at 40 percent off, sometimes with an additional 75 percent off that price.

Lands' End Outlet Store, 2121 N Clybourn St, Chicago, IL 60614, 312/281-0900, Mon–Fri 10 am–9 pm, Sat 10 am–6 pm, Sun 11 am–5 pm.

Fitting finds for large women

The Forgotten Woman

The name says it eloquently. In this age of fad diets, low-fat everything, crunching exercise regimes, and body toning and shaping, being large and/or heavy is no fun. And, let's face it, some will never be thin or trim. But, that shouldn't mean they can't be fashionable. This boutique caters to the fashion-conscious, full-figured woman, stocking sizes 14–24. The considerable inventory includes sportswear, sweaters, evening dresses, lingerie, shoes, and jewelry. Many items are designer-name fashions, and the boutique has exclusive contracts to produce larger-size designer fashions normally sold only in smaller sizes. For a specialty store, the prices are reasonable—designer dresses begin at $150 (but can range up to $2,000), with a wide variety available at the lower end of that spectrum. This store proves that the days of dull-colored oversize dresses can be banished for good.

The Forgotten Woman, 535 N Michigan Ave, Chicago, IL 60611, 312/329-0885. Mon, Wed, Fri & Sat 10 am–6 pm, Thu 10 am–7 pm, Sun noon–5 pm.

Best buys on bags

That's Our Bag

Accessorizing is the fashion buzzword for the 1990s, and one of the primary accessories is a matching handbag. In this shop, chances are good of finding just the right matching bag. Hundreds of bags are on display, including many famous designer-name bags (Bosca, Liz Claiborne, and Peil Latico, for example), constructed of natural and dyed leather, vinyl, sequined cloth, and numerous other materials. Also stocked are belts, evening purses, and attaché cases. Prices for handbags range from $20 to $300. Generally good quality merchandise, sold by a knowledgeable sales staff.

That's Our Bag, 734 N Michigan Ave, Chicago, IL 60601, 312/984-3517. Mon & Thu 9 am–7 pm, Tue, Wed, Fri & Sat 9 am–6 pm, Sun noon–5 pm.

Handiest glove shopping
Glove Me Tender

In the beautifully designed Avenue Atrium shopping center, this small boutique devotes 80 percent of its inventory to gloves. The remaining 20 percent includes accessories such as hats, scarves, and umbrellas. The store literally has a glove for any reason, any season—delicate lace gloves for brides, gloves for driving, designer-fashion dish-washing gloves, house-cleaning gloves, garden gloves, work gloves, sports gloves, car-washing gloves, and play gloves. Choice of material offers almost as much variety. Options include leather, acrylic, wool, cotton, plastic, rubber, cashmere, linen, fur, and rayon. And colors. Mittens, for example, come in a rainbow of hues, including red, blue, green, yellow, pink, turquoise, and melon. Chances are, if you don't find the glove you're looking for here, it doesn't exist. Sizes fit men, women, and children; prices range from $5 to $800 (the latter for detailed hand-worked leather). The store also stocks sun hats, visors, sunglasses, and umbrellas.

Glove Me Tender, 900 N Michigan Ave, Chicago, IL 60611, 312/664-4022. Mon–Fri 10 am–7 pm, Sat 10 am–6:30 pm, Sun 11 am–6 pm.

Best hose for your toes
This Little Piggy

This must be the market that the first little piggy went to—particularly, if he developed cold feet along the way. Greeting you at this Water Tower Place shop is a pink neon sign with a pig logo, and every item in this store has to do with covering your feet. Sold are socks and "footsies," hosiery and pantyhose, for men, women, children, and even infants. Choices ranges from socks emblazoned with logos from Chicago sports teams to women's fashion hose with fancy sequins stitched up the back. It's a fun shop to browse.

This Little Piggy, 835 N Michigan Ave, Chicago, IL 60611, 312/943-7449. Mon–Fri 10 am–7 pm, Sat 10 am–6 pm, Sun noon–6 pm.

Best-kept secret for your secrets
Underthings

This is the kind of shopping most of us prefer to do discreetly, and this sequestered boutique dedicated to women's lingerie is perfect for those who love lace and are seduced by silk and satin. According to proprietor Maria Ashby, the emphasis of this small boutique (which has been open since 1980) is on lingerie made with all-natural fibers. Items displayed throughout the store (in sizes petite to large) bear such familiar designer labels as Christian Dior, Eileen West, Calvin Klein, and Hanro of Switzerland. And although the selections aren't vast, service is excellent, and prices are competitive. The store does a large catalog business, meaning fine lingerie could be as close as your mail box.

Underthings, 804 W Webster Ave, Chicago, IL 60614, 312/472-9291. Mon–Fri 10 am–7 pm, Sat 10 am–6 pm, Sun noon–5 pm.

Best place to buy a suit—and get a manicure, shoe shine, and sandwich

Bigsby & Kruthers

The building is as good-looking as the stylish clothes it houses, and customers are treated like royalty, with a glass of wine or soda, a free shoe shine on weekends, and complimentary valet parking. There's a barbershop and manicurist and Bigsby's Bar & Grill, a sports bar with a good range of salads, burgers, chicken-breast specialties, and imported beers. The major attraction is a wide range of high-quality clothing—up to 2,000 suits, 1,000 dress shirts, and the famous "Tie Wall" with 1,000 choices. Labels include Oxford, Polo University, Georgio Armani, and other leading designers; prices run from $350 to $1,500 for suits, and up to $110 for shirts and $75 for ties. Housed in a handsomely restored former furniture warehouse with brick ceilings and reputed Capone connections, the clothier attracts the likes of former Governor Jim Thompson, basketball superstar Michael Jordan, and the *NFL Today* cast. Look for an attractive mural of a park scene on the north exterior wall.

Bigsby & Kruthers, 1750 N Clark St, Chicago, IL 60614, 312/440-1750. Mon & Thu 11 am–9 pm, Tue & Wed 10 am–8 pm, Fri & Sat 10 am–6 pm, Sun noon–5 pm.

Best shirts on your back

Riddle-McIntyre, Inc.

In a venerable red-brick building fronted by black fluted iron columns, Frank Hee Kang has been making custom shirts since 1977, just as the original owners did when they opened in 1916. Cabinets swing open to reveal bolts of 1,000 different fabrics, including broadcloth cotton from England and Switzerland and Sea Island cotton that has the look and feel of silk. Shirts range from $95 to $225, with a minimum order of four. After measurements are taken, a sample shirt is cut on the premises and the customer comes in for a fitting before the order is completed. Customer sizes are kept on file. The shop makes about 4,000 shirts a year, mostly dress shirts, but some casual shirts in various plaids, solids, and stripes. It also tailors suits and sells ties, scarves, and cuff links.

Riddle-McIntyre, Inc., 175 N Franklin St, Chicago, IL 60606, 312/782-3317. Mon–Fri 9 am–5 pm. Sat by appointment.

Best sea island shirts for Agent 007
Dunhill

Although the men's clothier is among 125 stores in the Water Tower Place shopping center (see separate listing), this second-floor shop has no trouble projecting an air of exclusivity. This probably is attributable to its diminutive size, the attentive sales help, and the intimidating prices, with suits ranging from about $900. But the old maxim "you get what you pay for" holds true, for Dunhill's quality is world renowned. Still famous is its line of men's Sea Island polo shirts, popularized by Ian Fleming's flamboyant spy extraordinaire, Agent 007. In Fleming's books, James Bond slipped on one of these comfortable shirts as readily as he did his chamois-holstered Berretta. The distinguishing characteristic of the shirt is the special silk-like cotton, originally grown in the Sea Islands off Georgia. This particular Bond fetish will set you back about $125.

Dunhill, 835 N Michigan Ave, Chicago, IL 60611, 312/467-4455. Mon–Fri 10 am–7 pm, Sat 10 am–6 pm, Sun noon–5 pm.

Best place to "tie" one on
Knot Krazy

Prepare to be dazzled when you enter this tie emporium. You are surrounded by walls of color provided by about 3,000 ties of every imaginable hue and design. You'll find florals and geometrics, vintage and paisley, and conservative stripes. Designers include Hugo Bass, Jane Barnes, Andrew Fezza, and Givenchy. Ties, imported and U.S.-made, are all silk and are arranged by price category—from $17 to $50, with a few ranging up to $98. There also is a selection of belts, suspenders, bow ties, and socks, plus a few shirts and sweaters. A central work station is equipped with lapels in a variety of colors and patterns to help customers match ties and other accessories with particular suits and jackets.

Knot Krazy, Wabash & Randolph Sts, Chicago, IL
60601, 312/606-0781. Mon–Wed 9 am–6 pm, Thu &
Fri 9 am–6:30 pm, Sat 10 am–5 pm.

Best barber shop if you're a gentleman or a prince

Truefitt & Hill

Forget about unisex hairdressers. It's strictly men
only at this sixth-level Avenue Atrium barber shop.
A visit is like stepping into a transporter and arriving
on Curzon Street, London, England, location of the
parent store (founded in 1805). The staff of barbers
adhere to a strict code of discipline on how a gentle-
man receiving a haircut should be treated. And who
better to understand tonsorial protocol than the
official barbers of Prince Charles and Prince Philip.
Truefitt & Hill barbers visit Buckingham Palace every
Tuesday to trim these royal locks. In addition to
haircuts ($37), this full-service shop offers other
grooming services such as stress massage, facials,
herbal facials, pedicures, manicures, hot-lather
shaves, and shoe shines (price range $3–$50). Gift
packages available in various denominations.

Truefitt & Hill, 900 N Michigan Ave, Chicago, IL
60611, 312/337-2525. Mon–Fri 7:30 am–7 pm, Sat
7:30 am–6 pm, Sun noon–6 pm.

Best hairdresser where you feel like a prince (or princess)

Russum Waters Salon

Mozart plays softly as you lie back and allow cleansing herbal steam to envelop your face as your brow
is gently massaged by the soothing fingers of Euro-
pean-trained Mina Demren. Applying masks and
ampules from Vienna and Paris, she is an expert at
cleansing the skin and helping rejuvenate it with a
range of European facial treatments including
ultralight Swedish massages. Facials are one reason
clients return to this salon. Hair styles that can be
recreated at home are another. Founded in 1991, the
salon occupies the upper floor of a fashionable
brownstone above an espresso bar. It is operated by
noted hair colorist Anita Russum and Graham
Waters, a hair stylist from England, who share the
philosophy that styles they create must not only look
good when a client walks out after an appointment—
but also the next morning, and the following week.
Client relationships begin with a consultation, to
gain an understanding of the needs, lifestyle, and
image. "We only do what a client can recreate," notes

Waters. "We work with the client to educate about the right hair products and the best way for looking after the style at home."

Russum Waters Salon, 10 E Delaware Pl, Chicago, IL 60611, 312/944-8533. Tue–Sat 9 am–5 pm.

Best shopping for maternity clothes

Pea in the Pod

This successful Chicago outlet (opened in 1989) of a national, 25-store chain specializes in upscale designer-name and private-label maternity clothes; it feels right at home in Chicago's ritzy Oak Street shopping area. The long, narrow boutique carries a large inventory of pants, dresses, sweaters, evening wear, and suits, as well as an interesting selection of earrings, necklaces, and pins, and hair accessories such as headbands, barrettes, and clips. Much of the inventory has been specially designed by such noted fashion designers as Joan Vass, Victor Costa, and Nicole Miller. The store also has exclusive and private contracts with other recognized designers to provide a steady stream of new styles. Prices range from $3 for inexpensive jewelry up to $350 for a Nicole Miller coat dress (average dress cost is $150 to $200). Prices are upper-strata, with service and quality correspondingly high.

Pea in the Pod, 46 E Oak St, Chicago, IL 60611, 312/944-3080. Mon–Wed, Fri & Sat 10 am–6 pm, Thu 10 am–7 pm, Sun noon–5 pm.

Best shopping for baby furniture

Bellini

As with many of the stores along North Halsted Street (which has evolved steadily from run-down to upscale since around 1975), this store caters to folks with money—or with large credit limits. Featured are high-quality infant and juvenile furniture and accessories. The furniture, all designer-fashion imported from Italy and Germany, is designed to stay with children from cradle to college—innovative designs allow cribs to transform into daybeds and diaper-changing stands into bookcases. Other merchandise in this "baby department-store" includes accessories such as armoires, lamps, and dressers, as well as baby toys, rocking horses, high chairs, car seats, and bedding.

Bellini, 2001 N Halsted St, Chicago, IL 60614, 312/943-6696. Mon–Wed & Fri 10 am–6 pm, Thu 10 am–8 pm, Sat 10 am–5:30 pm, Sun noon–5 pm.

Best "better bring your credit card" toy stores

F.A.O. Schwarz

Although doormen are not uncommon at the tony hotels and residential buildings along the Magnificent Mile, you know you're about to enter a very special place when you're greeted by the doorman at the F.A.O. Schwarz flagship on North Michigan Avenue. He's costumed like a grenadier, complete with high hat and red suit and two red rouge circles on his cheeks to give him that toy-soldier look. Once inside this three-story funhouse, you'll find Spanky, the talking Gund Where Bear, driving a car and providing information about where to find games, dolls, and the other wondrous variety of children's amusements contained in this kid's wonderland. Throughout the store, you'll find whimsical displays of talking animals as well as pianos you have to hop onto to play—just as Tom Hanks did in the movie *Big*. Riding up the escalator, you'll look out over an Erector-set version of the John Hancock Center as you pass beneath The Giant Swoop Gravity Loop, something of a perpetual motion machine in which multicolored balls roll down and around a swooping yellow track—only to be whisked back up for another trip. Upper-floor attractions include a doll shop, the Nickelodeon corner, and full lines of action figures, remote-control cars, and video and game boards, as well as the Barbie Boutique. And if you can't find the latest Mutant Morphin Teenage Power Ranger Transforming Turtle at the main store, head across the street to Water Tower Place, where a smaller version of F.A.O Schwarz is tucked into the northwest corner of the shopping center's second floor.

F.A.O. Schwarz, 840 N Michigan Ave, Chicago, IL 60611, 312/587-5000. Mon–Wed 10 am–7 pm, Thu–Sat 10 am–8 pm, Sun 11 am–7 pm. Water Tower store: 835 N Michigan Ave, Chicago, IL 60611, 312/787-8894. Mon–Fri 10 am–7 pm, Sat 10 am–6 pm, Sun 11 am–6 pm.

Best toy store for "educational toys" (just don't call them that in front of the kids)

Saturday's Child

Want to find good old-fashioned building blocks and stuffed animals? Looking for a place to shop for toys without battling the massive crowds and impersonal selection found at most of today's gigantic toy supermarkets? This comfortable Lincoln Park store provides both—and more. The decor is bright and inviting, soft music plays in the background, and toys and books are attractively presented, beckoning to the parents and children shopping together there. Especially popular at Saturday's Child are such challenging, educational, and fun toys as block sets, arts-and-crafts materials, and beautifully illustrated books for all ages. Here you'll also find the complete set and accessories for the BRIO wooden train system from Sweden, the Ravensburger Amazing Labyrinth Game (a challenging and fun goal- and problem–solving-oriented board game) from Germany, the Canadian-made "Skwish" touch-and-squeeze toy (as popular for adult desks as they are for babies' cribs), and the newly popular "pogs." Owner Marcia Nordine says, "We like to think of ourselves as Lincoln Park's neighborhood toy store." Saturday's Child is a relaxed family oasis in a bustling, often high-pressured area.

Saturday's Child, 2146 N Halsted St, Chicago, IL 60614, 312/525-8697. Mon–Wed Fri & Sat 10 am–6 pm, Thu 10 am–7 pm, Sun noon–5 pm.

Best jewelry store that's forever

Cartier

This French-owned chain (with 135 stores worldwide), founded by Louis Cartier in 1847, ranks as one of Chicago's (as well as the world's) finest and most-respected jewelers. At the tony Michigan Avenue store, you'll find traditional, trend-resistant styles that combine the best of Europe and the United States. There's an excellent selection of diamond wedding and anniversary rings, bracelets, watches, china, perfumes, and necklaces. Look, too, for such Cartier originals as the popular Pasha watch (designed in 1983 as the world's first water-resistant watch), the tank watch, and Cartier's unique rolling rings (an 18K gold ring utilizing three colors of gold intertwined into bands). Expectedly, prices tend to be high, but service and quality are outstanding. Don't be surprised to spot Chicago socialites visiting this top-drawer jewelry store.

Cartier, 630 N Michigan Ave, Chicago, IL 60611, 312/266-7440. Mon–Sat 10 am–5:30 pm.

Most original jewelry store

Lester Lampert

If you've a mind—and the money—to commission an exquisite, one-of-a-kind piece of jewelry, expertly designed to your specifications, you'll want to visit David Lampert, who along with his father, Lester, runs this fine jewelry store. The venerable jewelers, in business since 1920, stock their own designed products and also do a large custom-design business. The jeweler also is the exclusive Chicago-area representative of Hublot watches. Other Swiss-made watches are well represented, too, including Audemars Piquet, Blancpain, Piaget, Corum, Concord, Movado, and TAG Heuer. An estate jewelry collection as well as David Yurman designs are shown at their best at this unique designer and manufacturer. Expect to find high-quality merchandise, friendly, knowledgeable assistance—and something different.

Lester Lampert, 57 E Oak St, Chicago, IL 60611, 312/944-6888, Mon–Sat 10 am–6 pm.

Best jewelry stores an elevator ride away

Mallers Building

If you want to buy or sell, have repaired or altered a watch, ring, or other piece of jewelry, head for this 1911 Loop landmark. The 21-story building has 16 floors of jewelers. You can start with New York Jewelers in the Wabash lobby and work your way up aboard an elevator with etched art deco doors, pointers to indicate its passage, and a live operator to whom you call out your floor. The third floor has a good cross-section of about a dozen jewelers plus a must stop, the Mallers Building Coffee Shop & Deli (see separate listing in "Dining"). On three, you'll find specialists in imported diamonds, same-day gold casting, engraving, watch and jewelry repair, and antiques—plus lots of signs offering to buy silver, gold, platinum, and precious stones. Owners run the gamut from fashionable young men to stereotypical, frail old men with accents and jeweler's glasses.

Mallers Building, 5 S Wabash Ave, Chicago, IL 60603.

Savviest shopping for vintage jewelry

Hubba-Hubba

Stepping into this attractive, modern-looking shop is like finding Grandma's attic or a long-lost aunt's closet neatly arranged and ready to give up their treasures. Hubba-Hubba offers displays of vintage clothing, accessories, purses, and a large, fun selection of hats. The shop's highlights, however, are its long counters of vintage and costume jewelry: gaudy, sparkly pins; delicate handmade bracelets from China; earrings that dazzle, dangle, or both; and trays of rings that range from just beyond Cracker Jack-box baubles to gorgeous diamond-and-gold bands. The friendly sales staff (usually the owners or their family or friends) are always helpful, joking, and patient and have never been pushy in our repeated visits. Always a great place for perfect little gifts.

Hubba-Hubba, 3338 N Clark St, Chicago, IL 60657, 312/477-1414. Mon–Sat 11 am–7 pm, Sun noon– 5 pm.

Savviest shopping for vintage clothing

Flashy Trash

Where do you go to buy or sell a pair of bell-bottom jeans, a Hawaiian shirt adorned with wild-colored orchids, or a pair of blue glitter shoes (assuming the question of *why* you would want to)? At the largest resale shop in the city (covering more than 3,000 square feet), where you'll find a huge mix of vintage clothing dating from the 1920s through the 1970s. This store has been in business since 1978 and offers an impressive selection of everyday wear, tuxedos, men's suits, furs, beaded dresses, wedding gowns, and overcoats, much of which seems to be in mint condition. According to Flashy-Trash–meister Harold Mandel, the most popular items are found among a large collection of vintage costume jewelry that includes watches, earrings, necklaces, and rings. Clothing and jewelry are purchased daily, and the inventory changes at least weekly. Even if you don't plan to buy, the store is a fun browse (although, even the most determined "just looking" visitors seem to find at least one item that they simply must have).

Flashy Trash, 3524 N Halsted St, Chicago, IL 60657, 312/327-6900. Mon–Sat 11 am–8 pm, Sun noon– 6 pm.

Best place to get stuck in the 1970s

Flashback Collectibles

If you've been suppressing an urge to throw on those old bell-bottom jeans you found while cleaning out your closets, the time to do it is just before visiting the weird and wonderful world of Flashback Collectibles. Your trip back to the pop-culture wasteland of the 1970s begins with glossy photos of John Travolta, Kristy McNichol, The Brady Bunch, and The Bay City Rollers that grin out at you from the front window. Cheap thrills inside this small shop devoted to TV memorabilia from the era include black-and-white stills of Farrah Fawcett-Majors and Henry "The Fonz" Winkler for $1; stickers featuring "Charlie's Angels" and "Starsky & Hutch" for $1.50;

old issues of *TV Guide* for $3; and H.R. Puff 'n' Stuff T-shirts for $12.95 (Remember H.R.? He was the Sid & Marty Kroft puppet whose TV theme included the inexplicable line, "He can't get a little, 'cause he can't get enough.") There's also an assortment of eight-track tapes and board games, as well as collectible lunch boxes featuring icons as varied as Scooby Doo, the Bee-Gees, and The Six Million Dollar Man (otherwise known as the ex-Mr. Farrah Fawcett-Majors). Back issues of *People*, collector's cards from nearly every bad sitcom you can imagine, puffy stickers of Mick Jagger and Keith Richards—they're all lumped together here in one mind-blowing, kaleidoscopic jumble. (While you're in the neighborhood, you owe it to yourself to check out the vintage clothing at Strange Cargo next door. Maybe they'll give you a good price on those bell bottoms.)

Flashback Collectibles, 3450 N Clark St, Chicago, IL 60657, 312/929-5060. Mon–Thu noon–7 pm, Fri & Sat noon–10 pm, Sun noon–6 pm.

Top spot to escape to fantasy aisles

Fantasy Headquarters

Whether it is Halloween, Mardi Gras, or someone's birthday or retirement, whenever the calendar says it's time for a party, it is worth checking out this department store of the macabre. Sprawling over an entire city block and with more than one million items in stock, it is ready with an array of glittery, beaded, feathered, and far-fetched trappings. Woody Allen sits between Richard Nixon and Margaret Thatcher, their molded-latex likenesses among 600 masks. Owner George Garcia, who started the business more than 25 years ago selling wigs from the trunk of his car, now totes up annual revenues exceeding $1 million, about 30 percent from corporate clients such as IBM, Zenith, Alberto Culver, and Arthur Andersen. Inventory includes 30,000 wigs (Chicago's largest stock), 25,000 costumes, and a variety of makeup, accessories, and props. Celebrity customers range from Bozo and Diana Ross to female impersonator Chili Pepper. At the height of the Gulf War, Saddam Hussein masks were in demand. The following year, the staff makeup artist was getting requests for Teddy Kennedy, who, in turn, was destined to be supplanted by Bill Clinton and Newt Gingrich. How fickle fame! Yes, there are Jim Carrey masks, for those wanting to duplicate the actor's look in the movie *The Mask*. A 1995 addition created the "Character Room," where all costumes— Santa, animals, birds, Power Rangers, X-Men, Batman, and the like—will be located.

Fantasy Headquarters, 4065 N Milwaukee Ave,
Chicago, IL 60641, 312/777-0222, 800\USA-WIGS.
Mon–Fri 9:30 am–8 pm, Sat 9:30 am–6 pm, Sun 10
am–6 pm.

Best shop to launch your second childhood

Uncle Fun

On most days, "Uncle Fun" himself (otherwise known
as proprietor Ted Frankel) will serve as your personal tour guide to the mountains of toys, collectibles, and novelty gift items stacked throughout
this whimsical Wrigleyville store. Featuring weird
baubles and knickknacks such as dribble glasses,
all manner of Elvis paraphernalia, brain candles
(labeled "This is your brain on fire"), and fuzzy
mutant "squirrels with nuts" for fifty cents apiece,
there may be something here to intrigue patrons of
all ages. "Everybody who comes in here is a kid,"
Frankel says. "Some just have bigger bodies." The
large selection of greeting cards and postcards includes many with adults-only themes, however. More
than half the goodies come from old warehouses,
". . . so it's a vintage fun-house as well," Frankel
notes. With about 90 percent of the merchandise
priced at under $10, this is a great spot to find low-
cost gimcrackery. Catalog shoppers will find Uncle
Fun reminiscent of Seattle's goofy Archie McPhee
store, but Frankel pioneered the concept. And because the store runs solely on word-of-mouth advertising, Uncle Fun truly is one of Chicago's best-kept
secrets.

Uncle Fun, 1338 W Belmont Ave, Chicago, IL 60657,
312/477-8223. Wed–Sat noon–7 pm, Sun noon–6
pm.

Best shop to say g'day

Kangaroo Connection

If you're fresh out of Vegemite, stop by this brick
storefront with the kangaroo sign out front. It calls
itself the Australian and New Zealand general store
and has a vast inventory of food, dry goods, and
other merchandise from Down Under. Popular items
include didgeridoos (an aborigine wooden musical
instrument), "lollies," ('Strine argot for chocolate
bars, of which Violet Crumble and Smarties are
favorites), oilskin coats ($200), and boomerangs.
Shop for an Akubra rabbit-fur hat ("Crocodile"
Dundee wore one) or an unusual stuffed animal—
perhaps a Tasmanian devil, platypus, echidna (a
kind of anteater), or a wombat, which owner Kathy

Schubert calls "the essence of cute." If you're planning an Aussie-themed party, you can rent oversized stuffed animals, costumes (koalas, kangaroos, penguins, lobsters, and, of course, "Crocodile" Dundee), flags, music, and a life-size Paul Hogan cardboard standup (for photographing guests beside). The store has a mail-order catalog. *Note:* Americans either love or hate Vegemite, a brewer's-yeast spread—with the majority probably in the latter category.

Kangaroo Connection, 1113 W Webster, Chicago, IL 60614, 312/248-5499. Mon–Wed & Fri noon–6 pm, Thu noon–7 pm, Sat noon–5 pm.

Classiest shopping for gifts where you dine

Two Doors South

This interesting hybrid offers side-by-side rooms, with light, elegant dining on the right, and gift shopping on the left—or possibly the reverse, once you're seated. The gifts here run to jewelry (especially artfully made pins, earrings, and bracelets), music boxes, decorative items, picture frames, a wide variety of cards (many risque or gay-themed, without being vulgar), and other small, tasteful knickknacks. Most items are priced reasonably, with sales, "two-fers" among selected items, and stock-rotating discounts making buying even more painless. (We've never failed to buy a perfect something for someone when we've stopped here.) The unpretentious nouvelle cuisine-ish menu in the restaurant fares best in a fresh, affordable Sunday brunch.

Two Doors South, 3220 N Clark St, Chicago, IL 60657, 312/404-7072. Daily noon–8 pm.

Where to buy fake Chicago street signs

Accent Chicago

This store is strictly for those needing more than a memory or a photograph to commemorate a visit to Chicago—or for those with folk back home who might expect a tangible souvenir that "says" Chicago. In fact, if the name's the thing, this seventh-floor Water Tower Place store probably has just the right memento. Literally everything in the shop has Chicago written on it—or otherwise has something to do with the city. Selections range from standard items such as T-shirts, sweatshirts, and key chains to more unique neon signs, deep-dish pizza pans, and imitation street signs. (There are also Accent Chicago stores at Sears Tower and O'Hare Airport.)

Accent Chicago, Water Tower Place, 835 N
Michigan Ave, Chicago, IL 60611, 312/944-1354.
Daily 9:30 am–9:30 pm.

Where to buy real Chicago street signs
The City of Chicago Store

Retired street signs, parking meters, stoplights, route
signs from buses, "El" station placards, signpost
banners—if the great City of Chicago can pry it off
the public thoroughfare, you can bet it's for sale at
this unique North Pier boutique. Create your own
Comiskey Park package with an authentic brick from
the original Sox Park ($24.95) and street signs for
35th and Shields ($50 a pop). Or go the Wrigley Field
route with Clark and Addison street signs (no bricks
are available from the Friendly Confines—nor will
they be as long as true Cubs fans draw breath). Bulls
fanatics can buy books on Michael Jordan, Madison
Street signs, bricks from the old stadium ($24.95
each), along with the old wooden balcony seats.
Those who could care less about the mementos of
pro sports also will find a wealth of offbeat merchandise here, including copper desktop replicas of the
Daley Plaza Picasso sculpture; souvenir tickets from
the old Riverview Park amusement park; old-fashioned mechanical voting machines; a Chicago board
game patterned after Monopoly; and all manner of
mugs, maps, T-shirts, hats, books, posters, postcards, even napkins. (You'll definitely need plenty of
the latter if you plan to try out the recipes in a
cookbook featuring Chicago-style pizza.)

The City of Chicago Store, North Pier, 435 E Illinois
St, Chicago, IL 60611, 312/467-1111. Mon–Thu 10
am–9 pm, Fri & Sat 10 am–10 pm, Sun 10 am–6:45
pm.

Best bet for things you didn't know you needed
Brookstone

This chain store, with another branch at Water Tower
Place (fourth level), is genuinely fascinating. It's
almost always busy with people buying various and
sundry gadgets claimed to make life easier. As you
browse, you're likely to hear: "Great idea!" or "I could
use one of these." Among the more obscure gifts
carried are magnetic playing cards complete with
magnetic board (in case you're playing poker during
a hurricane), a cast-iron Roman sundial, an all-
aluminum clip board, and instant fresh air in a can.
But this fun store also sells more conventional items
such as miniature power tools, super-heavy-duty

flashlights, ultra-tough luggage, and hammocks.
Each item displayed in the showroom has its own
description card; items are purchased by filling out
a brief form, making shopping here seem like a walk
through a living catalog. There's something for nearly
every taste and budget.

Brookstone, 835 N Michigan Ave, Chicago, IL
60611, 312/943-6356. Mon–Fri 10 am–8 pm, Sat 10
am–7 pm, Sun 11 am–6 pm.

Best bet for things you didn't know existed

Hammacher Schlemmer

Although hardly "hidden" at its former location along
the Mag Mile, when in 1995 this store moved into
the spacious and highly conspicuous ground-floor
showroom in the Tribune Building, the rest of the
world soon discovered what aficionados already
knew—this is one of the most utterly fascinating
places to browse. It is the ultimate try-it-for-yourself
store, where you can swing a computerized golf club,
twirl the handles of a fussball game, and relax in a
cordless massaging chair. Chock-full of high-tech
electronic gizmos and toys for all ages, this pricey
gift store is a fun place to browse for things you'd
otherwise never know existed. How about a golf club
(the kind you keep in your bag) that dispenses cold
drinks, a drip-free umbrella, and dinosaur feet slip-
pers? Or a contraption that allows you to walk on
water, football helmets autographed by the likes of
Joe Montana and Walter Payton, and a range of
mechanical cast-iron banks? You'll also find such
items as a lightweight traveler's golf bag constructed
of crush-resistant polyethylene and a pocket-size
electronic language interpreter featuring a human-
like synthesized voice pronouncing words correctly
in six different languages. If you are interested in
purchasing an exact replica of the popular 1951
Schwinn Black Phantom bicycle, it will set you back
$3,500. With prices ranging from $20 on up to
thousands, shopping here requires either nerves of
steel or a credit card to match. Nevertheless, it is an
inspiringly creative place to shop for the person who
seems to have everything.

Hammacher Schlemmer, 445 N Michigan Ave,
Chicago, IL 60611, 312/527-9100. Mon–Sat 10 am–6
pm, Sun noon–5 pm.

Most elegant food hall

Neiman-Marcus Gourmet Department

Harrod's it ain't. But this fourth-floor epicure shop
is a great place to pick up cold cuts, pâtés, terrines,

pasta, and creative salads-to-go, as well as cakes, tarts, pastries, chocolates, and huge (but pricey) chocolate-chip and raisin-oatmeal cookies that are big enough for dessert for at least three. It is elegant, with gleaming white marble countertops and salmon marble-tiled floors. And it is tempting. A center island offers the likes of ravioli stuffed with lobster, double-baked potatoes, smoked-duck salad, and wild rice with mushrooms and onions. There is a Petrossian counter with caviar, smoked salmon, and foie gras, a good selection of cheeses, and an array of Neiman's Red River house brand of marinades, barbecue sauces, jalapeno jelly, and other Southwestern condiments. A small wine department carries a good selection of ports and sherries. *Cooking demos:* Phone for schedule of occasional lunchtime appearances by guest chefs.

Neiman-Marcus, 737 N Michigan Ave, Chicago, IL 60611, 312/642-5900. Mon & Thu 10 am–8 pm, Tue & Wed, Fri & Sat 10 am–6 pm, Sun noon–5 pm.

Best food emporium to eat lunch at

Bockwinkel's, The Food Market

Here's a spot where you can do a little grocery shopping—and eat lunch. In front of this gourmet supermarket, in a bright basement of glitzy Chicago Place, is a small area with greenery and eight black tables. Visit the deli counter and have a fat sandwich custom built from your choice of more than two dozen meats and salads—from smoked turkey (and even a truly low-salt turkey) and pastrami to capacola, shrimp salad, and a piquant black bean salad. Choose from a variety of breads and garnishes. Alongside the deli counter are urns of hot soup and a make-it-yourself salad bar with a huge array of vegetables, fruits, meats, pastas, and dressings. The store has a small selection of meats and seafood, gourmet coffee, wine and spirits, produce in big wicker baskets, and freshly baked breads. A bakery counter has a variety of tempting desserts, ranging from white chocolate mousse cake and hazelnut torte to elephant ears and almond bars.

Bockwinkel's, The Food Market, 700 N Michigan Ave, Chicago, IL 60611, 312/482-9900. Mon–Fri 8 am–9 pm, Sat 8 am–8 pm, Sun 10 am–8 pm.

Best shopping for caviar & smoked salmon

Petrossian Counter, Bloomingdale's

For that occasion when you entertain foreign dignitaries, a favorite (and/or rich) maiden aunt—or when you simply want the ultimate self-indulgent culinary experience—look no further than Bloomie's Petrossian food section on the sixth floor for ready-made French delicacies. Vegetable purées, Mediterranean fish soup, and cassoulet with pork sausage and goose are among the provisions offered at this upper-crust counter. Also direct from the Caspian Sea, in three distinct flavors (Beluga, Sevruga, and Ossetra), is a selection of the world's best caviar, starting at about $21 per ounce. You'll also find a large selection of Norwegian smoked salmon. At the small (25-seat) adjacent Petrossian Rendez-Vous Restaurant, which features a modern decor of slate blue and rose accented by fresh flowers on tables, you can sample some of these world-class tidbits before you buy.

Petrossian Counter, Bloomingdale's, 900 N Michigan Ave, Chicago, IL 60611, 312/440-4460. Mon–Sat 11 am–5 pm, Sun noon–5 pm.

Tastiest Midwest fish eggs

Carolyn Collins Caviar Company

Chilled vodka and caviar—it is about as elegant as you can get in terms of party food. And the comestibles' part of the combo can be expensive, too—if you opt for imported caviar. Enter Carolyn Collins who, in the space of a dozen years, has parlayed a hobby into a thriving business that produces wonderful domestic caviar at less than one-third of the price of the imported product. This company uses North American freshwater fish and produces caviar totally by hand, painstakingly separating individual caviar "berries." It offers whitefish, salmon, trout, and bowfin caviar, along with traditional sturgeon caviar. It also produces smoked caviar and a range of specialty caviar, including two based on golden-orange whitefish roe—one cured with fresh hot chili peppers and accented with pepper-flavored vodka, the other infused with the flavors of fresh citrus fruits with a dash of citron vodka. Also offered are lobster roe, flavored caviar butters, and a variety of smoked fish. Carolyn Collins suggests that people think of caviar as light fare, pointing out that it has little fat, only a trace of cholesterol, and only 50 calories per ounce. The entrepreneur also points to a misconception about caviar tasting too salty or too fishy. "Not true!" she says. "I don't even eat fishy-tasting *fish*." These products are also available by mail order.

Carolyn Collins Caviar Company, 925 W Jackson Blvd, Chicago, IL 60607, 312/226-0342. Hours by appointment.

Best fish market that smells like a seashore (and not like a fish store)

Burhop's at Plaza del Lago

For years, Burhop's downtown fish markets were the spots to pick up such favorites as California sand dabs and Rex sole, steamer clams from New England—plus cherrystones, filets of Alaskan sockeye salmon, soft-shell crabs and even finnan haddie. One by one these wonderful markets closed, so that now aficionados must journey to the North Shore for this wonderful fresh fish. It's worth the trip, because the quality and variety are first-rate and the surrounding Spanish-flavored Plaza del Lago offers other diversions (such as Convito Italiano—see separate listing—for Italian fare, and Betise, a charming French bistro full of paintings and sculptures). Try the fresh-tasting wild Gulf shrimp (superior to thawed farm-raised product) and Maine salmon (offered ten ways—eight ready to cook or heat, plus two versions that are smoked and ready to eat). This market also is a fun place to visit for seafood cooking demonstrations (learn how to stage a Wisconsin-style fish boil or make cioppino, the San Francisco Italian-style seafood stew), plus wine tasting—the store offers a decent selection of the stuff. It also carries fresh vegetables, so that you can throw hydroponically grown tomatoes or Portobello mushrooms on the grill with your fresh fish.

Burhop's Fisheries, 1515 N Sheridan Rd (at Plaza del Lago), Wilmette, IL 60091, 847/256-6400. Mon–Fri 9:30 am–6:30 pm, Sat 9 am–6 pm, Sun 9:30 am–5 pm.

Best place for pasta provisions

Convito Italiano

If you're provisioning an Italian meal, it may be worth a trip to the upscale Plaza del Lago shopping center in north suburban Wilmette. Here, you'll find everything you'll need here from antipasto to rare grappa, the fiery brandy distilled from grape pulp. There's a wide selection of Italian cured meats and sausage, imported cheeses, and ready-to-serve pasta salads. Homemade pasta comes in a variety of shapes and sizes and about a dozen different flavors, such as spicy red chili pepper, black pasta colored by squid ink, and red pasta with beet coloring. There are about 25 different freshly baked breads (pepper cheese bread is a big hit) and pastries such as hazelnut torte and flourless chocolate cake. The store's signature Italian cookies include *cantucci*, a Tuscan biscuit baked from the store's own recipe.

There's a selection of more than 1,000 different Italian wines, and various grappa in a cupboard kept under lock and key, not surprisingly since prices range from $25 to $3,500 a bottle.

Convito Italiano, Plaza del Lago, 1515 Sheridan Rd, Wilmette, IL 60091, 847/251-3654. Mon–Fri 10 am– 5:30 pm, Sat & Sun 11:30 am–5 pm.

Top spot for taramasalata

Athens Grocery Store

This is the neighborhood grocery store, and knowing that the neighborhood is Greek, you have some idea of what to expect. You're greeted by Greek music and rows of three-liter wicker-covered bottles of roditys and retsina. A showcase displays six different kinds and shades of olives, plus Salonika peppers and eggplant stuffed with pimiento and parsley. There are jars of pine nuts, pistachios, chick peas, and fat Jordan almonds, and containers of taramasalata and tarama caviar. A long shelf is bright with colorful cans of olive oil; another has a dozen kinds of sardines. You can buy mackerel in oil from the Black Sea, and, if you're up to making saganaki, the flaming-cheese appetizer so popular in Greek restaurants everywhere, there are appropriate sheep's-milk cheeses, including kasery (mild) and kefalotiri (sharp). You can also buy grape leaves (perfect for dolmades), ground lamb, and Greek sausage. There are packages of figs, plus pasta, fava beans, barley bread, and an array of exotically flavored cookies (grape syrup and orange) and a variety of preserves— quince, cherry, apricot, figs, banana-vanilla.

Athens Grocery Store, 324 S Halsted St, Chicago, IL 60606, 312/332-6737. Mon–Sat 8 am–8 pm, Sun 8 am–2 pm.

Best authentic Chinese market

Mei Wah Company

Chicago's cramped, hustling Chinatown (south of the Loop, centered around Cermak Road and Wentworth Avenue) is best known to nonresidents for a number of good authentic restaurants (as well as a few more-touristy ones). But, if you've a mind to provision your own Asian banquet, this cluttered neighborhood shop is a good place to start. From fresh fish (especially whitefish and catfish) to Chinese vegetables (bok choi, peapods, snow peas, bamboo shoots, et al) to exotic spices, sauces, and herbs (such as ginseng and dried seaweed), this grocery provides a fine variety of goods not as likely to be found at your local supermarket. Although this well-stocked Chinatown market has a potentially helpful staff, language problems sometimes are a barrier. Bringing a translator wouldn't hurt—otherwise, be prepared to point and nod.

Mei Wah Company, 2401 S Wentworth Ave, Chicago, IL 60616, 312/225-9090. Daily 9 am–7 pm.

Best authentic Vietnamese market

Viet Hoa Market

In Chicago's Little Saigon, Beng Prinh's authentic Vietnamese grocery (open since 1979) is a must-stop for those fascinated by unusual foods. On its cluttered shelves and along its narrow aisles are dry goods, fresh meat, fish, vegetables, and a selection of Vietnamese cooking and serving utensils. An array of fresh and frozen fish changes daily and includes jellyfish, eel, silver bass, and perch. There are vegetables such as *cailen* (Chinese broccoli), *yuchoy* (a soft green vegetable), and a sour, bitter vegetable, resembling a small orange, that is used largely in soups. In addition, you'll find a selection of exotic spices such as sweet basil and Lady Thumb, a large assortment of rice (including a jasmine-flavored variety), and a wide range of spiced tea. The store also stocks inexpensive ceramic bowls, chop sticks, Vietnamese cooking utensils, and Oriental hand-painted tea pots. The store's sales staff is friendly but extremely hard to understand.

Viet Hoa Market, 1051 W Argyle St, Chicago, IL 60640, 312/334-1028. Daily 8:30 am–7:30 pm.

Best wurst shopping

Lincoln Quality Market

In the delightfully Teutonic Lincoln Square area, amid a cluster of German restaurants, delis, and beer halls, this butcher shop has been fashioning plump wurst for way over half a century. Housed in a corner building with a bright brick-and-wood interior, it offers a wide range of meats and "hausmade" sausages. The latter include white, fully cooked bratwurst made mostly of veal, uncooked Sheboygan-style brats, knackwurst, smoked Thuringer, braunschweiger and country-style liverwurst, and paprika-and-garlic-flavored Hungarian sausage. You'll also find fresh Polish sausage and three different kinds of blood sausage, including a liver-blood sausage ring that traditionally is heated and served with sauerkraut. There also is a selection of smoked ham and bacon and *kassler rippchen*.

Lincoln Quality Market, 4661 N Lincoln Ave, Chicago, IL 60625, 312/561-4570. Mon–Fri 9 am–6 pm, Sat 8 am–5 pm.

Best German market

Paulina Market

This large and wonderful meat market, a Chicago fixture since 1949, may have the best sausage makers outside of Germany. This butcher produces more than 70 different kinds of sausage—closer to 100 kinds around the holidays. The range is incredible and includes German, Italian, Polish, Swedish, and Hungarian sausage (the latter spiked with garlic and red paprika), and a premier version of the New Orleans specialty, andouille. There are beer sausage, blood sausage, bockwurst, and bratwurst—plus duck sausage links (blended with pork and mild spices, gelbtwurst (white veal and pork sausage), and holsteiner (mildly seasoned German smoked pork sausage). Landjäger, the traditional hunter's smoked sausage of the Swiss and Germans, is made of beef seasoned with brandy and bacon bits and sold in linked pairs ready to snack on. Another specialty is *leberkäse*, a German version of meatloaf, great hot or cold (and sold either precooked or frozen, ready to cook at home). The meat market smokes its own mild-cured hickory boneless ham as well as boneless dry-cured Westphalian-style heavy ham. A great product for campers, hikers, and backpackers is beef jerky. Unlike the commercially packed brands that tend to be too salty and artificial tasting, this is made from beef sirloin tips that are trimmed of fat, cured, and then smoked.

Paulina Market, 3501 N Lincoln Ave, Chicago, IL 60657, 312/248-6272. Mon–Wed, Fri 9 am–6 pm, Thu 9 am–7 pm, Sat 9 am–5 pm.

Best German deli

Delicatessen Meyer

In the German Lincoln Square neighborhood, across from the tree-shaded benches of Giddings Plaza, this deli probably has the city's most comprehensive inventory of German goodies. Start with up to 200 kinds of sausages, made for Meyer by German butchers. Bestsellers include calves' liver sausage and *jagdwurst*, a garlicky sausage for slicing. *Leberkäse*, traditional companion to a pretzel roll, is baked daily and sold hot in three flavors—veal, mushroom, and Bavarian-style pork-and-beef. There are 30 different kinds of rye bread, 150 cheeses, and 30 homemade salads, including German potato salad and *fleischsalat*, a German-style meat salad. There is a big selection of German jams, candies, and cookies, plus imported fish, packages of spaetzel, and German toiletries, including colognes and soaps.

About 200 kinds of wine include German and Hungarian imports. You can buy Asbach Uralt grape brandy and Jägermeister, the famous herbal liqueur for curing what ails you (including overindulging in wurst).

Delicatessen Meyer, 4750 N Lincoln Ave, Chicago, IL 60625, 312/561-3377. Mon–Sat 9 am–9 pm, Sun 10 am–5 pm.

Best Scandinavian-style delis

Wikstrom's & Erickson's

In Swedish Andersonville, these two delis across the street from each other offer a smorgasbord of Scandinavian fare. I once was surprised to find a jar of cloudberries for a friend who had developed a taste for this exotic fruit on various visits to Sweden. You can buy Norwegian Jarlsberg cheese, with its distinctive nutty flavor and soft texture, cut fresh from a big yellow wheel, or Danish brie, Camembert, havarti, and samsoe. You'll find sacks of yellow peas, packages of potato dumplings, and in the fish section, schmaltz, lutefisk, and tempting trays of pickled herring. There are bottles of glug mix and Ramlosa Royal Swedish mineral water and bright packages of Scandinavian chocolate and candy. Wikstrom's claims the patronage of Sweden's Queen Sylvia during her visit to Chicago in 1988. "She bought some herring," reports owner Ingvar Wikstrom.

Wikstrom's, 5247 N Clark St, Chicago, IL 60640, 312/878-0601. Mon–Sat 9 am–6 pm, Sun noon–4 pm; Erickson's, 5250 N Clark St, Chicago, IL 60640, 312/561-5634. Mon 9 am–5 pm, Tue–Fri 9 am–6 pm, Sat 9 am–5 pm, Sun 9 am–4 pm.

Toughest bakery to walk past (without going in)

Swedish Bakery

With an abundance of fresh flowers, a wooden bench, counter help in blue-and-yellow Swedish aprons, and hand-painted pastoral wall trim, this resembles a country teashop more than a busy city bakery. And it *does* get busy, especially on Saturdays, jammed with customers waiting for their numbers to be called as they hungrily eye showcases packed with goodies and a revolving cake stand filled with cream-and-fruit–laden cakes and pies. There are petit fours, custard eclairs, marzipan cakes, strawberry logs, tortes, and 20 different kinds of coffee cakes, including apple-walnut, raisin streusel, and cardamom.

You can buy macaroon, Swedish blonde, and chocolate chip cookies with peanuts, and a variety of slices, including sour cream, apple, Italian plum, and custard streusel. Pie selections include chocolate silk, mincemeat, and lemon meringue. Behind the counter, neat rows of baskets contain crusty loaves of limpa bread, potato bread, and other varieties.

Swedish Bakery, 5348 N Clark St, Chicago, IL 60640, 312/561-8919. Mon–Thu 6:30 am–6:30 pm, Fri 6:30 am–8 pm, Sat 6:30 am–5 pm.

Best bakery to carry out cannoli

Scafuri Bakery

In the window are crusty loaves and pans of rich-red pizza bread. Inside, glass showcases are filled with a wonderful array of traditional Italian cookies—icing-coated butter cookies, honey balls, amaretto-flavored biscuits. On the walls are framed photographs of Mayor Richard M. Daley and former presidential candidate Michael Dukakis "helping out" in the kitchen (the latter wearing an apron inscribed "Duke"). But taking pride of place over the Irishman and Greek is a turn-of-the-century family portrait, colorized and indisputably Neapolitan, portraying the family that has owned this neighborhood bakery for more than 90 years. You'll find egg-twist bread and pan loaves, as well as Vienna and French loaves, plus absolutely delicious cannoli (as served at Mategrano's, the family restaurant a few doors east—see separate listing in "Dining"). Plus turnovers filled with ricotta cheese and apples, bags of bread sticks, cake donuts, and rich fruitcakes during holiday seasons.

Scafuri Bakery, 1337 W Taylor St, Chicago, IL 60607, 312/733-8881. Tue–Sat 7 am–5 pm, Sun 7 am–2 pm.

Best bakery to buy a party cake

Let Them Eat Cake

On the premise that Marie Antoinette may have had the right idea, this cake confectioner takes the art to the nth degree. You can buy a cake sculptured as a football helmet or a crescent wrench or practically any other shape you can imagine (including, perhaps, a guillotine). This upscale bakery specializes in made-to-order cakes for special occasions, weddings, and other assorted wing-dings, gaining a respected reputation with party planners as a purveyor of original-looking treats. Also sold here are ready-made cakes featuring heavy frosting and thick fillings, various cookies, and a large selection of pastries. Behind large glass display cases you'll find fresh-fruit tarts, banana-fudge walnut cake, cherry-cheese strudel, carrot cake, and fresh whipped-strawberry cake. (In fact, the bakery invites customers to test their confection-making versatility with the challenge: "Anything our customers can think up we can make.") Various locations through-out the city.

Let Them Eat Cake, 177 W Washington St, Chicago, IL 60602, 708/863-4200. Mon–Fri 6:30 am–6 pm. Closed Sat & Sun.

Best bakery to shop for yesterday's bread

The Corner Bakery

At $5 a pop, the chocolate-cherry bread, dark, rich, and studded with tart Michigan sour cherries, isn't cheap. But it's worth every penny. And it's an even better deal if you buy it day old, at half price. Most days, the bakery offers a good selection of day-old—buy a few loaves and stick them into the freezer. Along with crackly crusted baguettes and peasant-style country sourdough loaves, the bakery's full repertoire of freshly baked specialty breads is around 50. These include rosemary and olive, walnut, sesame semolina, raisin pecan, honey wheat, fig anise, cheese pepper, garlic thyme, and miller's rye. A favorite is olive bread, a Provençale-style rustic bread slightly salty with Greek Kalamata olives. The bakery offers a lunch menu that includes focaccia, sandwiches, soups, salads, and a selection of muf-fins, cookies, scones, and brownies. In warm weather, diners spill onto the sidewalks at shaded tables with cheerful red-and-white covers. (The bakery has several branches in Chicago and in sub-urban Skokie and Oak Brook.)

The Corner Bakery, 516 N Clark St, Chicago, IL 60610, 312/644-8100. Mon–Thu 7 am–10 pm, Fri 7 am–11 pm, Sat 8 am–11 pm, Sun 8 am–10 pm.

Choicest cheesecakes

Cheesecakes by JR Dessert Bakery

Next to ice cream, cheesecake is America's most popular dessert, and at this bakery it comes in almost as many flavors. Try mango cheesecake. Or white chocolate. How about pecan-caramel, pump-kin, hazelnut, or amaretto? These are among a score of flavors available at this shop that has made a name baking cheesecakes of uncompromising qual-ity. It operates its own bakery, which produces about four tons of pastries a week, including about 2,000 cheesecakes. Goods are baked from scratch using such high-quality ingredients as fresh fruit, bottled liquors, and instilled cappuccino. Although it built its reputation on cheesecakes, the bakery offers a diversified line of cakes, muffins, and other goodies. These include specialty cakes such as apple cobbler, carrot, German chocolate, chocolate mousse, and tiramisu, plus key lime pie, apple custard tart, caramel applebread pudding, plum crumb cake, and blueberry crumble. Health-conscious shoppers should know that at JR's you can have your cake and eat it, too. Responding to customer interest, the bakery developed a line of low-fat and no-fat items, such as 100 percent fat-free brownies and low-fat oatmeal cookies. Cakes are available whole or by the slice.

Cheesecakes by JR Dessert Bakery, 1001 W North Ave, Chicago, IL 60032, 312/266-9242. Mon–Fri 7 am–7 pm, Sat 9 am–6 pm, Sun 9 am–4 pm.

Choicest spot for choosing cheese, wine, and other delectable comestibles and potables

Chalet Wine & Cheese Shop/Gold Standard Liquors

This spacious North Side shop (or one of its other city branches) is just the thing for provisioning a cocktail party or selecting a spread of munchies for that big game on TV. A counter of domestic and imported cheeses includes varieties from England, Ireland, France, Denmark, Holland, Norway, and Germany. Among the cheese choices you'll find here are Huntsman from England, Crustin (with peppercorns) from France, and Pompadour from Holland. Gold Standard/Chalet offers a large selection of pâtés, crackers, chips, dips, snack meats (sausages, salamis, etc.), and various condiments as well. The store also carries a fine variety of wines (in all price ranges), liquors, and one of the city's most extensive stocks of imported and domestic "boutique" beers, such as fruit-flavored Lambic from Belgium (in peach, raspberry, and cherry varieties), Pechuer 36/15 from France (a supposedly aphrodisiacal beer containing ginseng), and Xingu, a black beer from Brazil. Does a large-volume business; discounts are often offered for case (or other bulk) purchases.

Chalet Wine & Cheese Shop/Gold Standard Liquors, 3000 N Clark St, Chicago, IL 60657, 312/935-9400. Mon–Sat 10 am–10 pm, Sun 11 am–6 pm. Other Chalet locations at 405 W Armitage, Chicago, IL 60614, 312/266-7155; 40 E Delaware Pl, Chicago, IL 60611, 312/787-8555; 1525 E 53rd St, Chicago, IL 60615, 312/324-5000.

Biggest best buys on booze

Zimmerman's

The man wearing the Stetson is Max Zimmerman, patriarch of the liquor supermarket that he founded in 1933. "I've worn this one for about 20 years," he told us. "I started wearing a hat in the store to keep my head warm, and it's become a trademark." Another trademark of Zimmerman's is its vast inventory and wide range—125 brands of beer, 30 brands of single-malt Scotch, 14 different kinds of vodka. If you can't find it elsewhere, it's probably somewhere in this 12,000-square-foot store, no matter how exotic or obscure, or whether it's from Poland or Peru. Pisco, for example, is a Peruvian liqueur popular for making whiskey sours. There is a fenced-in parking lot outside, shopping carts to tote your booze, and three generations of Zimmermans to provide counsel (you're likely to find one of them at your elbow politely suggesting a vintage and/or a bargain).

Zimmerman's, 213 W Grand Ave, Chicago, IL 60610, 312/332-0012. Mon–Sat 7:30 am–8 pm, Sun 11 am–5 pm.

Largest wine warehouse (to put you in good spirits)

Sam's Wine Warehouse

This huge warehouse offers Chicago's widest selection of wines plus hefty discounts. For sure you aren't paying for the ambience: Wine is displayed in cardboard boxes on bare, concrete floors. An inventory of about 20,000 bottles includes California wines from all of the major wineries. You'll also find good-value wines from the Southern Rhone, a variety of Loire wines, imported burgundies and bordeaux, 350 German wines, and a large selection of Italian reds and whites. Also discounted are 40-year-old tawny ports and a good selection of sherries, from bone-dry fino to dessert varieties. There are bargains, too, on a wide range of hard liquor and exotic cordials, on cases of imported beer stacked to the concrete ceiling, and on hard-to-find mixes, such as Bermuda ginger beer. You'll even find fat limes by the check-out, alongside piles of empty cartons. The store was started by Sam Rosen, and is run by his son, Fred, with help from grandson, Daryl. It's hard to miss Sam's—look for the massive lighted sign and exterior walls plastered with signs extolling deals on 750 ml Glenfiddich, Stoli, and such.

Sam's Wine Warehouse, 1000 W North Ave, Chicago, IL 60622, 312/664-4394. Mon–Sat 8 am–9 pm, Sun 11 am–6 pm.

Silliest-named (but good) card and gift shop

He Who Eats Mud

First of all—that name. Where does it come from? Some tribal rite? A childhood proclivity? The answer is more prosaic than you might think: The owner held a cocktail party for friends, and, when the group was well-oiled, suggested that they write down ideas for the store's name, which he would draw from a hat. Thus, He Who Eats Mud it randomly became. The store offers a truly staggering array of cards: Racks and racks of greetings for all seasons and tastes, from blank to bland to—potentially—banned (in a risqué adults-only section). Also stocked are (mostly clever, if not mainstream) T-shirts and buttons, stationery, gift wrap, and posters. A great place to find the distinctive touches that can add to an already-perfect gift.

He Who Eats Mud, 3247 N Broadway, Chicago, IL 60657, 312/525-0616. Mon–Fri 11 am–7 pm, Sat 11 am–6 pm, Sun noon–6 pm.

Shop with the most requests for plain brown wrappers

The Pleasure Chest, Ltd.

This is a store for adults. But it is not for the self-conscious—those with a tendency to look over their shoulders in case the people next door happen to be around (and, who knows, they may be, looking over *their* shoulders). The focus is on that three-letter subject and included in the store's interesting inventory are sexual aids, lingerie, toys, gifts, games, oils, lotions, potions, stimulants, books, magazines, and X-rated cards, all with adult orientation. Those who have never been to a sex store may be in for a surprise, but this shop and its matter-of-fact, bored-looking staff do their best to be tactful.

The Pleasure Chest, Ltd., 3143 N Broadway, Chicago, IL 60657, 312/525-7151. Daily noon–midnight.

Most magical carpets

Peerless Imported Rugs

But for a glass of mint tea and a salaam or two, this showroom of carpets and tapestries is for all the world like stepping into a Moroccan bazaar. Most of the carpets are handmade, such as the Imperial wool carpets from China, adapted from antique classics, that are the result of thousands of hours of hand-labor by weavers skilled in the ancient art of rug-making. More than 1,000 different carpets at this showroom originate from China, Pakistan, India, Turkey, Rumania, Portugal, Spain, and Belgium. This family business of more than 50 years directly imports most of its Oriental carpets and claims prices to be generally 20 percent or more lower than local dealers. In addition to carpets, the showroom carries more than 100 tapestries, intricately woven pieces of decorative art that are adapted from museum originals. Rugs and tapestries also are available from a mail-order catalog.

Peerless Imported Rugs, 3033 N Lincoln Ave, Chicago, IL 60657, 312/525-9034, 800/621-6573. Mon & Thu 9 am–7 pm, Tue, Wed, Fri & Sat 9 am–5:30 pm, Sun noon–5 pm.

Best hardware store that's more than a hardware store

The Great Ace

Those expecting the neighborhood hardware store to be cramped, a bit grungy, and offering merely paint, nuts and bolts, and various tools should consider the neighborhood. Located at the Webster Place Shopping Center in the gentrifying North Clybourn Corridor, this spacious outlet of the national Ace Hardware chain more than earns its trademarked name of The Great Ace. In its two well-lit, attractively laid out levels, shoppers can find the usual do-it-yourself supplies. . . . But this store also offers a wide selection of house- and bathwares, furniture (for house and lawn), lamps, electronics, decorative items, and tons of handy gadgets and knickknacks. If you combined a basic hardware store, a five-and-dime store, a Crate & Barrel/Pier 1, a Radio Shack, and a gift shop, you'd get close to what The Great Ace offers. It also has a good supply of free parking.

The Great Ace, 1455 W Webster Ave, Chicago, IL 60614, 312/348-0705. Mon–Sat 9 am–9 pm, Sun 10 am–7 pm.

Best office or business supplies

Horder's

Have a sudden need for a ream of peach-tinted copy paper? Or perhaps a set of 32 different-colored pens? Or even 5,000 #2 pencils? These—and much, much more—can be found among the massive inventory lining the shelves of this chain of office-supply stores. Horder's has become a trusted name with area businesses for its attentive service and reliability (if they don't stock it, they'll find it for you). Among the more unique items in the store are ready-to-use forms (leases, contracts, disclaimers) and a large selection of business books. The chain also publishes a giant catalog featuring high-ticket items such as office furniture and fax machines.

Horder's, 111 E Wacker Dr, Chicago, IL 60601, 312/648-7272. Mon–Fri 8 am–5 pm.

Best record store—jazz & blues

Jazz Record Mart

After 32 years, this Chicago landmark moved from its dingy River North storefront into fancy new digs around the corner. With 8,000 square feet to play with compared with the old store's 3,000 square foot, look for owner and musical pack rat Bob Koester to expand on an already unbelievable selection of music that includes some 15,000 CDs, 10,000 LP albums, 3,000 cassettes, and 5,000 78 rpm discs—purportedly the world's largest collection of jazz and blues recordings. In fact, Koester plans to turn the place into something of a jazz cultural center, with lots of related books, videos, magazines, T-shirts, posters, and even space for organizations dedicated to keeping the music alive. (Koester is also the proprietor of Delmark Records, a preservationist jazz and blues label he runs out of a North Lincoln Avenue location.)

Jazz Record Mart, 444 N Wabash Ave, Chicago, IL 60610, 312/222-1467. Mon–Sat 10 am–8 pm, Sun noon–5 pm.

Best record store—underground/independent

Wax Trax Records

Lovers of rock, punk, and post-punk music will find that Wax Trax, relocated from Lincoln Park to a small storefront in the near-West Side Wicker Park neighborhood, still offers the latest in new U.S. and import releases, old standards, some oldies, and an interesting selection of used music. A little light in cassettes and albums, but well-stocked in CDs (especially by hard-to-find alternative acts), the new location is festooned with posters for acts such as KMFDM, Pavement, and Hole. Although a pale imitation of its former self, decoration-wise, Wax Trax makes good use of gold spray paint, a stuffed blue marlin, and a big green cross propped behind the counter to recapture some of the in-your-face attitude of yore. Even if you don't know "Pop Will Eat Itself" from Iggy Pop (but would like to), this is the place to start.

Wax Trax Records, 1653 N Damen Ave, Chicago, IL
60647. Mon–Sat 11 am–10 pm, Sun noon–8 pm.

Best neighborhood for used record stores
North Clark Street

Looking for bargains on tapes and CDs? Head for a
short stretch of North Clark Street, between Fullerton Avenue and Diversey Parkway in the Lincoln
Park area, home to three of the city's best used
record stores. From south to north on Clark: Dr.
Wax (2523) has a huge selection of CDs (including
rare "bootlegs" of concert performances or previously
unreleased studio tracks) and albums, in all categories of music (with heavy concentrations of mainstream and alternative rock); 2nd Hand Tunes (2550)
offers used CDs and cassettes only, many of them
the latest chart hits; the other 2nd Hand Tunes
(2604) carries vinyl albums (and some 45s) only,
with large selections of 1970s and 1980s rock, and
some rare older material (and, incongruously, a
sizable rack of show tunes and movie sound tracks).
This stretch of Clark also contains two new record
stores: Gramaphone (2663), with good selections of
alternative rock; and Music World (2747), a large
chain store.

Dr. Wax, 2523 N Clark St, Chicago, IL 60614, 312/
549-3377. Mon–Sat 11:30 am–9 pm, Sun noon–6
pm; 2nd Hand Tunes, 2550 N Clark St, Chicago, IL
60614, 312/281-8813. Mon–Fri 11 am–8 pm, Sat 11
am–7 pm, Sun noon–7 pm (CDs and cassettes
only). 2nd Hand Tunes, 2604 N Clark St, Chicago, IL
60614, 312/929-6325. Mon–Fri 11 am–8 pm, Sat 11
am–7 pm, Sun noon–7 pm (albums only).

Best shopping in a building shaped like a barrel
Crate & Barrel

In a few short years, this gleaming store, opened in
the late 1980s, has become one of the best-known
shopping landmarks along the Magnificent Mile—
and one of the busiest. Aptly shaped like a rectan-
gular crate and cylindrical barrel, it may be the only
store on Michigan Avenue where you can buy a sofa.
In fact, two of the four floors are devoted to a line
of home furnishings, including everything from pictures and floor lamps to wall units and coffee tables,
in styles ranging from country classics and ultra-
modern to chic Southwestern styling. Floors one and
two of the slick, modern building display C & B's
unique brand of mix-and-match housewares. Here

you'll find bread baskets shaped like hens, blue-smoked water glasses, and shortbread molds, as well as a large selection of serving sets, utensils, and tablecloths. There's a selection of coffee machines, juice makers, and other appliances along with such kitchen gadgets as garlic presses and garlic bakers and pizza-making equipment. This newer version of an old standby has become such a favorite with Chicagoans and out-of-towners alike that you usually can expect a crowd (which knowledgeable wait staff and efficient wrappers are expert at handling).

Crate & Barrel, 646 N Michigan Ave, Chicago, IL 60611, 312/787-5900. Mon–Fri 10 am–8 pm, Sat 10 am–6 pm, Sun noon–5 pm.

Best bet to dress your bed

Private Lives

It's hard to imagine that there can be so many choices when it comes to dressing a bed. But this store, devoted to the latest fashions in bedspreads, comforters, duvets, sheets, and linens, is crammed with options. Many of the products carry the names of famous designers such as Ralph Lauren, Laura Ashley, and Liberty of London and are offered at discount prices. There is a wide choice of sewing materials, such as silk, cotton, and flannel. Also in the store is a large selection of bath accessories, including shower curtains, soap dishes, towels, and various knickknacks. New home owners can find decorating inspiration here.

Private Lives, 662 W Diversey, Chicago, IL 60657, 312/525-6464. Mon–Fri 10 am–7 pm, Sat 11 am–6 pm, Sun 11 am–5 pm.

Best place to buy the kitchen sink

Kitchen & Bath Mart

If there's art in plumbing, it's at this showroom of kitchen and bathroom cabinetry and fixtures. You'll find island kitchen countertops with built-in cooking units, gleaming white vanity sinks with futuristic bright red hardware, and bathroom sinks, tubs, and shower stalls in the latest contemporary colors—although the store says that neutral blacks and whites continue to be popular. For those rehabbing a kitchen or bathroom, this is a springboard of ideas that can set your imagination soaring. And, if you need help, there are consultants to take you through complete design and installation.

Kitchen & Bath Mart, 237 North Ave, Chicago, IL 60610, 312/943-7060. Mon–Fri 10 am–6 pm, Sat 10 am–4 pm.

Best place to art deco-rate your home

Steve Starr Studios

If you've ever fantasized about redecorating your home (or even an office) in art deco style, this is the spot that can help you realize your dream. Available here are mirrors and glassware (such as elaborate decanters), lighting fixtures, and a variety of other decorative accessories; also, a collection of sparkling jewelry. Starr himself can be found peddling his store's wares (in his trademark confident and excited fashion) most days; for fun, ask him about the store's semilegendary former window sign, which mock-barred clumsy, annoying, or otherwise clueless customers from entering.

Steve Starr Studios, 2779 N Lincoln Ave, Chicago, IL 60614, 312/525-6530. Mon–Thu 2–6:30 pm, Fri 2–6 pm, Sat noon–5 pm, Sun 1–5 pm.

Deepest stock of Depression glassware

Through-A-Glass

If you're looking for a particular item of Depression-era glassware, you'll likely find it in this store, the largest of its kind in the city. If you can't, the shop's owner, Mary Dillon, probably can obtain it for you. Using her nationwide network of contacts, Mary offers customers a free locator service. Displayed is a range of glassware priced from as little as $1 to as high as $1,000 and up. (Considering those upper-end prices, it's ironic to remember that Depression-era glassware dates back to the time when people earned one dollar a day, and a cup of coffee cost a nickel.) Opened in 1972, the store carries a huge collection of Depression-style glassware in the distinctive smoked and tinted shades popular in the 1920s, 1930s, and 1940s. Included are plates, cups, stemware, shot glasses—virtually any vessel made of glass. Merchandise is attractively displayed; this definitely is not a junk store.

Through-A-Glass, 2255 W Belmont, Chicago, IL 60518, 312/528-1617. Tue–Sat 1–7 pm.

Best antiquities and artifacts

Harlan J. Berk, Ltd.

You know the old gift-giving credo: "When in doubt, give money." Instead of writing a check the next time you're stymied for a gift idea, why not take it one step further and give money with a bit of background and history to it? How about a Roman coin depicting Julius Caesar or Nero, or a Russian ruble showing Catherine the Great? These and other rare and delightful antiquities are available at this unique downtown shop. While ancient coins are a particular specialty, Berk also carries a wide variety of amulets, pottery, lamps, jewelry, and other decorative pieces from throughout Northern and Southern Europe, the Middle East, South America, and Asia, as well as letters and autographs from historical figures and celebrities (ranging from Napoleon to Teddy Roosevelt to Elvis Presley). Quality and prices on all items vary; some are museum quality and priced to reflect it, and others may be less perfect or more common and therefore more affordable.

Harlan J. Berk, Ltd., 31 N Clark St, Chicago, IL 60602, 312/609-0016. Mon–Fri 9 am–4:45 pm (also some Sat hrs Thanksgiving–Christmas).

Best mart for Illinois art

Illinois Artisans Shop

For an unusual gift or a piece of artwork that you know wasn't mass-produced by sweat labor in Asia, check out this shop showcasing homegrown talent. Located on the second floor of the State of Illinois building (and part of the Illinois Artisans Program, which also has two outlets downstate), it draws from the work of the more than 1,500 artists and craftspeople throughout the state. Ranging from a 60-cent folk art postcard to woven wall hangings and quilts valued at thousands of dollars, this shop has a huge inventory and displays the work of about 500 Illinois artisans at any given time. Pick up a one-of-a-kind piece of jewelry for $20; choose from wrought-iron candlesticks, wood-turned bowls, stationery fashioned from handmade paper, and hand-painted wearable art in the form of jackets, capes, and vests. You'll also find blown and fused glass, raku, hand-made quilts and tapestries, masks, various other ceramics, prints, and fiber art, as well as boxes crafted from a variety of materials—wood, fabric, paper, stainless steel. Artists represent virtually every region of the state, many of whom produce in modern rendition such traditional craft and art forms as quilling, glass engraving, and lace-making.

Illinois Artisans Shop, James R. Thompson Center, Suite 2-200, 100 W Randolph St, Chicago, IL 60601, 312/814-1794. Mon–Fri 9 am–5 pm.

Most uncommon art mart

Uncommon Market

Stop at the Chicago Cultural Center (see separate listing in "Museums, Galleries, Theaters & Other Sites") to enjoy a free concert or movie, visit a free museum, and browse a free exhibition of paintings, photography, or sculpture. And head for the Randolph Street lobby to find this tiny shop offering unusual shopping for art-related items (you just might find that unique gift that has been eluding you). The kiosk has a selection of posters, postcards, notecards, T-shirts, and souvenir mugs relating to exhibits at the Cultural Center. Check out their glittering glass paperweights and a selection of CDs and tapes of artists who have performed at the center (or who are scheduled to). This also is the home of Uncommon Ground, an espresso bar where one usually can find an unoccupied table and enjoy a cup of coffee, cappuccino, tea, or soft drink, and choose from a selection of baked goods.

Uncommon Market, Cultural Center (Randolph St lobby), 78 E. Washington St, Chicago, IL 60602, 312/541-0077. Mon–Fri 9 am–5 pm, Sat 11 am–5 pm, Sun noon–5 pm.

Oldest apothecary

Merz Apothecary

It's not surprising that this good-looking shop, established in 1875, also is known as an *apotheke*. It's in the heart of German Lincoln Square and it's not unusual to hear a customer using German to discuss a prescription with the pharmacist. The redbrick storefront is trimmed in oak and green marble, with black-and-gold German lettering on the windows. Inside, the bright, attractive store has a tin ceiling, wood paneling, and brass chandeliers. As you walk up a ramp flanked by brass handrails, you are assailed by the fragrance of an extensive selection of imported soaps. The shop specializes in European herbs and toiletries, as well as allopathic and homeopathic medicines. You'll find boxes of sponges, rows of vitamins and imported elixirs, and bottles of German vegetable juices (sauerkraut, carrot, beet, and tomato). Two shelves contain handlabeled jars of bulk herbs, such as hops, agrimony, horehound, motherwort, and licorice root. Even if you're not in the market for some huckleberry leaves, you'll probably find this a fascinating place to browse.

Merz Apothecary, 4716 N Lincoln Ave, Chicago, IL 60625, 312/989-0900. Mon–Sat 9 am–6 pm.

Hottest tubs to try before you buy

GreatLakes Hot Tubs

If you've ever considered installing a hot-tub spa in your home, vacation home, or even your office, here's a dealer that lets you try before you buy. If you're interested only in dunking and not in buying, you can rent a hot-tub suite by the hour. There are five rooms with hot tubs, jacuzzi jets, showers, dressing areas, and music systems. They accommodate from two to four persons and cost $28 an hour (plus $10 per hour for the third and fourth soakers). For $33 an hour you can rent a VIP suite that has a sauna and other extras for up to eight tubbers. Speaking of extras, bathing suits are optional.

GreatLakes Hot Tubs, 15 W Hubbard St, Chicago, IL 60610, 312/527-1311, Mon–Thu 11 am–2 am, Fri & Sat 11 am–4 am, Sun noon–midnight.

ROMANTIC

Most romantic restaurant for breakfast
Boulevard, Hotel Inter-Continental

Tables for two in the second-floor dining room are
set out by windows that look down onto sun-dappled
Michigan Avenue with its pretty container plantings
of flowers and shrubs. Inside, the atmosphere is soft
and heavy, sound muted by thick carpet—the sort
of place where waking up comes slowly. With potted
palms, heavy drapes, and art deco chairs in striped
upholstery, this is a dining room that invites lingering. The menu is elegantly simple, with many heart-
healthy offerings, such as oatmeal with kiln-dried
cherries, *birchermuesli* or low-fat yogurt with fresh
berries, and vegetable frittata with tomato sauce.
There are buttermilk pancakes, fluffy, made-to-order
omelettes, and Belgian waffles—or splurge with a
traditional eggs Benedict or a version featuring
smoked salmon. There are potato cakes and house-
made grits as sides, plus a selection of pastries,
bagels, and muffins. Elegant china is embossed with
the hotel's signature golden lion. Pause to look over
ornate wrought-iron railings and admire the marble-
and-alabaster columns and Moorish embellishments
of the foyer. (For a detailed look at the restored 1929
decor of this former Medinah Athletic Club, take a
free tape-recorded tour—see separate listing for hotel
in "Accommodations"). *Make a date:* Peek in to The

Salon, off the foyer, and plan to return for traditional English-style afternoon tea (with Devonshire cream) or in late evening to listen to the soft music of a jazz trio.

Boulevard, Hotel Inter-Continental, 505 N Michigan Ave, Chicago, IL 60611, 312/944-4100. Breakfast daily.

Most romantic restaurant for lunch
Grappa

Just steps from the Magnificent Mile and Water Tower shopping, this restaurant, with light wood paneling, matching polished wood floors, and huge gilded mirrors, is a stylish luncheon spot—at once, bright, sleek, and contemporary and warm and companionable. Well-spaced tables are decorated with petite, colorful vases with sprigs of fresh flowers (sometimes orchids). Black-and-white fashion photography adorns softly lighted walls. Festooned clumps of garlic and sausages add a folksy touch to an exhibition kitchen featuring a pizza oven. A cozy terraced mezzanine dining area with a wood-burning fireplace overlooks the main dining room. The food is superb, quickly installing this newcomer as one of Chicago's top restaurants. Start with seared loin of rabbit with soft polenta and savoy cabbage or octopus on a bed of black beans with a piquant tomato broth. Then move on to veal scallopini served with braised spinach and a fennel tart, grilled medallions of beef tenderloin partnered with cannellini beans and Gorgonzola, or grilled tuna with raddicchio, lentil puree, and sage olive oil. Roasted grouper with vegetables is a simple luncheon choice. Or try the wonderful freshly made pastas, including potato gnocchi with goat cheese and tomato basil sauce and thin ribbons of pappardelle with roasted wild duck, portobello mushrooms, fennel, and port wine sauce. Rissotos are well made and change daily. Incredible desserts include warm apple cake, what may be the best tiramisu in the city, and an unusual blend of roasted and caramelized pears, dried figs, and caramel gelato served with a pistachio crisp.

Grappa, 200 E Chestnut St, Chicago, IL 60611, 312/337-4500. Mon–Sat 11:30 am–11 pm, Sun 5–10 pm.

Most romantic restaurant for dinner
Bella Vista

A former bank may seem an unlikely spot for a romantic meal, but that doesn't take into account the stunning, award-winning makeover of the landmark building once occupied by the Belmont Trust and Savings Bank. The architecture showcases a 30-foot ceiling, atrium skylight, hand-painted walls, inlaid marble floors, and—symbolizing the importance of wine—red and white woodwork blending African purple heart wood and blond wood. Five levels of dining include a European bar/café featuring a grape fabric motif. As the name suggests, the view is beautiful, and splendid food matches the ambience—innovative and delicious entrées such as grilled lamb loin layered with potato "sheets," smoked bacon, spinach, caramelized onion, and mint and rotisserie chicken with horseradish potatoes, tomatoes, peppers, and escarole. Pasta dishes, offered in appetizer- and entrée-sized portions, include pappardelle with duck, wild mushrooms, tomato, and peas, and linguini with wild mushrooms, artichokes and a rosemary-mushroom broth. For starters try grilled eggplant with smoked mozzarella, fontina, prosciutto, and lemon—or steamed mussels with cannellini beans in a tomato-white wine broth. Excellent pizzas include a blend of artichokes, wild mushrooms, roasted peppers, and smoked mozzarella. A popular salad combines endive, watercress, pears, peppered pecans, and Gorgonzola cheese with a red wine vinaigrette dressing. Romantic occasions, such as Valentine's Day, are celebrated in grand style with sensuous dessert creations such as liquid center espresso cake with white chocolate gelato and two chocolates. Wines are an important part of the dining experience here, with more than 250 American and Italian wines, including a dozen offered by the glass. A walk-through wine room has cast-iron gates shaped as wine bottles.

Bella Vista, 1001 W Belmont Ave, Chicago, IL 60657, 312/404-0111. Mon–Thu 11:30 am–11 pm, Fri & Sat 11:30 am–midnight, Sun 5–10 pm.

Most romantic dining room with a view
Cité

Step out of the elevator on the 70th floor of residential Lake Point Tower, enter the foyer of this restaurant converted from a former private club, and the view is sudden and startling. Spread before you are the shimmering blue lake, beaches, parkland, and the shoreline stretching into infinity. Close at hand is the hustle-bustle of Navy Pier with its gaudy new landmark giant ferris wheel. This arguably is the best restaurant view in all of Chicago. Indiana and Michigan are visible in the distance, and the flight path to O'Hare provides constant entertainment. At night, ant-like columns of cars on the busy outer drive create ribbons of red and white lights. This is a special-occasion restaurant, where the tableside cooking may be a little showy but is well executed to produce such classics as steak Diane, crêpe Suzette, and cherries jubilee. Start with crab cakes or mushrooms in puff pastry and continue with rack of lamb, châteaubriand, veal chop with mushrooms, red snapper, or baked salmon with fresh raspberry champagne sauce. The only real surprise here is the high quality of the food—a top view plus fine eats. You can make a meal from seafood-loaded bouillabaisse and finish with the chef's signature key lime tart. Sunday brunch is a treat, a time to watch the city at play far below.

Cité, Lake Point Tower, 505 N Lake Shore Drive, Chicago, IL 60611, 312/644-4050. Mon–Fri noon–midnight, Sat 5 pm–midnight, Sun 11 am–midnight.

Most romantic dining in a former hamburger joint

Tra Via

Although immensely popular with Chicagoans weekending in Michigan, Redamak's of New Buffalo (of hamburger fame) didn't make it at this near-north location. Nor did its immediate successor. But if justice prevails, the superb food and pretty ambience of Tra Via should bring success to the current tenant. Its name translates to "the meeting place," and with glass and antique yellow walls, faux-marble columns, and floors of light woods and marbles—designed to capture the casual warmth of a trattoria in Tuscany or Lombardy—it is a casual, romantic meeting place. Adding to the ambience are wide windows opening to Lincoln Avenue and, in one corner, a wood-burning pizza oven faced with fieldstone. Creatively prepared seafood is a good choice—sautéed halibut served with sweet corn, fennel, and arugula salad with roasted pepper coulis, and pan-roasted snapper with sweet corn, soft polenta, and red pepper aioli. The restaurant is vegetarian-friendly, with emphasis on such unusual varieties as fennel, rapini, baby artichokes, Jerusalem artichokes, and haricots verts. Yet the carnivore will find T-bone steak Florentine and grilled steak served with lemon and truffle oil and roasted garlic mashed potatoes. In fall, an intriguing variety of fresh mushrooms includes porcini, golden chanterelles, shiitake, and portobello. A not-to-miss dessert is warm, deep-dish apple pie with cinnamon buttermilk gelato. *Starter tip:* If available, order sea scallops—exquisitely prepared with roasted tomato aioli and basil oil.

Tra Via, 2263 N Lincoln Ave, Chicago, IL 60614, 312/348-7200. Sun–Wed 4–10 pm, Thu–Sat 4 pm–1 am.

Most romantic restaurant for a candlelight dinner

Geja's Cafe

Back in 1964, when John Davis opened Geja's, newlyweds could count upon receiving a gift of at least one fondue pot. More than 30 years later, the fad has faded, but the restaurant flourishes as one of Chicago's most romantic—perfect for proposals and anniversaries. It's an intimate, candlelit spot to share a booth, a fondue pot, and a special occasion with a significant someone. To heighten the romantic mood is music by a classical or flamenco guitarist. Combination dinners include cheese fondue (a spiced blend of Gruyere cheese, white wine, and kirsch), followed by a small salad, an entrée fondue, and a chocolate fondue dessert flamed with orange liqueur and served with assorted fresh fruit, pound cake, and marshmallows. Entrées include various combinations of beef, shrimp, lobster, scallops, and chicken, plus a fresh-vegetable fondue. Also available is a selection of international cheeses served with French and black bread and whipped butter. Owner Davis is an oenophile, so the wine list is thoughtfully assembled.

Geja's Cafe, 340 W Armitage Ave, Chicago, IL 60614, 312/281-9101. Mon–Thu 5–10:30 pm, Fri 5 pm–midnight, Sat 5 pm–12:30 am, Sun 4:30–10 pm.

Most romantic dining spot where you control the lighting

Nick's Fishmarket

Close enough to City Hall and Chicago's trading floors to be a power luncheon spot, this also is a popular locale for an assignation. Not only is there a phone jack at every table (for that wheeling and dealing), but every table also has its own rheostat with which to dim the lighting. You enter the restaurant by riding an elevator down from street level. The atmosphere of three dining areas with their burgundy leather seating, colorful oils, and etched glass is dark, clubby, and (depending upon your companion) romantic. With its gallery of celebrity photos (Nick's claims as patrons the likes of Clint Eastwood and MJ) Nick's also feels—and is—expensive. Emphasis is on fresh seafood, including more exotic varieties such as opakpaki and abalone. A range of appetizers includes many standards such as mussels marinara, shrimp scampi, oysters Rockefeller, and clams casino. Fish selections range from salmon and catfish to mahi mahi, swordfish, and Dover sole. Simple preparations such as grilling are best; sauces tend to be uninspired and smothering. This definitely is a special-event destination—especially an event involving just the two of you. There's piano entertainment in the bar Tue–Sat.

Nick's Fishmarket, 1st National Bank Plaza, Chicago, IL 60603, 312/621-0200. Mon–Thu 11:30 am–11 pm. Fri 11:30 am–11:30 pm, Sat 5:30 pm–11:30 pm (also a Rosemont location).

Most romantic spot for pretheater dinner

Cuisines (Stouffer Renaissance)

On the table is a single long-stemmed rose (just as if *you* planned it that way). Spacious booths are comfortably upholstered with floral coverings in muted green. Dark paneling, soft lighting, and wine racks along the walls give the room a moody, intimate feel. Yet an open grill with a counter decorated with platters of glistening peppers and tomatoes and massive jars of green olives tied with bright red cloth brings a casual touch. So do the Mediterranean accents of a café occupying the forecourt, where a deep blue skylighted ceiling with painted clouds and paddle fans overlook granite-topped tables in a terrace-like setting. A lively Mediterranean-accented menu features such entrées as paella, lamb brochette with Moroccan spices and minted cous cous, grilled swordfish with herb risotto, tomato, and leek, and filet mignon with four-cheese ravioli and portobello mushrooms. A wide range of starters includes artichoke and scallop risotto, polenta with asparagus and morel mushroom sauce, and Mediterranean fish soup. A creative selection of pasta and pizza is available in both appetizer- and entrée-sized portions. Dinner begins at 5:30 pm, and many take advantage of it for pre-theater dining (the Chicago Theater is right across street and the hotel offers special packages). Desserts are well worth considering, but, regardless, every table receives a bowl of fresh fruit—a nice touch from a class operation. Incredibly, most entrées are modestly priced in the $13–$19 range.

Cuisines, Stouffer Renaissance Hotel, 1 W Wacker Dr, Chicago, IL 60601, 312/372-7200. Mon–Fri 11:30 am–10:30 pm.

Most romantic Sunday brunch in a museum

Big Shoulders Café

Although the Chicago Historical Society is an obvious place to find out all you ever wanted to know about the city, it is an unlikely venue for Sunday brunch. This pleasant café occupies an airy white room, decorated in black and gray and framed by a circular wall of windows. There are ficus trees in the windows, pots of ivy on the tables, and a piano to provide soft background music—a little Gershwin, Porter, or Berlin. Order from the menu or from a modestly priced brunch buffet that includes salads, grilled vegetables, meats, seafood, egg dishes, quiche, fruit, and pastries. Menu selections include buttermilk pancakes, banana bread French toast with fresh fruit, curried chicken salad, and sandwiches. Flanking the doorway is a magnificent terra-cotta arch designed in 1888 for Chicago's famed Union Stockyards. Its ornamentation depicts a cowboy, a cattle rancher, and livestock. The menu prints Carl Sandburg's poem "Chicago" from which the restaurant takes its name. (There also is piano music on Tuesday afternoons.)

Big Shoulders Café, 1601 N Clark St, Chicago, IL 60614, 312/587-7766. Mon–Fri 11:30 am–3 pm, Sat & Sun 10:30 am–3 pm.

Most romantic champagne bar

Pops For Champagne

This is a bar with multiple personalities—and all of its facets are quite compatible. First and foremost, this is a champagne bar—one of the finest in the country. It offers more than 100 different types of champagne, by the glass or by the bottle, for big-spending and less-moneyed lovers of bubbly alike. Pops is also a great spot for live and recorded jazz in an upscale, intimate setting. And both of these add to the bar's third side—a romantic place. Dark and atmospheric, this is a winning spot for wooing someone special. Although champagne is the specialty, Pops also offers a good selection of other wines and fine cognacs. There is live music nightly (except Tuesdays) and a light jazz-and-champagne brunch on Sundays.

Pops For Champagne, 2934 N Sheffield Ave, Chicago, IL 60657, 312/472-1000. Mon–Fri 4 pm–2 am, Sat 4 pm–3 am, Sun 10:30 am–2 am.

Best sidewalk café—for people watching

Bistro 110

Romantically inclined couples be advised that both (or neither) should sample the complimentary hors d'oeuvre—soft roasted garlic cloves, delicious when spread on crusty bread and butter. This comfortable, casual bistro is known for preparation in a wood-burning oven—and for the view of the passing crowd from a glass-enclosed patio or from tables that spill out onto the sidewalk during warm weather. Top starters are petite whole-wheat pizza; mushrooms roasted with garlic, rosemary, and thyme; and a creamy goat cheese salad that combines spinach, frisse (a field green), and a sun-dried tomato vinaigrette dressing. The restaurant's signature dish is oven-roasted half chicken—also prepared with garlic, rosemary, and thyme. Standards include steak au poivre, leg of lamb, and filet of salmon. Desserts feature cherry-apple cobbler, bittersweet chocolate mousse, apple tart, crème brulée, and various sorbets and ice cream. Eight wines are served by the glass.

Bistro 110, 110 E Pearson St, Chicago, IL 60611, 312/266-3110. Mon–Thu 11:30 am–10 pm, Fri & Sat 11:30 am–midnight, Sun 11 am–10 pm.

Best sidewalk café—for an after-dinner drink or Italian ice cream
Carlucci

In a city with an overload of Italian eateries, everyone has his or her own favorites, and Carlucci remains as reliable as ever and commands a loyal following. Along fashionable Halsted Street, where bars and restaurants seem to spring up—and disappear—as quickly as mushrooms after a rainshower, Carlucci is a perennially popular alfresco spot. When warm weather finally smiles on Chicago, Carlucci opens its lovely garden area. Head there for a homemade *gelato* (Italian ice cream) served from an outdoor stand. Or choose, perhaps, an espresso or cappuccino. Either way, this is a perfect place of repose for two after dinner or before an evening of nightlife. Indoors, the main dining room is a stylish, high-ceilinged spot to enjoy inventive Italian cuisine. An attractive bar up front (separated from the restaurant), looking out on the people-parade of Halsted Street, is a just-right spot to share some conversation over a bottle of wine or an aperitif.

Carlucci, 2215 N Halsted St, Chicago, IL 60614, 312/281-1220. Mon–Thu 5:30–10:15 pm, Fri & Sat 5:30–11:15 pm, Sun 5–10 pm.

Best sidewalk café—European-style
Corner Bakery

Tables with traditional red-checkered tablecloths wrap around the front of this popular eatery. Even on workdays, this sidewalk café is a busy spot, with workers stopping off for a latte or maybe a low-fat muffin as tempting aromas waft out from the bakery. It is the baked-on-the-premises bread—the long, golden, crusty baguettes and the flour-dusted country loaves—that give this café its European flavor. On Sundays, things are more leisurely, with couples enjoying each other and taking time to spread out the Sunday papers. Sandwich selections include tuna salad, chicken pesto, and roasted vegetables—spinach, zucchini, squash, red peppers, and goat cheese on caramelized onion bread. Other popular choices include tomato mozzarella, made with red peppers, tomato, fresh basil, and balsamic vinaigrette and served on a baguette, and Mediterranean turkey, featuring Swiss cheese, olive salad, and honey mustard on Italian bread. Minestrone is offered daily (plus a changing soup selection) and salads include chicken curry, Caesar, and wild rice. The menu features a variety of pizzas, plus desserts that run the gamut from lemon squares, raspberry bars, and chocolate-cherry rolls, to pure vanilla pound cake, fudge brownies, and butterscotch Blondies. This also is a good spot to buy crusty loaves (up to 50 varieties are offered)—and find bargains in day-old bread (see separate listing in "Shopping").

Corner Bakery, 516 N Clark St, Chicago, IL 60610, 312/644-8100. Mon–Thu 7 am–10 pm, Fri 7 am–11 pm, Sat 8 am–11 pm, Sun 8 am–10 pm.

Best outdoor café for art's sake

McKinlock Court Garden Restaurant of the Art Institute

After enjoying Georges Seurat's famous "A Sunday Afternoon on the Island of Grande Jatte," spend part of your Sunday afternoon relaxing at a shaded table at this perennial summer favorite at the Art Institute. Surrounded by flowers and trees, the outdoor cafe encircles the Triton fountain, bubbling gently to provide a soothing background. Relax with a cappuccino or espresso and perhaps a refreshing sorbet or homemade ice cream. The menu features such selections as chilled melon soup, fried artichoke hearts, breast of chicken salad, pasta and albacore salad, quiche du jour, and baked filet of sole. Desserts include cheesecake, apple almond tart with caramel sauce, and chocolate nougatine torte with chocolate sauce. Entertainment includes harp music and Tuesday evening "After-Hours Jazz" concerts.

McKinlock Court Garden Restaurant of the Art Institute, S Michigan Ave at E Adams St, Chicago, IL 60603, 312/443-3500. Late May–Sept, Oct: Mon–Sat 11 am–3:30 pm, Sun noon–3:30 pm.

Best garden for Sunday brunch and jazz

O'Brien's

Although this old-town saloon has been around since 1979 (spot it by the landmark clock on the edge of the sidewalk), its pleasant garden café was created only in 1993. It's the spot to head on Sundays for brunch and live jazz—the likes of talented pianists Scot Holman and Mike Hanko and guitarists Peter Tye and Brian Scott. Nestled between two buildings and dominated by a magnificent elm, the garden is a cool, shady summer oasis, with seating for about 150, English teakwood furniture, a gazebo bar, and an abundance of flowers and greenery. Inside, the restaurant has a clubby feel with hunter green and dark wood decor. It has long been a favorite for good-quality steaks (but skip the shrimp de jonge; it's bland and not sufficiently garlicky). A piano bar draws a coterie of regulars late into the evening, as lyrics of "As Time Goes By" drift into the dining room. The garden serves a special café menu along with the regular menu (the restaurant does a good job with peach melba and produces a moist carrot cake). Jazz sometimes is scheduled on other days—phone for schedule. *Movie trivia:* This is one spot where Paul Newman and Tom Cruise filmed scenes for *The Color of Money.*

O'Briens, 1528 N Wells St, Chicago, IL 60610, 312/787-3131. Mon–Thu 11 am–10:30 pm, Fri & Sat 11 am–12:30 am, Sun noon–10 pm.

Best afternoon tea where you might bump into celebrities

Park Hyatt Chicago

Elizabeth Taylor, Barry Manilow, Bob Hope, and Pat Summerall all have signed the guest register at the elegant and exclusive Park Hyatt, so you never know whom you're likely to bump into if you decide to rendezvous in Le Salon lobby lounge for afternoon tea. Of course, if your assignation is with someone special, you probably don't care who else you might see, not as you sit close on a plush couch under the magnificent crystal chandelier, with classical piano tinkling in the background. But, to practical matters—tea is served Monday–Saturday 2–5 pm and includes a selection of six types of tea, scones, preserves, and Devonshire cream, plus selections from the pastry cart. Cost is $12.50 per person (sandwiches are extra).

Park Hyatt Chicago, 800 N Michigan Ave, Chicago, IL 60611, 312/280-2222.

Best bet to take a date to the French countryside (where you won't forguette your baguette)

la Madeleine

About every two months or so, Patrick Esquerre returns to his native France and drives a truck around the countryside, visiting village antique fairs. He buys up old furniture, clocks, lamps, tools, and farm implements—anything that will add character to the rustic bakery/cafés he has opened in Dallas, New Orleans, and now Chicago. Warm natural woods are used for floor, beams, and tables, complemented by exposed brick walls decorated with copper pots and pans and old wooden clocks. The charming Frenchman has a knack that makes his restaurants immediate hits in neighborhoods where locals come to buy fresh loaves shaped by hand and baked for six hours in wood-burning ovens (no short cuts here). There also is the lure of homemade pastries such as puffy éclairs, strawberry Napoléons, and fresh fruit tarts, and a pleasant, homey ambience in which to make a meal of a hearty bowl of soup, a luncheon salad, quiche, or rosemary rotisserie chicken. Bread not only tastes good but also is healthful: So-called "No No" breads are no-fat, no-cholesterol products that include baguettes, country wheat, whole wheat, and French sourdough (a separate menu is devoted to suggestions for low-calorie, low-fat meals). Daily soups always include French onion and a wonderful creamy blend of fresh basil and tomatoes. What is punningly called the "pizza de résistance" combines the flavors of Proveçale with an herb crust layered with onions and a base of herb-infused tomato sauce and topping of chicken, olives, and Swiss cheese. Other bread choices include olive, prosciutto-pecan, and walnut-macadamia. Breakfast options include eggs, meats, and baked goods.

la Madeleine, 2813 N Broadway, Chicago, IL 60657, 312/477-3173. Sun–Thu 7 am–10 pm, Fri & Sat 7 am–11 pm (also Wilmette location in Edens Plaza).

Best romance on cloud nine

Windy City Balloonport

Sweep that special someone off his or her feet with a flight in a hot-air balloon. In northwest suburban Fox River Grove, local balloonists have found an ideal launching area in a natural bowl sheltered from the wind. Launchings generally are held in early morning or late afternoon when wind conditions usually are most favorable. In approximately seven minutes, the 70-foot balloon is inflated and ready for flights, filled with air by powerful fans; propane burners heat the air inside to create buoyancy. Altitude of the flight will vary from a tree-skimming, hedge-hopping height to a lofty 3,000 feet. For romantic adventure, nothing compares with silently floating above the earth at sunrise or sunset. Upon landing—wherever that may turn out to be— the voyage is completed with a champagne toast. A one-hour balloon ride costs $250 for two persons.

Windy City Balloonport, 100 Ski Hill Rd, Fox River Grove, IL 60021. 847/639-0550. Winter months on stand-by basis only. Summer–fall early morning and evening flights arranged by reservation only.

Best romantic boats afloat

Lake Michigan Cruises

Chicago's distinctive skyline, bathed in soft moonlight, takes on a romantic perspective when viewed across the inky waters of Lake Michigan from the unobstructed vantage point of a lake cruise. The mood is enhanced as the sweet sound of a tenor saxophone filters out over the breezy deck. A variety of cruise lines offer packages that vary in luxury, length, and cost. Among them are *Spirit of Chicago* departing from Grand Avenue and Lake Shore Drive, a 600-passenger luxury yacht making lunch, dinner, and moonlight cruises; and, perhaps the most luxurious passenger craft to sail Chicago's lakefront, the *Odyssey*, a sleek, multideck, 800-passenger yacht offering gourmet brunch, lunch, dinner, and moonlight cruises, with live entertainment, a piano bar, and dancing on various decks. *For a very special evening:* Consider a cruise on the *Odyssey* as a different, fun, and romantic way to bring in the New Year.

Spirit of Chicago, 312/836-7899; *Odyssey,* 312/321-7620.

Most romantic view for cocktails

The Signature Lounge

For the price of a drink, you can enjoy spectacular views of up to 80 miles across four states from the floor-to-ceiling windows of the John Hancock Center's 96th-floor lounge (and thus avert the $4.75 admission fee to the skyscraper's observation center). As you walk around the bar, drink in hand, you can enjoy the changing panorama—the shoreline stretching north to Wisconsin and south toward the glowing steel mills of Gary, and the orderly grid of city streets to the west. The brilliant blue expanse of Lake Michigan is dotted with sails; freighters chug across distant shipping lanes. When the ceiling is low, "Big John" is enveloped with fluffy, billowy clouds. A pleasant time to visit is dusk, as the lights of the city twinkle on. Completed in 1970, this mixed-used skyscraper (office, residential, and commercial space) ranks as the world's fifth-tallest building, behind Chicago's Sears Tower (1) and Amoco Building (4) and New York's World Trade Center (2) and Empire State Building (3). Although not a fact to dwell upon while atop the 100-story, 1,127-foot-tall building, this behemoth is *expected* to sway in the wind. In a 60 mph blow, it has a sway factor of five-eighths of an inch. Its skin is made of black-anodized aluminum—enough to cover 12 football fields—and 11,459 bronze-colored window panes. The lounge has a one-drink minimum. A popular drink is Signature Punch, a concoction of light and dark rum and fruit juices served in a 32-ounce brandy snifter garnished with fruit.

The Signature Lounge, 835 N Michigan Ave, Chicago, IL 60611, 312/787-7230, Sun–Thu 11 am–12:30 am, Fri–Sat 11 am–1:30 am.

Best pampering pleasure palace

Sybaris Inn

Everything about this couples-only inn is designed to pamper guests and to do it in privacy—such as in cottages that deliberately exclude windows and telephones. With the emphasis on self-indulgence, guests control the lighting, the temperature, the music, and even the breeze in their rooms. The most popular style cottage comes with its own private 20-foot swimming pool, attached whirlpool, overhead waterfall, and steam room. Also featured is an expanded bedroom complete with king-size waterbed surrounded by thick carpeting and complemented by a flickering fireplace. The Sybaris may seem gaudily extravagant—or extravagantly extreme—but management claims this is an intriguing way to put spice back into a relationship. Maybe they're on to something, inasmuch as reservations need to be made about six months in advance.

Sybaris Inn, 3350 Milwaukee Ave, Northbrook, IL 60062, 847/298-5000.

Finest florist

Fertile Delta

This largest plant and garden center in Chicago is to green thumbs what a lumberyard is to carpenters. The store stocks literally everything to do with flora—

and also creates romantic bouquets in exotic, European, and traditional styles. Included in the massive inventory are most popular varieties of tropical plants, indoor and outdoor trees (including cacti and bonsai), garden supplies and tools, the largest seasonal selection of nonartificial Christmas trees and ornaments in the city, ceramic pots and planters, as well as plant fertilizer and "how-to" books. In addition to creating bouquets, a well-stocked flower shop offers an enormous variety of roses, orchids, daisies, and other beautiful fresh stem flowers, and a selection of silk and dried flowers, all of which can be transformed into bouquets. A selection of flowering plants includes bromeliads, azaleas, tulips, daffodils, kalanchoes, and Persian and African violets. The shop offers such services as FTD and Teleflower, as well as landscaping and "interiorscaping."

Fertile Delta, 2760 N Lincoln Ave, Chicago, IL 60614, 312/929-5350. Mon–Fri 8 am–8 pm, Sat & Sun 9 am–6 pm.

Best sweets for your sweetest

Godiva Chocolatier

Traditionally, chocolates have been the romantic gift of choice. And, while health and heart consciousness might dictate a low-fat, low-cal, no-cholesterol alternative, there is something sensuous and soul-satisfying about chocolates. Besides, you can always rationalize it by miserly apportioning them as special treats. Once you're past this hurdle, you might as well go first class. There is something special about receiving a box of Godiva chocolates, made from recipes perfected in Belgium and packaged in the distinctive gold foil–wrapped box with silk rose and ribbon. Maybe it's because the recipient knows they aren't cheap. A one-pound box of approximately 35 chocolates sells for $29—that's around 80 cents per sinful chocolate. The most traditional gift box includes a mix of solids, creams, and nuts coated with either delicious dark or milk chocolate. This premium-chocolate boutique has a small area set up with tables and chairs tempting Water Tower Place shoppers with coffee, cappuccino, espresso, and hot chocolate, plus gourmet ice cream, fresh pastries and, of course, Godiva's virtually irresistible chocolates.

Godiva Chocolatier, Water Tower Place, 845 N Michigan Ave, Chicago, IL 60611, 312/280-1133. Mon–Fri 10 am–8 pm, Sat 10 am–7 pm, Sun noon–6 pm.

Best place for a "sweet" deal
Fannie May Outlet

Not much compares with the gently wafting aroma of a confectioner, especially one as "sweet" as Fannie May. Chocoholics will find all of their favorites here—rich chocolate mints, creamy fudge, delectable chocolate-covered cherries, and, of course, Fannie May's popular Trinidads, butter-creams, and pixies (turtles) sold in half-pound, pound, and two-pound boxes. But as good as the chocolates are that attract the customers, it is the price that brings them back. At this outlet store, virtually the same merchandise that's sold in the chain's retail stores is offered at a 35 to 50 percent discount. What's the catch? Well, some of the candies are imperfect. They aren't stale, just a little misshapen, according to Fannie May's specifications. Don't be surprised if you walk out of here with several pounds of chocolate. (Unfortunately for penurious would-be suitors, boxes purchased here are marked "SECONDS," so they don't make very impressive gifts.)

Fannie May Outlet, 51 E Randolph St, Chicago, IL 60601. Mon–Fri 8 am–7 pm, Sat 9:30 am–7 pm, Sun 10 am–5:30 pm (does not accept phone orders).

Most romantic way to travel the Mag Mile
Carriage Rides

There is something undeniably romantic about a ride in a horse-drawn carriage. With a top-hatted, tuxedo-clad livery perched on an elevated seat, the well-trained horse clip-clops down Chicago's most fashionable streets and along quiet thoroughfares beside tiny parks, their greenery cloaked in evening's dark shadows, the illuminated skyline providing a backdrop as stars twinkle overhead. Carriages come in a variety of colors—black, white, maroon, blue; some are restored turn-of-the century antiques. They are available both in open and glass-enclosed versions—although, even in winter, many prefer to snuggle under a blanket, sipping coffee or hot chocolate. Although many riders choose soft summer nights, the period between Thanksgiving and New Year's is the busiest, when the Magnificent Mile throngs with shoppers, with windows dressed in their holiday finery, and tiny lights glinting on sidewalk trees. "It's the closest thing to a one-horse sleigh," said one cab owner. You can make reservations, flag down an empty carriage, or head to the carriage-ride equivalent of a taxi stand—such as the horse-watering trough/fountain on Chicago Avenue, just east of Michigan Avenue.

Carriage stands also at the SE and SW corners of Pearson St and Michigan Ave. (Cost runs to around $30–$35 a half hour, plus tip—depending upon the number of riders up to a maximum of six.) JC Cutters, Ltd, 875 N Orleans St, Chicago, IL 60610, 312/664-6014.

Most romantic spot to stroll (and highest spot to be wed)

Navy Pier

Year-round, newly renovated Navy Pier might just be the most romantic spot in the city for an afternoon or evening promenade. During warmer months, couples can enjoy the natural air-conditioning as they stroll the nearly two-thirds of a mile length of the Pier and admire a nonpareil view of the city skyline and flotillas of sailboats on the horizon. As the free trolley passes by, pedestrians can enjoy the antics of professional street entertainers (including magicians, comedians, improvisational actors, singers, and the obligatory mime acts) or take a ride on the beautiful new carousel or the 15-story Ferris wheel. On those days when the Windy City's weather is less than balmy, an indoor Crystal Gardens filled with palm trees and ringed with shops, restaurants, and pubs awaits. With the Chicago Children's Museum, the giant-size Iwerks Theater, an outdoor skating rink/reflecting pool, and the many cocktail and dinner cruises that depart from here, the historic Pier is looking more and more like *the* place to pass the day on Chicago's lakefront. In addition, the Teflon-roofed, 1,500-seat Skyline Stage hosts a variety of musical acts as well as entertainers such as Bill Cosby and Penn & Teller. And the Festival Hall Exposition Center at the Pier's East End offers several open-to-the-public events every year, including flower shows, the Art Chicago art fair, and the Generation Xpo sponsored by the Chicago *Sun Times*. *Historical note:* The world's finest Ferris wheel debuted at the 1893 World's Columbian Exposition in Chicago, a full 23 years before Navy Pier opened. *Contemporary note:* It didn't take long for Navy Pier to experience its first wedding atop the 148-foot-high Ferris wheel—on July 4, 1995, only weeks after the attraction opened, Ursula Wonn wed John Elrod (the couple had met via the Internet).

Navy Pier, Grand Ave at Lake Michigan, 312/595-PIER.

Most romantic rendezvous

Palm Court, Drake Hotel

Long before Tom Cruise used this elegant area in the Drake's upper lobby for a movie assignation (*Risky Business*, 1983), Chicagoans and visitors were choosing the Palm Court as a favorite meeting spot. It's a tranquil setting, with greenery, original paintings, warm, russet tones, and couches with floral-print fabrics. A bronze French urn, around 300 years old, is the centerpiece of a marble-based fountain, where cherubs are perched on dolphins that spray streamlets of water. Meet for a light lunch, cocktails (11 am–11:30 pm), or an English-style afternoon tea with accompaniment by a harpist (3–5:30 pm). Jazz trios play every Friday and Saturday (9 pm–midnight).

Palm Court, Drake Hotel, 140 E Walton St, Chicago, IL 60611, 312/787-2200.

PARKS & GARDENS

Best prairie-in-the-city

Bob-o-Link Meadows

When the covered prairie schooners rolled westward, much of the area now occupied by the sprawling metropolis of Chicago was blanketed with wildflowers and waving stands of tall prairie grass. Offering a glimpse of what pioneer families encountered, this recreated vest-pocket prairie, tucked away on Chicago's south side near the Museum of Science and Industry, contains more than 200 varieties of native plants. Planted in 1988, this experiment in turning back the clock has produced a six-acre preserve that is patrolled periodically by naturalists who uproot nonprairie plants seeded by birds, allowing the prairie to flourish. (Future plans include burn-offs to control aggressive nonnative plants.) Among more than 22 species of prairie grass is turkeyfoot (also known as big bluestem), the tallest of these grasses, reaching heights of at least 10 feet. There are wild oats, fleabane (used by pioneers to banish fleas from bedding), and knotted wild onion, a plant with delicate purple flowers from which the city took the name *Chekagou*, derived from the Ojibwa for "wild onion place." Look for milkweed with large pods containing thousands of fluffy seeds, and the rare compass plant with leaves that orient to the points of the compass as the plant seeks to conserve moisture. Paths and signs direct visitors; markers

identify species. This is "Prairie State" prairie the
way it might have looked when Marquette and Jolliet
first paddled its waterways.

Bob-o-Link Meadows, just south of the Museum of
Science and Industry, E 57th St & S Lake Shore Dr,
312/294-2241.

Most tranquil garden
Osaka Garden

"To enter through the Osaka Garden gate is to re-
fresh the spirit. . . ." This tranquil Japanese garden
is as historic as the 1893 World's Columbian Exposition (it and the neighboring Museum of Science
and Industry are among the last surviving remnants
of the famous fair) and as contemporary as its Osaka
Gate, constructed in 1995 to celebrate Osaka's sister
city relationship with Chicago, its Japanese design
influenced by the traditions of Buddhism and
Shintoism. This is a traditional "stroll garden" (a
form developed during the Edo period, 1615–1867)
and features elements of revelation, with paths that
lead a visitor from view to view. A circuitous route
over rough stone paths directs attention to sudden
changes in the garden's vistas. Ultimately, the path
leads to a teahouse, symbolically isolated from the
outside world. Among garden features are Turtle
Island, which represents the traditional island of
happiness on which people do not walk; Moon
Bridge, used for viewing the moon's reflection in the
water; and the Pavilion, patterned after a classic Noh
stage. The Kasuga Lantern remains from the 1893
Exposition (the original pavilion was destroyed by
fire in 1944).

Osaka Garden, Jackson Park, 57th & Lake Shore
Dr, Chicago, IL 60637, 312/747-6187. Daily 6 am–11
pm. Free.

Most surprising rooftop garden
Bergen Garden

In the heart of Hyde Park is this high park. Set atop
a three-story parking garage between two apartment
towers, this stunning garden began as a way to
improve the view of the complex's in-facing apartments. Today, it is a flourishing, one-acre living
garden, full of delights and surprises. The grounds
have been landscaped to rise and fall in gentle, green
hills; leafy crabapple, oak, and birch trees rustle in
the breeze; marigolds and petunias bloom brightly;
bushy shrubs and creeping vines provide ground-
clinging cover; four fountains gurgle and splash;
and, perhaps most amazingly, are two side-by-side
"lakes" (actually, ponds less than a foot deep, with

bottoms painted dark to project an illusion of depth),
complete with rustic footbridges, small waterfall, and
a resident duck population—a pretty amazing trans-
formation for a one-time concrete eyesore. A series
of pathways meanders through this surprising garden, providing a perfect opportunity for a quiet stroll
among more than 30,000 plants and trees (with
benches for quiet contemplation or to spend time
with a book)—only 30 or 40 feet above the hectic
rush of Lake Shore Drive.

Bergen Garden, 5050 S Lake Shore Dr, Chicago, IL
60615, 312/288-5050. Self-guided tours available;
inquire for dates, times.

Best garden walks

Dearborn & Sheffield Garden Walks

Garden lovers mark their July calendars with the
dates of two popular garden walks, when the owners
of private gardens open them to public visitation.
The annual Dearborn Garden Walk and Heritage
Festival, opening up formal gardens and hidden
coach houses and patios, has been going on for
nearly 40 years. The oldest garden walk in the
nation—with its gardens judged by professional
horticulturalists—it has blossomed into a major
festival and an eagerly awaited annual event. It now
includes 50 gardens, and such attractions as entertainment by an orchestra, a dance recital, choreo-
graphed team tumbling, free carriage rides, puppets,
a clown, face-painting, a plant market, floral-arrang-
ing and plant-care demonstrations, and an architectural tour of the neighborhood. About a decade later,
the Sheffield Garden Walk, near the DePaul University campus, got underway. This annual event also
has expanded to include more than 90 gardens,
musical entertainment, and children's activities such
as a petting zoo and miniature train rides.

Dearborn Garden Walk and Heritage Festival,
North Dearborn Association, Dearborn & State
Pkwys and LaSalle & Astor Sts between Division St
& North Ave, 312/472-6561. $5 donation. Sheffield
Garden Walk and Festival, Webster (2200 N) and
Sheffield (1000 W) Aves, 312/327-4988. $4 donation.

Chicago's best shot at Versailles

Buckingham Fountain

Chicago's penchant for "big"—from shoulders to skyscrapers—holds true even when it is imitating French
palaces. The baroque, pink-marble fountain in the
north end of Grant Park is patterned on the "Latona"
at Versailles—but was built about twice the size of
the original. It was back in 1927 that a crusty

heiress, Kate Sturges Buckingham, donated this fountain to the city. Since then, during warm-weather months, the fountain had entertained Chicagoans and visitors with a symphony of dancing water, now orchestrated by a computer. Every evening, a special display features colored lights, prettily illuminating the changing patterns of water as it is propelled more than 100 feet into the air by 133 jets. Speaking of superlatives, the fountain can use up to 14,000 gallons a minute, and the base can hold 1.5 million gallons. Best of all, in the early 1990s the fountain was restored to its original splendor.

Buckingham Fountain, Grant Park, May 1–Oct 1, daily 11 am–11 pm, illumination 9–11 pm.

Best concerts in the park
Grant Park Concerts

Beethoven and Schubert, Gershwin and Porter, Gilbert and Sullivan. During summer, the Grant Park Music Festival offers music to suit a variety of tastes. Concerts, held in the evening when Lake Michigan breezes air-condition the lakefront park, are perfect occasions for a family picnic or a romantic evening. Musical fare ranges from "Pops in the Park" with Lou Rawls to "A Night in Vienna"—Mozart conducted by Peter Maag with an appearance by white Lipizzan stallions. The Grant Park Symphony Orchestra and Chorus combines 81 musicians and 134 voices. Admission is free—or prime seats in the Petrillo Music Shell may be reserved for the entire festival for less than $1 a concert with membership in the Grant Park Concerts Society. Membership perks include discounted parking and a reserved seat for Chicago's Independence Day Eve celebration. This huge party features a memorable fireworks display and a concert highlighted by Tchaikovsky's "1812 Overture" and Sousa's "Stars and Stripes Forever." A separate concert series introduces children to classical music, ballet, and opera. The kids' series includes such presentations as Stravinsky's "The Firebird," Prokofiev's "Peter and the Wolf" performed with life-size puppets, "Highlights from the Nutcracker," and "The Mikado."

Grant Park Concerts Society, 520 S Michigan Ave #343, Chicago, IL 60605, 312/819-0614.

Most diverse music in the park
Petrillo Music Shell

From rock to classical, blues to jazz, folk to gospel—virtually all types of music can be heard at some time or another during the summer months at this open-air site in Grant Park. The stage of this clamshell-shaped bandstand plays host to the Grant Park

Symphony (Wednesday and weekend evenings—see separate listing), as well as the headline acts featured in the city's annual music festivals that enjoy international renown and patronage—gospel (early June), blues (early–mid June), and jazz (late August–early September). Another Petrillo highlight is the annual Fourth of July concert, sponsored by radio station WXRT-FM, and featuring big names in progressive rock music. All Petrillo Music Shell concerts are free. *Scenic note:* The buildings of Michigan Avenue provide a breathtaking backdrop to any concert here.

Petrillo Music Shell, Grant Park, E Jackson Blvd & S Columbus Dr, Chicago, IL 60604, 312/742-7638.

Best park for music

Ravinia Festival

Stretch out on the grass under the stars as you listen to the world-renowned Chicago Symphony Orchestra—which performs weekly concerts at Ravinia. Or reserve a pavilion seat to watch the likes of Ringo Starr; the Neville Brothers; Lyle Lovett; Peter, Paul, and Mary; and Harry Belafonte. This delightful music festival, with pavilion seating for about 3,500 and a 36-acre lawn area where patrons spread out blankets or relax in folding lounge chairs they tote in, is the perfect spot for a picnic, simple or elegant. Ravinia attracts a mix of top-name classical, jazz, country, pop, and folk music artists. Attending concerts are Chicago's elite, dressed to the height of the season's fashion, and toting elegant china, flatware, folding tables and chairs with crisp linen, candelabra, and expensive picnic hampers provisioned with pâté, caviar, cold salmon, imported cheeses, vintage champagne, and other fine wines. But equally at home at Ravinia are the proletariat in jeans, T-shirts, and sweats, happily munching on fried chicken and sipping Italian red. If you prefer to eat in but not carry in, there are four restaurants on the grounds. Concerts sell out early, so be sure to make reservations for pavilion seats. A Ravinia bus runs from downtown on performance nights and costs $12 roundtrip, and the Metra Union Pacific Chicago train stops at the gate. If you drive, there are shuttle buses serving remote parking lots.

Ravinia Festival, Green Bay & Lake Cook Rds, Highland Park, IL 60035, 312/RAVINIA.

Best sports in the park

Daley Bicentennial Plaza, Grant Park

This area, at the north end of Grant Park, is a good spot for a variety of all-season sports. During winter, a rink is flooded and frozen for skating, and there is cross-country skiing over the park's smooth expanses. The plaza also offers 12 lighted tennis courts, which are usually available on a first-come, first-served basis, but reservations can also be made (a good idea during the busiest, warmest months). This park also offers a "Tennis Academy" designed for youngsters ages 8–13 years (offered on numerous days June through August) as well as a "Play Camp" for children four to seven years of age. And if these pursuits sound a little strenuous—or if you'd rather exercise your mind than your body—the plaza has special chessboard tabletops (with bench seating), which attract a core of players, both fanatic and casual.

Daley Bicentennial Plaza, Grant Park, 337 E Randolph, Chicago, IL 60601, 312/742-7648.

Best art in the park

Lincoln Park

Chicago's largest park, Lincoln Park—50 percent bigger than New York's Central Park—is said to be host to more than 17 million visitors each year (but it is unclear whether that figure includes neighborhood residents walking their dogs twice a day). And although most visitors journey to the popular park for its zoo, jogging/bicycling/skating paths, and broad, rolling expanses of green, the park also offers history and art in its collection of more than 20 sculptural monuments. Dating from the late 19th and early 20th centuries, many of these works are beginning to show the wear and tear of years of rain, grime, and auto exhaust. Accordingly, the Friends of Lincoln Park advocacy organization has started a program wherein corporations and individuals can contribute to "adopt" monuments, helping to provide them with needed restoration and maintenance. Some of Lincoln Park's most notable statuary (all included in the "Adopt-A-Monument" program) are Saint-Gaudens' majestic standing Lincoln (Stockton Drive and North Avenue); the popular seated Shakespeare, whose lap beckons to adults and children alike (Lincoln Park West at Belden Avenue); the heroic equestrian statue of General Philip Sheridan (Sheridan Road at Belmont Avenue); and the 1884 work known as "The Alarm," which depicts a Native American family and is the oldest monument on Park District property (east of Lake Shore Drive at Wellington Avenue). A poster-sized foldout brochure from Friends of Lincoln Park includes photos of and historic details about each monument.

Friends of Lincoln Park, 1760 N Wells St, Chicago, IL 60614, 312/787-7275.

Best park among the art

Art Institute Gardens

Not all of the fine art is *inside* this world-class museum. For example, the Stanley McCormick Memorial Court at the corner of Michigan Avenue and Monroe Street is designed to provide a setting for Alexander Calder's "Flying Dragon," a monumental sculpture of red steel acquired in 1990. Included are a planting of eight skyline locust trees and indigenous prairie grasses, plants, ground cover, and three river birch trees. Also in this area is Henry Moore's "Large Interior Form." On the east facade of the building (Columbus Drive between Monroe Street and Jackson Boulevard), connecting a fountain and reflecting pool, is Isamu Noguchi's "Celebration of the 200th Anniversary of the Founding of the Republic," a granite-and-stainless steel sculpture commemorating the American Bicentennial. Of course, the most recognizable sculptures are the 10-foot-high bronze lions of Edward Kemeys that have guarded the entrance to the museum for more than 100 years and seasonally are treated to such whimsical dressings as Santa hats or (honoring rare championship seasons) Bears' football helmets.

The Art Institute of Chicago, S Michigan Ave at E Adams St, Chicago, IL 60603, 312/443-3600.

Best park to admire more than 4,000 roses

Marquette Park

It is not unusual to walk the streets of this southwest side neighborhood and see women vigorously sweeping the steps *and* the sidewalk in front of their homes. Marquette Park, an area of well-kept streets lined with neat, squat bungalows, is focal point of Chicago's 150,000-strong Lithuanian community. Lithuanian immigrants began arriving in the late 1880s and found work at the stockyards and Pullman Works. The neighborhood developed such a distinctive ethnic character that the section of 69th Street between California and Western avenues was renamed "Lithuanian Plaza Court" by proclamation of the late mayor Richard J. Daley. Sprinkled with tiny European-style cafés, delicatessens, and ethnic gift shops, it more resembles a small town than a big-city neighborhood. Enjoy hearty, inexpensive Lithuanian cuisine—sauerkraut soup, roast duck, and potato pancakes and dumplings—in such restaurants as Tulpe, or delis such as the Talman Grocery. A neighborhood landmark is a massive church, Nativity of Blessed Virgin Mary, showcasing exterior mosaic murals by a Lithuanian artist. Horticulturally speaking, a famous neighborhood attraction is the Marquette rose garden, one of the largest municipal rose gardens in the Midwest. Its spectacular display features more than 4,000 roses in 80 varieties in rich and delicate reds, pinks, and yellows. *Neighborhood note:* Sadly, Marquette Park is losing its ethnicity as surrounding neighborhoods crowd in.

Marquette Park, 6700 S Kedzie, Chicago, IL 60629, 312/776-9879.

Best park to admire 4,000 species of trees

Morton Arboretum

Whether you enjoy the great outdoors through the windows of your car or up close during an invigorating hike, this 1,500-acre living museum of flora provides opportunity for both. You can drive through on a system of one-way roads, or hike miles of marked trails. There's an orientation program for first-time visitors and guided tours during spring blossom time and the fall color season. Highlights include a fragrance garden, Japanese collection, displays of hedges, woody herbs, and dwarf shrubs, the Ground-Cover Walk (with more than 50 different kinds), and the Pinetum, with cultivated pines and other conifers. You want woods? The arboretum contains 40,000 trees classified into 4,000 different species. It attempts to grow every species of woody plant that will survive the harsh climate and clay soil of northern Illinois. There are year-round classes on botany, photography, landscaping, and other topics, and bird-watching and other field programs; also, a restaurant, snack shop, and gift shop.

Morton Arboretum, Rte 53 (near I-88), Lisle, IL 60532, 630/719-2466. Winter: Mon–Sun 7 am–5 pm; summer: Mon–Sun 7 am–7 pm.

Best vest-pocket park for noontime jogging

Lake Shore Park

Within the shadow of the John Hancock Center and with easy access to the hotels of North Michigan Avenue, this vest-pocket park is ideal for running, jogging, and speed walking. It's immediately south of the Illinois National Guard Armory and across the street from the gray Gothic towers of Northwestern's University McGaw Medical Center and Northwestern's ivy-covered School of Law—so you'll probably have a few med and law students as exercise mates. A track encircles the green swath of a softball field (for 16" softball only), with two sets of benches. Alongside are two public tennis courts and three concrete chess tables. An adjacent Chicago Park District field house has locker rooms and washroom facilities. (The park also offers play camp, day camp, and athletics camp for kids and teens.) The park is bounded by Chicago Avenue, Pearson Street, Fairbanks Court, and Lake Shore Drive.

Lake Shore Park, 808 N Lake Shore Dr, Chicago, IL 60611, 312/742-7891. Open daily 9 am–10 pm.

Best bet for every blooming thing
Chicago Botanic Gardens

This is a place to explore, listen, smell, learn, and participate. Awaiting exploration is an oasis of rolling woods and grassland and placid lagoons. You can listen to a carillon concert, smell the fragrance of hundreds of orchids, and attend classes to learn how to raise hanging vegetables and make natural Christmas-tree ornaments and wreaths. You can participate in an annual Bike Day, with trail rides and seminars, and enjoy the Japan Days Festival with music, dance, bonsai demonstrations, flower arranging, and tea ceremonies. You can visit an herb garden, vegetable gardens, and the Arid House, which simulates a desert, complete with a 100-year-old, 15-foot-tall saguaro cactus. You can walk a nature trail through woodlands planted with wildflowers, ferns, and rhododendrons; admire tranquil Japanese islands; visit a prairie restoration; and enjoy the many types of wildlife within the gardens—ducks, geese, raccoons, fox, deer, and many species of birds. In May, the forest floor is carpeted with brilliant white trillium; in autumn, its canopy is burnished with red and gold.

Chicago Botanic Gardens, P.O. Box 400, Glencoe, IL 60022, 847/835-5440. (entrance at Lake Cook Rd, 1/2 mi E of I-94). Daily 8 am–sunset. Free (parking $4).

Wettest rain forest
Brookfield Zoo

Within a short, pleasantly strollable distance of this zoo's huge indoor Tropic World exhibit, you can travel through recreated rain forests representing those found in South America, Africa, and Asia, complete with native foliage, birds, and wildlife, and intermittent rain pouring down from ceiling sprinklers (stand away from the railing, unless you don't mind catching a bit of this faux precipitation). One of the country's top zoos, Brookfield is gorgeously landscaped and displays its collection of animals in barless recreations of their natural settings (it was one of the first zoos in the country to do so). Other top attractions include the entertaining dolphin shows of the Seven Seas Panorama, an extensive Children's Zoo, and special safari tours in open-air buses decorated in animal stripes or spots. Every summer, the zoo hosts a lively Teddy Bear Picnic, with parades, music, and plenty of (stuffed) furry friends.

Brookfield Zoo, 8400 W 31st St (at First Ave), Brookfield, IL 60513, 708/485-2200. Mon–Fri 10 am–4:30 pm, Sat & Sun 10 am–5:30 pm. $4.50 adults, $1.50 seniors & children 3–11 (half price Tue & Thu); $4 parking.

Dandiest desert

Garfield Park Conservatory

Explore an arid desert where cacti flash their fleeting, delicate blooms; step into the tropics where the humid air smothers like a blanket and vines hang to within inches of visitors' heads. The hothouse flora of such diverse climates await exploration at the largest public-owned botanical garden under glass in the world. Although this landmark structure, completed in 1907, is showing its years (the Park District has plans for renovation) and is a bit off the beaten track in the seen-better-days neighborhood of East Garfield Park, this conservatory is one of the remaining gems of Victorian-era Chicago. It is a wonderful spot for an outing close to the heart of the city—particularly during winter, when its bright tropical blooms may be especially welcome. This free attraction displays 3,000 species and varieties of plants conservatively valued at $1.8 million. The Palm House, perhaps the most spectacular, contains a variety of its namesake plants, including ancient date palm, coconut palm, Chinese fan palm, and a rare palm collected during a 1926 expedition to Brazil. There are giant bamboos, clumps of bananas, and the curious double coconut palm, the two-lobed fruits of which may weigh up to 50 pounds. Other houses showcase ferns, cacti, tropical vegetation, and plants known for their economic value. There are four annual flower shows: chrysanthemums (November), poinsettias (Christmas), azaleas, camellias, and rhododendrons (January), and lilies (Easter).

Garfield Park Conservatory, 300 N Central Park Blvd, Chicago, IL 60624, 312/746-5100. Daily 9 am–5 pm. Free.

Most ferns not in a restaurant

Lincoln Park Conservatory

On bleak and blustery winter days, when the gray snowscape merges with the gray sky, escape to a tropical clime where sweet-scented orchids bloom. This conservatory, nestled against the Lincoln Park Zoo, has been providing a warm taste of summer to winter-weary Chicagoans since 1891–92. Although the exteriors of the four massive greenhouses show a century of wear and tear, the horticultural collections remain first-class. In the Palm House, the 50-foot-tall fiddle-leaf rubber tree has been around as long as the building, and the fishtail palm yields a wine-like liquid tapped from the flower stalk which is prized as a beverage in its native India and Malay. The Fernery is glade-like and contains specimens of cycads, the oldest known plant, and the cactus collection, displayed in a setting of sand and sponge rocks, includes succulents from the American desert and such diverse countries as South Africa, Brazil, and Zimbabwe. A number of annual seasonal shows include spectacular Spring & Easter and Christmas shows (see separate listings, "Sightseeing").

Lincoln Park Conservatory, 2400 N Stockton Dr, Chicago, IL 60614, 312/742-7736. Daily 9 am–5 pm (special hrs during major shows).

SIGHTSEEING

Top spot for traders

Chicago Board of Trade

Stepping into an elevator in this massive building, designed in 1930, provides a glimpse of what the Chicago Board of Trade is about. Passengers usually include traders wearing outlandish jackets festooned with badges and IDs, pockets stuffed with pens and trading documents. With a trading area equal to the size of a football field, this is the world's largest and oldest futures exchange, formed in 1848 by 82 merchants to stabilize the grain-trading marketplace. Traders work out of "pits," with trading accompanied by animated shouting and hand signals denoting the price and number of contracts being bought or sold. Jackets and ties are mandatory—the lightweight jackets worn by traders were developed to allow maximum freedom and comfort during the frenetic trading sessions packed between the opening and closing bells. A massive clock above the entrance is ornamented with a distinctive agrarian motif. The art deco lobby gleams with contrasting black and light-colored marble; elevator doors are masterpieces of art deco in silver and black. Ceres, the Roman goddess of grain and harvest, receives due homage with a 31-foot-tall statue atop the original building and a monumental mural in the new atrium. A visitor center offers information, tours, and an eight-minute audiovisual presentation. The most fascinating diversion for visitors, however, is watching the action on the trading floor below.

Chicago Board of Trade, 141 W Jackson Blvd, Chicago, IL 60604, 312/435-3590. Mon–Fri 9 am–2 pm (tours every 30 min until noon).

Prime spot for pork bellies
Chicago Mercantile Exchange

The average person probably has heard of "pork bellies futures"—albeit not knowing exactly what they are. These are among the commodities bought and sold on the trading floor of this noisy, frenetic exchange. From the visitors' gallery, outsiders get an overview of what's going on—with help from an informative booklet, "The Merc at Work." They can watch action in the trading pits—the bullpens where actual trading takes place with a system known as "open outcry." This free-form auction has been described as combining "primal scream, aerobic dancing, and the Battle of Hastings." Visitors learn that there is a futures market for just about anything, from dried cocoons to crossbred wool (both of which are traded commodities), including agriculture commodities such as feeder cattle and broiler chickens, foreign currencies, interest rates, and stock indices (Will the stock market go up or down?). They'll learn the difference between a trader and a broker and discover that a CME seat can cost as much as a half million dollars. Visitors discover that trading also is done through a series of hand signals and learn the significance of the various colored jackets worn on the floor.

Chicago Mercantile Exchange, 30 S Wacker Dr, Chicago, IL 60606, 312/930-8249. Mon–Fri 7:30 am–3:15 pm.

Prime place for pierogi & Pulaski
Avondale Polish neighborhood

It is said that Chicago's Polish community is second in size only to Warsaw. Many Polish immigrants are insular, clinging to pockets of ethnicity where older inhabitants have little understanding of English—despite having lived the largest part of their lives in the United States. One such enclave is Avondale, dubbed "Little Warsaw." Snuggled in a triangle west of the Kennedy Expressway and bounded by Addison, Pulaski, and Diversey, Avondale is where you'll hear Polish spoken in the neighborhood stores that carry Polish newspapers and magazines, videos of Polish movies, and tapes of Polish music. The

Polish community tends to shop on Milwaukee Avenue and worship at St. Hyacinth's Roman Catholic Church. Milwaukee Avenue is dotted with storefront restaurants offering filling and remarkably inexpensive meals featuring pierogi, cabbage rolls, stuffed cabbage, pork tenderloin, and cheese blintzes. There are lively Polish nightclubs, delis with homemade sausages and fiery slivowitz, bakeries with tempting breads and fruit-filled pastries, and assorted Polish grocery stores, meat markets, gift shops, and travel agencies. On Milwaukee Avenue (but much farther south of Avondale), The Polish Museum of America (see separate listing in "Museums, Galleries, Theaters & Other Sites") is a storehouse of Polish culture. It hosts such annual events as the Pulaski Day Reception and Polish Art Fest.

Best bet for borscht and Byzantine
Ukrainian Village

In a nondescript west-side neighborhood, Ukrainian markets ply twist bread and beets and restaurants dish up hearty dumplings and lively folk songs. There are *two* Ukrainian churches and *two* museums where you can view avant-garde art and learn about the folk art of decorating egg shells. This is Ukrainian Village, centered around Chicago Avenue and Oakley Boulevard. With copper-clad domes and Byzantine-style architecture, neighborhood churches are straight out of the European steppe. Modeled after the cathedral in Kiev, St. Nicholas Cathedral dates back to 1913. St. Volodymyr, built in the mid-1970s by parishioners at odds with the older church's conversion from the Julian to the Gregorian calendar, has gilded domes and a two-story mosaic mural depicting its eponymous saint. In January, a children's choir in traditional costume performs Christmas songs at locations along Chicago Avenue. There are also choral singing, native dancing, and ethnic food at other annual celebrations. The earthy soul of Ukraine flourishes at Galan's, a large restaurant with filling feasts of borscht, cabbage rolls, sausages, kabobs, sauerkraut, dumplings, and potato pancakes, and a lively stage where professional entertainers and sometimes audience members perform. A couple of doors east, a local market sells Ukrainian specialties.

Littlest (and boldest) "Little Italy"
Taylor Street

"Little Italy," centered around short stretch of Taylor Street at the south end of the Loop, wears its ethnicity boldly. There's the red, white, and green–painted woodwork of Mario's Italian ice stand. There are

Italian-American celebrities—the likes of Tony
Bennett and Frank Sinatra—dining at the trendy
New Rosebud Café. There are pans of rich-red pizza
bread, hot crusty loaves, and amaretto cookies at
Scafuri Bakery. And homemade cannoli at
Mategrano's family-owned restaurant, where the
cheerful wait staff dish up incredibly light cheese
ravioli and sing along with recorded 1950s music
(see separate listings, "Dining"). As one of Chicago's
oldest Italian neighborhoods, "Little Italy" dates back
to the late 19th century when thousands of immigrants poured into the area. Then, in the early 1960s,
large segments were supplanted by the sprawling
new campus of the University of Illinois. Today, the
compact neighborhood retains its strong Neapolitan
flavor. Lining its streets are Italian sausage-and-beef
joints, a clutch of excellent restaurants, many specializing in Southern Italian cuisine, and stores with
imported olive oil, sausages, cheeses, and wines.
Just as in the old days, cloth-capped men linger over
strong coffee and black-draped elderly women tote
shopping bags to neighborhood bakeries and gossip
on stoops.

Best bet for saris and chutney

"Little Bombay"

It has an English name, but the stretch of Devon
Avenue between Western and California avenues is
as Indian as downtown Bombay. It is lined with sari
shops, grocery stores crammed with pungent spices,
and restaurants with vegetarian dishes and delicate
curries, and is shopped by women with caste spots
on their foreheads, silver bracelets jangling on dusky
arms. There are thin veneers of other cultures—
Kosher butchers that served the neighborhood's
earlier residents, Russian delis, Greek and Syrian
markets, and a Croatian community center. But,
more than anything else, this street has become a
center of Chicago's Indian and Pakistani communities. As such, it is teeming with immigrants, bursting
with pungent smells, and alive with the tongues of
the populous subcontinent and a background dirge
of Indian pop music. Many of Chicago's 70,000-
strong Indian community shop here for rainbow-
hued bolts of silk, diaphanous saris, Indian videos
and cassettes, cumin seeds, jars of chutney, and
sacks of rice. "Little Bombay" restaurants such as
Viceroy of India and Natraj offer bargain meals on
buffet tables, popular tandoori-grilled meats and
breads, and dishes such as mulligatawny soup and,
from southern Indian, crepes filled with a piquant
mixture of onions and potatoes.

Best bet for a bit of Bavaria

Lincoln Square

One of the best-selling foodstuffs in Lincoln Square is Bavarian-style leberkäse, a sort of liverwurst meatloaf, served hot. Find it at Meyer's German-style deli, along with trays of herring, strings of plump sausages made by German butchers, shelves of grainy German rye bread, homemade salads, and imported cheeses, jams, candies, and cookies. Meyer's (see separate listing in "Shopping") and nearby Kuhn's and Inge's delicatessens are among a cluster of German shops, restaurants, and beer halls in the German enclave centered around Lincoln Avenue at Western Avenue. Originally settled by German immigrants, the neighborhood is regaining its Teutonic flavor. An outdoor mural depicts a rural scene in medieval Germany, a brass-ornamented cast-iron lantern was donated by the city of Hamburg, and Giddings Plaza has tree-shaded benches where one is likely to hear German spoken.

Those who prefer to buy their sausages at a butcher's shop head for the Lincoln Quality Market (see separate listing, "Shopping"). It offers a wide range of meats and the "haus-made" sausages it has been fashioning for more than 50 years. Red-brick Merz Apothecary (see separate listing, "Shopping") looks as though it might have been transported intact from Munich. It has a tin ceiling, brass chandeliers, and German lettering in the window, and stocks European toiletries, herbs, and allopathic and homeopathic medicines. Even tiny Bavarians are provided for along what has been dubbed "Sauerkraut Boulevard"—at Small Fry, which sells *lederhosen* and *trachten* in small sizes.

Most bittersweet Latin quarter

Pilsen/Little Village

Festive mariachi bands parade through the mean streets of Hispanic Chicago. Buildings colorfully painted with larger-than-life Mexican murals hide the sorry, cramped apartments of new immigrants. In Pilsen and Little Village, bright hope and grim despair live side-by-side. Wedged into the southwest side between Ogden Avenue and the Stevenson Expressway, these neighborhoods once were the center of Chicago's Bohemian population. Now they are the main point of entry for floods of Mexican immigrants, legal and illegal. Along 18th and 26th streets, once Slavic arteries, are storefront restaurants with authentic Mexican fare, bakeries with warm bread and sugar-coated pastries, and markets with tortillas, tomatillos, and chorizo. Casa Aztlan

at 1831 South Racine Avenue, once a settlement
house for Bohemian immigrants, now is daubed with
murals painted in the early 1970s by Ray Patlan
depicting Mexican folk heroes. It serves as a Mexican
cultural center offering classes in English and promoting folk art, dance, and theater. Art and culture
also flourish at the Mexican Fine Arts Center Museum (see separate listing, "Museums"). Mexican
food, music, and folkloric dances are featured at the
annual *Fiesta en la Villita* in September. It culmi-
nates in the Mexican Independence Day Parade
winding through the heart of Little Village.

Best memories of Nam
Little Saigon

Chicago's least-assimilated ethnic neighborhood may
be the Vietnamese enclave, dubbed "Little Saigon,"
centered around a short stretch of Argyle Street and
bisected by the "El" tracks—where even the station
is pagoda-like. Although predominantly Vietnamese,
the neighborhood does include shades of other Asian
cultures and sometimes is known as "New Chinatown." This compact neighborhood, with streets that
often seem to be as teeming with humanity as those
in Hong Kong, offers a heavy concentration of Vietnamese restaurants, markets, and shops. The bustling Viet Hoa Market, drenched in spicy aromas, is
the equivalent of a corner grocery store, offering a
selection of seafood, Oriental vegetables, teas, rice,
and exotic spices not found in the average supermarket, plus hand-painted tea pots and Vietnamese
cooking utensils (see separate listing in "Shopping").
Dining choices—mostly inexpensive, storefront restaurants—include Nhu Hoa Café (which includes
Laotian specialties) and Hua Giang (stop by for an
iced coffee). Pasteur (see separate listing, "Dining")
on nearby Sheridan Road is arguably the best Vietnamese restaurant in the city. Named after a street
in Saigon, it is attractively decorated with hanging
globe lamps and photographs of Vietnam. Nearby (at
954 W Carmen Ave) is the Vietnam Museum, founded
by a vet and commemorating that unpopular conflict
with uniforms, photos, and other memorabilia.

Prettiest neighborhood where the presses stopped
Printers Row/Burnham Park

At the south end of the Loop, what once was the focal
point of Chicago's printing industry has been res-
cued from urban blight and transformed into a quiet

residential neighborhood, its tree-lined streets scattered with outdoor cafés. It is a living example of architectural history, with landmark structures that include the famous Monadnock Building (see separate description) and the Burnham-designed Fisher Building at 343 South Dearborn Street, with sea creatures sculpted in the terra-cotta and fish images cut into the main glass doors. Two old brick printing plants from the 1880s and 1890s now house the charming Hyatt on Printers Row, where the Prairie restaurant has architecture inspired by Frank Lloyd Wright and heartland food (see separate description, "Dining"). Recalling the neighborhood's past, Printers Row Printing Museum recreates a working 19th-century print shop. At the foot of Dearborn Street, beautifully restored Dearborn Station (see separate description) is a romanesque building of red brick and terra-cotta dating to 1885. Each June, the neighborhood buzzes with one of the nation's largest book fairs. Featured are poetry readings, panel discussions, street theater, book-craft demonstrations, children's programs, and appearances by such literary luminaries as Kurt Vonnegut, Jr., and Susan Sontag.

Most popular (and unreliable) timepiece

Wrigley Building

When the Wrigley clocks were taken out of service for repair in 1995, hundreds of Chicagoans called in to complain. So much is the Wrigley Building part of the Chicago scene. This ornate, white wedding cake of a building sits on the north side of the Chicago River at the Michigan Avenue bridge, guarding the gateway to the elegant emporia of the Magnificent Mile. At nighttime, the building is a dazzling sight, with its white terra-cotta-clad facade brilliantly floodlit—as it has been from its earliest days. (The building dates from 1921, when it became the first skyscraper on North Michigan Avenue; an annex was added in 1924). Designed by the architectural firm of Graham, Anderson, Probst & White, the building is heavily ornamented in the baroque style popular during that period. Its distinguishing feature is the long, narrow, and exceedingly elaborate clock tower that points its finger skyward and serves as a time check (albeit seldom a precise one) for the office workers, shoppers, and sightseeers who throng Michigan Avenue. Between the main building and its annex is a narrow plaza. It has a small fountain and garden and is a pleasant—and usually cool—spot to relax on a summer's

day. The building is, of course, named for the family
that made its fortune manufacturing chewing gum.
The company still maintains its corporate offices in
the Wrigley Building.

Wrigley Building, 400 N Michigan Ave, Chicago, IL
60611, 312/923-8080.

Most Gothic gargoyles

Tribune Tower

This is the tower that the Colonel built. In 1922,
Chicago Tribune publisher Robert R. McCormick
conducted a $100,000 international competition to
design a new home for the newspaper. The winning
architects were John Mead Howells and Raymond
M. Hood of New York, who designed this 33-story,
Gothic revival building that opened three years later.
There was some criticism of the design by those who
believed that such a prominent new building should
be more modernistic. Nonetheless, the structure,
with its distinctive flying buttresses and gargoyles
carved into its soaring stone tower, has survived as
one of Chicago's most endearing landmarks. There's
a bit of the world in the Trib Tower. Embedded in
its facade are pieces of stone extracted from some
of the world's most famous edifices, including Co-
logne Cathedral, Notre Dame, Westminster Abbey,
the Parthenon, the Arc de Triomphe, the Vatican,
and the Taj Mahal. Inspection of these mementoes
makes a fascinating street-level tour. On the southwest corner of the building is a showcase studio
from which WGN radio personalities often do live
broadcasts, sometimes involving window-watchers.
Adjoining the south face of the building is an ex-
pansive square, the scene of noontime concerts and
art shows.

Tribune Tower, 435 N Michigan Ave, Chicago, IL
60611, 312/222-3994.

Handsomest station sans trains

Dearborn Station

This superannuated station at the south end of the
Loop is a quiet spot where office workers munch on
croissants and sip cappuccino in a skylit atrium
decorated with banners evoking famous names in
railway history. It wasn't always thus. Opened in
May 1885, this red sandstone and brick building
was one of three downtown railway stations built in
the late 19th century. By 1900, it connected 25
railroads with a daily load of 122 trains and 17,000
passengers. In the 1920s it was served by streetcars
clanking down the stretch of Dearborn Street known

as "Printing House Row." Even a fire in 1922 failed to close the busy terminal as it was rebuilt without disrupting service (although it did lose its gabled roof). During two world wars, the station was the heart-rending scene of sad farewells and joyous reunions. Chicago's oldest surviving railway station served passengers until 1971. It was painstakingly restored in 1986 to house offices and shops. Highlighting the building are Romanesque terra-cotta arches and a distinctive clock tower that is a landmark in the revitalized Printers Row/Burnham Park residential neighborhoods. In warm weather, patrons of Lindas Margaritas spill into a sidewalk café with their guacamole and margaritas.

Dearborn Station, 47 W Polk St, Chicago, IL 60605, 312/554-4400.

Noisiest day on the beach

Air & Water Show

There's thunder in the skies and foam in the lake when Chicago gives itself over to the annual Park District Air and Water Show and a wide range of aerial and aquatic stunts and demonstrations. Crack precision flying teams, such as the U.S. Air Force Thunderbirds, perform tight maneuvers overhead, while teams of skydivers leap from speeding aircraft and water-skiers crisscross the lakefront. Head for North Avenue Beach for a front-row seat. Although the schedule and performers vary year to year, included are such events as wind-surfing demonstrations, wing-walking, stunt kite-flying, air-sea rescue, hang-gliding, fly-overs by a variety of airplanes (including state-of-the-art military aircraft, such as the Stealth fighter), a fire department colored-water display, and tours of a U.S. Coast Guard cutter. The event runs Wednesday through Sunday in early July and includes a free beach party with music and dancing at Oak Street Beach. *Tip:* Consider a 70th-floor vantage point from Cité restaurant (see separate listing in "Romantic"), but be sure to reserve early.

Best boat for commuters

Wendella Commuter Boats

If not the best, this certainly is the least expensive cruise in Chicago. Passage costs only $1.25. For this fish's-eye view of downtown Chicago, join the hurrying hordes of work- or home-bound commuters onboard the boats which ply the Chicago River between the Northwestern Train Station (Madison Street and Canal Street) and the Wrigley Building (at the Michigan Avenue bridge). Boats leave every 10 minutes during morning and evening rush hours for a seven-minute ride along the river, avoiding traffic snarls, stop lights, and standing-room-only CTA buses and trains. These mini-cruises can be a nice way to get a feel for the scope and sprawl of the city's central district. Wendella boats also offer weekly cocktail cruises and Friday night (no-alcohol) cruises during prom season.

Wendella's Commuter Boats, 400 N Michigan Ave, Chicago IL 60611, 312/337-1446. Commuter service: late Apr–late Sept/early Oct. Mon–Fri 7:45–8:45 am & 4:45–5:15 pm. $1.25 one-way passage; $10 book of 10 tickets.

Best boat for architectural buffs

Architectural Lecture Tour

On this boat tour, there are coffee, rolls, and an extraordinary look at the architecture that makes up Chicago's spectacular skyline. A 90-minute river ride aboard the *Fort Dearborn* or the *Innnisfree* can be a perfect way to spend a Sunday morning—or any morning when the weather is good and the air is clear. On board, as you slip under 24 bridges and explore three branches of the Chicago River, is a knowledgeable guide from the Chicago Architecture Foundation. You'll admire ever-changing reflections in the modernistic dark-green curved glass of 333 West Wacker Drive, study the city's industrial riverfront and its 19th century bridge houses, and get a back-door glimpse at some of the city's most-admired waterside homes. The guide provides a knowledgeable, entertaining, and sometimes witty commentary ("we take old warehouses and fill them up with yuppies"; "the State of Illinois Building [which had widely publicized air-conditioning problems in its early days] is the world's largest microwave oven") on Chicago's melange of architectural styles.

Chicago from the Lake Ltd., North Pier Chicago, 455 E Illinois St, Chicago IL 60611. 312/527-1977. Daily 10 am, noon, $16.

Best tours for architectural buffs

Architectural tours by bus, bicycle, and on foot

If Mrs. O'Leary's cow did kick over a lamp to start the Great Fire of 1871, she was also unwittingly responsible for a wave of new architecture. In the wake of the fire, talented architects arrived with their portfolios and dreams of rebuilding the city.

Out of the ashes rose the prototype of the modern industrial metropolis. "Early Skyscrapers," a Loop architectural walking tour, is one of more than 50 tours offered by the Chicago Architecture Foundation. Participants view the city's architecture on foot and by bus, bicycle, and boat, led by trained docents who provide informative—and often witty—commentary. Tours cover historic, modern, postmodern, and contemporary structures in downtown Chicago. Others focus on historic movie palaces, cemeteries filled with architectural surprises, and Chicago's neighborhoods and suburbs, including Frank Lloyd Wright's Oak Park. For bicyclists, there are tours of Lincoln Park; the wooded and winding roads of Lake Forest; and Riverside, one of America's earliest planned suburbs with examples of the work of Wright, Frederick Law Olmsted, and other architectural luminaries.

Chicago Architecture Foundation, 224 S Michigan Ave, Chicago, Il 60604, 312/922-3432.

Best building (and shop) for architectural buffs

Railway Exchange Building

When Chicago really was "hog-butcher to the world" and a major railway hub, this building (also known as the Santa Fe Center) contained the offices of a number of railroads. Besides the intrinsic artistic qualities of the architecture itself, there are two significant reasons that prompt architectural buffs to visit this 18-story building located just south of Orchestra Hall. First are its associations with architect Daniel Burnham—recognized as a pioneer of city planning and author of a far-sighted beautification scheme, the famous "Plan for Chicago." Not only was the building designed by Burnham, but he was also an investor in the property and maintained his firm's offices on the 14th floor. Second, this building is the headquarters of the Chicago Architecture Foundation. Show up here for one of its more than 50 architectural tours or to browse a wonderful shop with an extensive collection of books, gifts, and architectural memorabilia. Clad in white terra-cotta, the square-shaped building has a delicate, ornamented facade. Worth noting is an elegant, spacious two-story lobby, surrounded by a handsome gallery that has been converted into an attractive skylit atrium. A large, distinctive "Santa Fe" sign, illuminated at night, crowns the building.

Railway Exchange Building, 224 S Michigan Ave, Chicago, IL 60604.

Best block for architectural buffs

Prairie Avenue Historical District

Bounded by urban blight and industrial desolation, this time-warp neighborhood, with gaslights and cobblestone streets, provides an oasis of tranquility. Step back into the 1800s to what once was one of Chicago's wealthiest neighborhoods. The Prairie Avenue District once was a lonely strip of sandy prairie south of brash, frontier Chicago. In 1812, it was the site of the Fort Dearborn massacre. Seventy years later, it was the home of millionaires. The Glessner House is one of only a dozen mansions remaining. Built of pink granite, it has been called the "finest urban residence" designed by important American architect H. H. Richardson and is said to have influenced Louis Sullivan, Frank Lloyd Wright, and others. The Clarke House, Chicago's oldest, which escaped the Great Fire of 1871 and twice has been moved, has been meticulously restored and authentically furnished. It serves as a museum for the Chicago Architecture Foundation and provides insights into Chicago's pioneer days. Neighboring houses include a replica of a French chateau.

For information call the Chicago Architecture Foundation, 312/922-3432. Glessner House open Wed–Sun. Tours leave from Glessner Coach House, 18th St & Prairie Ave 1, 2 & 3 pm; Clarke House noon, 1 pm & 2 pm (Admission: 1 house: $5 adults, $2 seniors; both houses: $8 adults, $4 seniors).

Right place for the Wright stuff and the write stuff

Oak Park, Illinois

This suburban community, approximately 10 miles west of the Loop, has two primary claims to fame: the architecture of Frank Lloyd Wright (who lived and worked there for a number of years) and as birthplace and boyhood home of Ernest Hemingway. Oak Park offers a fine selection of buildings designed by Wright, in his distinctive "Prairie" style of low roof lines and open areas, most notably the Wright Home and Studio (951 Chicago Avenue) and the Unity Temple (875 Lake Street), Wright's first monumental structure. If not as revered in his own hometown (which he supposedly disparaged as being a town of "broad lawns and narrow minds"), Hemingway has not been forgotten. You'll find the house where the author was born in 1899 (339 N Oak Park Avenue) and his home as a boy and young man (600 N Kenilworth Ave) as well as significant displays of Hemingway memorabilia at the local library and historical society. Before you start exploring the haunts of these two legendary figures, you can get orientation at the Oak Park Visitors Center. *Event:* An annual festival celebrates Hemingway and includes readings and a look-alike contest.

Oak Park Visitors Center, 158 Forest Ave, Oak Park, IL 60302, 708/848-1500. Daily 10 am–5 pm.

Wright place not in Oak Park!

Robie House

Two items of good news for architectural buffs: (1) They need not travel to the near-western suburb of Oak Park (see separate listing) to find a prime example of Frank Lloyd Wright's world-famous "Prairie School" architecture. This 1909 Hyde Park house is one of Wright's most famous—and, among critics, considered one of his most successful—structures. (2) It was announced in 1995 that the house will undergo an estimated $2.5 million refurbishing and open as a museum. "It's probably one of the world's greatest houses," noted John Engman, executive director of the Chicago Architecture Foundation. "It was the culmination of the Prairie School, which was really the basis for a lot of the residential architecture that came after it." Currently, daily one-hour public tours show only the living and dining rooms. These will continue until the museum opens, perhaps in 1997. Meanwhile, the strong, low, cantilevered lines of this ahead-of-its-time building are well worth a sidewalk view for architecture and history buffs.

Robie House, 5757 S Woodlawn Ave, Chicago, IL 60637.

Ugliest buildings to survive the "great fire"

Water Tower & Pumping Station

Amid the gleaming steel and glass high rises and glittering shops of the Magnificent Mile is Chicago's best-known—and oddest—landmark. The Water Tower was built two years before the Great Fire of 1871 swept catastrophically through Chicago and was one of the rare buildings to survive the blaze, along with its companion waterworks across the street. Architect W.W. Boyington was commissioned to design a lake pumping station and a structure to hide its unsightly standpipe. But the odd sandstone castle that resulted was considered by many to be an even greater eyesore. Oscar Wilde called it "a castellated monstrosity with pepper boxes stuck all over it." Later, it was described as a naive imitation of Gothic architecture. Today, it houses a visitor center (with a state-of-the-art interactive computer kiosk), and the waterworks offers a 45-minute audiovisual orientation on Chicago and a shop of Chicago souvenirs. . . . And, much like the city's Picasso sculpture (see separate entry in "Museums, Galleries, Theaters & Other Sites"), it has survived early denigrations to become a revered symbol of the city. *Worth a look:* A new mosaic floor titled "Water Cosmology" was designed by Spanish artist Carlos Vega and incorporates water iconography of indigenous cultures around the word.

Water Tower & Pumping Station, 806 N Michigan Ave; Pumping Station, 163 E Pearson, Chicago, IL 60611. Visitor Welcome Center: Mon–Fri 10 am–6 pm, Sat 10 am–5 pm, Sun noon–5 pm.

Best spot prominent Chicagoans are dying to get into

Graceland Cemetery

If you could've ever gotten such Chicago luminaries as Potter Palmer, Marshall Field, Cyrus McCormick, George M. Pullman, Philip Armour, and Daniel Burnham together in one place, you'd have called it one successful party. Today, put all of them in one place, and you'd have to call it Graceland Cemetery. No ordinary burying ground, Graceland is 119 acres of gently rolling, delicately landscaped cemetery, offering a fascinating look at the sendoffs famous Chicagoans got during the boom years of the late 19th century. Graves are decorated with elaborate sculptures, columned arches, Gothic crypts, and even pyramids. A booklet available at the cemetery's office reveals locations of the graves of the notables listed above, as well as those of detective-agency founder Alan Pinkerton, architects Mies van der Rohe and Louis Sullivan, and William Hulbert, founder of baseball's National League (atop his grave is a granite baseball bearing the names of the National League teams of his era). Expectedly, this park-like spot is a quiet place for strolling and discovering.

Graceland Cemetery, 4001 N Clark St, Chicago, IL 60613, 312/525-1105. Daily 8 am–4:30 pm.

Best company town

Pullman Historic District

Tour the town that Pullman built! That's railroad magnate George M. Pullman, whose company town was designed to be to be the most modern self-contained community, with schools, churches, parks, shops, recreational and cultural facilities, and houses with indoor plumbing, running water, and illuminating gas. That was in 1880, and within six years the town had 14,000 residents. But within another 15 years, economic strain and a bloody strike finished the venture and Pullman became just another Chicago neighborhood. Today, it is a neighborhood dedicated to preservation. More than 90 percent of the original buildings remain, many neatly kept rowhouses built with bricks fashioned from clay found on the company site. An architectural highlight is Greenstone Church, built of green serpentine rock. Combine your trip with Sunday brunch at the Hotel Florence, the community's Grande Dame. Built in the Pullman era, it once provided gracious accommodations for the rich and famous, such as Ulysses S. Grant and Robert Todd Lincoln. Named after the daughter of the railway tycoon, it has been restored with turrets and gables intact. Dining rooms have dark cherry paneling, white-painted tin ceilings, and stained-glass windows.

Pullman Historic District, Hotel Florence, 11111 S Forestville Ave, Chicago, IL 60628, 312/785-8181. Tours May–Oct. first Sun of month, 12:30 & 1 pm. Annual house tour, second weekend Oct.

Best helicopter ride

Helicopter Transport Services

Whether you're in a rush on important business or just in the mood for a spectacular overview of Chicago, this outfit can lift you above the city in style. Based at Midway Airport (on the city's Southwest side), Helicopter Transport Services will take passengers to and from any available helipad, including downtown at Meigs Field on the lakefront. The price is also sky-high—$600 per flight hour for a four-passenger helicopter, $750 per flight hour for a six-passenger model—making this a splurge best defrayed by a group of adventure-seekers. These rates are only charged for the time the helicopter is in the air (plus $75 per hour for on-ground waiting time if any—after the first hour), but flight time is figured from the moment the chopper lifts off from Midway to the time it returns to the airport. So, while it may be more convenient to have your sky chariot pick you up downtown, you can save money by getting out to the airport.

Helicopter Transport Services, 5040 W 63rd St, Chicago, IL 60638, 312/585-9800.

Best "taken for a ride"

Untouchable Tours

Although Chicago civic boosters have spent years trying to combat the city's Al Capone/rat-a-tat/Elliot Ness/gangster image (which has been fostered around the world by TV and movies), this fun tour outfit has put the bang back into big, bad Chicago. A small black bus, hosted by a guide sporting a Prohibition-era outfit, shuttles visitors to and from more than 15 city hot spots and hit spots. These include (among others) the former Lexington Hotel (Al Capone's old HQ—site of Geraldo Rivera's infamous empty vault), the Biograph Theatre (where Dillinger caught his last movie—and last breath), and, of course, the now grassy lot at 2122 North Clark Street that was the location of the S-M-C Cartage Company garage—better known as the site of the St. Valentine's Day Massacre. A good tour for some indelible city history and for some macabre laughs.

Untouchable Tours, 10030 S Charles St, Chicago, IL 60643, 312/881-1195. Tours daily at varying times, $20 adults, $15 children.

Most haunting tour

Tour of Haunted & Legendary Places

Explore the unexplainable with Richard T. Crowe, collector of unusual folk- and ghostlore, and the only full-time professional ghost hunter in the United States. On this five-hour, personally guided coach tour, Richard Crowe provides a wealth of history and gives you the opportunity to meet Chicago's scariest spooks, spirits, and specters. Since 1973, Crowe (who holds BA and MA degrees in English Literature) has been conducting his supernatural tours with great success. He has appeared on television and radio in the United States and England and has become sought after as an expert in the field of paranormal occurrences. Tours depart from DePaul University's Lincoln Park Campus and visit such reportedly haunted sites as Robinson Woods Indian burial grounds; the Melody Mill Ballroom haunted by the "Flapper Ghost"; Archer Avenue, supposedly patrolled by the spectral "Resurrection Mary," Chicago's most famous ghost; Peabody's Tomb; a ballroom in Bridgeport, claimed to be the favorite haunt of the devil; and various psychic spots in the western suburbs.

Tour of Haunted & Legendary Places, PO Box 29054, Chicago, IL 60629, 312/499-0300. Tours depart at various weekend times. $28 per person.

Best place to welcome Christmas

Christmas Show, Lincoln Park Conservatory

Guaranteed to get you in the mood for the holidays is the conservatory's annual Christmas Show of poinsettias, when the seasonal blooms fill the Show House with bold and subtle hues of red, pink, white, and yellow. Arrangements include pots of red, white, and pink poinsettias stacked to form a 12-foot-tall Christmas tree, and arbors built of evergreen boughs and decorated with poinsettias. There are reflecting pools, a waterfall, picket fence, complementary plantings of cyclamen and Jerusalem cherries, and decorative frosted Christmas trees. Look for unusual marbled varieties of poinsettia, particularly a hybrid called Jingle Bells, a traditional red poinsettia marbled with pink. The show runs from about mid-December through the first week in January. It's warm, and it's free!

Lincoln Park Conservatory, 2400 N Stockton Dr, Chicago, IL 60614, 312/742-7736. Daily 9 am–5 pm. Free.

Best place to welcome spring

Spring & Easter Show, Lincoln Park Conservatory

When cabin fever gets you down, here's a nice way to welcome spring and get you in the mood for Easter. This is the most popular of all of the seasonal shows staged annually at this grand old Victorian conservatory (see separate listing in "Parks & Gardens"). On Easter Sunday it can draw a crowd of up to 25,000, so if you arrive mid-afternoon, you may find a line. Around 2,000 plants are used in the exhibit, which runs for about three weeks or so (but varies according to when Easter falls). This is a bright, fragrant, sensual show, a delight to the eye and nose. You'll find multicolored tulips, crocuses, snapdragons, and sweet-scented hydrangeas in white, pink, and blue. There are masses of fragrant Easter lilies and displays of tiger lilies. Layout for the show includes arbors over walkways, still pools, a small waterfall, and a well.

Lincoln Park Conservatory, 2400 N Stockton Dr, Chicago, IL 60614, 312/742-7736. Free.

Best place to meet the Irish (and the Irish-for-a-day)

St. Patrick's Day Parade

Shamrocks and shillelaghs, fair colleens and kilted pipers—these, along with high visibility of local pols—

are key ingredients of Chicago's annual ritual of March 17 (or the closest Saturday, thanks to a recent mayoral edict). A parade in Chicago has been a St. Patrick's Day tradition since the 1840s, although it is only since 1956 that is has been held downtown— currently along Dearborn Street from Wacker Drive to Van Buren Street. Related events include a 9 am mass at Old St. Patrick's Church (Adams & Des Plaines Streets), an Irish breakfast in the parish hall, the choosing of a grand marshal, and the crowning of a queen (sometimes from as many as 500 hopefuls). For a jar of Irish suds, a taste of Irish cooking, and a look at a collection of shillelaghs carried by prominent Irish-Americans in St. Patty's parades, stop by Kitty O'Shea's Pub in the Hilton Hotel & Towers (see separate listing in "Notable Potables").

Best intact turn-of-the-century street that's a mirror image of itself

Alta Vista Terrace

It's only a block north of Wrigley Field, but this immaculately kept, one-block-long street may be one of Chicago's least-known architectural finds. Built around 1900–1904, the two-story, black-iron–gated rowhouses of this block reflect a variety of architectural styles that were popular around the turn of the century. That alone does not make it particularly notable. But the two facts that do distinguish Alta Vista Terrace from all other streets in Chicago are: (1) It has survived intact—all of its houses have remained from that one period, and (2) The houses on the east and west sides of the street mirror each other's styles diagonally—that is, the first house on the east side is the same as the last house on the west side. The overall effect of the street is that of a charming, off-the-beaten-path London mews. Until, of course, you look to the south, and catch a glimpse of the upper-deck and light towers of Wrigley Field rising above the row of handsome houses.

Alta Vista Terrace (1050 W), between Grace St (3800 N) and Byron St (3900 N).

Least-known neighborhood of historic mansions

Hutchinson Street District

Since the early 1980s, the Buena Park neighborhood north of Irving Park Road and east of Broadway has seen considerable renewal and gentrification among its massive courtyard buildings. But one tucked-away pocket in this area never needed sprucing up, since it is home to a collection of some of the most varied, attractive, and undiscovered mansions in the city. The landmark Hutchinson Street District contains a high concentration of 1890–1920 mansions (some sprawling only four to six to an entire square block), many designed by noted architect George Maher, who was heavily influenced by Wright's "Prairie School." The mansions—adorned with stained glass, cupolas, verandas, and huge cast-iron gates—combine Prairie aspects with the more ornate Historical Revival style. These attractive homes line Hutchinson Street, Hazel Street, and Junior Terrace, mostly between Broadway on the west and Clarendon Avenue on the east (with some continuing east of Clarendon on Hutchinson). The district is perfect for casual strolling, especially, we've found, during winter—on snowy evenings, with flakes drifting gently down, it can seem eerily of a different time and place.

Hutchinson Street District, Hutchinson St (4232 N) and Clarendon Ave (800 W).

Best Victorian rowhouses hidden behind DePaul University

The McCormick Rowhouses

When the resident brothers of Chicago's McCormick Theological Seminary decided to raise money in the 1880s, they did it in a way that would make 1990s developer-capitalists proud: They built houses. But not just any houses—they built two facing ranks of Queen Anne-style red-brick rowhouses (a style not common to Chicago architecture), with a private street and park nestled between them. Today, the site of the seminary is the home of DePaul University, and the McCormick Rowhouses are a delightfully hidden city sanctuary. The private street is now known as Chalmers Place, and is only accessible by a fenced-and-gated (for seclusion purposes, rather than for security) entrance off Belden Avenue. To see the houses, park on Belden and enter at the DePaul University sign pointing to Chalmers Place; notice that the house numbers above each door indicate both the current street address and the old, original 19th-century numbering. The residents of this street seem to cherish their privacy (and their street's anonymity), but, on weekends, some can be found in their yards or out in front of their buildings; perhaps persistent and flattery-minded architecture buffs can wangle a tour.

The McCormick Rowhouses, on Chalmers Pl (2335 N), just north of Belden Ave (2300 N) and west of Halsted St (800 W).

Best view from on high
Sears Tower

No great ape has ever scaled the heights of Sears Tower, but one of the world's tallest buildings is ascended by about 11,000 office workers and legions of sightseers (almost 25 million in the first 18 years of its life). Designed by Skidmore, Owings, and Merrill and opened in 1974, the staggered-profile, 110-story building is 1,454 feet above ground (1,705 feet including twin antenna towers). In 1992, the Sears Tower Skydeck underwent a complete renovation. Visitors now enter by a dedicated entrance on Jackson Boulevard and relax in a 285-seat theater for a five-minute audiovisual show describing the views they will see from above. Also on the ground floor is an exhibit containing a nine-foot-tall model of the Sears Tower, a photographic essay on how it got to be the world's tallest building, facts about its construction, and a cartoon series of fun superlatives about it. Companion exhibits provide an overview of the city and showcase Chicago's ten most architecturally significant buildings. High-speed elevators whisk visitors to a pair of observatories—on the 100th and 103rd floors. Free fold-out maps pinpoint buildings that can be seen from the Skydeck. On one of those mythical clear days, several neighboring states are visible.

Sears Tower, 233 S Wacker Dr. (Skydeck entrance on Jackson Blvd), Chicago, IL 60605, 312/875-9696. Daily 9 am–11 pm.

Shortest "tallest" building
Monadnock Building

As tall towers go, this 16-story, 197-foot-high office building doesn't scrape much sky. But for a while, before the turn of the century, it did claim the "world's tallest" title that has been bantered back and forth between Chicago and New York. Even today, the Monadnock, built in 1891 and named after a mountain in New England, remains the highest wall-bearing structure in Chicago. The north section, designed by Burnham and Root, supports its prodigious weight with six-foot-thick base walls. The south half of the building, added two years later by architects Holabird and Roche, incorporates a conventional full steel frame. Adding visual appeal to this stark masonry structure is a facade that looks, in profile, like a woven basket. Alternating

vertical rows of deeply recessed windows contrast
with columns of protruding window bays. In design-
ing the original dark-brown brick building, principal
architect John Wellborn Root, a pioneer of the
"Chicago School" of modern architecture, was chal-
lenged with a site at the extreme south end of the
Loop adjacent to a notorious red-light district. This
stern, unadorned building, which Louis Sullivan
called "an amazing cliff of brickwork," occupied a
city block and served as an effective buffer.

Monadnock Building, 53 W Jackson Blvd, Chicago,
IL 60604, 312/922-1890.

Best spot for Harold and the blues

Harold Washington Library Center

Honoring Chicago's first black mayor, this handsome, hulking ten-story library (America's largest)
is decorated with the artwork of 19 African-American artists. A "Chicago blues" archive has an extensive collection of music, photographs, and
memorabilia relating to this distinctive music form.
On the eighth floor, street signs "W. Maxwell Street"
and "E. Muddy Waters Drive" recall significant
names from Chicago's cultural history. A permanent exhibition chronicles the political and private
life of charismatic mayor Harold Washington (who
died in 1987 during his second term). Included are
photographs of a young, lithe Washington as a track
athlete and a miscellany of political memorabilia
including a button collection (one that reads
"Honkies for Harold" symbolizes the late mayor's
universal appeal). On the one-hour guided tour view
a mosaic by Jacob Lawrence titled "Events in the life
of Harold Washington" and visit the winter garden
on the ninth floor. With a skylight rising 52 feet
above benches and greenery, this pretty, sun-
dappled public space is a spot for quiet contemplation (a restaurant is planned here). A glass curtain
at the rear lets in a view of the Chicago skyline. On
the ground floor, don't miss a stop at Second Hand
Prose, the wonderfully named shop that offers at
next-to-nothing prices books retired from circula-
tion.

Harold Washington Library Center, 400 S State St,
Chicago, IL 60605, 312/747-4300. Free guided tours
Mon–Sat noon, 2 pm, Sun 2 pm (747-4136).

World's largest microwave oven?

State of Illinois Center

Resembling a giant upturned teacup, the massive
glass curves of Helmut Jahn's design house 70 state
agencies. Inside the 17-story, 160-foot-diameter

rotunda, the grid-like pattern of a 10,000-ton steel frame is visible through the thousands of glass panels of the walls and roof. Opened in 1985, this radically designed building has many fans and detractors. Pulitzer Prize–winning architecture critic, the late Paul Gapp, described it as "no less than breathtaking." An acerbic guide on an architectural tour dubbed it "the world's largest microwave oven" (see separate listing). From the lobby, visitors gaze up at a web of salmon-colored metal below a glass skylight—and down on a black and white marble rosette in the center of a granite floor surrounded by a 900-seat food court. A glass elevator glides up dramatic free-standing shafts. Glass-clad circular balconies reflect the salmon and blue metal frame and gleaming chrome railings. Dominating the southeast plaza is Jean Dubuffet's black and white fiberglass sculpture, *Monument with Standing Beast.* Within the building is a permanent collection of specially commissioned works by Illinois artists. The work of state artists also is showcased in the Illinois Artisans Shop and the State of Illinois Art Gallery. Lunchtime concerts are a popular attraction.

State of Illinois Center, 100 W Randolph St, Chicago, IL 60601, 312/793-3500.

Best Victorian dowager

The Rookery

Soaring, light-filled atriums, the hallmark of many modern architects, also took the fancy of master architects of the 19th century. So it was during the years 1885 to 1888 when architects John Wellborn Root and Daniel Burnham created this heavily ornamented 12-story office building of red brick, granite, and terra-cotta. They installed a skylit art nouveau lobby full of engaging ironwork. Adding to the building's cachet as an architectural gem was the hiring in 1905 of Frank Lloyd Wright to redo the lobby in his redoubtable Prairie style with a gold and ivory motif and signature marble urns and light fixtures. Yet another hand entered the architectural mix when Wright protégé William Drummond fashioned attractive elevator doors. The whole is an architectural textbook that was shuttered for a number of years pending restoration. It reopened in 1992, after $80 million was spent to restore the Victorian dowager to its former splendor with delicate ornamentation of gilded marble, glass, and filigree ironwork, and dramatic spiraling staircases wrapped in detailed grille work. Today, imported hawks circle the Loop helping keep in check the pigeon population. In the 1870s, when a city hall temporarily occupied this site, this was a favorite pigeon roost—thus the name, The Rookery.

The Rookery, 209 S LaSalle St, Chicago, IL 60604, 312/553-6150.

Best building to recall the explorers

The Marquette Building

Four bronze panels over the doors of this restored 1894 office building portray the adventures of eponymous French Jesuit explorer Pere Marquette. They show the launching of the voyageur's canoe, an Indian attack, the campsite near the Chicago River, and the burial of Marquette. This tapestry of history continues in the rotunda lobby, where brilliantly colored Tiffany mosaics dramatically unfold the history of early French exploration of Illinois. Completing this portrayal of history are sculptured heads above the elevator doors on the first and second floor that commemorate members of the French expedition and important Mississippi Valley Native American chiefs. Executed by Edward Kemeys, who sculpted the famous Art Institute lions, these sculptures include explorers Marquette and Louis Jolliet, and Native Americans Chicagou and Little Panther. The building was designed by Holabird & Roche in 1894, and is an excellent example of the "Chicago School," pioneering use of steel columns and spandrels to usher in the era of the modern skyscraper. Ornamenting the doors of the Dearborn Street entrance are gleaming tomahawks and panther heads; in front are ornate black metal planters. An old-style arcade of shops connects with the Edison Building.

Marquette Building, 140 S Dearborn St, Chicago, IL 60603, 312/422-5500.

Moodiest modern architecture

333 West Wacker Drive

Chameleon-like, this elegant office building, which sits on a curve of the Chicago River, changes color to match the mood of the day. As light conditions change with varying cloud cover, sunshine, morning mists, or fog rolling in off the lake, its majestic curved wall of sheer glass adopts different hues of green-gray, reflecting the river and its neighbors. Its bold and subtle changes also vary according to vantage point and time of day. Built in 1983, this 36-story, steel-framed crystal tower was designed by William Pedersen, a New York architect making a stunning Chicago debut. Its 365-foot-wide curved wall of reflective, tinted gray-green glass is complemented by a four-story base of gray, green, and black granite and marble. Aesthetically pleasing and architecturally innovative, it is perfect for its time and for its place—on the curve where the Chicago River joins up with its north and south branches. To neighbors, such as the monolithic old Merchandise Mart across the river, it is a flattering addition to the skyline. Lacking historic pedigree and a gimmicky moniker, this bowed-glass building makes its statement with becoming modesty—it is known simply by its street address or as "333."

"333," 333 W Wacker Dr, Chicago, IL 60601.

Most ornate department store

Carson Pirie Scott & Company Store

As well as being one of the long-time anchor stores along State Street, this department store also is architecturally significant. When holiday-time window dressers are ready to work their magic, ready to showcase their work are ornate windows designed in 1899 by Louis Sullivan, a pioneer of modern architecture whom young Frank Lloyd Wright called "the Master." This building pairs unadorned form and function with whimsical embellishment. Step across the street to admire the strong, clean lines of the upper floors, where long, horizonal windows—so-called "Chicago windows"—flood the store with daylight. Then, step up close to examine the elaborate detail of the main entrance and the lower two floors. Sullivan used ornamental iron to create a floral motif of intricately entwined leaves, flowers, and vines. Restoration stripped layers of gray paint to return the finish of this rich ornamentation to its original luster—the architect used coats of red and green paint to simulate oxidized bronze. Glass panels flood the attractive rotunda entrance with light, complementing its restored mahogany. The building reflects the work of three architectural firms. After Sullivan built the store between 1899 and 1903, extensions were designed by Daniel Burnham's firm in 1905 and by Holabird and Root in 1960. Both subsequent architects retained the integrity of the original Sullivan design.

Carson Pirie Scott & Co, 1 S State St, Chicago, IL 60603, 312/641-7000.

BEST OF THE 'BURBS
(AND BEYOND)

Best outdoor music festival for listening *and* watching

Firefly Festival, South Bend, Indiana

Those who like their food and entertainment alfresco—including those who spend some of their
summer evenings at the Ravinia Festival (see separate listing in "Parks & Gardens")—might like to
consider a weekend visit to the Firefly Festival (truly
one of the region's best-kept secrets). Here, on a
summer evening, you can stretch out with a picnic
on a grassy knoll and enjoy performers such as The
Platters, Dave Brubeck, Ray Charles, The Supremes,
and Tom Jones, or listen to performances of the
Indianapolis Symphony Orchestra and the Sym-
phonic Pops Orchestra of Chicago. Firefly's mixed
bag of entertainment also may include such diverse
offerings as Gilbert and Sullivan, ballet, folk music,
zydeco, and performances of Shakespeare. Unlike
Ravinia—where you can lie on the lawn and *listen*
to music or buy a seat in the pavilion and *watch* the
performance—at Firefly you can do both at once.
Opened in 1981, the summer festival occupies a
natural amphitheater where audiences can spread
blankets or place lawn chairs (there are separate
areas for each) and enjoy an unobstructed view of

the performance. The stage is housed in a rustic red barn that is equipped with state-of-the-art sound and lighting systems. *Diversion:* Just across the Michigan line, near Niles, visitors to Madeline Bertrand County Park can play 18 holes of golf—without benefit of clubs or balls. The game is Disc Golf, where the object is to toss a Frisbee-like disc into pole-mounted baskets.

Firefly Festival, St Patrick's County Park, 50651 Laurel Rd (nr IN/MI state line), South Bend, IN 46601, 219/288-3472, 800/830-2489. Tickets $8 to $20.

Closest world class resort

The American Club, Kohler, Wisconsin

Golfers match skills with links carved artfully into rugged unglaciated landscape. Anglers cast flies into cold-running trout streams. Weekenders sleep in late in the most luxurious beds in the most welcoming rooms you'll find anywhere. The American Club truly is a world-class resort that would be a standout anywhere—and easily is the best in the Midwest. Resembling a Tudor-style English manor house, the resort once provided shelter for immigrant workers. Today, it offers state-of-the-art amenities—from luxurious accommodations to superb dining. Adjoining the resort, the enormous expanse of Kettle Moraine State Forest carries the distinctive imprint of the immense ice sheet that covered the upper Midwest 20,000 years ago. Its rugged terrain, scarred by Ice-Age glaciers, has deep woods with gnarled oaks, open meadows carpeted with wildflowers, and glacial lakes. Some 500 acres of this unspoiled wilderness are encompassed within the resort's River Wildlife preserve. Seven miles of the scenic Sheboygan River meander through the preserve, which protects native flora and fauna and offers nearly 30 miles of hiking and cross-country ski trails. Nearby is a reserve for pheasant hunting and trap shooting. Clear, fast-running streams offer excellent trout fishing. Two 18-hole championship golf courses were designed by Peter Dye. Located on the shores of Wood Lake, the Sports Core is a splendidly equipped spa, fitness center, and racquet club. Dining options include the top-of-the-line Immigrant Restaurant & Winery, ranking among the best in the country and offering a European-accented menu in six rooms decorated to salute the European mix of early Wisconsin settlers; The Horse & Plow, originally a tap room for the club's immigrant residents, decorated in rich wood, brass, and stained glass, and providing well-made sandwiches and a large selection of beers; and the River Wildlife Lodge, a rustic log cabin with

a natural fieldstone fireplace, serving "gourmet country" fare—pheasant in applejack cream, barbecued
rabbit, and broiled stuffed brook trout.

The American Club, Highland Dr, Kohler, WI 53044,
414/457-8000, 800/344-2838.

Best chocolates and antiques
Richmond, Illinois

Before the super highways, weekend travelers en
route to resorts in Wisconsin stopped at this tiny
crossroads town for ice cream, sandwiches, and
homemade candies. Today, Richmond is a destination in its own right, attracting antique collectors,
foodies, and chocolaholics drawn to Anderson's
Candy Shop, where three generations have produced
hand-dipped chocolates, candy, and fudge since
1926. Visitors can hunt for antiques at close to two
dozen shops, many of them specialists in such
collectibles as advertising signs, vintage clocks and
watches, and early-American furniture. They can
tour a pottery, order a custom-made cabinet, and
shop for honey (bring your own container and buy
it bulk). The International House of Wine & Cheese
is three destinations in one. It is a wine shop (with
300 selections from California alone), a deli with an
array of sausages and cheeses, and an attractive
restaurant (try a Napa Valley breakfast dish blending potatoes with three different kinds of onions,
spices, and a topping of melted cheese). *Lagniappe:*
At Genoa City, just a few miles north and barely
across the Wisconsin line, you can experience a Door
County-style fish boil at Fitzgerald's Genoa Junc-
tion, which occupies a remarkable octagon-shaped
Federalist house, circa 1853.

The Richmond Merchants Association, PO Box 411,
Richmond, IL 60071.

Best route to the north 'burbs
Sheridan Road

Sometimes getting there *is* a big part of the fun—
such as following Sheridan Road northwards. As
spectacular parkways go, Sheridan Road is a mere
street. But it is a *long* street, twisting and turning
from Diversey Avenue, virtually in the shadow of
Chicago's skyscrapers, northward toward the Wisconsin line. Like a surgeon's knife, it opens up the
belly of Chicago and its northern suburbs. Never
straying far from the Lake Michigan shoreline, it
begins in gentrified Lincoln Park, runs through the
condominium canyons north of Foster Avenue, and
glides past Evanston's Victorian mansions. Heading

north, it showcases the multimillion-dollar frontage
of waspish "North Shore" communities Kenilworth,
Wilmette, and Winnetka. As it crosses into Evanston
from Chicago, Sheridan kisses the lake atop high
rocky bluffs, skirts downtown, and travels through
a section of sprawling Northwestern campus reminiscent of an English university town. At Lighthouse
Park, there are tours of a nature center with a
wildflower walk, small museum, and experimental
greenhouse, and of an 1873 lighthouse, built after
the tragic wreck of the *Lady Elgin*. An art center
occupies a replica 16th-century manor house. *The*
architectural landmark is Wilmette's shimmering
white Baha'i House of Worship. The nine-sided
building has ornate columns, decorated with scroll-
work and bas-relief, supporting an intricate filigree
dome that also has nine identical sides. Also in
Wilmette is the attractive Plaza del Lago shopping
center—well worth a stop to visit the fine Italian
grocery Convito Italiano (see separate listing in
"Shopping"), where you can relax at an outdoor café
with a cappuccino, glass of wine, or a sandwich built
from the store's wonderful bread and imported Italian meats and smoked sausages.

Rolling on the riverboat

Hollywood Casino, Aurora

Forget about string ties, ruffled shirts, and derrin-
gers tucked into boots. Riverboat gamblers these
days prefer Reeboks and T-shirts as they test Lady
Luck on the Midwest's emerging fleet of floating
casinos. Vying for the Chicago-area gaming business
is the Hollywood Casino in downtown Aurora, 38
miles west of the city. This themed casino is designed to reflect the Golden Era of Hollywood, with
staff uniforms inspired by movie costumes, celebrity
look-alikes, and movie memorabilia such as a John
Wayne hat, Jean Harlow tiara, and Zorro robe.
Complementing two riverboat casinos that cruise the
Fox River is a four-story pavilion with Hollywood-
themed restaurants. These include the Fairbanks
Steakhouse and Bar, based on Douglas Fairbanks,
Sr.'s role in that perennial favorite *Don Q, Son of
Zorro*, offering prime beef and showcasing Hollywood
estate memorabilia, with movie-inspired seating and
film-reel accents. The Café Harlow is a more intimate
restaurant, while the Epic Buffet (with Vegas-style
buffet values) includes a giant gorilla scaling the
Chicago skyline (having presumably tired of the
Empire State Building), a 30-foot shark crashing
through the wall, and the clipper ship from *Interview
With a Vampire*. Superstar entertainment at Aurora's
beautifully restored Paramount Theater—one block

from Hollywood's pavilion—includes the likes of Frank Sinatra, Bill Cosby, Willie Nelson, and Liza Minnelli. If you've the urge to gamble, this is a likely spot with good food and a fun ambience.

Hollywood Casino, on the Fox River between the New York St & Illinois Ave bridges, Aurora, IL 60506, 630/801-1234, 800/888-7777. Thirteen gaming sessions daily 8:30 am–2:30 am. Admission free (must be 21 years of age).

Best mall that was raised from the dead

Old Orchard Shopping Center

This 1950s North Shore landmark lays claim to being the first modern shopping mall in the United States. Although still charming, Old Orchard began showing its age in recent years, and a massive $100 million renovation was undertaken in the early 1990s. In addition to a full remodeling job for the Marshall Field's and Sak's Fifth Avenue anchor stores, the upgrade saw the demolition of a down-at-the-heels Montgomery Ward's outlet—supplanted by a gorgeous new Nordstrom department store. The quaint, covered walkways remain, but the mall's landscaping has been upgraded to show the nearly 100 stores in their best light. Recent additions include a spacious Barnes & Noble bookstore and coffee shop, a valet parking service, and Old Orchard Gardens, one of the Chicago area's nicer multiplex movie theaters. *Food stop:* Just a few minutes drive from the Center is Bistro Europe (see separate listing in "Dining"), occupying the old Tower Restaurant space and offering an intriguing blend of French, Italian, and other European fare in a light, bright, colorfully accented setting.

Old Orchard Shopping Center, Skokie Blvd and Old Orchard Rd, Skokie, IL 60076, 847/673-6800. Mon–Fri 10 am–9 pm; Sat 9:30 am–5:30 pm; Sun 11 am–5 pm.

Best shopping center that blew Mall of America off the map

Woodfield Mall

Woodfield, in northwest suburban Schaumburg, is no secret to Chicago residents, or to most visitors for that matter. But even many regular patrons don't realize that in 1995 the fully enclosed, multilevel Woodfield overtook Minnesota's over-hyped Mall of America as the nation's largest shopping center. With the addition of 65 new shops (including Tiffany's and Nordstrom) to a mix that includes anchors such

as Marshall Field's and Lord & Taylor (as well as a
wide array of specialty shops such as the Art Institute Store, Rand McNally, and Warner Brothers and
Disney studio stores), Woodfield now offers 2.7
million square feet of retail space. And as if this
center's nearly 300 stores didn't offer enough plas-
tic-melting opportunities, neighboring One Schaumburg Place (with a Filene's Basement branch and a
Chernin's Shoes that is the largest shoe store in the
Chicago area) and Woodfield Village Green (with a
Lands' End Outlet and the Midwest's first Nordstrom
Rack, a store packed with top-flight clearance items)
offer plenty of additional diversions for the shop-'til-
you-drop crowd.

Woodfield Shopping Center, Golf Rd at Route 53,
Schaumburg, IL 60173, 847/330-1537. Mon–Fri 10
am–9 pm, Sat 10 am–6 pm, Sun 11 am–6 pm.

Best place to tap a maple tree

Pilcher Park

It's almost spring and cabin fever is starting to get
to you. Recognize the feeling? A pleasant antidote is
an outing to Pilcher Park during maple-sugar time
(check for dates). You can inspect sap being collected
and transformed into maple syrup through a wood-
fired evaporation process and sample the product at
a Saturday- and Sunday-morning pancake breakfast (usually held the second or third weekend in
March). Plan a stop at the nearby park district
conservatory to enjoy the displays at four exhibit
areas filled with trees, flowers, cacti, and succulents.
Check the schedule for special seasonal floral shows.

Pilcher Park, US 30 & Gougar Rd, Joliet, IL 60435,
815/741-7277. Greenhouse, daily 8 am–4:30 pm.

Friendliest river to paddle a canoe

Fox River

Although one of the drawbacks of canoeing the Fox
is the frequency of dams, the nine-mile stretch
between Sheridan and the village of Wedron is
uninterrupted. It is easy paddling, well suited to a
novice—in fact, you may find people floating lazily
down this section of the Fox in tiny rubber dinghies
and even on inner tubes. Depending upon how much
exploring and drifting you do, the trip will take
anywhere upward of about three hours. Edging the
river are high bluffs of St. Peters sandstone, pocked
with the nesting holes of swallows. There are caves
and feeder streams to explore and quiet pools where
you can wet a line. At Wedron, Chet and Mary's Fox
River Tavern is a local watering hole—a place to

enjoy a post-trip drink. The owners also operate
C & M Canoe Rental, including shuttles to the put-
in spot upstream.

Chet and Mary's Fox River Tavern (C & M Canoe
Rental), Wedron, IL 60557, 815/434-6690.

Wildest river to paddle a canoe

Vermillion River

White water in Illinois? While it can't match such
storied rivers as the Colorado, Cheat, or Salmon,
there is a fast-running stretch of the Vermillion River
just south of where it joins the Illinois River close
to Starved Rock State Park. Many canoeists regard
the ten-mile stretch between the Lowell Bridge and
Highway IL 71 as one of the most beautiful and
challenging in the state. However, this is a wild
stretch of river with a frothy Class II rapid (scouting
from the shore recommended) and a tricky chute
through a hazardous dam. It is not for novices unless
they share a canoe with an expert. Then a wet suit,
personal flotation device, and helmet are essential.
If you don't have a paddling expert with whom to
share—and survive—this thrilling experience, contact a Chicago-area canoe club; the Chicagoland
Canoe Base can help you find a club or group.

Chicagoland Canoe Base, 4019 N Naragansett,
Chicago, IL 60634, 312/777-1489. Mon–Sat 9 am–5
pm, Sun 9 am–9 pm.

Best Amadeus

Mozart Festival

Paul Newman, Geraldine Page, Orson Welles—each
of these theatrical luminaries, and many others,
received early training on the boards of the
Woodstock Opera House, a landmark steamboat
Gothic building which never has been dark since it
opened in 1889. Both Woodstock and the restored
opera house, with its stenciled ceiling and classic
horseshoe balcony, are well worth a visit, particular
during the annual Mozart Festival in July and
August. Welles once dubbed Woodstock the "grand
capital of Victorianism in the Midwest." And so it
remains, with its thoughtful preservation of charming Victorian mansions. Head for the cobbled streets
of the town square, with its park, pretty gazebo, and
clutch of shops, boutiques, and restaurants. (If you
saw the film *Groundhog Day*, you may remember
seeing this distinctive square—over and over.) Also
on the square is the Opera House, an intimate
theater (429 seats) with excellent acoustics that
makes it perfect for Mozart. Held since 1986, the

annual festival attracts international guest conductors and performers who play to sold-out houses.

Woodstock Opera House, 121 Van Buren St, Woodstock, IL 60098, 815/338-2436. Mozart Festival, Jul & Aug; Fri & Sat 8–10:30 pm.

Best place to visit the trenches of World War I

Cantigny

War and peace? You'll find both represented at the 500-acre country estate of the late Col. Robert R. McCormick, where field-artillery pieces and tanks are nestled among beautifully landscaped gardens. You can wander through a series of ornamental gardens and tour the house of the former *Chicago Tribune* publisher. On Sundays May through September there are free outdoor concerts, ranging from jazz and bluegrass to barbershop quartets and piano recitals, plus demonstrations of military techniques, such as parachuting and helicopter rappelling. McCormick commanded an artillery battalion in World War I that fought a bitter engagement at the French town of Cantigny. A museum recreates a front-line trench and chronicles the history of the legendary First Division. Cantigny also offers a golf-tennis center, built in the late 1980s.

Cantigny, 1 S 151 Winfield Rd, Wheaton, IL 60187, 630/668-5161. Feb–Dec Tue–Sun (hours vary), $5/vehicle.

Best place to visit a French airfield of World War I

94th Aero Squadron Restaurant

Crossing a creaking wooden bridge, you step back in time more than 75 years to a bombed-out French farmhouse, HQ for American fliers. Outside is a 1918 Newport monoplane, with a stretched-canvas skin. Inside the sandbagged entrance is a popular restaurant on the edge of Palwaukee Municipal Airport. From the picture windows of the three wood-beamed dining rooms, it's fun to watch activity on the runways, using headphones to eavesdrop on the control tower. Mementos of WWI include hundreds of historic photographs, weapons, and helmets—even the actual wing of a German plane. Prime rib is popular, with an all-you-can-eat special Sunday through Tuesday. Seafood dishes are a specialty, with all-you-can-eat crab legs served Wednesdays and Thursdays. The patio, appropriately "bomb-damaged," is a nice spot for a drink—served by waitresses in nurses' uniforms.

94th Aero Squadron Restaurant, 1070 S Milwaukee Ave, Wheeling, IL 60090, 847/459-3700. Lunch Sun–Thu 11 am–2:30 pm; dinner Sun–Thu 4–10 pm, Fri & Sat 4–10:30 pm.

Best soar spot

Phoenix Skydiving, Inc.

If you believe that the only reason to jump out of an airplane is if it no longer is able to fly, then this adrenaline-pumping sport probably is not for you. But, if you yearn to pitch out into the wild blue yonder—after intense instruction and with the considerable help of an experienced teacher—this is the spot to give skydiving a try. For an introduction to the sport, this skydiving center just beyond the far western suburbs (near the town of Hinckley) offers tandem jumping, allowing novices to make their first few jumps in a double harness that literally straps them to their instructor's back. After a quick climb to 14,000 feet in a single-engine Cessna, it's time for the moment of truth—a leap from the large bay door into the sky. With the instructor's help, the huge canopy (more like a wing than the old round parachutes and better for precise maneuvering) is released, and the tandem team floats gently to the ground, usually with ultra-soft upright landings. But first-timers beware: The exhilarating experience has been known to become addicting. Cost of first-jump training, equipment rental, and the jump itself is $165; participants must be at least 18 years of age.

Phoenix Skydiving, Inc., 6N162 Weber Dr, St Charles, IL 60174, 800/404-JUMP. Open year-round (weather permitting).

Best spot to find Dorothy, Toto & friends

The Yellow Brick Road

Amid the dusty cornfields of northwestern Indiana, the Yellow Brick Road transports motorists to the Land of Oz. Although it's a long way from Kansas, you'll find all of the characters from *The Wizard of Oz* at Jean Nelson's shop of Oz memorabilia. The store, on a street of the same name officially renamed by city fathers, carries toys, dolls, puppets, models, games, puzzles, collector's plates, ceramic Munchkins, and hand-painted music boxes; a museum of Ozmorabilia houses rare collectibles such as many of the three dozen or so editions of L. Frank Baum's book and the Parker Brothers' game issued in 1921 that uses pewter figures of the key Oz characters. There's a diorama of the Land of Oz and movie stills and posters, many of them autographed, and a "wall of fame" with photos of famous visitors. Actors who portrayed Munchkins in the 1929 film classic sometimes drop by—particularly during Chesterton's big Oz festival in September.

The Yellow Brick Road, 109 E 950 N, Chesterton, IN 46304, 219/926-7048. Mon–Sat 10 am–5 pm, Sun 11 am–4 pm.

Woolliest wanderers

Opportunity Llama Treks

Here's a relaxed approach to backpacking—you do the walking, a llama does the packing. Choose from a number of treks into the Kettle Moraine State Forest of southeast Wisconsin. Although the terrain varies in difficulty, none is rugged and many easy trails make llama treks popular with seniors. Lunch treks ($25/person) last about four hours and include a picnic of croissants, meats, cheeses, salads, vegetables, dessert, fruit juices, wine coolers, and other goodies. Two-hour snack treks ($15) include a break for an ice cream sundae. A naturalist's commentary describes flora and fauna. You'll learn to identify animal tracks, bird songs, and wild edibles such as purple clover and cattails, and how burdock burrs inspired the invention of Velcro. Perfect companions for a hike, llamas were bred by Incas to carry 100-pound loads over the rugged Andes. They're friendly, gentle creatures with soft alpaca coats.

Opportunity Llama Treks, 974 Hwy S, Kewaskum, WI 53040, 414/965-5262.

Spoofiest spy spot

The Safe House, Milwaukee

The innocent sign outside reads "International Exports, Limited." It's a cover for The Safe House, opened in the 1960s when James Bond was ordering his martinis "shaken, not stirred." The spot thrives, although it covers the clandestine capers of conventioneers, not spies. You enter through a sliding bookcase after performing some embarrassing act— imitating a plane or performing a pirouette—which is relayed via TV monitors for the amusement of patrons. Inside, you can join an instructional card game (to prepare for that trip to Vegas) and swap lines with resident magician Sneaky Pete. The "Dirty Tricks Officer" will help you arrange for a suitable victim to be raised in an elevator chair through the barroom floor with a 21-gun salute, the screening of a risqué movie, and a quart of his or her favorite potable. There is an "alibi" phone for calling home against a background of airport sounds, stuck-in-traffic noises, or another suitable fabrication. And for when you really must leave—in a hurry—a secret phone-booth escape route. *Stayover option:* If you decide to spend the night in Milwaukee, plan to take advantage of two unique experiences: (1) A room at the Pfister hotel, a meticulously restored Victorian landmark with state-of-the-art amenities; and (2) Dinner at Karl Ratzch's, arguably the best German restaurant in the country (roast goose and sublime schnitzel are don't-miss entrées).

The Safe House, 779 N Front St, Milwaukee, WI 53202, 414/271-2007. Mon–Thu 11:30 am–1 am, Fri & Sat 11:30 am–2:30 am, Sun 4 pm–midnight. Milwaukee info: 800/231-0903.

Most gorgeous gladiolus

Momence Gladiolus Festival

Head about 60 miles south to Momence for one of the region's prettiest floral displays and biggest floral parades. Gladiolus have been raised commercially in the area since the early 1900s. These tall-stemmed perennials with their beautiful trumpet blooms come in a wide range of colors—bright reds, pale yellows and greens, and a kaleidoscope of pastel hues. Tour the roads of St. Ann township south of Momence and east of IL 1 for a view of about 500 acres of spectacular gladiolus fields (in bloom from about July 4 through mid-September). Local growers produce about 60 varieties and ship across the United States. The three-day Gladiolus Festival in Momence is held in mid-August and includes a parade of blossom-laden floats, a flower show, flea market, and an antique-car show. *Dining option:* Dionne's French Cafe & Gallerie is a charming country French restaurant decorated with the paintings of co-owner Betty Dionne and featuring the cuisine of husband Gene (related to Quebec's famous Dionne quintuplets). Stellar bread pudding is served with Southern Comfort sauce and is also packaged to go. The café occasionally features cabaret and operatic singers (815/472-6081). *Float trip:* In nearby Kankakee, Reed's will rent all the equipment you need for a canoe trip lasting a couple of hours or two days. Ideal for families with youngsters, the Kankakee River has a gentle current and is shallow enough to wade in many places.

Kankakee County Convention & Visitors Bureau, 1711 Rte 50 N, Suite 1, Bourbonnais, IL 60914, 815/935-7390.

Best country bar (nearest the country)

Nashville North

In the words of the waitress at Bob's Country Bunker in *The Blues Brothers*, "We have both kinds of music here—country and western!" Approximately 500 miles north of its namesake city, this northwest suburban bar recreates the music, fashions, and down-home fun of Music City. Nashville North offers live music (Wednesday through Sunday), country dance lessons three nights a week (for those who want to brush up on their Two-Step or Cotton-Eyed Joe), lunch and dinner specials (chicken, barbecued ribs, and steak are the most popular offerings), and a complete Western-wear shop to outfit the weekend cowboy and cowgirl inside you.

Nashville North, 101 E Irving Park, Bensenville, IL 60106, 630/595-0170. Tue–Sun 8:30 pm–2 am.

Closest former bunny warren

Grand Geneva Resort & Spa

The bunnies have gone, and so has Hef (although his suite remains, available for rent). Also gone is the rather seedy image of the former Playboy Resort and its ill-fated successors. Rising Phoenix-like in its stead is totally made-over resort (with a $20-million face-lift) that is comfortable and functional (and vaguely rustic) without being stuffy. Renovations have retained the Frank Lloyd Wright Prairie School architectural style but opened up the building to allow more light and more views of the resort's rolling 1,300-acre estate. Same thing with guest rooms: each with a full wall of windows looks out onto the scenic property. The 355 guest rooms, including 37 suites, are brightly decorated in a color scheme that combines yellow, peach, cobalt blue, and red. Three restaurants provide variety. The Grand Café features heartland food: the Newport Grill is a Chicago-style steakhouse specializing in steaks, chops, and sea-food; and Ristoranté Brissago offers a mix of regional and contemporary Italian cuisine (try lobster-filled ravioli or saltimbocca—slices of veal and prosciutto with sage and white wine). The spa and sport center offer a wide variety of services including massages, facials, body and bath treatments, and a special Swiss shower room. There's a lap pool, indoor and outdoor tennis courts, and racquetball and volley-ball courts. There are stables and riding trails and downhill and cross-country skiing with a full ski lodge—plus sledding, sleigh rides, and ice skating. Two PGA championship golf courses feature the Scottish-style layout of the Briar Patch and the

7,258-yard challenge of the Brute, one of the longest courses in the United States. Now that the property has been thoroughly revamped and has so much to offer, location adds another major drawing card. Just across the Wisconsin line, within easy driving distance of Chicago, it offers a close-in opportunity to ski and play golf in a resort setting.

Grand Geneva Resort & Spa, 7036 Grand Way at Hwys 50 E and 12, PO Box 120, Lake Geneva, WI 53147, 414/248-8811.

INDEX

NOTES

NOTES

NOTES